ISBN 978-1-332-49543-6
PIBN 10256901

Similar Books Are Available from
www.forgottenbooks.com

PREFACE

THE Scottish History Society is indebted to Colonel J. A. S. Cuninghame, of Caprington Castle, Kilmarnock, for permission to print the text of the Chartulary, and to photograph the specimen pages which appear in this volume. The editor has to add his thanks to Colonel Cuninghame for personally verifying some doubtful readings after the manuscript had been returned to Caprington. The thanks of the Society and of the editor are due to Mr, Alexander Gibb, F.S.A. (Scot.), for the observations on place-names and persons which he has been so good as to furnish to the Notes and Illustrations; and to Mr. William Rae Macdonald, F.S.A. (Scot.), for his valuable Appendix on the Seals of Lindores, and for procuring the impressions of the seals which have been photographed and are here reproduced.

In the course of this work acknowledgment is made of the obliging services of several gentlemen who have aided the editor in elucidating points of more or less difficulty. The editor's special thanks are due to a distinguished charter and record scholar, who, so long as health allowed him, was unfailing in his help, but who has forbidden the mention of his name. This gentleman's labours unfortunately extended to only the earlier charters of the volume. Subsequently the

editor has enjoyed the invaluable assistance rendered by Mr J. Maitland Thomson, Curator of the Historical Department of H.M. General Register House. The editor has been, he fears, barefaced and unblushing in his demands; but Dr Thomson's generosity has condoned his innumerable impor-

tunities. Mr. J. T. Clark, Keeper of the Advocates' Library, was so good as to assist both with wise counsel and the loan of books in regard to the difficult task of verifying the authorities cited in the 'Legal Opinion' (No. CXLIX.), which was a line of research quite outside the circle of the editor's ordinary studies. The editor is also under innumerable obligations to Dr. T. G. Law, Secretary of the Society.

The editor in the course of many years has had frequent struggles with printers, who for the most part like to follow their own ways rather than those of the authors whose 'copy' they are employed to set up. But in the present case he is compelled to acknowledge that he has been saved from many an error by the intelligent and keen proof-reading, both of the Latin and the English, in the office of the Edinburgh University Press.

The Index has been prepared by Mr. Alex. Mill of the Signet Library.

One of the most delightful of the compensations for labours, such as those demanded by the task now brought to a conclusion, is the vivid sense of brotherly fellowship created by the ready generosity of others engaged in similar lines of research. And, if he may trust his own feelings, the editor is certain that he is not justly liable to a δίκη ἀχαριστίας, should the Court of Session, like the judicatories of ancient Athens, entertain such an action at law.

J. D.

CONTENTS

THE CHARTULARY OF LINDORES

INTRODUCTION

THE transformation of Scotland in its political, civil, social, and ecclesiastical aspects, accomplished by Anglo-Norman influence during the course of the twelfth century, was wide in extent and far-reaching in its consequences. It has indeed no parallel in the history of the kingdom. Confining our view to the changes which took place in the organisation and life of the Church, we find the century opening with the ancient Celtic Church of the country in a stage of advanced decrepitude, feeble in its energies, relaxed in discipline, and largely denuded of its temporal possessions. There was but one episcopal see, that of the ' episcopus Scottorum,' situated at St. Andrews, and hopelessly incapable of exercising a competent supervision over a diocese (if we may use that term) as extensive as the whole mainland of Scotland. At the close of the century the entire country was sub-divided and portioned out into no less than eleven effective bishoprics. Dunkeld was reconstituted and Moray founded as early, perhaps, as 1107. Glasgow, Galloway, Ross, Caithness, and Aberdeen followed in quick succession. The erection of Dunblane and Brechin marked the middle of the century, and after an interval of some fifty years the tale was completed by the sub-division of the diocese of Dunkeld, and the creation of a new see, that of Lismore or Argyll, out of its western district. Cathedral

centre of civilising influence in the region in which it was placed.

Following close on the erection of the early bishoprics was the establishment of the parochial system, hitherto unknown, with its grouping of parishes for disciplinary purposes into archdeaconries and 'deaneries of Christianity.' Before the close of the twelfth century the organisation of the Scottish Church and its secular clergy was indistinguishable, save for the lack of a metropolitan, from that of the Church of England.

Not less remarkable was the rapid spread of new monastic establishments throughout the country. The ancient Celtic Church in Scotland had indeed in its origin been essentially monastic in character; but in the course of centuries its energy had failed; its missionary zeal was extinct; it was suffering from internal decay. Its weakness had yielded to the greed of the great landowners; its possessions were to a large extent alienated; and such little as remained was handed down by hereditary descent in petty communities of married ecclesiastics, who were the representatives in law of the early monasteries of the Church of St. Columba. Such a state of things did nothing to satisfy the religious conceptions of the English settlers and Norman knights who crowded into Scotland in the reigns of Alexander and David, and whose influence with these monarchs was dominant. The sons of St. Margaret had inherited her love for the ecclesiastical arrangements of the southern kingdom. Their intimate relations with the English court made them keenly sensible of the painful contrast presented by the state of the Church in their own country. The vigour and beneficent labours of the great monastic houses of England and Normandy could not have failed to impress

them; and they resolved that Scotland should particulate in what was then universally regarded as the most excellent form of religious devotion.

We need not here delay to investigate the causes, but the

fact is unquestionable that piety and religious zeal among the wealthy and powerful of that day took shape in the erection and endowment of monasteries. Excluding from consideration the houses of the mendicant orders of friars, the great monasteries of Scotland, and, with a few unimportant exceptions, even those of secondary rank, can trace their foundation to the twelfth, and earlier years of the thirteenth, century. As founders, the kings and other members of the royal family led the way; and they were speedily followed by the great nobles, whose power and influence were at that period scarcely inferior to those of the Crown. Alexander I. erected the houses of Canons Regular at Scone, Loch Tay, and Inchcolm. To his successor, David, are to be attributed the monasteries —some of them of the first importance—of St. Andrews (Priory), Dunfermline (new foundation), Selkirk (soon to be transferred to Kelso), Jedburgh, Holyrood, Newbottle, Cambuskenneth, Urquhart, the May, and Kinloss. The great lords of Galloway founded Dundrennan, Soulseat, Lincluden, Glenluce, St. Mary's Isle, Tongland, and Whithern (new foundation). Walter Fitz-Alan, the Steward, established the great abbey of Paisley, and the house of Mauchline, afterwards attached to Melrose. Dryburgh and Kilwynning were due to Hugh de Morville, the Constable; Coldstream and Eccles to the Earl of Dunbar. Other foundations will be referred to hereafter.

The wave of religious zeal, which in this form was distinctly of Anglo-Norman origin, does not seem at first to have largely affected the Scottish Earls north of the water of Forth. There are many indications of their instinctive jealousy of English ideas and English ways. It could not be with unmingled satisfaction that they witnessed the settlement of English

monks from Canterbury at Dunfermline, from Pontefract at Kelso, from Rievaulx at Melrose and Dundrennan, from Wenlock at Paisley, and from Alnwick at Dryburgh. In the council of the king then held Constable used generally ...

cessful rivals in the Anglo-Norman knights who were filling
so many of the great offices of state.   And it would seem that
the Church in like manner was now being handed over to the
control of Anglo-Norman ecclesiastics.   The castles of the
Anglo-Norman laymen seemed to have their counterparts in
the monasteries garrisoned with monks from south of Scotland.   At any rate, for some time the great nobles of the
north did not lend themselves to this new form of piety.[1]
After a generation or two the feeling of distrust wore off.

Earl David, the founder of the Abbey of Lindores, came of
a family especially addicted to this form of pious munificence.
We have seen something of the profuse liberality in this
direction of his grandfather, David i.   His father, Prince
Henry, though cut off in the years of early manhood, had
time, some two years before his death, to erect the monastery
of Holmcultram.   His brothers, Malcolm, 'the Maiden,' and
William, 'the Lion,' can each be credited with the erection of
a famous house : the former founded the Cistercian Abbey
of Cupar in Angus ; the latter, the splendid and richly endowed
Benedictine Abbey of Arbroath ; while his mother, the
Countess Ada, had founded the Cistercian nunnery at Had-
dingtou.[2]

At the latest, early in the year 1195, the first abbot had
been chosen for the new foundation at Lindores.[3]   This fact
is known to us through an original charter preserved in the
collection known as the 'Campbell Charters' (xxx. 16), in

---

[1] Earl Duncan's nunnery at North Berwick can scarcely be reckoned an

the library of the British Museum. It is somewhat earlier than the earliest writ directly connected with Lindores in our Chartulary; and the reader owes its appearance here to the courtesy of Mr. J. Maitland Thomson, who not only called the attention of the editor to its existence, but was also so good as to transcribe it from the original. It may be added that a fragment of the seal remains attached. It is now reproduced (Appendix I.) for the first time, it is believed, in type.

THE FOUNDER OF THE ABBEY OF LINDORES AND HIS FAMILY

Earl David, the founder of the Abbey of Lindores, was the third and youngest son of Earl Henry, younger son of King David I. Earl Henry's elder brother Malcolm had met a violent death when a child, and Henry thus became the heir to the Scottish throne. He married in 1139 Ada, daughter of William, Earl of Warenne, second Earl of Surrey, and by her had six children, three sons and three daughters. Of the sons, Malcolm and William were successively kings of Scotland, and the third, the subject of this notice, became Earl of Huntingdon, by which title he is commonly known in history.[1]

Earl Henry's untimely death, in the flower of his youth, and possessed, as he was, of qualities well fitted to win and hold the affections of the people, plunged the whole nation into grief. He died, 'amid the lamentations of both the English and the Scots,' on 12th June 1152. He was buried in the Abbey of Kelso. Fordun describes him as particularly handsome, of a kind and affectionate disposition, devout and pious, and most tender-hearted towards the poor; and summing up

---

[1] The blunder which Fordun made in representing David as being William's elder brother (*Chronica*, lib. v. cap. 33, Skene's edit. p. 232) reappears in his *Gesta Annalia* (§§ i. and xii.) as written in 1363; but it was corrected in the

his virtue, he declares him to have been in all respects like his father, only more attractive.[1]

The place of the burial of his father may have contributed to determine the choice of Earl David that the monks of his new foundation at Lindores should be 'de ordine Kelkoensi.' (Nos. II. III.)

As to the date of Earl David's birth, Sir Archibald H. Dunbar, who in the careful and laborious investigation of the chronology of the royal families of Scotland stands *facile princeps*, places it as 'about 1144.'[2] This figure, which I believe is correct, is probably based upon a reasonable correction of an allegation in Fordun's *Chronica*,[3] that of the three sons of Earl Henry, Malcolm was born in the eighteenth year of the reign of David I., Earl David in the nineteenth year, and William in the twentieth. The error that David was William's elder brother was, as we have seen, subsequently corrected. Making this correction, we are probably justified in substituting the name of David for that of William in the original passage where Fordun records the dates of the births of the three brothers. Now the twentieth year of the reign of David I. began on April 23, 1143; and accordingly Sir A. H. Dunbar has come sufficiently near when he places Earl David's birth as 'about 1144,' that is, to be precise, in the year ending April 23, 1144. But it would be foolish to look for exact precision.

Authentic history has not much to tell of the life of Earl David, and little can now be done beyond piecing together in chronological order the brief notices which may be found scattered in the pages of the public records, of Fordun, the Chronicles of Melrose, Roger de Hoveden, and Walter de

Coventry.

If we may trust Fordun, David was in England at the time

when his brother Malcolm 'the Maiden' was causing serious discontent among his people by his neglect of his duties as king. David must have been then a mere youth. The first unquestionable fact in his story is his visit in the train of his brother King William to the court of Henry II. at Windsor. This took place in the spring of the year 1170. The brothers spent Easter with the English king, and their stay in the south extended over several weeks, for on the octave of Whitsunday (Trinity Sunday, May 31) David received, after the manner of the time, the honour of knighthood from the hands of the King of England. During the visit of the royal brothers Henry II. took a step fraught with the gravest consequences in the immediate future. He caused his son Henry to be crowned, and on the following day required King William and David to do homage, and on the relics of the saints to swear fealty to the newly crowned, with the reservation of fealty to himself. This homage was no doubt for possessions in England, of which more will be said hereafter. William during this visit made fruitless efforts to obtain from Henry the restoration of the earldom of Northumberland, and returned with much chagrin to his own kingdom. Two years later, when the younger Henry, supported by Louis of France and a formidable array of English Barons, engaged in the great conspiracy against his father, William and Earl David joined the confederacy on the conditions that if the plot were successful William should receive Northumberland as far as the Tyne, and David the fief of Huntingdon, and in addition (*in augmentum*) the whole of Cambridgeshire.

King William's futile invasion of the north of England in 1173, his renewed attack in the following year, his capture at Alnwick, and the unhappy treaty of Falaise are familiar facts of history. David had also taken an active part on behalf of the younger Henry. The castle of Huntingdon was held by

Earl David against the old king. After the capture of the

rebel Earl of Leicester David succeeded him in the command
of his forces. He was engaged in military operations near
Leicester when the news reached him of the capture of his
brother at Alnwick, whereupon he immediately retreated with
precipitation to Scotland. Shortly after his return, as security
for the fulfilment of the terms of the treaty of Falaise, hostages
from the great Scottish nobles were demanded. Of these the
most distinguished was Earl David.

After the release of King William consequent on the treaty
of Falaise, we next find Earl David accompanying his brother,
the king, to York, and there doing homage to the elder
Henry, whose authority had been by this time safely secured.

In 1179 Earl David accompanied King William, when with
a large force he marched into Ross to quell a rebellious rising
in that remote part of his dominions. The expedition was
successful, and two fortresses were erected for maintaining the
royal authority in that lawless district.

In 1180 contentions of a less formidable kind demanded the
consideration and intervention of the king. The monks of
Melrose, whose possessions consisted largely of their vast flocks
of sheep, had come into collision with the men of Wedale in
regard to the boundaries of their respective pasture-lands.
The dispute was brought to a close at Haddington in the
presence of the king and Earl David.[1]

In the following year, according to the Chronicle of Melrose,
'matters of business required that William, King of Scots, and
Earl David his brother, should go to parts beyond sea, to King
Henry, the elder.' The nature of the business does not appear.
In the spring of 1185 the two brothers met the King of England
in council at London, when the question of a new crusade for
the relief of the Holy Land was under consideration. In the

*following year William and David again visited the court of
Henry. It was on this occasion that Henry offered to his*

unwilling King of Scots his future wife, Ermengard de
Beaumont.[1]   After consultation with his friends William (who
aspired to a higher alliance) thought it prudent not to resist
the wishes of the King of England.

The next notice we have of Earl David is his appearance at
the stately coronation of Richard I. at Westminster (3rd Sept.
1189).   In the splendid procession David, as Earl of Huntingdon, bore one of the three swords of state, the sword in the
centre being carried by the king's brother, John, Earl of
Moreton (afterwards King John), and that on the other side
by Earl David's future brother-in-law, the Earl of Chester.[2]

On 24th June 1190 Richard confirmed to Earl David in the
amplest manner the liberties of the honour of Huntingdon.[3]
It was not till Earl David was well advanced in life that he
took a wife.   On Sunday, 26th August 1190, he was married
to Matilda (Nos. II. III.) daughter of Hugh, Earl of Chester.
This was a great alliance quite worthy of his station.   By
Matilda he had a family of (at least) three sons and three
daughters, of whom more will be said hereafter.

If any credence is to be given to the story of Earl David
having accompanied Richard I. of England to the Crusade,
told very circumstantially by Boece, it is at this point of the
earl's history we must insert it.   But as the story is connected
in Boece's narrative with the founding of the Abbey of Lindores,
it is proper that we should examine it in detail, and form
some judgment on its credibility.   This will be done in a
separate section, and we here resume the chronicle of Earl
David's life as it appears in authentic history.

In 1194 we find David actively espousing the cause of King
Richard in his struggle with John.   In opposition to John's
partisans, with the assistance of his wife's brother Ranulph,

Earl of Chester, he is found engaged in the siege of Nottingham. On 30th March in the same year he was present at a council held by Richard.

John, on his accession to the throne of England, and after the arrangement of a truce with France, resolved to attempt a settlement of the claim made by King William to the northern border counties. To this end he despatched David, Earl of Huntingdon, with the Bishop of Durham and others of noble rank, bearing letters patent of safe-conduct for King William to come to meet him at Lincoln on the morrow of St. Edmund (21st November) 1200. William, accompanied by the Earl of Huntingdon, attended on the day named. There in the presence of a remarkable assemblage of great prelates and nobles William did homage 'salvo jure suo,' and afterwards demanded the counties of Northumberland, Cumberland, and Westmoreland. John put him off with the promise that he would return an answer at the following Whitsunday.[1]

There are some notices in Bain's *Calendar*, under the year 1202, which reveal that Earl David had incurred debts to the Jews.[2]

In 1205 Earl David swore fealty to his nephew Alexander, the heir to the throne of Scotland, then a boy of seven years.

In the summer of 1210 Earl David and his son Henry are found in Ireland, with several of his knights in attendance on King John.[3] In 1212 King John seems to have suspected the fidelity of Earl David, for he required from him his son John as a hostage. Among the English possessions of Earl David was the castle of Fotheringhay in Northamptonshire, the place where, after three centuries and a half, his unhappy descendant Mary, Queen of Scots, met her tragic death. King John demanded of the earl the surrender of this fortress, and gave commands that it should be at once besieged and taken, if there were any delay in yielding it.[1] Its restoration three years later is closely connected with one of the greatest events in the constitutional history of the English people. The English barons, among whom was the Earl of Huntingdon, at length brought the king to bay. On 15th June the Great Charter was signed and sworn to by John. Less than a week later, on 21st June, John, still at Runnymede, signed the order for the restoration of Fotheringhay, together with the delivery of the earl's son and other hostages.[2]

It was probably the illness of King William which brought David to Scotland at the close of 1214. At any rate he appears to have been with his brother when he died at Stirling on 4th December. He was present at the crowning of Alexander at Scone, and accompanied the young king to attend the obsequies of his father. The chronicler tells us how Earl David met the body of William at the bridge of Perth, and how, dismounting from his horse, though now beset by age and infirmities, he insisted on lifting one arm of the bier upon his shoulder and acting for a while as bearer. He accompanied the funeral cortege to the appointed place of sepulture in the church of the abbey of Arbroath, and stood by the grave 'lamenting as became a brother.'[3]

The lives of the brothers give every indication of genuine brotherly affection. And in this respect they present a happy contrast to the jealousy and strife exhibited in the family of Henry ii. of England.

Earl David survived his brother by four years. He died

at Yardley (Yardley-Hastings in Northamptonshire), aged some seventy-five years, on Thursday, 17th June 1219. On the day following his death he was buried in the abbey of Sautrey in Huntingdonshire, a foundation of Simon de St. Liz, a former Earl of Huntingdon.   Fordun asserts that it had been David's desire to be interred in his own foundation of Lindores, but that ' on the advice of certain persons' his wishes were not carried out.[1]   This statement as having an air of probability has, I think, been universally accepted.   But an entry in the Assize Roll of Huntingdon, which will be found summarised in Mr. Bain's invaluable *Calendar*[2] dispels the illusion.   A question of land-holding brought the abbot of Sautrey into court in April 1228.   In the course of the proceedings the abbot produced Earl David's will, in which, *inter alia*, he bequeathed his body to the church of St. Mary of Sautrey.

According to Bower, Abbot of Inchcolm, in his additions to Fordun, Earl David had by his wife three sons.   Of these Robert died young, and was buried at Lindores.[3]   The next son is simply named as Henry, but nothing more is said of him.   The name of the third son was John, 'called,' says Bower, 'by the English the Scot.'   But we have to add that he styles himself ' Johannes de Scotia ' in many of the charters of our Chartulary.[4]   Earl David resided chiefly on his English possessions, and perhaps the word 'the Scot' or 'of Scotland' may have indicated that John had been born in Scotland. As John succeeded his father in the earldom, it may be assumed that Henry, like Robert, had died young.

Among the ruins of the Abbey of Lindores there are now to be seen two small stone coffins placed in the choir of the abbey church, in front of the high altar. They are close together, and are said t occuby the exact position which they had when they were originally unearthed. They are carefully wrought. Each coffin is cut from a single block, and each has the circular recess for the head. The internal measurements give twenty-seven and a half inches as the length of one, and thirty and a half inches as the length of the other. The place of honour assigned to them falls in well with the natural suggestion that they had contained the remains of the children of the founder. Robert, we know, was buried in the abbey.[1] May not one of the coffins have been that of Henry ?[2]

The three daughters of Earl David by his wife made marriages suited to their high rank. Margaret, the eldest, was wife of Alan, Lord of Galloway.[3] Through the marriage of her daughter, Devorgulla, she was grandmother of John Balliol, King of Scotland. The second daughter, Isabella, married Robert Brus, Lord of Annandale. Her son Robert was one of the 'Competitors' in 1291; and the grandson of the latter was Robert i. of Scotland. The third daughter, Ada, was wife of Henry de Hastynges. Her grandson John was one of the 'Competitors.'[4]

Among the benefactors of Lindores is the founder's son, 'John of Scotland,' several charters of whom are transcribed in our Chartulary (Nos. xv. to xxi. inclusive, xc. and cxxxix.). David's daughter, Isabella de Brus, granted her messuage of Cragyn and other lands near Dundee (No. xl.)—grants confirmed by her son Robert, afterwards the 'Competitor' (No. xli.). Another grandson of the founder, Henry de Hastynges, the son of his daughter Ada, granted his vill of Flanders in

---

[1] *Scotichronicon* (Hearne's edit.), lib. ix. cap. 27.
[2] Or, possibly, of David, who is named in Charter 11. See the ground-plan of the abbey in Macgibbon and Ross's *Ecclesiastical Architecture of Scotland*,

the Garioch to the abbey in exchange for second tithes (No. cxviii.) ; while the Gocelin de Balliol, who appears in an agreement with the abbey in 1260 (No. cxxiii.), was a brother of John de Balliol, presumably the husband of Devorgulla.

John 'of Scotland,' or 'the Scot,' succeeded his father as Earl of Huntingdon. On Whitsunday 1227 he received the honour of knighthood from King Alexander ; and on the death of his maternal uncle, the Earl of Chester, in 1232, he succeeded to the dignities of the great Palatine earldom. After that date he styles himself Earl of Chester and Huntingdon. The Chartulary affords examples of his charters both before (Nos. xv., repeated in cxxxix., and xvi.) and after (Nos. xvii., xviii., xix., xx., xxi., and xc.) his succession to Chester. He died 5th June 1237, without issue, and both his earldoms reverted to the English crown. Soon after the estates and dignities of the earldom of Chester became centred in the royal family. At a later period it was assigned to the eldest son of the King of England. As is well known, the title of Earl of Chester has long been borne by successive Princes of Wales.[1]

Beside the children by his marriage with Matilda, we possess evidence for the existence of three (perhaps four) illegitimate children, two (perhaps three) sons and one daughter. The dates or approximate dates of some of the charters in which their names occur point to the conclusion that these children were the offspring of a connection or connections formed previous to his marriage, which, as we have seen, was entered upon rather late in life. Henry of Stirling and Henry of Brechin occur not infrequently in the testing clauses of charters. And Ada,[2] daughter of Earl David and wife of Malise, son of Earl Ferteth and brother of Earl Gilbert of Stratherne, appears as granting a ploughgate of land to Lindores together 'with my body' (No. xxxvi.).[1]

A charter of Earl David (No. v.) is tested by 'duobus Henricis filiis comitis.' Charters of Earl John 'of Scotland' (Nos. xv. xvi. xvii. xviii. xix.) are tested by 'Henrico de Strivelyn' or 'Henrico de Strivelyn fratre meo.' The charter of Henry of Brechin (No. lx.) is tested by 'Domino Henrico de Strivelin fratre meo.'[2]

The son David (Nos. ii. iii.) was perhaps illegitimate, or perhaps, being legitimate, died in infancy. He is not mentioned in Fordun.

THE CONNECTION OF THE EARLDOM OF HUNTINGDON WITH THE SCOTTISH ROYAL FAMILY.

For our purposes it is unnecessary to enter on any minute or elaborate investigation of the history of the earldom of Huntingdon in its connection with the royal family of Scotland. It may suffice to say that it first came to be held by David, afterwards David i. of Scotland, by his marriage with Matilda, daughter of and heir of Waltheof, Earl of Huntingdon, and widow of Simon de St. Liz, Earl of Northampton. It was by right of his wife that David held this English fief. After his accession to the throne David seems to have transferred (doubtless with the consent of his feudal superior, the King of England) the earldom of Huntingdon

---

[1] See also Nos. ix. and xv.

[2] Henry of Stirling and Henry of Brechin, 'my brothers,' witness a charter of Earl John.—*Registrum de Aberbrothoc*, i. 57. We find both Henry of Stirling and Henry of Brechin, 'sons of Earl David,' present at Forfar in October 1225.—*Lib. de Balmerinach*, p. 5. Henry of Stirling and Henry of Brechin were witnesses in the nineteenth year of Alexander ii. (that is the year ending 3rd December 1233)—*Ibid.* pp. 18 and 31. And we find Henry of

to his eldest son, Prince Henry.[1] On the death of Prince
Henry the earldom seems to have gone to his eldest son
Malcolm.   Not long after Malcolm's accession to the throne,
whose stability was seriously affected by the internal dissen-
sions of the kingdom, Henry ii. of England seized the
opportunity for demanding the cession to him of the counties
of Northumberland, Cumberland, and Westmoreland. The
offer was made that Malcolm's claim to Huntingdon would be
admitted if he surrendered the northern counties.   His
weakness perhaps left him no alternative but to comply with
the discreditable proposal. If we may trust *Scotichronicon*
(viii. 1) Earl David held Huntingdon in the reign of his
brother Malcolm.   But it is certain that on King William
and David joining the confederation of the supporters of the
younger Henry in his rebellion against his father, Henry ii.
forfeited the English fiefs held by both brothers, and in 1174
bestowed the Earldom of Huntingdon on Simon de St. Liz,
the second of that name. It was not till 1184 or 1185 that,
on the death of St. Liz, Henry conferred the earldom of
Huntingdon on King William, who immediately in the
presence of Henry (*coram rege*), and therefore with his consent, gave the earldom to his brother David.[2] From that
time the earldom remained with David, and after him with
his son John 'the Scot.' The history of the earldom after
the death of Earl John (1237) does not concern us.   He died,
as has been said, without issue.

EARL DAVID AND THE EARLDOM OF LENNOX.

Our Chartulary contains (No. i.) a grant by King William
to Earl David, conferring on him, *inter alia*, 'comitatum de

Levenaus, cum omnibus pertinenciis suis.' The date of the charter can be approximately determined as between 1178 and 1182.[1] The account commonly accepted, and probably correct, of this grant is that the earldom had fallen to the king in ward owing to the minority of Alwyn, second Earl of Lennox.[2] Lennox is not among the grants recorded in *Scotichronicon*[3] as having been made by William to David after the return of the former from his captivity in England. On the other hand, the same authority elsewhere,[4] when recording Earl David's death, describes him as 'Earl of Huntingdon, Garioch, and Lennox.' A notice of Earl David's administration of Lennox is to be found in the Register of the Monastery of Paisley, where we read that when he held and possessed the earldom of Lennox he sought to obtain an 'aid' from the lands of the church of Kilpatrick, 'as from the other lands of the earldom, but he could not obtain it as these lands were defended by the Church.'[5] The grant is quite of a piece with other indications of the affection that subsisted between the two brothers. Wardship was one of the most valuable of the feudal casualties of the Crown; the dues payable in respect of it often amounted to very large sums, and in England wardship was commonly assigned at this time to the highest bidder. When Earl David granted to Lindores (No. II.) the tithe of 'all my gains which come to me of the gains of the king my brother,' the tithe of the profits arising from 'ward' would, of course, be included.[6]

---

[1] Hugh, Bishop of St. Andrews, one of the witnesses, was appointed to that see not earlier than 1178, when his predecessor died (*Chron. de Mailros*, s. a.). And Earl Waldeve, another witness, died 1182 (*ibid.* s. a.).

[2] Douglas, *Peerage*, ii. 81.   [3] Lib. ix. cap. 27.

[4] Lib. ix. cap. 33.   [5] *Reg. Monast. Passel.*, pp. 166-8.

[6] Earl David's life in England affords an example of his payments to Richard I.

EARL DAVID AND THE THIRD CRUSADE

The foundation of Lindores has been supposed by some to have been in fulfilment of a vow made by Earl David when in peril of shipwreck on his voyage to Scotland when returning from the Third Crusade. The historical value of the story upon which this supposition is based claims investigation. Hector Boece[1] supplies a long and circumstantial story of Earl David with five hundred knights having accompanied Richard of England on the great expedition for the relief of Palestine in 1190.

Bower[2] represents Guido, first abbot of Lindores, as having ruled his monastery for eight and twenty years, and places his death on 17th June 1219, from which we gather that Guido was appointed in 1191, which, of course, if we accept it, is fatal to the story of Boece.

But it is right to examine more minutely the account given by that author. David is represented as sailing with Richard's followers from Marseilles. The capture of Cyprus is then recounted ; after which David appears with Richard at the siege of Acre, and as commander of the troops who, by the aid of a friendly Scot named Oliver, in the Saracen garrison, succeeded in getting entrance to the city. On the return voyage Earl David is shipwrecked, carried captive to Alexandria, released by the efforts of Venetian merchants, carried first to Constantinople and then to Venice, where he is redeemed by certain Englishmen who were trading in that city. He makes his way to Flanders, whence he sails for Scotland. The ship is blown by the tempests of winter 'near to Norway and Shetland.' In his peril he vows that if he returns home in safety he will build a church in honour of the

Blessed Virgin Mary. By the aid of the Virgin his ship enters the estuary of the Tay, and comes to Aberdour (?) with...

or sails, not far from the rock on which there is now the chapel dedicated to St. Nicholas. He leaps on shore, and in gratitude calls the town of Alectum by a new name—Dei-donum [Dundee], and immediately founds a church dedicated to St. Mary in the field called Triticium [? Wheatfield], and makes it a parish church. King William hears of the return of his brother, whom he had mourned as dead, and hurries to Dundee. His joy is almost inexpressible. He orders prayers to be made, and great festal rejoicing, with public sports. He summons a great council of the magnates of the realm, and therein grants permission to his brother to build a monastery wherever he may choose. David thereupon builds and richly endows an abbey in Fife, dedicated to St. Mary, called in the vulgar tongue Lindores.

Such, in outline, is the story told by Boece, which, borrowed from him, is repeated by Holinshed and by George Buchanan, and has been accepted by more than one recent writer of repute. Are we to give it any credence, and if so, to what extent?

First of all, it must be acknowledged that such a story coming to us from the inaccurate and credulous Boece gains no presumption in favour of its truth by reason of its source.

But, again, the *Historiae Scotorum* of Boece was written in the early part of the sixteenth century; and there is no reason to suppose that the genuine sources of history on the matter before us, to which he had access, were other than those possessed by ourselves. Now the honest Fordun and his continuator, Bower, who were never inclined to keep back anything that made for the honour of the royal family of Scotland, and who record several of the more noteworthy incidents in the lives of King William, the Lion, and his brother, David, are silent as to this chivalrous and romantic episode in the

history of the latter. There is not the slightest hint that David had engaged in the Third Crusade. While the account of king Richard's colle...in to...aud his subsequent adventures are given with some fulness (lib. viii. cc. 51, 53) it is scarcely conceivable that if Fordun or Bower had heard of Earl David's expedition to Palestine it would have failed to find a place in *Scotichronicon*.   Of perhaps no less weight in the argument is the silence of the *Chronicle of Melrose,* which does not omit to notice King Richard's expedition. The names of some of the men of rank who joined in this Crusade are entered in the *Chronicle*, but the name of Earl David is not among them.   The same silence marks the English chroniclers, Roger de Hoveden and Walter de Coventry.   The chroniclers of the events of the Third Crusade make no mention of the brother of the King of Scots as among the princes and nobles who took part in that enterprise.   And most notable is the absence of any mention of David in the *Itinerarium* of King Richard.   If ever the argument from silence is entitled to carry weight, here is a clear example.

As it happens, none of the references to Earl David, so far as I know,[1] represent him as in Scotland or England between the date of his marriage (26th August 1190) and the beginning of the year 1194, so that we are not in a position to disprove the story by positive evidence.   It is certain indeed that he did not accompany the English troops who had proceeded by ship across the Bay of Biscay; but Boece's story represents him as joining the fleet at Marseilles.   The facts of authentic history, however, reveal that Richard Cœur de Lion sailed from Marseilles on 7th August.[2]

In Wyntoun's *Cronykill* (viii. 6) we are told, with evident disbelief on the writer's part, that, ' as sum men sayd,' Earl David was the elder brother of King William.   This notion, as we have seen, was given currency by the earlier form of

Fordun's *Chronica*, but was afterwards corrected. But Wyntoun goes on, speaking of Earl David—

> 'And, as men sayd, in Sarzines
> He trawalyd quhen Willame crownyd wes.'

Assuming that 'Sarzines' means the country of the Saracens, it would seem that in the early years of the fifteenth century the notion which Fordun in his first (and erroneous) statement was content to express in the form that David was 'in partibus transmarinis' at the time of the death of King Malcolm and that therefore William was made king instead of David, assumed a more definite shape, but was still not generally accepted. But as William succeeded to the throne in 1165, this journey 'in Sarzines' (if it ever took place) is not to be confused with the Third Crusade in 1190. At a later period there was a story current, probably originating in a French romance, that a Scottish prince named David had fought in the Holy Land, and it appears that he was identified by some with David, Earl of Huntingdon. Major, in his *Historia Majoris Britanniae* (lib. iv. cap. 5), after recording the foundation of the monastery of Lindores by David, Earl of Huntingdon, goes on to say : 'This was the David of whom mention is made in a book that is rather popular (*satis vulgaris*) among the French, entitled, "Of the Sons of the Three Kings, to wit, of France, England, and Scotland "; and we have a book in our vernacular tongue not differing from it.'[1]

Once more, if the founding of Lindores was in fulfilment of a vow made in peril at sea (though this does not seem necessarily implied by the story as told by Boece) it is strange that there is not the slightest allusion to the fact in the foundation charter (No. ii.).

---

[1] Sir David Dalrymple (*Annals*, vol. i. p. 159), has doubtless correctly identified the French book to which Major refers. He gives the title thus :—

On the whole I am disposed to regard the account not only as 'not proven,' but as wholly fictitious.   It can only be said, that if Boece has perverted history, he has, at all events, had the good fortune of supplying Sir Walter Scott with a figure for the romantic story of *The Talisman*.[1]

The munificence of Earl David towards the Scottish Church was not confined to the foundation of Lindores.   The *Register of the Priory of St. Andrews* reveals several benefactions of his bestowed upon that house.   He gave land in Garioch;[2] land in Forgrund;[3] the whole of the cane and conveth[4] which the canons of the priory owed to him from his lands at Eglesgirg;[5] and a toft in Dundee;[6] and a mark from the rents of the same town.[7]

THE EARLY EARLS OF STRATHERN[8]

There is a group of charters in the Lindores Chartulary in

---

[1] Scott would himself have been the first to laugh, and laugh long and loud, if any one had pointed out that his gallant young Earl of Huntingdon was an elderly married man, and that his espousal with the Princess Edith was bigamy.   With a genuine feeling for the general correctness of his historic colouring, Scott was very indifferent to details.

[2] Pp. 226, 239.   [3] P. 237.

[4] 'Cane' in this connection is to be understood as rent payable in kind. 'Conveth' was the allowance for the hospitable entertainment of the feudal superior when passing through his lands.

[5] P. 238.   [6] *Ibid.*   [7] P. 240.

[8] *THE EARLS OF STRATHERN to* A.D. 1270.

Note.—Names occurring in the Lindores Chartulary are printed in small capitals.

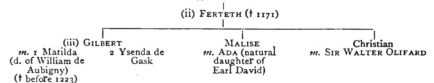

(i) Malise

(ii) FERTETH († 1171)

| (iii) GILBERT
m. 1 Matilda
(d. of William de
Aubigny)
(† before 1223) | 2 Ysenda de
Gask | MALISE
m. ADA (natural
daughter of
Earl David) | Christian
m. SIR WALTER OLIFARD |

which the family of the Earls of Strathern makes its appearance. Some members of the family appear as benefactors of the abbey, while others confirm or attest the grants. With a view to some approximate dating of these charters it is necessary to know something of the history of the early earls and their sons.

The first of the Celtic chieftains of Strathern, who appears under the name of earl, is (i) Malise, who is found witnessing the foundation charter of the Priory of Scone in 1114 or 1115,[1] and a grant made to the same monastery a few years later.[2] He was one of the witnesses of a charter of King David giving land in Partick to the Cathedral of Glasgow on the occasion of the dedication of the building in 1136.[3] And some grants to Dunfermline are witnessed by Earl Malise.[4] In the account of the battle of the Standard (22nd August 1138) given by Ailred, Abbot of Rievaulx, the Earl of Strathern is described as refusing to adopt the armour ordinarily worn by the Norman followers of King David.

The successor of Malise was (ii) Earl Ferteth or Ferquhard, referred to as the father of Earl Gilbert and of Malise in our Chartulary (Nos. xxix., xxxiii., xxxiv., and xxxvi.).

In 1160 Ferteth led five other of the seven Earls of Scotland (Earl Duncan of Fife, who generally heads the list of the seven earls, probably not being associated with them)[5] in an attempt to capture King Malcolm, who was then in his castle at Perth. The attempt was unsuccessful, and after a few days, on the intervention of the clergy, the king and the earls came to amicable terms. Fordun (viii. 4) explains this rising of the six earls as originating in the dread caused by the king's extreme devotion to English ways and to the English King, Henry ii., with regard to whom, Fordun (with an ecclesiastic's reminiscence of the language of Luke xix. 14), represents the earls as saying within themselves, 'Nolumus hunc regnare super nos.'

That Earl Ferteth should alone be mentioned by name among the six earls points, it would seem, to his having taken a leading part in this affair. The same national spirit which had shown itself in opposition to the newly introduced methods of warfare in the case of his father Earl Malise, seems to have asserted itself again in the conspiracy against a king, who had, in opposition to the wishes of many leading men in Scotland, a short time before attached himself to the army of the King of England, while it was engaged in the siege of Toulouse, and had received from the King of England the distinction of knighthood.

According to the *Chronicle of Melrose*, Earl Ferteth died in 1171. He was succeeded by (iii) Earl Gilbert, who witnessed or confirmed the grants made to Lindores by his brother Malise and by his own son Robert (Nos. xxx., xxxi., xxxii.) while he himself showed his interest in the Abbey by undertaking the military service (*onus exercitus*) due from the land of Exmagirdle in the parish of Dron, some few miles from the Abbey, which had been assigned to the monks. It was not Earl Gilbert but his brother Malise who was the chief benefactor of Lindores at this period. Earl Gilbert, who was munificent in his ecclesiastical benefactions, was founder of Inchaffray and did much for the cathedral of Dunblane,[1] and probably his resources were taxed to the uttermost in support of these establishments. The special interest of Malise in Lindores can be easily accounted for when we remember that he had married Ada, daughter of Earl David, the founder of the Abbey. Ada herself, ' daughter of Earl David, and wife

body should find sepulture (No. xxxvi.). And Malise makes the grant to the Abbey of the lands of Rathengothen for the souls of his ancestors, 'and for the soul of Ada, my wife, daughter of Earl David' (No. xxix.).

Earl Gilbert had married Matildis, daughter of William de Aubegni, and by her had a numerous family. Our own Chartulary has references to his sons, Robert, afterwards earl (No. xxxi.), and as earl (Nos. xxv., xxvii., etc.); Fergus, a considerable benefactor of Lindores (Nos. xxiii., xxiv., xxvi., xxviii., xxxii.); Gilbert (among the witnesses of No. xxviii.); and Malise, 'parson of Gask' (among the witnesses of Nos. xxvii. and liii.; and see xxviii.). From other sources we know that Earl Gilbert's eldest son Gilchrist had died in his father's lifetime, and was buried in Inchaffray;[1] and there are notices of two other sons, William and Ferteth.[2] Mr. Cosmo Innes in his Preface to the *Registrum de Inchaffray* accepts for the date of the death of Earl Gilbert the year 1223, on the authority of a chronicle 'which seems to have been written in the diocese, or to be in some other way peculiarly connected with Dunblane.'[3]

Gilbert was succeeded by (iv) Earl Robert, who appears, as has been observed, several times in our Chartulary. His son Malise, who afterwards succeeded, appears in our Chartulary during the life of his father as a-witness to a charter (No. xxvii.). He must have succeeded as (v) Earl of Strathern before 1244; in which year he appears as one of the guarantors of the treaty between Alexander ii. and Henry iii. of Eng-

---

[1] The principal charter of Inchaffray is dated in the year 1200, 'ab obitu prenominati filii nostri Gilcrist anno secundo.'—*Registrum de Inchaffray*, p. 5.

[2] Among the witnesses of the principal charter of Inchaffray, we find 'Willelmius, Ferthead, Robertus, filii comitis.' The order in which the names appear is presumably that of seniority; and as Robert succeeded his father in

land.[1] He died, according to Bower, in France, in the year 1270.[2] This slight sketch of the family of the early Earls of Strathern is sufficiently full for our special purpose, and will be helpful in determining more or less nearly the dates of the charters.[3]

The relation of the Earls of Strathern to the bishopric of Dunblane was peculiar. Whatever measure of truth there be in the story told by Bower [4] that Earl Gilbert divided his earldom into three parts, one part being given to the bishop and church of Dunblane, one part to Inchaffray, which he had founded, and the third being reserved for himself and his heirs, his relation and that of his successors to the church was one of great and peculiar influence. They are styled the ' patrons' of the church,[5] and, what is much more remarkable, the Pope when appointing, or confirming an appointment, to the bishopric, intimated the fact (as in other cases to the king) to the Earl of Strathern. Thus Pope Martin iv. when appointing Bishop William in 1284 sends concurrent letters to the chapter, to the clergy and people, and to Malise, Earl of Strathern, ' patron of the church of Dunblane.' [6] We find the same course followed in the case of the papal confirmation of the election of Alpin (1296) ; [7] and again in the confirmation of Nicholas de Balmyle,[8] and again in 1347.[9] In 1361 an appointment is reported by the Pope to the earl and to the king. [10]

EARL DAVID'S ORIGINAL ENDOWMENT OF LINDORES

From the various lands held by Earl David in Scotland, the names of which are recorded in the charter of King William's

---

[1] See *Foedera*, i. 257.

grant to his brother (No. I.), he selected Lindores as the site of his monastery. The lands lie on the southern banks of the Tay, and the Abbey is beautifully situated about five hundred yards from the river and half a mile eastwards from the little town of Newburgh, the 'nostrum burgum' and 'novum burgum' of our Chartulary. The extent of land here granted was considerable. Its marches are not fully indicated in the Chartulary;[1] but from notices of the leasing of various holdings and from the 'Rentaill of the Abbey of Lundoris,' now preserved in the charter-chest of Mugdrum, and assigned to the close of the fifteenth century, Mr. Alexander Laing, who on questions of the topography of Lindores and its neighbourhood is entitled to speak with high authority, describes the property as 'a stretch of about four miles in length and upwards of two miles in breadth, of fine upland pasture, and of rich and diversified arable soil.'[2] These lands included the land of the church of Lindores, which church was at the same time made over to the monastery.

The foundation charter also grants the whole island called 'Redinche,' which one cannot doubt has been correctly identified as the large island in the Tay facing the monastery and now known as Mugdrum island. Tall reeds grow in great abundance on the shores of the island; and Mr. Laing's conjecture that the word Redinche is a form of 'Reedinch' will perhaps commend itself to those who view the island from the ruins of the Abbey.[3] The island and the fishings round the island were granted to the monastery with the reservation

---

[1] Lindores Loch—the *magnus lacus* of Charter II., now skirted by the railway from Ladybank to Perth, is more than three-quarters of a mile in length, and more than a quarter of a mile broad in its widest part. The stream (*rivulus*) from the lake to the Tay which formed the eastern boundary of Earl David's grant falls into the river near the abbey. But see Notes on CXL.

(1) of the earl's 'yare,' a word signifying an enclosure of stake-nets in which fish were caught as the tide ebbed; and (2) his right of pasturing his cattle on the island. But apparently this right of pasture was not to be to the exclusion of the cattle of the monastery, for in the Bull of Celestine III. (No. XCIII.) it is stated that the 'easements' of the island were to be common to the earl and the monks.

The other lands granted to the monastery at its foundation were the lands of Fintray (in Aberdeenshire); and 'in Garioch, Lethgauel, and Malind'; and in Perth all Earl David's land that was called Inch (*insula*);[1] and a ploughgate of land in Newtyle granted by Earl David's natural daughter, Ada, wife of Malise, son of Ferteth, Earl of Strathern.[2]

Earl David also granted to the monastery three tofts, one in Perth, one 'in my burgh of Dundee,' and one 'in my burgh of Inverury.'

Some time after the foundation Earl David added the gift of certain lands on the coast of Kincardineshire close to its southern boundary.[3] They lie within, or close to, the parish of St. Cyrus (Eglesgirg); and they appeared to have remained in possession of Lindores down to the dissolution of the monastery.[4]

Earl David's grants of parish churches with their church-lands and tithes were numerous; indeed, as he states, all the churches in Scotland which were in his gift he made over to the Abbey.[5] These were the churches of (1) Lindores (already referred to), which is almost certainly to be identified with the

---

[1] In 1236 the monastery surrendered Inch to Alexander II. in exchange for other land, see No. XXII.

[2] Compare No. II. with No. XXXVI. One is led to suppose that these were not two gifts of Ada (though that is just possible), but that the 'vill of Balemagh'

old parish church of Abdie,[1] the ruins of which lie close to the north-west corner of the Loch of Lindores, about two miles from the abbey; (2) the church of Dundee,[2] followed by the churches in Aberdeenshire, namely, (3) the church of Fintray; (4) the church of Inverury, with its chapel of Monkegie;[3] (5) the church of Durnach (Logie-Durno); (6) the church of Prameth (Premnay); (7) the church of Rathmuliel, or Rathmuriel;[4] (8) the church of Inchmabanin (Insch); (9) the church of Culsamuel (Culsalmond); and (10) the church of Kilalcmond (Kinnethmont). All these, with their chapels, lands, and tithes, were made over to the monastery 'ad proprios usus et sustentaciones eorundem monachorum.' The significance of this phrase will be dealt with by and by.[5]

In addition to lands and churches, Earl David made an important augmentation to the revenues of the monastery by grants of another kind. First, casualties of various sorts would accrue to him from time to time as feudal superior and lord of Garioch, wards, 'aids,' fines on subinfeudation, and such like; of these a tithe was granted to Lindores. Secondly, he granted to Lindores a tithe of his 'pleas,' that is, a tithe of the fines, escheats, and other issues of his baron's court.

---

[1] The 'Ebedyn' of No. LXII.

[2] Mr. A. Laing states that the first mention of the town of Dundee in authentic record is to be found in the foundation charter 'certainly executed before A.D. 1198' (*Lindores Abbey*, etc., p. 55). The bull of Celestine III. (No. XCIII.) enables us to point to the mention of Dundee early in 1195.

[3] In the bull of Celestine III. the language used is 'the church of Rothket, with its chapels, namely, Inverury and Monkegie,' and this is repeated in the bull of Innocent III. In King William's charter (No. CXXXVIII.) there is no mention of Rothket; and we have 'the church of Inverury with the chapel of Monkegie.' Monkegie does not appear as a separate parish in the thirteenth century. In 1481 'the paroche Kyrk of Monkege' is mentioned. See *Collections for a History of the Shires of Aberdeen and Banff*, vol. i. p. 569.

[4] There is now no parish corresponding to Rathmuriel. Its situation can be inferred approximately from Charter LV. The form of the word is Rothmuriell in the valuation of churches in the thirteenth century printed in *Registrum Aberdonense*, ii. p. 54. In *Retours* for 1626 (No. 178) we find ' Christiskirk de Rothmurielle.' The ruins of Christ's Kirk are in the parish of Kinnethmont.

Thirdly, he granted a tithe of the gains which came to him
of the gains of his brother the king.   An example of such
is afforded in the gains accruing from the wardship of
the Lennox already referred to.[1]   Fourthly, be granted a
tithe of all things capable of tithe on his manors beyond
the Mounth, 'of grain and meal, of butter and cheese, of
flesh and venison, of food and drink, of the skins of animals
caught in hunting, of wax and salt, of fat and tallow,' etc.

All the grants of Earl David, like the great majority of the
grants made in early times to the Church in Scotland, were
'in free, pure, and perpetual alms,' and nothing was to be
asked in return 'save only prayers for the weal of the soul.'
The monks were to be free of all secular services such as lay
vassals were required to render to their lord, and were expressly exempt from the vexatious demand of 'aids' (*auxilia*).[2]
We have already seen an instance of Earl David, as holding
the Earldom of Lennox, attempting to obtain an 'aid' from
churchlands of Kilpatrick.[3]

Lastly, the foundation charter confers on the monastery
their 'court free in all respects, and the dignity of peace.'
The word 'dignitas' in this connection is probably to be
understood in the sense (familiar to students of mediæval
Latin) of 'privilege,' and perhaps refers to the Abbey having
the earl's protection.   Its equivalent in the bull of Celestine
iii. is 'firmam pacem' (No. xciii.).   As 'dignitas pacis' is
confirmed by King William (No. cxxxviii.), the Abbey was
secured of royal protection.   In another charter (No. v.), the
earl grants the abbot and convent a court of jurisdiction over
'their men' living in the churchlands of Culsalmond and
Monkegie in the north.

---

[1] P. xxix.

Such are the grants made in the foundation charter. Other benefactions, though not very many or extensive, were made by others, which will be noticed hereafter. But this seems a suitable place for considering more particularly the character and the value of the grant of the ten parish churches—Lindores, Dundee, and the eight churches in the lordship of Garioch. What is said of these may be applied *mutatis mutandis* to other churches granted to the monks *in proprios usus.*

Immediately on the first notices we possess of the establishment of parish churches in Scotland, we meet with the beginnings of the practice of patrons conferring them upon monasteries. Such a transfer, when not merely a grant of the advowson (that is, merely of the right of presenting a priest to the bishop for institution to the church with its cure of souls), was intended to convey the whole revenues of the church from lands, tithes, oblations, and dues to the monastery. This could only be effected with the sanction of the bishop in whose diocese the church was situated; and it was his duty (if he sanctioned the transfer) to secure that a decent maintenance should be allowed by the monastery to the priest who was to have cure of souls in the parish. This priest was instituted by the bishop, and when once appointed was irremovable except by legal process in the ecclesiastical courts. He was the 'perpetual vicar,' or, more briefly, the 'vicar' of the parish, the monastery obtaining all the rights of 'rector.' The monastery had the right to present the vicar, who received for his maintenance such an allowance as was agreed on between the parties, with the concurrence and assent of the bishop.

As can be easily understood, it was a temptation to the abbot and chapter to appoint a cheap man, one who would take as little as possible in remuneration for his services; and then leave as much as possible to be added to the means of the monastery. The bishop appear constantly as endeavouring to secure good terms for the vicar of each church. And such efforts on his part contributed not a little to the strained relations, or open antagonism, that we find frequently subsisting between the bishops and the monasteries.

The growing evil of the aggrandisement of the monasteries at the cost of the parochial clergy soon made itself felt in various parts of Western Christendom, and we find injunctions by the Popes issued with a view to restrain or mitigate the injury. Not long before the foundation of Lindores we find Pope Alexander III. writing to the Archbishop of York that he should refuse the presentation made by monasteries to parish churches unless in his presence an income was assigned to the presentee which would afford him a fitting maintenance (*congruam sustentacionem*), and enable him to pay his dues to the bishop.[1] Some ten years later the same Pope rebuked the monasteries of the diocese of York for their 'covetousness which is idolatry,' as manifested by their cutting down the incomes of the parish clergy serving the churches which had been appropriated to them.[2] The Scottish Church was painfully sensible of the evil. In the body of Statutes enacted in Scotland in the thirteenth century, we find a canon on the subject enjoining that the vicars of churches should have a sufficient and decent maintenance (*sufficientem et honestam sustentacionem*) from the revenues of the churches whose altars they served. It fixes the minimum income for a vicar at ten marks (6 lib. 13s. 4d.), after meeting all the 'ordinary burdens,' such as procurations and other dues of the bishop, and adds that in the case of rich churches (*in pinguioribus ecclesiis*) there should be a suitable increase of the amount.[3] But the struggle between the vicars (supported by the bishops) and the monasteries continued to manifest itself from time to time. In the case of some of the Lindores

certain of the vicars of three of the churches in the diocese of Aberdeen, which we seem justified in identifying with Culsalmond, Rathmuriel, and Kinnethmont (Kilalcmond), claiming an augmentation to their incomes, and proceeding to litigation on the subject (No. xcii.). The question was appealed to the Apostolic See, and the Pope, according to a sensible practice, common at this time, referred the matter to certain Scottish ecclesiastics delegated by him to examine into the dispute and pronounce judgment. One of the vicars, the vicar of Kinnethmont, had taken the law into his own hands, and for three years had refused the payment to the monastery, out of his tithe, of thirty lambs of good quality (*pacabiles*) which he was bound to render. The papal delegates were, as usual, chosen from among persons who might be presumed to have no personal interest in the disputed question. They were the chancellor of Moray, and the treasurer, and a canon of Dunkeld.

In the bull appointing the delegates (No. cv.) we find brought out clearly the action of the Bishop of Aberdeen in the matter. He had learned that Lindores and other monasteries had been demanding increased payments from their 'appropriate' churches, and he had forbidden the vicars, on pain of suspension, to pay anything in addition to the old pensions, that is, the annual payment fixed at the granting of these churches to the monks *ad proprios usus*. It was a test question of great importance. Not only Lindores, but also three other, much more important, religious houses were affected. The priory of St. Andrews and the abbeys of Kelso and Arbroath had their 'appropriate' churches in the diocese; and the three monasteries (a formidable combination) united their forces with Lindores to bring the question to an issue.[1] The curious will not find it difficult to understand the contentions of the parties if they read the bulls (Nos. cv. and cvi.) and the adjudication pronounced five years later by the delegates, but not finally confirmed by the Pope for two more years.[1] Appeals to Rome were tedious as well as costly.

Differences between the monastery and the vicars of their 'appropriate' churches were not confined to the diocese of Aberdeen. About the same time trouble of a like kind arose as to the proper valuation of the vicarage of St. Mary's Dundee. The abbot and convent of Lindores had presented one William Mydford to the vicarage, and the bishop of the diocese (Brechin) had admitted the presentee with the reservation that the bishop should have the right of determining the proportions of the revenues of the church which should be assigned to the monastery and the vicar respectively. The bishop had a formal hearing in the spring of 1252, the parties being present; the revenues of the church were carefully considered, and the bishop, *de consilio proborum virorum*, pronounced his decision that the vicar should have the whole altarage, and out of it should pay annually a 'pension' of ten marks sterling[2] to the monastery. Mydford appealed to Rome against this decision, and refused, despite the frequent admonitions of the bishop, to pay the assigned pension. Somewhat complicated litigation continued to drag its slow course for more than four years. Finally the vicar submitted, and agreed to pay his ten marks and all arrears, together with interest and law expenses, which were taken as amounting to fifty marks, though it was admitted that they really amounted to a larger sum.[3]

There is preserved in the Register of the Diocese of Aberdeen a valuation of the parishes of the diocese, which has

---

[1] See *Regist. Aberdon.*, i. pp. 19-26.

[2] After more than two hundred years it was this sum—vi lib. xiii s. and iv d.—which continued to come to Lindores from 'the wiccarag of Dundy.' See

been assigned by Mr. Cosmo Innes to 'about 1275.'[1] It is of much value to us as enabling us to gain a tolerably correct notion of the revenues of the churches in the Garioch which were 'appropriate' of the abbey of Lindores, and of the proportion of such revenues which went respectively to the abbey and to the vicars. Whether the valuation should be assigned to 'about 1275' I shall not discuss; but it is certain that it was before Boiamund's valuation, of which some account will be given later on. If conjecture is permissible it may be supposed that it was a valuation which it was hoped that Boiamund would accept; but, as will be seen, he was required by his commission from the Pope to take a valuation on oath, and the real revenues (*verus valor*) so ascertained were considerably larger than represented in the old valuation. For the convenience of the reader, and the purpose of comparison with Boiamund's valuation, in which pounds, shillings, and pence is a frequent denomination, the marks of this valuation have been reduced to the more familiar form.

Extracting from this Register the churches of Lindores, we have the following results. The word 'Rector' is to be understood as the community of Lindores, which enjoyed the rectoral rights.

Fintray, .	Vicar, 6lib. 13s. 4d.	Rector, 1lib. 13s. 4d. and 20 chalders of meal.
Inverury,	Vicar, 11lib. 7s. 8d.	Rector, 6lib. 10s. and 24 chalders of meal.
Premnay,	Vicar, 2lib. 13s. 4d.	Rector, 10lib. 13s. 8d.
Rathmuriel, .	Vicar, 2lib.	Rector, 6lib. 6s. 8d.
Insch, .	Vicar, 4lib.	Rector, 14lib. 13s. 4d.
Culsalmond, .	Vicar, 4lib.	Rector, 17lib. 13s. 4d.
Kinnethmund,	Vicar, 4lib.	Rector, 16lib.
Durnach, .	Vicar, 13lib. 6s. 8d.	Rector, 7lib. 6s. 8d. and 30 chalders of meal.
Leslie,[2] . .	Vicar, 3lib. 6s. 8d.	Rector, 10lib.

It is perhaps now impossible to determine with precise accuracy the value of a chalder of meal in the third quarter of the thirteenth century;[1] but from those cases where simply a money value is given to the vicar's and the rector's portion it can readily be seen to what a large extent the parish revenues of the Garioch churches were diverted to the abbey of Lindores. Even allowing for the great purchasing value of money in those days it is plain that some of the vicars were but poorly paid.

In 1275 the new valuation of the ecclesiastical property of Scotland, demanded by the Pope with a view to exacting a tithe for the relief of the Holy Land, again furnishes us with material for estimating the increases to the vicars of the appropriate churches and comparing them with the revenue received by the monastery. Boiamund, or, as he was called in Scotland, Bagimont, was sent from Rome to Scotland to make the valuation and collect the tithe. This proceeding was excessively distasteful to the clergy. A valuation which had served for many years was beyond question far too low, and Boiamund was empowered to compel the clergy to give their oaths to the accuracy of the returns they made. This he did; and 'Bagimont's Rolls' (imperfect though they are) form a most valuable record. In making my calculations I have followed the Roll as given from the copy preserved at Rome and published (1864) in Theiner's *Vetera Monumenta*.[2] While the record is deficient in many particulars, fortunately the return for the deanery of Garioch (in which all the northern churches of Lindores were situated) is complete; and the accounts are rendered for two years. The denomination in which the accounts are given varies; it is sometimes in marks, sometimes in pounds, shillings, and pence. I have reduced all the figures to the more familiar denomination. What is entered is the tithe of the *true value* as actually paid to Boiamund or his agents.

The tithe of the *verus valor* of the vicarages of the churches in the deanery of Garioch which belonged to the Abbey of Lindores, extracted from the accounts of Boiamund as printed in Theiner's *Vetera Monumenta Hibernorum et Scotorum Historiam illustrantia*, pp. 110-11 and p. 115 :—

	For the year ending 24th June 1275.			For the year ending 24th June 1276.		
	lib.	s.	d.	lib.	s.	d.
Fintray, . . .	0	17	4	1	7	4
Inverury, . . .	1	4	0	1	4	0
Premnay, . . .	0	10	0	0	10	0
Rathmuriel,	0	6	8	0	6	8
Insch, · . .	0	17	4	0	17	3
Culsalmond,	0	10	0	0	10	0
Kinnethmund,	0	13	4	0	13	4
Durnach, . . .	1	6	8	1	10	0
Leslie, .	0	10	0	0	10	0

It is to be regretted that we have not a larger number of years from which to construct an average. A good year or a bad year for the farmers meant a good year or a bad year for the Church. But taking the average on the two years we find the vicar's income to be as follows :—

	lib.	s.	d.
Fintray, ...	11	3	4
Inverury, ...	12	0	0
Premnay, ...			
Rathmuriel			
Insch, ...	8	12	11
Culsalmond, ...	5	0	0
Kinnethmund, ...	6	13	4
Durnach, ...	14	3	4
Leslie .	5	0	0
Total	70	19	7

how we also have a record in Boiammund's accounts the tithe paid each year by the abbot of Lindores for his ecclesiastical income from the deanery of Garioch. This for the first year of Boiamund's taxation was 33lib. 3s. 8d., and for the second 23lib. 3s. 8d.; giving us the average of 28lib. 3s. 8d., representing an income of 281lib. 16s. 8d. This, perhaps, included the revenue from the lands in Garioch as well as the churches, so that we are still uncertain as to the proportion of revenue at this date which came from the churches of the Garioch to Lindores; but the earlier record in the Register of Aberdeen makes plain that the proportion was large.

In the case of the·parish of Dundee, Gregory, Bishop of Brechin (*circa* 1224) granted the whole revenues of the church to Lindores, but required that 10lib. sterling should be paid yearly to the vicar.[1]

To the benefactions of Earl David recorded in the foundation charter he soon added other grants. The monks were allowed (No. VII.) to take as much stone as they needed for the building of the church and conventual buildings from the earl's neighbouring quarry in Hyrneside.[2]

From his English possessions Earl David granted two churches—Wissendene (Whissendine) in the north-west of Rutlandshire, and Cunington (Conington) in the north of Huntingdonshire, both churches being then in the vast diocese of Lincoln.[3]

In or adjoining the latter parish was the abbey of Sautry in which the body of Earl David found its resting-place.

At the period of the foundation of Lindores, when so many

---

[1] *Lib. S. Marie de Lundoris*, p. 17.

[2] This is the Irnsyde or Earnside of later documents. For a discussion on the derivation of the word—which it is contended is not to be connected with the name of the river Earn—see Laing's *Lindores Abbey*, p. 87 note. I am dis-

of the barons of Scotland held fiefs in England, it was not uncommon to confer land and churches in England on Scottish monasteries, and Scottish land and churches on monasteries in England. A notable example of the latter was the grant of the church of Annan and five other parishes in the south-west of Scotland by an early Robert de Brus (who held the lordship of Guisborough in the north-riding of Yorkshire) to the abbot and canons of Guisborough.[1] The great Benedictine Abbey of Reading not only drew a 'pension from the Isle of May, but was entitled by a grant of David i. to the surplus of the revenues of the vill of Rindalgros, at the junction of the Earn and the Tay a few miles west of Lindores.[2]

The abbey of Jedburgh had the churches of Abbotsleigh, in Hunts, and Bassenthwaite and Kirkanders in Cumberland.[3] The priory of canons regular of St. Andrews obtained by the gift of Hugh de Lacy, Earl of Ulster, 'the churches of Carlingford and Ruskache, and the churches of all Caling,' in Ireland which were confirmed to the priory by Henry iii. in 1237.[4]

It was often more convenient to take a fixed 'pension' from a parish church in places remote from a monastery than to undertake dealing with the collection and disposal of tithes.[5] At any rate it was so in the case of Whissendine, where the arrangement sanctioned by the Bishop of Lincoln was that Lindores should have the patronage of the church and an annual pension of ten marks (No. cii.). In 1248 the incumbent of that parish was Master Rolandin, a chaplain of the Pope. Out of 'reverence' to the Apostolic See the

---

[1] See *Reg. Glasguen.*, ii. 620 and i. 105.
[2] See *Records of the Priory of the Isle of May*, p. 1.
[3] Originally the two latter churches were in the province of Cumbria when subject to the Scottish crown.

monastery did not in his case require the payment· of the pension ; but it was thought well to obtain from the Pope a bull (No. cii.) to the effect that this act of remission on their part was not to create a prejudice against the rights of the monastery in the future.[1]

The right of advowson to the church of Whissendine is distinctly acknowledged in the bull to belong to Lindores ; but at an earlier date (1213) that right was disputed in an imparlance before King John by Elena de Moreville and her son Alan de Galweia on the one part and the abbot of Lindores on the other.[2] The patronage was in Lindores in the reign of Edward i.; but it is said that during the wars of independence it was alienated to the prior and convent of Sempringham in Lincolnshire.[3] We certainly find nothing as to either of the English churches in the records of the monastery after that date.[4]

This is not an inappropriate place to observe that, when a parish church made over to monks *in proprios usus* was situated in the neighbourhood of the monastery, it was not unusual to serve the church by one of the monks and so avoid the appointment of a vicar. This would seem to have been the arrangement in the case of the parish of Abdie, in which the monastery of Lindores was placed, for we find mention, not of

---

[1] In this bull Master Rolandin is styled 'rector' of Whissendine ; and other instances could be cited where the instituted priests of monastic churches are so called. See what is said in the legal opinion (p. 214) : those having care of souls, 'qui ad modum patrie dicuntur vicarii, set pocius *veri rectores* sunt ?' Could this Master Rolandin be the Master Rolland, Primicerius of Sienna, to whom on the petition of Pandulph, Bishop of Norwich, a dispensation to hold benefices and serve them by vicars was granted in 1226 ? See *Calendar of Papal Registers*, vol. i. p. 111.

[2] Bain's *Calendar*, vol. i. No. 594.

a vicar, but of a 'chaplain,' ministering in the parish church.[1] In this way the whole of the xxxiv. marks (22 lib. 13s. 4d.) at which the church at Lindores (or Abdie) was rated would go to the monastery.[2]

In the interval between the bull of Celestine III. and that of Innocent III.[3] the church of Muthill in the bishopric of Strathern, that is, of Dunblane, was granted to Lindores; and as we learn elsewhere in our Chartulary (Nos. cxxvII. and xLI.) the donor was Malise, brother of Gilbert, earl of Strathern. Malise, it will be remembered, was married to Ada, (illegitimate) daughter of the founder of the abbey, who herself had made a grant of land to the monastery, and bequeathed her body for burial in that place.

Interests of a material kind, affecting various persons, were involved in this grant. Muthill was a ' mensal ' church of the Bishop of Dunblane; that is, it was a church the revenues of which, after making suitable provision for the cure of souls in the parish, went to the bishop's ' table,' or, in other words, to the episcopal income. On the subject of the grant litigation arose between the bishop and Guido, first abbot of the monastery. The question in dispute was appealed to Rome; and Innocent III. commissioned as judges-delegate the prior of St. Andrews, the prior of May, and the archdeacon of St. Andrews to try and determine the cause. The nature of the proceedings, the judgment, and the amendment of the judgment will be found in detail in Charters xLII.-L.

Some Early Notices of Schools

Any notices of the efforts of the Church at an early date on behalf of the cause of education are of peculiar interest. We find that there was a school at Dunblane, which had been accustomed to receive ' conveth,' which is pro-

---

[1] No. LXIII.

bably to be understood as an allowance in the form of food, in the vill of Eglismagril. Its head, who styles himself 'Rex scolarum de Dumblayn,' together with the scholars (*scolastici*) quitclaim their 'conveth' for two shillings to be paid yearly at Whitsunday (No. XLVI.). At Muthill there was another school with its 'rex' and its scholars who quitclaimed their 'conveth' for a like amount (No. XLVII.). One is less confident that the clerks (*clerici*) of Methven, who are mentioned in the next charter as also relinquishing 'conveth' on the same terms, were students of some establishment for education; but it is not improbable that it was so, for the word *clericus* is not infrequently used in this sense. The name Macbeth borne by the 'rex' of the schools at Dunblane, and the name Malduueny, which belonged to the 'rex' of the schools of Muthill, suggest that these schools were a survival of the ancient Celtic Christianity of that part of the country.

We also learn (No. XXXII.) that the chapter of Dunkeld had been accustomed to receive 'conveth' and rent out of the lands of a place called Rathengothen 'ad opus Macleins et Scoloccorum.' Here the 'scoloc' or 'scolog' of Celtic records is very apparent. And it has been suggested that the word 'Macleins' is here not a proper name but the Gaelic equivalent of scholars.[1] Dr. Dickson in the notice of the Chartulary of Lindores which was within a few days of its discovery communicated to the Society of Scottish Antiquaries[2] writes: 'In the early Celtic Church of Scotland as of Ireland, the lector or teacher was known as "ferleighinn," while the scholar or student was "macleighinn" (pronounced maclane) *filius lectionis*, and in a subordinate degree of proficiency "scoloc," *scholasticus*.'[3]

---

[1] Mr. Alexander Gibb in the notes which he has supplied to the editor

The notices here recorded of schools at Dunblane, Dunkeld and Muthill make a valuable addition to the notices of schools at Abernethy, Arbuthnott, Perth, Stirling, Lanark, Ayr, Elgin Glasgow, St. Andrews, Roxburgh, and South Berwick (Berwick-on-Tweed) collected by Mr. Joseph Robertson in his erudite essay on *Scholastic Offices in the Scottish Church in the Twelfth and Thirteenth Centuries.*[1]

It may be observed that none of these appear to have been, strictly speaking, monastic schools. And it may be reasonably believed that such schools were more numerous than the notices preserved in written records might lead some to imagine, for our knowledge of the existence of schools in some of the places mentioned is due solely to such accidents as that a master of a school was called to test a charter, or was appointed to serve on some ecclesiastical commission

About, perhaps, 1224 Gregory, Bishop of Brechin, conferred on Lindores the right to appoint the masters to the schools of Dundee and the neighbourhood;[2] and that the abbey exercised the right we have evidence in a notarial instrument of 22nd August 1424, dealing with a dispute (the details of which are obscure) between the bishop and a priest named Gilbert Knycht, who claimed the mastership of the school of Dundee.[3]

It is, perhaps, worth observing that there seems to be evidence that 'Master Laurence, archdeacon of St. Andrews,' who was one of the judges delegate in the cause concerning the land of Eglesmagril and the church of that vill (No. XLII.), was

MacConglinne, who is a wandering scholar, is usually called *scolaige*, but also *mac legind* (pp. 47, 52, 54, etc.). The *s* at the end of the word 'Macleins' looks as though the writer of the charter had put the sign of an English plural

himself 'Ferleighinn' of St. Andrews. Pope Innocent III., in a controversy between 'the Master of the schools of the city of St. Andrews and the same city,' on the one part, and the prior and convent of St. Andrews, on the other, had appointed judges delegate with the assent of Master Laurence, who was 'archdeacon and *Ferlanus* of St. Andrews.'[1] Before leaving the notices in the Chartulary of schools in the thirteenth century we may call attention to the school of Aberdeen in 1281, the master of the schools being also at the time the rural dean, or, to use the more common Scottish term, 'the dean of Christianity' of that place (No. cxxv.).[2]

BENEFACTORS OF THE MONASTERY

Not long after the foundation of the abbey the patronage of the church of Leslie in the Garioch was granted to Lindores by 'Norman, son of Malcolm,' of the family which afterwards assumed the name of Leslie (No. LXXXI.).[3] This Norman is 'Norman, the Constable' (Nos. LXXXIII., LXXXIV.). He survived Earl David, for we find Earl John confirming to him the lands of Leslie with the exception of 'that gift of the church of Leslie which the said Norman gave to the Abbey of Lindores and the monks there serving God, as the charter of Norman which the said monks possess testifies.'[4]   It was to Norman's father,

---

[1] *Reg. Prior. S. Andr.*, pp. 317, 318.   He is mentioned as distinct from the Master of the Schools, to whom he was superior in office.   Master Laurence appears again (No. XCVI.) as among those who by friendly intervention brought to a termination a dispute between the monks of Lindores and the bishop of St. Andrews as to the revenues of certain lands in Garioch.   He is probably the Master Laurence who in 1207 was Official of St. Andrews.—*Calendar of Papal Registers*, i. 28.

[2] The full term 'dean of Christianity' distinguishes this person from the dean of the Cathedral.   The 'dean of Christianity' of Aberdeen had in his deanery the parishes of Balhelvy, Banchory Devenick, Culter, Banchory Ternan, Echt,

'Malcolm, son of Bartholff,' that the lands of Leslie had been granted originally by Earl David.[1] In Charter LXXXIV. 'Norman, son of Norman, the Constable,' styles himself 'Norman de Lescelin.' This is a considerably earlier date for the assumption of the surname than that given in Macfarlane.[2]

NEYFSHIP

The little group of Leslie charters supplies a glimpse of the existence of bondmen on the estate of Leslie. In 1253 John, son of Thomas, and all the *sequela*, the issue of his own body, are quitclaimed to the Abbey of Lindores, and released from all *jus ligacionis* which Norman, son of the Constable, possessed over them (LXXXIV.). The word *sequela* applied to the offspring of bondmen is the word commonly used in the old charters for the young of animals still following the dam.[3] The passage before us is a particularly clear example of the application of the word to the young of bondmen. If Ducange had known it, we should have had a less vague and hesitating article on the word in the *Glossarium*. Cosmo Innes, speaking of the application of the word to bondmen, remarks that it is used 'just as a horse-dealer now sells a mare with her *followers*.'[4] It would seem that the grant of the church lands in Garioch *cum hominibus manentibus in ipsis terris et eorum sequela* (No. IV.) was a transfer of the lands and the neyfs astricted to those lands. I have not investigated the question of how long such transfers of neyfs continued in Scotland ; but in 1375 we have a grant by Robert II. of all and singular his lands of the Thanage of Kintore to the Earl of Moray and Marjory his wife, in fee and heritage 'in bondis, bondagiis, nativis et eorum sequelis.'[5] And in 1413 the same language in a charter by Robert, Duke of Albany, to John Stewart, Earl of Buchan.[1]   Yet while the old language of the charters persisted, the institution of neyfship was dying out.[2]

The process of the transfer of Parish Churches to Monasteries *in proprios usus*

To return to the subject of the grants of parish churches to monasteries *in proprios usus*, it may be observed that our Chartulary illustrates the steps of the transfer in more than one case.   The amplest details occur in the case of the last of the parish churches noticed in our Chartulary as added to the 'appropriate' list of Lindores.   Collessie, adjoining the parish of Lindores or Abdie (Ebedyn), was granted to the monastery in 1262.   Roger de Quincy, Earl of Winton, Constable of Scotland,[3] had his chief seat in Scotland at Locres (Leuchars) in the neighbourhood.   The property in Fife, besides other Scottish estates, had come into possession of the family by the marriage of his grandfather, Robert de Quincy, with Orabile, daughter and heir of Ness, Lord of Leuchars.   The moor of Kyndeloch (Kinloch) near Collessie, the moor of Edyn, and the peat-moss of Monagrey (mentioned in Charter cxxxvii.) had already afforded Earl Roger the opportunity of doing a kindness to the monks of Lindores by his grant of broom, heather, and peats from these places, together with other privileges, such as commonage for some of their cattle, and a right-of-way (*liberum chymnachium*) through all his lands.   To these benefactions he, as patron, now added the church of Collessie with all its pertinents, *in usus proprios*, if they can obtain in any measure leave for this transfer.   The consent of the bishop of the diocese is what is pointed to.   He made the grant as far as it lay in his power to make it, or, as it is expressed in the bishop's charter of concession, *quantum in ipso fuit.*[1]

But at the time of the grant the church of Collessie was not vacant.   The rector was a well-known man in his day, Master Adam of Malcarviston, a chaplain of the Pope, and provost of St. Mary's Church in the city of St. Andrews, who a few years before had been employed by Alexander III. as an envoy to the court of Henry III. of England.[2]   The grant accordingly could only be effective on the rector's resignation or death (*cedente vel decedente*).   His resignation had, no doubt, been anticipated and arranged for.[3]   The Bishop of St. Andrews, Gamelin, confirmed the grant, with the usual reservation of a sufficient and decent maintenance for the vicar, and of his own and his successors' episcopal dues.   One may suspect that it was not a scruple as to being a pluralist which induced the provost of St. Mary's to resign, for a notice in the *Calendar of Papal Registers*[4] shows him in the following year as rector of the neighbouring parish of Syreys (Ceres).

The Bishop of St. Andrews seems to have secured rather good terms for the vicar of Collessie, for we find him paying a tithe of twenty shillings to Boiamund in 1276.[5]   But what was the share that fell to Lindores it seems impossible to say.

Shortly afterwards (in 1263) additional security was obtained by a confirmation granted by the king.[6]

Whether technically it was absolutely necessary for a bishop to obtain the assent of his cathedral chapter to such transfers of parochial churches may not be clear; but the practice seems

---

[1] P. 189.

[2] In 1258.   See Bain's *Calendar of Documents relating to Scotland,* i. Nos. 2126, 2127.

[3] The Bishop of St. Andrews confirms De Quincy's grant, subject to the resignation of Malcarviston, on 5th June 1262, and Malcarviston resigned the

to have prevailed, and in the present case the prior and convent of canons regular at St. Andrews who formed the chapter of the cathedral did, as a matter of fact, confirm the grant of Earl Roger and the concession of the bishop. This may have been, however, only *ad majorem cautelam*; for in questions of property, ecclesiastical as well as secular, the lawyers seemed never weary of obtaining confirmations from every one who could by any possibility be supposed to have an interest in raising objections. Successive confirmations of the same grant by successive bishops were common, as though the force of the original confirmation terminated with the life of him who granted it. Thus in respect to the original grant of the parish church of Lindores we have episcopal confirmations by successive bishops of St. Andrews : Roger de Beaumont (1198-1202); William Malvoisine (1202-1238); David de Bernham, (1239-1252); and Gamelin (1255-1271).[1] In like manner the appropriation of the parish church of Collessie is confirmed not only, as we have seen, by Bishop Gamelin, but subsequently by Bishop William Wiseheart (1273-1279) [2]

The bishops had a personal interest in securing to the vicars of appropriate churches a sufficient maintenance. There were certain ' burdens ' on the parish which went to the upkeep of the diocesan establishment ; and these had, as a rule, to be met by the vicars. The heaviest of these burdens was what was known as 'procurations,'—a term originally applied to the hospitable entertainment of the bishop and archdeacon, with their respective retinues, when engaged on their official visitations of the churches of the diocese. Such hospitable entertainment was at a later date commuted to an annual payment in money, the amount of which was often considerable. The *Register of the Bishopric of Aberdeen* enables us

the thirteenth century.   Fintray, Inverury, Kinnethmond, Culsalmond, Insch, and Durnach paid 2lib. each ; Leslie and Premnay 1lib. 6s. 8d. each ; and Rathmuriel 13s. 4d.[1]   The Bishop of Aberdeen received from procurations throughout his whole diocese the then very considerable sum of 117lib. 10s.[2]

Another burden was a small payment made annually to the bishop by way of recognition of subjection.   This was commouly known in Scotland and England as a ' synodal,'[3] and corresponds to what is sometimes styled ' cathedraticum.' The name 'synodal' has been supposed to have originated from the payment being made when the clergy attended the diocesan synod, while ' cathedraticum' is, doubtless, employed to signify the recognition of the bishop's chair.   These two charges—' procurations' and 'synodals'—formed the bishop's dues (*episcopalia*), referred to in the bull of Gregory IX.[4]

In addition to 'ordinary burdens' there were ' extraordinary burdens' to be met by the beneficiaries in the case of parish churches.   Thus the cost of the building of the manse was to be defrayed by the rector and the vicar in proportion to the share of the revenues of the parish which they respectively received.   The upkeep of the manse fell wholly on the vicar.[5] The repair of the chancels of parish churches had to be borne by the clergy, and, according to the Scottish statutes of the thirteenth century, by the ' parsons,' that is, the rectors.[6] But it is evident from the Chartulary[7] that the monastery of Lindores demanded of their vicars in the Garioch that they should pay their proportion *de fabrica cancellarum suarum ecclesiarum*.   And it appears that this demand, though dis-

---

[1] *Reg. Aberdon.*, ii. 55.   There is reason to believe that the incomes of the vicars as stated at p. xlvii, represent the incomes *after* the payment of procurations and other dues.

[2] *Ibid.* p. 56.

[3] See p. 129.   While *Synodale* is the more frequent form, we also find the

puted by certain of the vicars, was allowed by the decision of
the judges delegated by the Pope to determine the question.

It may be added, that in England we find it ordered (A.D.
1305) in the constitutions of Robert Winchelsey, Archbishop
of Canterbury, that the repair of the chancels of parish
churches should be borne by the vicars as well as the rectors ;[1]
and it is possible that there may have been some alteration
of the Scottish statute before the time (A.D. 1375) when the
dispute between the monastery and their vicars was settled

During the earlier part of the period with which we
are concerned no doubt was entertained that the owner
of the land from which tithe was derived could, after due
provision for the performance of the spiritual duties of the
parish, determine the destination of the revenue to a religious
house. It was a way in which powerful friends might be
made.[2] But, distinct from such motives, the records are
practically unanimous in showing that the desire for prayers
pro salute animarum which might be secured from the monasteries formed a potent factor in these grants. With the then
universal belief that such prayers could benefit the souls in
Purgatory, natural affection no less than rational self-interest
suggested or encouraged the bestowment of gifts that would
secure this end. At first the terms of the charters of conveyance were general and somewhat vague. The donors looked
for ' devout prayers for the weal of the soul'; and further
specification is often lacking. The names, indeed, of those
for whose benefit the gift was made are entered in the record ;

---

[1] Wilkins, *Concilia Magnae Britanniae*, ii. p. 280.
[2] In Thomas Gascoigne's entertaining *Liber Veritatum*, we have several
examples of the granting of churches to monasteries *in proprios usus* in England
in the fifteenth century where material advantages as well as ' devout prayers '

but, as years ran on, it seemed to be recognised that it was safer to specify the times, and often the place or particular altar where Mass, on the 'anniversary,' or weekly, or twice or three times a week, or daily, was to be celebrated. What could be done by any one at any time might come to be forgotten or but imperfectly attended to.

For the illustration of this subject our Chartulary is singularly barren when compared with several of the Scottish registers, but there are two or three cases which may be noticed. At an early date (for three sons of Earl David are witnesses to the instrument) William de Campania grants three marks a year for the singing of a Mass every day for the soul of his father, Robert de Campania, who was buried in the abbey church of Lindores. The Mass was to be celebrated at the altar of St. Nicholas.[1] The three marks were made a charge on the land of Stokes in the county of Leicester.[2] The Lady Ysabel de Brus (second daughter of Earl David) makes a grant of land near Dundee on condition that the revenue derivable therefrom should be for the maintenance of one monk who at Lindores would in all time coming celebrate Mass for the souls of herself, her ancestors, and successors.[3] The fifteenth century presents us with charters generally much more full and specific than those of early date in declaring the exact character of the religious services which were expected in return for grants of money or land. Such

---

[1] It is often only from notices of this kind that we learn the dedications of the altars of cathedrals, collegiate churches, and monasteries. The *piscinae* and ambries of several altars still remain among the ruins of Lindores. Mr. Laing has recorded notices of altars of St. Mary, St. Dionysius, and St. John. *Lindores Abbey*, pp. 92, 192, 195. To these we can now add the altar of St. Nicholas. I have not been able to find the authority for an altar of St. Michael in the abbey, and suspect that Mr. Laing has made a mistake in

documents are to be found in abundance in the records of the Scottish cathedrals and collegiate churches, and not infrequently in the registers of the monasteries. One specimen of that period is preserved in the Lindores Chartulary. In 1479, Thomas Rossy, vicar of Inchestur,[1] professes his belief that by pious prayers and the celebration of Masses sins were remitted, the pains of Purgatory mitigated, souls released from such pains, and carried to the joys of Paradise, and therefore grants to Lindores certain lands and a dwelling-house on the condition that every year on the anniversary of his dearest uncle, James de Rossy, late abbot of Lindores, a solemn Mass of requiem should be sung at the great altar of the monastery for his own soul, the soul of his uncle, and the souls of all the faithful departed, which Mass was to be preceded, on the night before, by the vigils of the dead.[2]

Second Tithes

In the pages of the Chartulary there are several references to what are styled ' second tithes' (*decimae secundae*). The term was applied to certain grants made to the Church over and above the tithes which were obligatory under the general law of tithe. Such grants were purely voluntary and dictated by motives of piety. Rents and dues, ordinarily payable in kind, came to the lord of the soil after the customary tithing of farm produce. He was under no obligation to make any grant for religious purposes from such. But there are many examples of the devotion of kings or nobles tithing this revenue. Again there were gains (*lucra*) coming to the crown, or to the great feudal lords, from other sources. There were the fines and escheats of their respective courts, and there

cases we find that even as much as an eighth was so granted.
The dues known as 'cane' were also not infrequently tithed.

Early grants to the bishoprics or the monasteries made by
the crown commonly included a 'tenth penny,' sometimes an
'eighth penny,' of all the fines and escheats of the courts of
the Justiciar, Chamberlain, and Sheriff; and even when a fine
was remitted to the offender by the crown the Church was still
treated as though entitled to the tenth, or the eighth, as the
case might be. As the fines of the courts were, in early times,
ordinarily paid in cattle, it is not difficult to understand how
the term 'second tithe' came to be used of such tithings.

The example set by kings came soon to be followed by the
great lords. They had their own courts and their own canes,
which piety suggested that they too should tithe.

Of royal grants of this kind we have examples in the king's
grant of the tithe of his cane (or custom dues) of ships coming
to the port of Aberdeen, of his rents from the burgh, and
from his thanages in the country, and of the fines and escheats
of all his courts in the sheriffdom of Aberdeen and Banff, all
these being made over to the bishop and cathedral of Aber
deen.[1] Subsequent records leave no doubt that the tithe of
the 'reliefs' due to the crown was paid to the Bishop of
Aberdeen. Thus, in 1395 the 'relief' of the lands of Strath
bolgy, on the death of Sir John de Gordon, due to King
Robert III., amounted to seven hundred marks. The king
ordered a tithe, viz. 46lib. 13s. 4d., to be paid to the Bishop
of Aberdeen from his treasury.[2] The profit of 'wards,'
it is also stated, was tithed to the bishopric of Aberdeen.[3]
Similar grants, though not quite so extensive, were made
to the bishop and cathedral of Moray.[4] The loss of the
ecclesiastical records in the cases of Ross and Caithness

Exchequer Rolls, from which it appears that these two bishoprics benefited at least from the fines of the king's courts.[1]   The bishopric of Brechin enjoyed second tithes from the gains pertaining to the king out of the shire of Kincardine, derivable not only from fines and escheats, but also from the feudal casualties of ward, relief, and marriage. And it is clearly implied that these latter also furnished a tenth penny in other cases.[2]   The see of Glasgow was more particularly honoured.   David, the restorer of the bishopric, added to numerous endowments an *eighth* penny from his courts throughout the whole of Cumbria; while it had a tithe of the king's cane *in animalibus et porcis* in Strathgrif (Renfrewshire), Cunningham, Kyle, and Carrick.[3]   Dunkeld had a tithe of the issues of the king's courts in Strathern and Stormonth.[4]

Certain of the monasteries were granted favours of a like kind.   The Abbey of Holyrood had, by its foundation charter, a tithe of the issues of the courts and of others of the king's *lucra* from the Avin (Amond Water) to Colbrandspade (Cockburnspath), that is in the counties of Mid-Lothian and East-Lothian, and half the tithe of similar ʻperquisites of the king' in Kintyre and Argyll.   The abbey of Scone had a tenth of the issues of the courts in Gowrie.[5]   The priory of Restennet had a tenth from the courts of Forfarshire.[6]   The Abbey of Dunfermline had an eighth from the courts in Fife.[7]   The priory of the Isle of May was entitled to a tenth penny of the king's cane from the ports of Anstruther and Pittenweem.[8]

. These examples of royal munificence (and they could be easily multiplied) may now be supplemented by a few illustrating the action of the nobility.   Gilbert, Earl of Strathern, was the founder of Inchaffray, and to that monastery he granted a tithe of all his canes and rents in wheat, malt, meal, and cheese, a tithe of the fish which came to his kitchen, a tithe of his venison, a tithe of all the gains from his courts and of all 'obventions,' including, perhaps, under the latter term his feudal casualties.[1] Malise, brother of Gilbert, Earl of Strathern, was a generous benefactor of the monastery of Lindores, founded by his wife's father; and he gave to it second tithes from his 'cane and rents.'[2] Morgrund, Earl of Mar, granted to the canons-regular of St. Andrews a tithe of all the revenues from all his land and a tithe of all his courts and of his 'reliefs.'[3]

As lord of Garioch, Earl David made a grant to Lindores as munificent in spirit, if not as great in extent, as that of any kingly founder.[4] On his death there appears to have been some disinclination or neglect in rendering the second tithes from Garioch. Earl John's bailiff—or, to use the more common Scottish term, bailie,—Simon of Garentully seems to have been remiss, and then litigious. In 1234 the value of the arrears of the second tithes was computed, and, not payment, but an acknowledgment of his indebtedness given by Earl John to the monks of Lindores, together with a mandate to his bailiffs to pay the second tithes of Garioch in the future.[5]

Second tithes, from their nature, must have been difficult to collect, and were probably a source of annoyance to both parties. At all events at an early date we find an inclination on the part of the monastery to accept some equivalent in the shape either of a money payment made yearly, or of a grant of land given them in exchange. Thus, Simon of Garentully, already referred to, who had been granted by Earl John certain lands in his northern lordship, burdened, of course,

with second tithes, seems to have refused to pay them. Litigation ensued, and the question was appealed to Rome. The
Pope appointed judges delegate to determine the dispute;
but at this stage the matter was amicably settled on the
intervention of friends, Simon taking on himself the obligation to pay annually eight shillings sterling in lieu of the
second tithes due out of his holdings at Cremond and Eden-
gerrock. It seems probable that after the death of Earl John
his Scottish property, like that in England, was divided
among the families of his three sisters. At any rate we now
find members of the families of Brus, Balliol, and Hastinges
holding property in the Garioch. Robert de Brus, lord of
Annandale, grandson of Earl David through Isabel, his second
daughter, exchanged his land, called the 'vill of William'
(Williamstown), in the Garioch for the second tithes which
the abbot and convent of Lindores had been accustomed to
receive from his lands, profits, pleas, and escheats.[1] A similar
course was adopted by Henry de Hastinges, a grandson
through Earl David's youngest daughter, who gave his whole
vill of Flandres in exchange for the second tithes of his
property. Something of the same kind (though here there
are certain reservations) took place in the case of the property
of Gocelin de Balliol, on whom his brother, John de Balliol,
descended from Earl David's eldest daughter, had bestowed
certain lands in the same lordship.[2] Lastly, the second tithes
of the property of Malise in Stratherne were redeemed by his
nephew Fergus (son of Earl Gilbert) with a grant of the lands
of Fedal.[3]

PRIVATE CHAPELS

"The law and usage of the Church with respect to the
erection of private chapels are well illustrated from
entries in the Chartulary. The essential principle on
which the ecclesiasti

cal authorities insisted was that the parish church, or mother-church (*matrix ecclesia*), as it was styled, should not suffer.

Early in the thirteenth century Simon of Garentully desired a chapel at his manor of Cremond, in the parish of Inverury, the church of which was appropriate of Lindores. The abbot and the convent consent on the conditions that it was to be used only by the members of his private family, who were nevertheless to attend the mother-church on the principal feasts, that the tenants were, *more debito*, to continue to attend the parish church, and that all the 'obventions' coming to the chapel were to be paid in full to the parish church. Simon, his heirs, and his chaplains were to do fealty to the parish church, and, as 'recognition,' Simon and his heirs engaged to give yearly to the parish church two pounds of wax (No. LVIII.).

About the same time Sir Bartholomew Fleming (*Flandrensis*) sought permission for a chapel at Weredors (Wardhouse), in the parish of Insch (Inchemabanin). In consideration he granted certain lands and a right of commonage to the church of St. Drostan at Insch and the 'rectors' of the same,[1] and further undertook that that church should suffer no loss (No. LIX.).

William of Brechin, grandson of Earl David, had a chapel in his castle at Lindores, situated apparently on the north of the loch. He obtained leave for the celebration of divine service in the chapel on condition that the chaplain should render canonical obedience to the mother-church of Abdie, and pay over to it all the oblations made in the chapel. The 'recognition' of the mother-church was the yearly gift of a pound of incense (No. LXII.).[2]

---

[1] The gift was not to the Vicar of Insch, but to the convent of Lindores,

The case of the chapel of Dundemore (Dunmore) in the same parish of Lindores, or Abdie, is somewhat different. It seems to have existed as a chapel of Lindores as early, at least, as 1198.[1] It was not, apparently, a private chapel, but was for the convenience of the parishioners in its neighbourhood; but it would seem that the services there had been discontinued by the monks, and the matter was brought by Sir Henry de Dundemor[2] to the notice of the Bishop of St. Andrews, David de Bernham, whose pontifical offices form the solitary liturgical relic of Scotland in the thirteenth century.[3] The bishop heard the cause in his synod at Perth in 1248, and pronounced his decision. The monks were to pay yearly to Sir Henry twenty-five shillings for the maintenance of a chaplain, and to provide in the first instance a chalice, and the necessary books and vestments. Afterwards the *ornamenta* of the chapel were to be kept up at the cost of Sir Henry. As usual, it was stipulated that all the oblations of the chapel should go to the mother-church. And all the parishioners at Dundemore, with the exception of the household, were to attend the mother-church at Christmas, Easter, and the feast of St. Andrew.

There is an interesting memorandum (No. LXIV.) of the *ornamenta* of the chapel of Dundemore supplied according to agreement by the convent. They were a silver chalice, a full vestment,[4] and a missal.[5]

---

[1] Indeed it would seem that there was more than one chapel in that district of the parish at that date,—'capellas de Dundemore,' p. 108.

[2] Several notices of the family of Dundemore will be found in Laing's *Lindores Abbey*, pp. 434-6.

[3] Scotland has not the honour of possessing the precious manuscript, which is deposited in the Bibliothèque Nationale in Paris (No. 138 *fonds du Supplément, Latin*). It was printed at the Pitsligo Press, and published in 1885 under the

It would seem that in the thirteenth century there was a considerable growth of the fashion of having private chapels in the castles and manors of the nobles and lesser barons. It was naturally looked on with dislike by the parochial clergy; and the matter was thought worthy of being made the subject of synodical legislation. In the statute, 'De capellis non construendis,' in the body of Scottish canons enacted in the thirteenth century, it was laid down that no chapel or oratory should be built without the consent of the diocesan, and in those which had already been built divine service should not be celebrated without a like consent and authority. To this a little later an addition was made to the effect that, inasmuch as the foregoing statute was in many places not fully observed, the bishops should, each in his own diocese, carefully inquire by what right and by whose authority such chapels had been built; and, if they were dissatisfied as to the results of their inquiries, the chapels were to be suspended. And it is further provided expressly that by whatever authority a chapel had been built it was of obligation that the mother-church should suffer no loss. If there was a special privilege alleged in any case it should be exhibited to the satisfaction of the Ordinary. Otherwise those offending should be suspended *ipso jure*.[1] The practice of having private chapels in the houses of the great continued to grow; and as late as 1521 John Major,[2] an unprejudiced witness, tells us that

kindness of Dr. Swete, Regius Professor of Divinity at Cambridge, and Canon Christopher Wordsworth, the editor is able to state that missals of the type above described occasionally, but rarely, occur. The Dean of Sarum in 1224 found on one of his visitations 'Missale vetus inordinate compositum continens psalterium et ympnarium: collectarium cum notula et cum troponio.'—*Register of St. Osmund* (Rolls Series), i. 314. The 'missal' given to the chapel at Dundemore is so described as to suggest that possibly it may have contained the whole

every little laird (*infimus quisque dominus*) kept one chaplain, and sometimes more, according to his means. He contrasts, very unfavourably to his own country in this respect, the condition of England and its numerous and comparatively small parishes with the parochial arrangements of Scotland, and points out how in many cases parishioners in remote districts were dependent on private chapels for the hearing of divine service.

From the first the Abbey of Lindores had been specially protected by bulls from Rome [1] against the erection of places of worship within the parishes appropriated, unless with the consent of the convent and the diocesan, *salvis privilegiis Romanorum Pontificum.* Here, as in so many other matters of administration, the Pope claimed the power of granting leave, though it was refused by others having ordinary authority. And it is perhaps to this right that reference is made in the statute of the Scottish Council cited above where it speaks of the exhibition to the bishop of an alleged 'special privilege.' In England certainly it was not uncommon to obtain from Rome the authority for the erection of a private chapel. In the petitions to the Pope for this privilege distance from the parish church is commonly pleaded; or sometimes the badness or dangerous character of the road; and it is commonly promised that there shall be no loss to the parish church.[2] Opposition from parish churches was so sure to be expected that even the colleges of Oxford, when petitioning for permission to have a chapel, sometimes stipulated that the rights of the parish church would be respected.[3]

---

[1] See Nos. XCIII., XCIV.

[2] Reference to the volume of 'Petitions' in the *Calendar of Papal Registers* will supply many illustrations. One must here suffice. William de Clinton, Earl

The general usage in Scotland with respect to the erection of private chapels may be illustrated by a few examples from sources other than the Chartulary of Lindores. In 1243, with the consent of Bishop David de Bernham and of the prior and convent of St. Andrews, Alexander of Stirling founded a chantry in his chapel of Laurenston in the parish of Egglisgrig (St. Cyrus) which belonged to the convent: he pledging himself that he would bear all the expenses; that all the oblations and obventions coming to the chapel should be paid in full to the mother-church; and that, in 'recognition of subjection,' he and his heirs would pay a pound of wax annually. The chaplain before he celebrated there was to take an oath of fealty to the mother-church; and any failure to fulfil the obligations set forth was to be followed by the cessation of the celebration of divine service in the chapel.[1] Sometimes the right to have a private chapel was practically bought for a grant of land, or an annual payment, oblations, and obventions at the chapel going, as in other cases, to the parish church. Of such an arrangement we have examples in Bernard Fraser's chapel of Drem in the parish of Haddington, and in the private chapel at Ochiltree in the parish of Linlithgow.[2]

EXEMPTIONS OF THE LANDS OF RELIGIOUS HOUSES FROM MILITARY SERVICE

Students of the ecclesiastical records of the Church of England in the mediæval period when they turn to the corresponding Scottish records must be struck by the generally prevailing advantages of the form of land-tenure in the Scottish Church. While the church-lands of England were

very largely held by military tenure, and is true quitclaim from that of fiefs held by secular persons, such cases were in Scotland rare and exceptional. Almost universally when land was

granted in Scotland to the Church, it was granted in frankalmoign (*in liberam elemosinam*); and when granted by
sub-infeudation, the military service due from the land was
ordinarily undertaken by the immediate superior who made
the grant.   It is not implied, of course, that the vassals of
the Church were exempt from the obligations of joining in a
general levy to resist foreign invasion; but it was no small
advantage to be freed from thé necessity of supplying the
attendance of armed men to the ordinary 'hostings' of the
kings.   It was a heavy burden on the English monasteries to
supply their annual quota to the army, which varied with the
extents of their lands.   Thus, to cite a few examples, Abingdon
had to furnish thirty knights (that is, thirty heavy-armed
horsemen) for a forty days' service in the year; Glastonbury,
forty (at one time sixty); St. Edmundsbury, forty; Hyde,
twenty; Coventry, ten; St. Albans, six; Evesham, five; Peterborough, sixty.   The lands of the cathedrals were similarly
burdened.   Bath furnished twenty knights; London, twenty;
Salisbury, thirty-two; Canterbury, sixty; Winchester, sixty;
Lincoln, sixty; Worcester, fifty; Norwich and Ely, forty
each.[1]

The rare exceptions to the general immunity of the religious
houses of Scotland only help to emphasise the contrast.   Thus
the monks of Melrose held land at Halsingtun, in the Merse, of
William de Alwentun for the twentieth part of the service
of one knight, *quando commune servicium exigetur per totum
regnum Scocie*.[2]   This indeed was scarcely more than a
'recognition,' or acknowledgment of dependence; and it is
not to be wondered at that the grant is said to be *in liberam
et puram elemosinam*.   From our Chartulary it will be seen
that Earl David held his Scottish possessions of his brother,

the king, for the service of ten knights.[1] But when Earl David made grants from these possessions to Lindores the sole reddendo consists of 'devout prayers.' Other benefactors are equally liberal, while in some cases military service due from the lands granted is expressly undertaken, so that the monastery of Lindores might be exempt. Thus the burden of hosting (*onus exercitus*) due from the lands of Eglesmagril was undertaken by Gilbert, Earl of Strathern, and this undertaking was confirmed by his son, Earl Robert.[2] Again, when Robert de Brus, Lord of Annandale, gives Williamstown in exchange for second tithes, for which he was liable to the monastery, he frees that land *ab exercitu*, that is, he undertakes the military service due therefrom. And in the confirmation of the exchange granted by Alexander III., he implies by the words '*salvo servicio meo*,' that the military service should be fulfilled.[3] A similar exchange was made by Henry de Hastinges; and he adds with respect to the lands of Flandres, '*ab omnibus auxilio, exercitibus, et aliis omnimodis forinsecis serviciis adquietabimus.*'[4] Here also the king's confirmation contains the words, '*salvo servicio nostro.*'[5] The land was conveyed; the monks were exempted from the military service due from the land, which service, though still to be rendered to the king, was to be rendered by the superior, Henry de Hastinges.[6]

A charter (No. LV.) of William of Brechin, grandson of Earl David, is witnessed by David de Lochore, Michael de Munchur, and others, designated by the grantor as 'my knights.' It has been suggested, with what seems reasonable probability, that this form of expression was used of those who discharged the military service due from their lord's land.[1]   In another of our charters (No. LXXXVI.), Constantine de Mortemer is described as 'Earl David, knight'; and Gilbert, Earl of Strathern, styles Roger de Luuethot, 'my knight' (No. XXVI.); expressions which are, presumably, to be interpreted in the same manner.

THE PAPAL BULLS

The bulls transcribed in our Chartulary are fifteen in number—one of Celestine III., two of Innocent III., one of Honorius III., three of Gregory IX.,[2] and eight of Innocent IV. Only one of these is, in the language of diplomatics, a 'great bull' (No. XCIV.).   It is dated with all the formalities, and is fortified by the subscriptions of the Pope and of fourteen members of the College of Cardinals.[3]   In the style of the Pontifical Chancery, the 'great bulls' were commonly designated *Privilegia*;[4] and the Lindores scribe in his rubric entitles No. XCIV. as 'Magnum privilegium Innocencii Tercij,' but it would be hazardous to assume that he used the word 'privilegium' in a technical sense, for the 'little bull,' No. XCIII., appears also as 'Magnum privilegium' in the rubric.

With the exception of the great bull of Innocent III. (No. XCIV.) none of the bulls recorded in the Chartulary are noticed by Mr. Bliss in the *Calendar of Papal Registers*, and, presumably, are not recorded in the extant Papal *Regesta*.   Our Chartulary therefore affords material for supplying some of the deficiencies in the early archives of the Vatican.   The great bull was printed by Baluze in 1682 in his *Epistolae Innocentii Papae III.*, but without the subscriptions, and with the *formulae* indicated only by the opening words; and (from the text of Baluze) it was printed by Mr. Turnbull in his *Liber Sancte Marie de Lundoris*.[1] All the other bulls are (so far as the editor is aware) now printed for the first time.

THE PRIVILEGES GRANTED BY THE POPES TO THE ABBEY OF LINDORES

The papal privileges to Lindores follow the usual lines.

1. The earliest charter connected with Lindores[2] shows that from the outset the monastery of Kelso, from which the first monks of Lindores appear to have been drawn, did not claim any jurisdiction over this daughter house. From the outset it was not a 'cell' of Kelso, but a wholly independent establishment. Celestine III. conferred on the monks the right to choose their own abbot on the death of the first abbot, Guido, and of each of his successors. So far as the evidence, as yet available, throws light on the subject, the direct appointment or 'provision,' as it was called, by the Pope to the office of abbot does not appear in the case of Lindores till the beginning of the sixteenth century, when (12th June 1502) Henry Orme was 'provided' by Alexander VI. Again, on Henry's resignation, John Philips was 'provided' (21st July 1523) by Pope Adrian VI.[3] But it is not improbable that, had we the evidence, it would be found that the system of direct appointment by the Pope commenced, as in the case of several other Scottish monasteries, much earlier. Theiner's *Monumenta*[4] supplies an example of Clement VI. setting aside an election made by the monks of Dunfermline, and 'providing' a nominee of his own as early as 1351. Dr. Brady's extracts from account-books and Consistorial Acts of the Roman *Curia*, preserved in the libraries of Rome, Florence, Bologna, Ravenna,

and Paris,[1] are not continuous or complete, and do not com-
mence till the year 1400; but they are sufficient to show that
the system of 'provision' by the Popes was largely prevalent
in the case of the monasteries, as well as in the case of the
bishoprics, in the fifteenth century. Thus we find 'provisions'
to Newbottle in 1422, to Deer in 1423, to Paisley in 1423, to
Holyrood in 1424, to Iona in 1426, to Dunfermline in 1427,
to Inchaffray in 1429, to Kinloss in 1431, to Arbroath in
1449, to Inchcolm in 1450. Other illustrations could be
added, but these will suffice for our purpose. It is reasonable
to conclude that the gradual processes by which the appointments to the headships of the religious houses passed in
practice from the chapters of the monasteries to the Pope
followed the same lines which mark the transfer to the Pope
of the appointment to bishoprics from the capitular bodies
of the cathedrals. In the earlier period the chapters elected,
and the Pope, as a rule, confirmed. At a later time, the Pope
claimed to 'reserve' the appointments to his own 'provision';
but ordinarily gave effect to the wishes of the chapters as
manifested by *de facto* elections.[2] Lastly, appointments both
to monasteries and bishoprics came to all intents and purposes
to be mere nominations from Rome.

2. Among the other privileges conferred on Lindores, in
common with many other religious houses, was the exemption
from paying tithes on the crops of fallow-lands (*novalia*)[3] which
they had brought into cultivation either by the actual labour
of the monks themselves or at their charges. Other lands
would, as in other cases, pay tithes to the church of the parish
in which they were situated. This exemption was a strong
incentive to the advance of agriculture and the reclaiming of
waste lands.

A further privilege of importance was the exemption from tithe of all the cattle, sheep, horses, etc., of the monastery.[1] There is no evidence to show that the monks of Lindores did much in the way of breeding cattle and sheep. The land in their neighbourhood did not afford such facilities for the pasturing great flocks of sheep as were enjoyed by the monks of Melrose; but still the privilege granted was an appreciable gain to the monastery.

The Chartulary presents us with an instance where the privilege now under consideration caused serious loss to those interested in the revenue from parochial tithes. The church of Muthill was a mensal church of the Bishop of Dunblane. When lands were granted to Lindores in that parish the flocks and herds on these lands were exempted from tithe, and the income of the bishop was diminished. How the matter was dealt with will be found in No. LIV.

3. The right of the monastery to receive *ad conversionem* and retain, without the gainsaying of any, laymen or clerks who desired to leave the world and place themselves under monastic rule is, as usual, qualified by the provision that such persons should be freemen, or formally released from serfdom.[2] From early times the Church, though it did much to mitigate the hardships of slavery, recognised the institution of slavery as not incompatible with the divine law.[3] The existence of serfdom in Scotland at the time (as witnessed to in No. LXXXIV.) shows that the limitation was no mere archaic survival of an unmeaning formula.[4] In Sir E. M. Thompson's recently issued volume *The Customary of the Benedictine Monasteries*

---

[1] The word *nutrimenta*, in mediæval Latin, means the young of animals, those still sucking the dam, from which only the tithe was exacted, or as Ducange expresses it, ' *Nutricatus animalium, ex quo decimae penduntur ecclesiis.*'

of St. Augustine, Canterbury, and St. Peter, Westminster,[1] we
find the following questions (among others) put to novices:
'Si sint liberæ condicionis, videlicet non serviles personæ?
Si unquam fuerunt professi in arciori religione ista?'[2]

4. The brothers of the monastery, after having been formally
professed, were forbidden to leave the house where their profession was made without the formal sanction of the abbot,
except in the case of their seeking to be admitted to an order
subjected to a stricter rule than that to which they had pro
fessed obedience.[3]   How early the exception here noted was
recognised it is not easy to say, but before long it appears as
part of the general Canon Law.[4]   For a time it had been a
special privilege of certain orders (among them the Templars
and Hospitallers) that a professed member could not, against
the will of his superiors, pass to any other order, even
though of stricter rule; but this privilege was abrogated
by Gregory ix.[5]

5. The privilege of the permission granted to the monasterv
to celebrate divine offices during the time of a general interdict was very commonly granted to religious houses.   The
permission was qualified by the condition that the services
should be said *suppressa voce,* with closed doors, and without
the ringing of bells.   Not many years before the foundation
of Lindores the contest of King William with the Pope as to
the appointment to the bishopric of St. Andrews had caused
the whole kingdom of Scotland to be placed under interdict.
The sentence was soon reversed; but its memory was fresh.

---

[1] Henry Bradshaw Society, 1902.
[2] P. 6.
[3] See the second of the questions put to novices at Canterbury.
[4] *Decretals* of Gregory ix. (lib. iii. tit. xxxj. cap. 18).
[5] The decretal letter embodied in the Canon Law, as cited in the preceding

The horrors of the better-known interdict of the whole kingdom of England, in the reign of John some fourteen years after the foundation of Lindores, revived the sense of the value of the privilege.[1]

6. It was assumed that for the performance of such religious offices as were confined to bishops—the conferring of orders on such of the monks as were to be ordained, the consecrating of churches, the consecration of altars, the blessing of the chrism and holy oil—the bishop of the diocese should be applied to ; but Lindores, in accordance with a very common privilege granted to monasteries, had the right to resort to any Catholic bishop in communion with the Apostolic See in the event of the bishop of the diocese attempting to bargain for such services. The diocesan bishop was expected to render such services *sine pravitate*.[2]

7. Another common privilege which Lindores possessed by grant from the Pope was the right to afford sepulture to any (not being excommunicated or under interdict) whose devotion prompted the wish to be buried in the monastery. This privilege was qualified by the condition that the rights to certain dues possessed by the parish church of the deceased should be respected. Beside the ' mortuary ' or ' corse-present ' —the best beast (*preciosius animal*), or, in the case of the very poor, the ' umaist claith ' (*major pannus et melior*),[3]—a proportion of the movable goods of the deceased, after the payment of debts and the provision for the widow and children, was assigned by custom and canon law to the church.

---

[1] The privilege as conferred on Lindores was the common form. The monastery of St. Augustine at Canterbury was specially honoured by Pope Celestine III. in the permission 'celebrare cantus *clarissime* quando terra est interdicta.' See Dugdale's *Monasticon*, i. 145.

[2] Pp. 104, 109. The phrase *sine pravitate* was understood as equivalent to

It is to dues of this kind that reference is made in the Chartulary (No. LIV.), where an agreement is made with the monastery that the parish church of Muthill should receive from the seculars living on the lands of the monastery, in Fedale, Beny, and Concrag, 'obventiones debitas tam pro vivis quam pro defunctis.' The Scottish Church of the thirteenth century dealt with the subject by statute. It was enacted that if the deceased had chosen a place of burial other than his parish church, the body should be first carried to the parish church (*ad matricem ecclesiam*), and, 'when all dues had been there paid,' it should be borne to the place chosen.[1]

Among those who chose the abbey of Lindores for a place of burial were Henry of Brechin, the son of the founder, and his wife, Juliana,[2] and William Wascelyn and his wife, Mabel. The two latter expressly direct that, wheresoever within the realm of Scotland they might die, their bodies were to be brought for burial to the monastery of Lindores.[3]

The possession by any church of the right of sepulture carried with it a privilege of much importance. Such churches, as well as 'baptismal churches,' that is, parish churches (for monasteries were as a rule forbidden to have a font) were allowed to afford temporary protection to certain classes of criminals fleeing there for safety.[4]

This important, though limited, right is not to be confounded with the enlarged and special privilege of 'sanctuary' possessed by such highly honoured places as Wedale, Lesmahago, Torphichen, and Innerleithen in the south, Dull in Atholl, and Applecross and Dornoch in the north, within whose 'girth' the worst criminals had immunity.

---

[1] *Concilia Scotiae*, ii. 44.   No. LX.

8. The papal prohibition of any one pronouncing against the monastery sentence of excommunication, suspension, or interdict, without evident and reasonable cause, cannot properly be styled a privilege; but it would serve as a wholesome reminder to the bishop in whose diocese a monastery was situated to be wary and discreet in taking action of this kind. There is unhappily more than enough of evidence to show that the weapon of spiritual penalty, even to the extreme of excommunication, was at times used with little scruple against opponents.[1]

9. From a bull (not preserved in our Chartulary) of which a transcript was made by the scribe of the Lindores writs preserved in the Advocates Library, and printed for the Abbotsford Club,[2] we learn that in March 1289 Pope Nicholas iv. granted to the monks of Lindores the privilege of wearing caps suitable to their order during divine service on the great festivals, and in processions, when they were according to custom vested in albs and silk copes, with the restriction that at the reading of the Gospel and the elevation of the Host in the Mass due reverence was to be observed. The monks had pleaded in the letter to which the indult of Nicholas was the response that some of the monks had suffered frequent and protracted illnesses from having their heads uncovered in the cold climate of Scotland. The monastery of Kelso, in a sense the mother-house of Lindores, had obtained (1257) this privilege more than thirty years previously. The monks of that house had represented that Kelso was 'in frigida zona regionis Scotiæ,'

---

[1] Treating of the thirteenth century in England, a competent authority, Mr. W. W. Capes, writes, 'Excommunications were always in the air. They passed to and fro between ecclesiastics in high places; were expected even by Peckham [Archbishop of Canterbury] when he could not pay his debts; they were flung broadcast at times like the curses of a scolding tongue; were hurled even at a

and that some of the brethren had died from the effects of the exposure of their heads to the cold.[1]   The papal rescript in the case of Kelso did not specify any limitations on account of reverence in the use of the cap.   But when, still earlier (1245), the privilege was granted to the monks of Dunfermline, the Elevation and the Gospel are, as in the case of Lindores, particularly mentioned as times when due reverence should be shown.

The permission to wear caps during the celebration of Mass was regarded as a distinction and an honour; and, quite apart from considerations of health in a cold climate, and in large churches which were not artificially heated, was sought after as a mark of favour.   It could be granted only by the Pope.[2] The privilege was not due to the exceptional coldness of the climate of Scotland.   The monks of Glastonbury obtained the indulgence in 1247,[3] those of Peterborough in 1249,[4] and at about the same time the monks of St. Augustine's Canterbury.[5]

The fact is that as a token of the Pope's favour the permission to use the cap was eagerly sought.   When one monastery had obtained this mark of distinction, others were unwilling to be lacking.   It was just like the papal privilege, granted to certain abbots, of wearing the mitre and ring. When conferred on one house the jealousy of other houses was roused, and no efforts were spared to secure the honour.   The abbot of Lindores does not appear to have ever been accorded the latter distinction.[6]

The Mills and Multures of the Abbey

The somewhat singular survival to the present day of rights arising out of the ancient obligations connected with mills has served to make the subject of thirlage and multure more generally familiar in Scotland than many other topics of feudal law and usage. It will accordingly suffice to deal briefly with the matters brought before the reader in the Chartulary.

In the mediæval records of Scotland mills and the servitudes connected therewith make a frequent appearance. They were made the subject of legislation, and they formed a constant source of dispute and litigation. The possession of a mill was a valuable piece of property, because ordinarily the neighbouring vassals of the superior who possessed the mill were required to grind their corn at that mill, and to pay for the use of the mill amounts that commonly far exceeded the cost of the labour involved. The demands may often have been excessive, but it must be remembered that the cost of erecting the mill was considerable. These payments (ordinarily a proportion of the grain or the flour) were the 'multures.' Such vassals were compelled to attend, or (in technical language) to give 'suit' (*secta*)[1] to that mill, and, in the vernacular, were said to be 'thirled' to it.

In Earl David's foundation-charter there is a grant to the monastery of 'the mill of the vill of Lundores.'[2] There is also evidence in the charter that beside this mill there was another mill, which the earl refers to as 'my mill,' and it was stipulated that if the earl's mill could not grind, his corn was to be ground at the monks' mill, free of multure, and, similarly, if the monks' mill could not grind, they were to enjoy the right of grinding their corn free of multure at the earl's mill. The vill of Lindores was doubtless what came to be called 'old Lindores,' some two miles from the abbey; and the mill was

---

[1] In a similar sense *secta* is used of the obligatory attendance of vassals at the

probably in its neighbourhood at the Den of Lindores, from which the name of Denmylne was given to the old castle with which the name of Sir James Balfour, Lyon-King, antiquary and annalist, is associated.[1] The mill of the vill of Lindores had, as usual, lands astricted or thirled to it, and all the suit and multure of the mill was conveyed by the earl to the monastery.

About half a century after the foundation of Lindores, the neighbouring priory of Cistercian nuns, which had been recently founded at Elcho, came into collision with Lindores on the subject of suit and multure which the abbot claimed from tenants of the nuns on their lands of Kynhard (Kinnaird), a couple of miles south-west of the abbey. For four and thirty years the nuns succeeded in preventing their tenants giving suit at the abbey mill. Probably litigation had gone on during some years, for at last we find this dispute between the two neighbouring religious houses was carried to the Pope. According to the not uncommon and sensible practice of the papal Curia, the Pope appointed an ecclesiastic in Scotland to try the question and give judgment. The abbot of Dunfermline was named as judge delegate. It would seem that the prioress and other senior members of the convent had, during the course of the proceedings, been guilty of contumacy, possibly in disregarding the citation of the court. At any rate, ' for contumacy' the prioress and other ' majores personae' of the nuns were suspended by the judge delegate, armed with the authority of the Pope, from entrance to their church, and under this pressure they abruptly surrendered their whole case. The monks of Lindores had calculated the arrears of multure due from the tenants of Kinnaird for thirty-four years as amounting to a hundred and twenty marks sterling; but it seems that the

monks did not insist on the immediate payment of these, but were content with the formal agreement that so long as the nuns of Elcho had no mill of their own, the tenants of Kinnaird should grind and pay their multure-dues at the abbot's mill; and after the nuns had made a mill on their lands at Kinnaird, for which the abbot gave permission, they were to pay to the abbot three marks a year in lieu of multure.

It is interesting to find that three hundred years later the arrangement seems to have held good, for in a rental of Lindores (of about 1580) we find Kinnaird still paying 'dry multure,' a term applied to multure-dues payable by those who had been relieved, in consideration therefor, of thirlage to the mill.[1]

This case points to what may reasonably be regarded as the true origin of 'dry multures.' The learned Scottish feudalist of the sixteenth century, Sir Thomas Craig of Riccarton, in a rather off-hand manner attributes 'dry multures' (*siccas multuras*) to the grasping injustice (*iniquitas*) of the feudal superiors.[2] But there must have been some reasonable, or at least some plausible, plea for such an exaction; and such a plea we find in the exemption of land, originally astricted to a particular mill, in return for a payment made, which payment was designated 'dry multure.'

It is obvious that on the terms agreed to, the nuns of Elcho had but little inducement to go to the expense of building a mill at Kinnaird, for the yearly average of the multure for the thirty-four years was only a little over three and a half marks.

The arrears of a hundred and twenty marks and the costs of litigation were held over the nuns *in terrorem* for the faithful fulfilment of the agreement. The monks may on the whole be regarded as having acted with generosity, for they had been compelled in defence of their rights to appeal to Rome; and an appeal to Rome was a costly proceeding. In the suit before the papal delegate they had indeed, in the usual form, claimed '*expensas in lite factas et de cetero faciendas.*' But, the agreement between the litigants being made before judgment was pronounced, the costs like the arrears were not to be demanded if the terms of the agreement were fulfilled.

We possess so little material for the history of the Cistercian nunnery at Elcho that any new light on the subject is to be welcomed. The instrument (No. cxxv.) with which we have been dealing is dated 25th January 1281-2; and the nuns' tenants at Kinnaird not having paid multure for thirty-four years is proof that the lands of Kinnaird had been granted to the nuns at least as early as 1258; but probably not earlier, for if multure had been paid from Kinnaird at an earlier date during its possession by the convent at Elcho, it is all but certain that the important fact would have been mentioned in the formal charge made against the nuns by the monastery of Lindores.

The permission granted to the monks by Gocelin de Balliol (for the blench-duty of a pair of white gloves), for the formation of a mill-lade, the exact measurement of which is prescribed, from the river Ury to the mill at Insch (Inchmabani), indicates that the abbey contemplated erecting a mill at that place.[1]

In the rental (about 1480), printed by Mr. Laing,[2] we find the following mills in the possession of Lindores and bringing in rents : (1) Williamstown (vi lib. xiij s. iv d.); (2) Fintray (vij lib. v s. viij d.); (3) Leslie (xxvj s. viij d.); (4) Feddelis (viij lib.); (5) Eglesmagyrdill (viij lib. xiij s. iv d.); (6) Denemylne (liij s. iv d.); (7) Cregmylne (iiij chalders of victual).

The last-named of these mills—Craigmill[3]—was the mill to

which the burgesses of Newburgh were thirled; and according

to the terms of their infeftment the multure paid by them was 'the sexteind corne of quheit, and the twenty-ane corne of bere, malt, and mele.'[1]

Beside the payment of multure-dues there were services connected with the lord's mill to which vassals were commonly obliged. Among these was the carriage of the mill-stones, often from a considerable distance, when they had to be renewed.[2] Another service was the repairing of the mill-lade, mill-stank, and mill-dam. To works of this kind reference is made by William Wascelyn when he grants to Lindores that the monks and their 'men' should be held quit or exempt of the 'work of the mill,' due from their land at Newtyle, though they were not freed of multure.[3] And an allusion to similar obligations seems to be made in the foundation charter[4] when Earl David granted the mill of Lindores to the monastery, ' *ita ut homines mei faciant omnia que pertinent ad molendinum sicut solent facere tempore quo habui illud in manu mea.*'

Sometimes in a grant of land to a monastery the mill was excluded. Thus, in the grant of the lands of Rathengothen made by Malise, brother of Gilbert, Earl of Strathern, the mill and the water of the stank of the mill are excepted ; but the monks and 'their men' were to enjoy the privilege of having their corn ground at the mill free of multure.[5]

Lastly, when a grant of land was made, if the clause *cum multuris* appeared in the writ of infeftment, the thirlage of such land was thereby extinguished.[6] An example of this

will be found in the grant to Lindores, made (*in excamb.*) by
King Robert de Brus, of the lands of Kynmuk, etc.[1]

THE MS. OF THE CHARTULARY OR REGISTER OF LINDORES,
PRINTED IN THE PRESENT VOLUME

The manuscript from which the Latin text in this volume
is transcribed has been long in the possession of the family of
Cuninghame of Caprington.   In February 1886 Mr. R. W.
Cochran-Patrick, while on a visit to Caprington Castle, seems
to have accidentally got sight of the little volume, and at once
perceived the general character of its contents.   By permission of the owner it was transmitted to Dr. Thomas Dickson,
then Curator of the Historical Department of H.M. General
Register House, Edinburgh, who after a few days communicated to the Society of Scottish Antiquaries of Scotland [2] an
account of the volume.   The high value and importance of
the discovery was at once established.

'The volume,' writes Dr. Dickson, 'consists of eighty-six leaves
of vellum measuring seven and a half by five inches.   Its ancient
binding is now so dilapidated that only a part of one of the
oak boards remains attached to it, and their leather covering
has disappeared with the exception of a minute fragment,
only sufficient to show that its colour was red; still the stout
leather bands and the strong sewing are unbroken, and the
book remains firm and well-preserved.[3]   The first twenty-six
leaves form five unequal gatherings, from which eight or nine
leaves have been cut away, apparently because they had been
written upon, suggesting either that the volume was at first
devoted to a different purpose, or that the first portion had
once formed part of another book.   The remainder of the

volume consists of five equal gatherings, each containing
twelve leaves.' It may be added that the quality of the
vellum of folios 29-88, containing the earlier script, is superior
to that in the first part of the volume, lending some support
to, or at least falling in with, the second suggestion of
Dr. Dickson, that the first portion once formed part of
another book.[1]

The earliest part of the manuscript, beginning at fol. 29,
and running on to the middle of fol. 74 *verso*, is (with the
exception of a few places where later scribes have utilised
blank spaces) written in a beautiful and uniform hand, which
Dr. Dickson assigns to the middle of the thirteenth century.
The lines (twenty-five to the page) have been carefully ruled.
The initial letters appear ordinarily in red and blue or red
and green alternately, though in a few instances the initial
letter which had been left blank for colouring has not been
supplied in colour. The titles are rubricated in this part; but
in the other parts of the volume they have in general been
added (sometimes very carelessly and unintelligently) in the
current script of a later date, and in ordinary ink of an inferior
quality.[2] After fol. 74 *verso* the entries are by a large variety
of hands, perhaps as many as fourteen or fifteen, varying much
in character. A page of the earliest handwriting, and two
pages from other parts (the latter two pages selected rather
for their affording good subjects for the photographic camera
than as representing the script of any large part of the
manuscript) have, by permission of Colonel Cuninghame, been
reproduced.

What has been said may suffice for the general reader.
Mr. Maitland Thomson, Curator of the Historical Department of H. M. General Register House, has been good enough

to furnish the editor with a fuller and more detailed description
of the manuscript.   This will be found in Appendix II.

The question as to how the Chartulary of Lindores came
into the possession of the Cuninghames of Caprington must
be left to conjecture.   Dr. Dickson observes, 'It is conjectured
that it may have been acquired by Sir John Cuninghame when
he was engaged, towards the end of the seventeenth century,
in collecting the library which is still preserved at the family
seat, or, with more probability perhaps, it may have come
nearly a century earlier, through the marriage of John
Cuninghame of Brownhill, father of the above-mentioned
Sir John, with Janet, fourth daughter of Patrick Leslie,
commendator of the abbey and first Lord Lindores.'   It may
be remarked that Sir John Cuninghame is known to have
been much interested in antiquarian pursuits.

In a blank space on the *verso* of fol. 62 there is written
in what may be sixteenth or seventeenth century hands,
'Iacobus fairful,' and beneath this, 'IHOИ KILgoure.'
Possibly these names may be found to afford some hint as to
the story of the ownership of the book, or of the hands
through which it passed.

The text of the Chartulary has been transcribed for the
Scottish History Society by the competent and experienced
charter-scholar, the Rev. Walter Macleod.   In cases of doubt
I have tested the transcript with the original, and have
occasionally availed myself of the aid generously afforded by
expert charter-scholars.   The writ entitled 'Dauid Comes
de Hunthyngton' (cxlix.) presented special difficulties; and
much labour has been expended by the editor in producing
a transcript as exact as possible.

The punctuation is wholly editorial.   To have been content

in the edition of the *Chartulary of the Church of St. Nicholas, Aberdeen,* recently issued by the New Spalding Club. The employment of capitals, though also to some extent capricious, will not mislead, and the use of the original has in this respect been retained. Readings which were doubtful either because of uncertainty as to the word intended by the scribe, or because of the obscurity of the sense, have been marked with an obelus (†). When any alteration of the text has been made the original is indicated in the margin, or, in the case of additions, by square brackets. The spelling of the original has been retained, except in a few cases noted in the margin.

THE ABBOTSFORD CLUB'S (SO-CALLED) *Chartulary of Lindores.*

In 1841 the Abbotsford Club issued to its members a volume under the editorship of Mr. W. B. D. D. Turnbull, bearing as title *The Chartularies of Balmerino and Lindores, now first printed from the original MSS. in the Library of the Faculty of Advocates.* Confining ourselves to the part of the volume relating to Lindores, which appears with separate pagination and a separate title-page (inscribed *Liber Sancte Marie de Lundoris*), it may be observed that the manuscript in the Advocates' Library from which it is transcribed has no just claim to be called the 'Chartulary of Lindores,' being merely, as Dr. Dickson has pointed out, 'a transcript, made apparently so late as the time of James iv., of twenty-five documents relating to the abbey and its burgh, ranging in date from the end of the twelfth century to the beginning of the sixteenth, and selected without any appearance of method.'[1] Three of these documents are records of obligations to various Scottish merchants in 1502 for money transmitted abroad. Of these more will be said hereafter.[2] As regards the others, if one

may venture on conjecture, I would recon that the interest of the person who made the transcripts, or for whom they were made, were mainly occupied with the possessions and rights of the abbey in its own immediate neighbourhood, or in parts not very remote. Four relate to Newburgh, six to the neighbouring fisheries, the quarry, the grange, and the woods of Lindores, two to the internal arrangements of the monastery, and seven to Dundee and its church and neighbourhood. With the exception of a grant of *libera foresta* in the woods of Fintray, and of a toft in the burgh of Aberdeen, no notice is taken of the extensive rights and possessions of the abbey in Aberdeenshire. Nor is there any reference to the churches of the abbey in the diocese of Lincoln. The foundation charter is not transcribed. Some of the charters copied appear also in our Chartulary. Abstracts of those which do not so appear will be found in Appendix III.

The Cuninghame Chartulary an incomplete Register of writs connected with Lindores

Not only have we evidence from the Abbotsford Club book that the record of writs in our Chartulary is not complete, but from other sources we find that there were several writs (some of them of much importance) which one might naturally expect to find in such a register, but which are absent from our manuscript. Thus in the *Registrum Aberdonense*[1] there is entered a bull of Pope Alexander IV., dated 13th September 1257, addressed to the abbot and convent of Lindores, and bearing on the income of the monastery derivable from their churches in the Garioch. Again (as we find in the same register)[2] two years later (1st August 1259) a deed of agreement was drawn up between the Bishop of Aberdeen and the abbot and convent of Lindores as to the boundaries of certain lands in Aberdeenshire,

which, contrary to what one might expect, is lacking in our Chartulary. Other late writs (including an important mandate of King Robert II.) will be found calendared in Appendix III.

It is plain that if the convent followed the usual practice of registering important deeds relating to rights, privileges, and property, the recently discovered volume must have been supplemented by one or more other books. It is perhaps too much to hope that another volume may yet be rescued from some obscure hiding-place ; but it is well that the attention of antiquaries should be drawn to the probability that at least one other volume of the register once existed.

The latest writ entered in our register by the scribe who wrote the earlier portions of the manuscript (ff. 29-74 *verso*), with the exception of a few writs entered on blank spaces by later hands, is dated in July 1253.[1] The bull of Alexander IV. referred to above as preserved in *Registrum Aberdonense* is dated in September 1257. One cannot but suspect that between these two dates the whole of the earliest part was transcribed, in other words, that it was transcribed at a time when the bulls of Innocent IV.[2] were the latest bulls in the possession of the monastery. This conjecture falls in sufficiently well with the judgment of Dr. Dickson, based on palæographical considerations, that the earliest portion was written 'about 1260.'

The dull details connected with the succession of the abbots, together with some few historical notices of the abbey, have been relegated to Appendix IV.

J. D.

THE CHARTULARY OF LINDORES

I

Carta Comitis Dauid de Rege Willelmo.

W. Dei gracia Rex Scottorum Episcopis, Abbatibus, Comitibus, [*fol.*
Baronibus, Justiciariis, vicecomitibus, prepositis, ministris, et
omnibus probis hominibus tocius terre sue clericis et laicis,
salutem. Sciant presentes et futuri me Dedisse et concessisse et
hac carta mea confirmasse Dauid fratri meo comitatum de
Leuenaus cum omnibus pertinenciis suis, et Lundors et Dunde,
et forgrund et petmothel, et Neutyle, et fintreth, et Rothiod,
et Inuerurin, et Munkegyn, et Boverdyn, et Durnach, et
Uuen et Arduuen, et Garuiach, et Mertonam que est in
Laudonia iuxta castellum puellarum. Volo itaque et precipio
ut predictus Dauid frater meus et heredes sui de me et heredi
bus meis in feudo et hereditate teneant et possideant omnes
terras istas prenominatas per Rectas Diuisas suas quas
habuerunt quando illas ci dedi, et cum omnibus iustis pertinenciis suis in bosco et plano, In terris et aquis, In pratis
et pascuis, In molendinis et stangnis, In moris et Maresiis,
In viis et semitis, et omnibus aliis iustis pertinenciis suis tam
non nominatis, quam nominatis; cum sacca et socca, cum
tol et Tem, et Infangenthefe, bene et plenarie et honorifice,
et ita libere et quiete in omnibus sicut ego ipse unquam terras
illas tenui et possedi, faciendo inde mihi et heredibus meis
seruicium Decem militum. Testibus H. episcopo Sancti Andree;
Jocelino episcopo Glasguensi; M. episcopo de Aberden; S.

de Vere; Ricardo de Munfichet; Willelmo de Lindesey; Malcolmo filio comitis Duncani; Patricio filio comitis Waldevi; Willelmo filio Ricardi de Moreuille; Rand. de Solis. apud Perth.

'CHARTER of EARL DAVID from KING WILLIAM.'

W[ILLIAM] by the grace of God King of Scots to the bishops, abbots, earls, barons, justiciars, sheriffs, provosts, officers, and all good men of his whole land, clerical and lay, greeting. Let those present and to come know that I have given and granted, and by this my charter have confirmed, to David, my brother, the Earldom of Lennox with all its pertinertts, and Lundors, and Dundee, and Forgrund, and Petmothel, and Neutyle, and Fintreth, and Rothiod, and Inverurin, and Munkegyn, and Boverdyn, and Durnach, and Vuen, and Arduuen, and Garviach, and Merton, which is in Lothian near the Castle of Maidens. I will, therefore, and command that my brother David aforesaid and his heirs should hold and possess, in fee and heritage, of me and my heirs all those aforenamed lands, by their right marches, which they had when I gave them to him, and with all their just pertinents in wood and plain, in lands and waters, in meadows and pastures, in mills and stanks, in moors and marshes, in roads and paths, and all other their just pertinents both named and unnamed, with sac and soc, with thol and them, and infangthef, well and fully and honourably, and as free and exempt in all things as I myself ever held and possessed those lands, by rendering to me and my heirs the service of ten knights. Witnesses, H[ugh], Bishop of St. Andrews; Jocelin, Bishop of Glasgow; M[atthew], Bishop of Aberdeen; S[imeon], Bishop of Moray; A[ndrew], Bishop of Caithness; Earl Duncan; Earl Gilbert; Earl Waldeve; Malcolm, Earl of Atholl; G. Earl of Angus; Earl Colban; Richard de Moreville, Constable; Robert de Quincy; Walter Olifer; Alan, son of Walter Steward (senescalli); William de Haya; Ralph de Vere; Richard de Munfichet; William de Lindesay; Malcolm, son of Earl Duncan; Patrick, son of Earl Waldeve; William, son of Richard de Moreville; Randolph de Solis. At Perth.

II

Magna Carta Comitis Dauid de fundacione Monasterij.

Dauid Regis aui mei, et pro salute anime comitis Henrici patris mei, et comitisse Ade matris mee, et Malcolmi Regis fratris mei, et pro salute anime Regis Willelmi fratris mei et Regine Ermegard, et omnium antecessorum meorum, et pro salute anime mee et Matilde comitisse sponse mee, et pro salute anime Dauid, filii mei, et omnium successorum meorum, et pro salute animarum fratrum et sororum mearum. Dedi eciam et concessi et hac presenti carta mea confirmaui predicte abbacie de Lundors. et monachis ibidem Deo seruientibus, in liberam et puram et perpetuam elemosinam, ecclesiam de Lundors cum omnibus iustis pertinenciis suis, et terram ad predictam ecclesiam pertinentem per rectas diuisas suas in bosco et plano, sicut magister Thomas eandem terram tenuit et habuit. Preterea dedi eis omnem terram ab occidentali parte riuuli descendentis de magno lacu usque in they, et totam insulam que vocatur Redinche. preter vnam piscariam meam, scilicet vnam Jharam : Boues autem mei et vacce mee proprie | *fol.*| de Lundors utentur pastura dicte insule. Dedi eciam eis molendinum predicte uille de Lundors cum omni secta sua et multura, ita ut homines mei faciant omnia que pertinent ad molendinum sicut solent facere tempore quo habui illud in manu mea. Si autem molendinum meum non potuerit molere, molam proprium bladum meum ad molendinum corum sine mulctura. Et si molendinum monachorum non potuerit molere, ipsi molent proprium bladum suum ad molendinum meum sine multura. Concedo eciam eis ecclesiam de Dunde cum omnibus iustis pertinenciis suis, et vnum toftum in burgo meo de Dunde liberum et quietum ab omni seruicio et auxilio, et consuetudine et exaccione ; Et ultra muneth fintreth per rectas diuisas suas cum omnibus pertinenciis suis, et ecclesiam eiusdem uille cum pertinenciis suis omnibus ; Et in Garuiach lethgauel et malind cum omnibus pertinenciis suis, et per rectas diuisas suas. Concedo eciam eis ecclesiam de Inueruri cum capella de Munkegin et cum omnibus aliis pertinenciis suis, et ecclesiam de Durnach. et ecclesiam de Pramet et ecclesiam de

cedo eciam eis totam terram meam de Perth que uocatur
insula cum omni plenitudine sua, et libertatibus suis sicut eam
plenius et melius tenui et habui, et vnum plenum toftum infra
uillam de Perth, quod euerardus flandrensis de me tenuit,
tenendum sibi in libero | burgagio liberum et quietum sicut
illud liberius et quiecius tenui et habni. Concedo eciam eis

ol. 30,
erso.]

vnam carrucatam terre in uilla de Neutile quam ada filia mea,
uxor malisij filij comitis fertheth eis dedit, tenendam sibi in
liberam et puram et perpetuam elemosinam, Ita libere,
quiete, plenarie et honorifice, sicut carta predicte filie mee ade
testatur. Concedo cciam eis vnum plenarium toftum in burgo
meo de Inuerurin liberum et quietum ab omni seruicio et
auxilio, et consuetudine, et exaccione. Concedo eciam eis
decimam omnium lucrorum et placitorum meorum infra terram
meam et extra ultra moneth quam habui tempore quo feci
donacionem istam ; et decimam omnium lucrorum meorum
que mihi proueniunt de lucris Domini Regis fratris mei, in toto
regno suo ; et decimam omnium rerum mearum et heredum
meorum ultra moneth, scilicet decimacionem Bladi et farine,
Butiri et casei, carnis et venacionis, cibi et potus, coriorum
ferarum cum mota canum captarum, Cere et salis, vncci et
sepi, et omnium aliarum rerum que decimari possunt, et que
dabuntur uel uendentur uel ad firmam ponentur de maneriis
meis ultra moneth, uel cciam que in eis expendentur, scilicet
in maneriis meis et terris quas habui tempore quo feci donacionem istam. Quare uolo et concedo ut predicta ecclesia de
Lundors, et monachi ibidem Deo seruientes, habeant et teneant
in liberam et puram et perpetuam elemosinam, de me et
heredibus meis, prenominatas terras, ita libere, quiete, plenarie,
et honorifice, sicut ego eas unquam liberius, quiecius, plenius,

l. 34.]

et honorificencius | tenui et habui. Concedo eciam eis curiam
suam omnino liberam et dignitatem pacis, et omnes alias libertates quas abbacia habere debetur. Volo eciam et concedo ut
predicti monachi habeant et teneant predictas terras et

et exaccione, in liberam et puram et perpetuam elemosinam, bene et in pace, libere, quiete, plenarie, integre et honorifice sicut aliqua abbacia uel domus religionis in toto regno Scocie, melius, liberius, quiecius, plenius, et honorificencius, aliquam elemosinam habet et possidet. Haec autem omnia prenominato monasterio de Lundors, et monachis ibidem deo seruientibus ita libere et pacifice iure perpetuo possidenda confirmaui, ut michi succedencium nullus aliquid ab eis nisi solas oraciones ad anime salutem exigere presumat. Hiis testibus, Willelmo Rege Scottorum, Rogero episcopo Sancti Andree, Jocelino episcopo Glasguensi, Johanne episcopo Dunkeldensi, Matheo episcopo Aberdonensi, Hugone cancellario Regis, Dunecano Comite de fyfe, Comite patricio, Gilberto comite de Strathern, Roberto de Lundors,† Malcolmo filio Comitis Duncani, Seier de quinci, Philippo de Valuniis, Willelmo de Lindesey, Willelmo Cumyn, Dauid de Lindeseie, Waltero Olifer, Walkelino filio Stephani, Willelmo Wacelin, Roberto Basset, Henrico filio comitis, Ricardo capellano comitis.

'EARL DAVID'S GREAT CHARTER of the FOUNDATION of the MONASTERY.'

To all the sons of Holy Mother Church and to the faithful, as well present as to come, Earl David, brother of the King of Scots, greeting. Know ye that I have founded an abbey at Lundors, of the order of Kelko, to the honour of God and of St. Mary and of St. Andrew and of All Saints, for the weal of the soul of King David, my grandfather, and for the weal of the soul of Earl Henry, my father, and of Countess Ada, my mother, and of King Malcolm, my brother, and for the weal of the soul of King William, my brother, and of Queen Ermegard, and of all my ancestors, and for the weal of my soul, and of Countess Matilda, my spouse, and for the weal of the soul of David, my son, and of all my successors, and for the weal of the souls of my brothers and sisters.

I have also given and granted, and by this my present charter have confirmed to the aforesaid Abbey of Lundors, and to the monks there serving God, in free and pure and perpetual alms, the church of Lundors, with all its just pertinents, and the land pertaining to the said church by its right marches, in wood and plain, even as Master Thomas had

them the mill of the aforesaid vill of Lundors, with all its suit (*secta*) and multure, so that my tenants shall do all things that pertain to the mill as they were accustomed to do when I had it in my possession. But if my mill shall not be able to grind, I shall grind my own grain at their mill without multure. And if the mill of the monks shall not be able to grind, they shall grind their own grain at my mill without multure.

I also grant to them the church of Dundee with all its just pertinents, and a toft in my burgh of Dundee, free and discharged of all service, aid, custom, and exaction : and beyond the Mounth, Fintreth by its right marches, with all its pertinents: and in Garviach, Lethgavel, and Malind, with all their pertinents, and by their right marches. I also grant to them the church of Inveruri, with the chapel of Munkegyn and all its other pertinents : and the church of Pramet, and the church of Rathmuriel, and the church of Inchmabanin, and the church of Culsamuel, and the church of Kelalcmond, with the chapels of the same churches, with their lands, teinds, and all pertinents, for their own uses and for the maintenance of the same monks.

I also grant to them the whole of my land at Perth which is called the Island [Inch] with all its full liberties, as fully and completely as I had and held it ; and a full toft within the town of Perth, which Everard Fleming (*flandrensis*)[1] held of me, to be held by them in free burgage, as free and discharged of service as when I had and held it.

I grant also to them one ploughgate of land in the vill of Newtyle, which Ada, my daughter, wife of Malise, son of Earl Ferteth, gave to them, to be held by them in free, pure, and perpetual alms, as freely, quietly,[2] fully, and honourably as the charter of my daughter, Ada, aforesaid, testifies. I likewise grant to them one full toft in my burgh of Inverurin, free and discharged of all service, aid, custom, and exaction.

I also grant to them the tithe of all gains and of my pleas both within and without my lands beyond the Mounth, which I had at the time when I made this gift ; and the tithe of all gains which come to me from the gains of my brother, the king, in his whole realm ; and the tithe of all the property of me and my heirs beyond the Mounth, namely the tithes of grain and meal, of butter and cheese, of flesh and venison, of food and drink, of the skins of the animals of the chase caught by packs of hounds, of wax and salt, of fat and tallow, and of all other things which can be tithed and which shall be given, or sold, or granted for a rent out of my manors beyond the Mounth, or even which shall be expended in my manors and lands which I had at the time when I made that gift.

Wherefore I will and grant that the aforesaid church of Lundors and the monks there serving God shall have and hold of me and my heirs, in free, pure, and perpetual alms, the lands aforenamed, as freely, quietly, fully, and honourably as I ever had and held them most freely, quietly, fully, and honourably.

I also grant to them their court wholly free, and the dignity of the peace, and all other liberties which an abbey ought to have. I will also and grant that the aforesaid monks should have and hold the aforesaid lands and the churches with their chapels, lands, tithes, and all other pertinents, in wood and plain, in meadows and pastures, in waters and mills, in stanks and live-pools (*vivariis*) and fisheries, in roads and paths, with all liberties and free customs, without any service, custom, secular aid, and exaction, in free, pure, and perpetual alms, well and in peace, freely, quietly, fully, perfectly, and honourably as any abbey or religious house in the whole realm of Scotland, most completely, freely, quietly, fully, and honourably has and possesses any alms. I have confirmed that all these shall be possessed by the aforesaid monastery of Lundors and the monks serving God there so freely and peaceably and of perpetual right, that none of my successors may presume to exact anything from them save only prayers for the weal of the soul. Witnesses, William, King of Scots; Roger, Bishop of St. Andrews; Jocelin, Bishop of Glasgow; John, Bishop of Dunkeld; Matthew, Bishop of Aberdeen; Hugh, the King's Chancellor; Duncan, Earl of Fife; Earl Patrick; Gilbert, Earl of Strathern; Robert of London; Malcolm, son of Earl Duncan; Seir de Quincy; Philip de Valoniis; William de Lindesay; William Cumyn; David de Lindesay; Walter Olifer; Walkelin, son of Stephen; William Wacelin; Robert Basset; Henry, son of the Earl; Richard, chaplain of the Earl.

III

Carta Comitis Dauid de Ecclesiis de Lundors, de Dunde, et de Garuiach. |

Vniversis sancte matris ecclesie filiis et fidelibus tam presentibus quam futuris Comes Dauid frater Regis Scottorum, Salutem. Sciatis me fundasse quandam abbaciam apud Lundors de ordine Kelkoensi ad honorem dei et sancte marie virginis, et Sancti Andree apostoli, omniumque sanctorum, pro salute anime Regis aui mei et pro salute anime Comitis

[*fol.
vers*

pro salute anime Dauid filij mei, et omnium successorum meorum, et pro salute animarum fratrum et sororum mearum. Concessi eciam et hac carta mea confirmaui predicte abbacie de Lundors et monachis ibidem deo seruientibus in liberam et puram et perpetuam elemosinam ecclesiam de Lundors cum omnibus pertinenciis suis, et terram ad candem ecclesiam pertinentem in bosco et plano sicut eam magister Thomas tenuit et habuit; et ecclesiam de Dunde cum omnibus pertinenciis suis; et ecclesiam de fintreth cum omnibus pertinenciis suis, et ecclesiam de Inuerurin cum capella de Munkegyn, et cum omnibus aliis pertinenciis suis; et ecclesiam de Durnach; et ecclesiam de prameth; et ecclesiam de Rathmuliel; et ecclesiam de Inchemabanin; et ecclesiam de Culsamuel; et ecclesiam de Kelalcmund cum capellis earundem ecclesiarum, et terris et decimis et omnibus aliis pertinenciis carum ad proprios usus, et sustentaciones eorundem monachorum. Quare uolo et concedo ut predicti monachi habeant et teneant in liberam et puram et perpetuam elemosinam predictas ecclesias *l. 3½.*] cum capellis,| terris, et decimis, et omnibus aliis pertinenciis suis, sine omni seruicio et consuetudine, et auxilio seculari et exactione, bene et in pace, libere, quiete, plenarie, integre, et honorifice, sicut aliqua abbacia uel domus religionis in toto regno Scocie melius, liberius, quiecius, plenarius, et honorificencius aliquas ecclesias, uel aliquas alias elemosinas habet et possidet. Has autem ecclesias prenominato monasterio de Lundors et monachis ibidem deo seruientibus ita libere et

(Abstract)

'CHARTER of EARL DAVID concerning the CHURCHES of LUNDORS, DUNDEE, and GARVIACH.'

EARL DAVID, brother of the King of Scots, to all the sons of Holy Mother Church . . . greeting. Know ye that I have founded an abbey at Lundors of the order of Kelko, to the honour of God, and of St. Mary the Virgin, and of St. Andrew the Apostle, and of All Saints, for the weal of the soul of the king, my grandfather, and . . . I have given and by this my charter have confirmed to the aforesaid abbey of Lundors and the monks serving God there, in free, pure, and perpetual alms, the church of Lundors with all its pertinents, and the land pertaining to the same church in wood and plain, as Master Thomas held and had it, and the church of Dundee . . . and the church of Fintreth, and the church of Inverurin, with the chapel of Monkegyn . . . and the church of Durnach, and the church of Frameth, and the church of Rathmuliel, and the church of Inchmabanin, and the church of Culsamuel, and the church of Kelalcmund, with the chapels of the same churches, and the lands, tithes, and all other their pertinents, for their own uses (*ad proprios usus*) and the maintenance of the same monks. Wherefore I will and grant that the monks aforesaid should have and hold the aforesaid churches, in free, pure, and perpetual alms, with their chapels, lands, and all other pertinents, free from all service, custom, secular aid, and exaction, well and in peace . . . so that none of my successors may presume to exact anything from them, save only prayers for the weal of the soul. Witnesses : William, King of Scotland. . .

IV

Carta Comitis Dauid de terris ecclesiarum de Garuiach.

OMNIBVS hoc scriptum uisuris uel audituris comes Dauid frater Regis Scottorum, salutem. Sciatis me dedisse, concessisse, et hac carta mea confirmasse deo et abbacie mee de Lundors

predicte abbacie contra hanc meam concessionem. Hiis testibus, Dauid de Lindeseie, Walkelino filio Stephani, Willelmo Wascelyn, Roberto Basset, Roberto filio Roberti, Willelmo et Dauid capellanis, Walkelino de Nuers, Gilberto Dolepain, Roberto filio Martini, et multis aliis.

(Abstract)

'CHARTER of EARL DAVID concerning the LANDS of the CHURCHES of GARVIACH.'

To all who shall see or hear this writ Earl David, brother of the King of Scots, greeting. Know ye that I have given, granted, and by this my charter confirmed to God and my abbey of Lundors all the churches which were in my gift in Scotland, with the chapels, tithes, and lands to them pertaining, by those marches which they had when I caused the land of Garviach to be measured ; together with the men and their families (<i>eorum sequela</i>) residing on those lands ; and that they should possess all the liberties on my lands which others residing on the lands of other churches in the realm of Scotland possess. Wherefore I will and strictly command that none of my successors cause any grievance or trouble to the aforesaid abbey contrary to my grant. Witnesses . . .

V

Carta Comitis Dauid de Culsamuel et Munkegin.

SCIANT presentes et futuri quod Ego comes Dauid, frater Regis Scocie, dedi et concessi et hac presenti carta mea confirmaui deo et ecclesie Sancte Marie et Sancti Andree de Lundors et monachis ibidem deo seruientibus pro salute anime mee, et uxoris mee, et antecessorum et successorum meorum omne ius quod habui in culsamuel et in Munkegyn, saluo cano quod pertinet ad episcopum Sancti Andree, scilicet, vj. solidos et vj. denarios, de culsamuel ; et iiij. solidos et iiij. denarios de Munkegyn, in liberam et puram et perpetuam elemosinam. Concedo eciam eis curiam suam liberam et quietam de hominibus suis qui manent in terris ecclesiarum suarum.

fice, sicut aliqua abbacia in regno domini Regis fratris mei elemosinam liberius, et quiecius, plenarius, et honorificencius tenet et possidet. Hiis testibus, domino J. episcopo de Aberdon, Roberto decano de Aberdon, Malisio filio comitis fertheth, W. Olifart, duobus Henricis filiis comitis, Roberto de parco, J. de Wiltune, W. Wascelyn, R. capellano, [*fol.* Kineth iudice, H. de Bouilla, N. filio Malcolmi, Waldeuo clerico, H. de Noiers clerico comitis, Gilberto clerico comitis.

(Abstract)

' CHARTER of EARL DAVID concerning CULSAMUEL and MUNKEGIN.'

LET men present and to come know that I, Earl David . . . have given . . . to God and the church of St. Mary and St. Andrew at Lundors, and the monks there serving God, for the weal of my soul, of the soul of my wife and of my ancestors and successors, all right which I have in Culsamuel and in Munkegyn, save the cane which pertains to the Bishop of St. Andrews, namely vj. shillings and vj. pence from Culsamuel, and iiij. shillings and iiij. pence from Munkegyn, in free, pure, and perpetual alms. I grant to them also their court for the men residing on their church-lands, free and exempt. Moreover I grant to them that their own men should be free from all toll and secular custom. But I forbid the said monks receiving any of my tenants or men on their lands. Wherefore I will that the aforesaid monks should hold and possess the said aforesaid as freelv . as any abbey Witnesses

VI

Carta Comitis Dauid de Redinch.

VNIVERSIS sancte matris ecclesie filiis et fidelibus comes Dauid frater Regis Scocie, salutem. Sciant tam presentes quam futuri me dedisse et concessisse, et hac carta mea confirmasse, deo et ecclesie sancte Marie et sancti Andree de Lundors, et monachis ibidem deo seruientibus et seruituris totam insulam que uocatur redinche et omnes piscarias in they iuxta prenominatam insulam preter vnam piscariam meam, scilicet, vnam iharam ad colcrike. Tenebunt autem predictam insulam in

filio Stephani, Nicholaio de Anas, Roberto Basset, Johanne de Wiltun, W. Olifer, Radulfo de Cameys.

(*Abstract*)

' CHARTER of EARL DAVID concerning REDINCH.'

To all the sons of Holy Mother Church and the faithful, Earl David, brother of the King of Scotland, greeting. Let men, present as well as to come, know that I have given . . . to God and the church of St. Mary and St. Andrew of Lundors, and the monks who serve or shall serve God there, the whole island which is called Redinch, and all the fisheries in the Tay near to the afore-named island, except my one fishery, namely, one yare at Colcrike. They will hold the aforesaid island in pure and perpetual alms as freely, etc.   Witnesses

VII

Carta Comitis Dauid de Quarrario.

OMNIBVS hoc scriptum uisuris uel audituris, comes Dauid fra ter Regis Scottorum, Salutem. Sciatis me dedisse, concessisse, et hac carta mea confirmasse monachis meis de Lundors, ut capiant lapidem in quarrario meo in byrneside quantum uolue-rint in perpetuum, ubi melius eis uisum fuerit, tam ad ecclesiam suam, quam ad omnia alia edificia que sibi fuerint necessaria construenda. Hiis testibus, Willelmo Wascelin, Walkelino filio Stephani, Roberto Basset, Nicholaio de Aness, Waltero Olifard, Philippo clerico, Henrico de Neueris, et aliis.

(*Abstract*)

' CHARTER of EARL DAVID concerning the QUARRY.'

To all who shall see or hear this writ Earl David, brother of the King of Scots, greeting. Know ye that I have granted . . . to my monks of Lundors that they may take as much stone as they wish from my quarry in Hyrneside in all time coming, where it shall seem to them best, as well for their church as for all other buildings necessary for them to be afterwards constructed. Witnesses . . .

VIII

carta mea confirmasse deo et ecclessie Sancte Marie et Sancti
Andree de Lundors et monachis ibidem [deo] seruientibus, pro
salute anime mee et animarum antecessorum et successorum
meorum totam terram de pethergus per rectas diuisas suas, et
terram que iacet inter torrentem de Matheres et torrentem de
eglesgirg, sicut cadunt in mari, et duas bouatas terre in
Pethannot, pro centum solidatis terre, in liberam et puram, et
perpetuam elemosinam, in bosco et plano, In pratis et pascuis
et pasturis, In moris et mariciis, In stagnis et uiuariis, in
aquis et molendinis, et in piscariis; et in omnibus aliis libertatibus predictis terris iuste pertinentibus. Quare nolo et
concedo ut predicti monachi de Lundors habeant et possideant predictas terras, cum omnibus iustis pertinenciis suis, ita
libere, quiete, plenarie, et honorifice, sicut aliqua abbacia uel
domus religionis in toto regno Scocie aliquam elemosinam
liberius, quiecius, plenius, et honorificencius, tenet et possidet.
Hiis testibus, Waltero Olifard, Henrico filio Comitis Dauid,
Walkelino filio Stephani, Willelmo Wascelyn, Roberto filio
Roberti, Johanne de Wiltun, Gilberto Scoto, Willelmo filio
Orme, Roberto de Inuerkileder, Alano clerico de Munros,
Simone Albo, cum multis aliis.

(Asbtract)

'CHARTER of EARL DAVID concerning WICHESTON, etc.'

EARL DAVID grants to Lundores 'the whole land of Pethergus by its
right marches, and the land which lies between the stream (<i>torrentem</i>) of
Matheres and the stream of Eglesgirg, as they fall into the sea, and two
oxgates of land in Pethannot, for one hundred shilling-lands (<i>pro
centum solidatis terre</i>), in free, pure and perpetual alms, in wood and
plain . . . mills and fisheries—and in all other liberties justly pertaining
to the lands aforesaid. Witnesses '

IX

Confirmacio Comitis Dauid de Carucata terre de Balemawe.

seruientibus illam carucatam terre quam ada filia mea, uxor Malisii filij comitis fertheth, eis dedit, Tenendam in liberam et puram et perpetuam elemosinam, ita libere, quiete, plenarie et honorifice, sicut carta predicte ade testatur. Hiis testibus, Henrico abbate de aberbrothoc, Malisio filio fertheth, Henrico filio comitis Dauid, Willelmo Beuel, nicholayo de anes: Willelmo burdeth, Roberto basset, Galfrido de Wateruile.

(*Abstract*)

'CONFIRMATION of EARL DAVID concerning a PLOUGHGATE of LAND of BALEMAWE.'

EARL DAVID confirms to Lundors 'that ploughgate of land which my daughter, Ada, wife of Malise, son of Earl Ferteth, gave to them.' It is granted in frankalmoign, 'as the charter of the aforesaid Ada testifies.' Witnesses. .

X

Confirmacio Comitis Dauid de terra de Neutyl.

OMNIBVS ad quos presens scriptum peruenerit Comes Dauid frater Regis Scocie, Salutem: Sciatis me concessisse et hac presenti carta mea confirmasse, deo et ecclesie Sancte Marie et Sancti Andree de Lundors et monachis ibidem deo seruientibus et seruituris donacionem illam quam Willelmus Wascelin illis fecit de una bouata terre in villa de Neutile que iacet proxima terre ecclesie illius uille, inter superiorem uiam et collem, cum communi pastura cum hominibus eius in eadem nilla ad decem aueria, et triginta oucs et vnum equum. Quare uolo et concedo ut predicti monachi teneant et habeant prenominatam terram cum predicta pastura, Ita libere, quiete, plenarie et honorifice sicut carta predicti Willelmi testatur. Hiis testibus, Ernaldo capellano meo, Philippo clerico de Dunde, Henrico filio meo, Bartholomeo de Mortemer, Roberto filio Roberti, Constantino de Mortemer, Adam filio Alani, Willelmo Gubiun, Henrico filio Walkelini.

which lies next to the land of the church of that vill, between the high
way and the hill, together with common pasture [to be enjoyed in
common] with his [Wascelin's] men in the same vill, for ten beasts
(*averia*), thirty sheep, and one horse.' To be held as freely, quietly,
etc. as the charter of the aforesaid William testifies. Witnesses.

XI

Carta Comitis Dauid de ecclesia de Wissindene.

VNIVERSIS sancte matris ecclesie filiis et fidelibus tam presentibus quam futuris, Comes Dauid frater Regis Scottorum,
Salutem: Sciatis me dedisse et concessisse, et hac carta mea
confirmasse deo et ecclesie Sancte Marie et Sancti Andree de
Lundors et monachis ibidem deo seruientibus in liberam et
puram et perpetuam elemosinam ecclesiam de Wyssindene Nota
cum omnibus ad eam iuste pertinentibus. Quare nolo ut pre- eccles
dicti monachi habeant et possideant prenominatam ecclesiam Angli
ita libere, quiete et honorifice, sicut aliqua abbacia in episcopatu lincolniensi aliquam ecclesiam quiecius, liberius, et
honorificencius tenet et possidet. Hiis testibus, Henrico
abbate de Sancto Thoma, Willelmo et Ricardo capellanis
comitis Dauid, Gaufrido clerico eius, Philippo clerico eius,
Henrico filio comitis, Roberto Basset, Willelmo burdet,
Gaufredo Wateruile, Waltero Olifard, Radulfo Cames, Gille-
berto Olepain, Walchelino Nuerres.

(*Abstract*)

CHARTER of EARL DAVID concerning the CHURCH of WISSINDENE.

EARL DAVID declares that he has 'given, granted, and confirmed to
Lundors in pure and perpetual alms the church of Wyssendene, with all
its just pertinents,' to be held as freely 'as any abbey in the diocese of
Lincoln holds any church.' Witnesses. . . .

XII

caritatis intuitu et pro salute anime mee, et antecessorum et successorum meorum, dedisse et concessisse et hac carta mea confirmasse deo et ecclesie Sancte Marie et Sancti Andree de Lundors et monachis ibidem deo seruientibus, in puram et perpetuam elemosinam, ecclesiam de Wissendene cum omnibus ad eam iuste pertinentibus. Quare uolo quod predicti monachi habeant et possideant prenominatam ecclesiam ita libere, quiete, et honorifice sicut aliqua abbacia in episcopatu lincolniensi aliquam ecclesiam quiecius, liberius, et honorificencius tenet et possidet. Hiis testibus, Henrico abbate de Sancto Thoma, Willelmo et Ricardo, capellanis, Magistro Petro de Paxton, Ricardo filio Willelmi, Philippo clerico, Petro de Hach, Henrico de Scotte, Roberto basset, Simone de Seynlez, Roberto de Basingh, Ricardo de Lindesei, Willelmo Burdet, Galfrido de Water|uile, Waltero Olifard, Radulfo de Kamais, Gilberto de holepen, Walkenio de Nuers, Henrico de Nuers.

35.]

(Abstract)

DOUBLE of the CHARTER concerning WISSENDENE.

EARL DAVID repeats the Charter granting Wissendene to Lundors, adding that the gift was made 'at the prompting of charity, and for the weal of the souls of myself, and my ancestors and successors.' Witnesses. . . .

XIII

Carta Comitis Dauid de ecclesia de Cuningtoun.

VNIVERSIS sancte Matris ecclesie filiis et fidelibus Comes Dauid frater Regis Scottorum, Salutem : Nouerint omnes tam presentes quam futuri me dedisse et concessisse, et hac mea carta confirmasse deo et ecclesie Sancte Marie et Sancti Andree de Lundors et monachis ibidem deo seruientibus, in liberam et puram et perpetuam elemosinam, ecclesiam de

H. abbate de Sancto Thoma, Willelmo et Ricardo, capellanis comitis Dauid, Galfrido clerico, Simone de Seynliz, Walkelino filio Stephani, Roberto de Betun, Malcolmo filio Bertolfi, Nicholao de adles, Bartholomeo monacho, Roberto Basset, Willelmo Burdet, Willelmo filio Walteri, cum multis aliis.

(Abstract)

'CHARTER of EARL DAVID concerning the CHURCH of CUNINGTON.'

EARL DAVID declares that he has given . . . to Lundors in pure alms 'the Church of Cunington with all its just pertinents to be possessed for their own uses,' to be held as freely as any abbey in the diocese of Lincoln holds any church. Witnesses . . .

XIV

Duplicacio carte de Cunington.

COMES Dauid frater Regis Scottorum omnibus sancte matris ecclesie filiis presentibus et futuris, Salutem: Noueritis me caritatis intuitu, et pro salute anime mee et antecessorum et successorum meorum, dedisse et concessisse, et hac carta mea confirmasse deo et ecclesie Sancte Marie et Sancti Andree de Lundors, et monachis ibidem deo seruientibus, in puram et perpetuam elemosinam, ecclesiam de Cunington, cum omnibus ad eam iuste pertinentibus. Quare uolo quod predicti monachi habeant et possideant prenominatam ecclesiam Ita quiete, libere, et honorifice, sicut aliqua abbacia in episcopatu lincolniensi aliquam ecclesiam quiecius, liberius, et honorificencius tenet et possidet. Hiis testibus, Henrico abbate de sancto Thoma, Willelmo et Ricardo capellanis, magistro Petro de Paxton, Ricardo filio Willelmi, Philippo clerico, Petro de Hach, Henrico de Scott, Roberto Basset, Simone de Seynliz, Roberto de Basingh, Ricardo de Lindesei, Willelmo Burdet, Galfrido de Wateruile, Waltero Olifard, Radulfo de Camais, Gilberto de Holepen, Walkelino de Nuers, Henrico de Nuers.

(Abstract)

XV

Confirmacio Comitis Johannis de terra de Lundors et de Garuiach et de carum ecclesiis.

OMNIBVS hoc scriptum uisuris uel audituris, Johannes de Scocia Comes huntedun, salutem : Sciatis me concessisse et hac presenti carta mea confirmasse deo et ecclesie sancte Marie et sancti Andree de Lundors, et monachis ibidem seruientibus, donacionem illam quam bone memorie pater meus Comes Dauid fecit eisdem, scilicet, totam terram que iacet ab occidentali parte riuuli descendentis de Magno lacu de Lundors usque in they, et totam insulam que uocatur Redinche, preter vnam ibaram, molendinum et predicte uille de Lundors, cum omni secta sua et multura ; Terram quoque quam tenent in Mernes ex dono eiusdem, patris mei ; terram de Perth que uocatur insula ; Et ultra munethe fintreth, lethgauel et malind, cum omnibus pertinenciis, et per rectas diuisas predictarum terrarum, ecclesias quoque de Lundors, de Dunde, de fintrefe, de Inueruri, de Durnach, de Prameth, de Rathmuriel, de Inchemabanyn, de Kulsamuel, de Kilalcmond, et de dono Normanni constabularij ecclesiam de Lescelin, cum terris et decimis et omnibus ad predictas ecclesias iuste pertinentibus ;

36.] et vnum plenarium | toftum in uilla de Perth quem euerardus flandrensis quondam tenuit ; et vnum plenarium toftum in Dunde ; unum plenarium toftum in inueruri ; unam carucatam terre in Neutyl de dono ade sororis mee. Concedo eciam eis decimam omnium lucrorum et placitorum meorum infra terram meam et extra, ultra moneth, et decimas omnium rerum mearum et heredum meorum ultra moneth, sicut in carta predicti patris mei continetur. Quare nolo et concedo ut predicta ecclesia de Lundors et monachi ibidem deo seruientes habeant, teneant, et possideant omnia predicta cum omnibus suis pertinenciis, et curiam suam liberam omnino et dignitatem pacis, et omnes liberas consuetudines, quas aliqua abbacia habere debetur in regno Scocie, sine omni seruicio et consue-

salutem pertinentes, sicut carta predicti patris mei eisdem facta testatur. Hiis testibus, Henrico de Striuelin fratre meo, Roberto de Campaniis, Johanne de Brus, Henrico Tuschet, Normanno constabulario, Henrico de Dundemor, Thoma de Lindeseia, Anketilo de foleuilla, Henrico de Boyuilla, Henrico de Wincester, Nicholao de Inuerpeffyn, Nicholao Meuerel clerico, et multis aliis.

EARL JOHN'S CONFIRMATION of the LAND of LUNDORS and of GARRIOCH, and of their CHURCHES.

To all who shall see or hear this writ John of Scotland, Earl of Huntingdon, greeting. Know ye that I have granted and by this my present charter have confirmed to God and the church of St. Mary and St. Andrew of Lundors, and to the monks there serving [God] that gift which my father, Earl David, of good memory, made to the same, namely, the whole land which lies on the west of the burn flowing down from the great lake of Lundors as far as the Tay, and the whole island which is called Redinche, except one yare, the mill also of the vill of Lundors with all its suit and multure : the land also which they hold in Mernes, of the gift of the same my father : the land in Perth which is called Inch (*insula*) : and beyond the Mounth, Fintreth, Lethgavel, and Malind, with all their pertinents, according to the right marches of the aforesaid lands; also the churches of Lundors, Dundee, Fintrefe, Inveruri, Durnach, Frameth, Rathmuriel, Inchemabanin, Culsamuel, Kilalcmond, and, by the gift of Norman, Constable, the church of Lescelin, with the lands, tithes, and all things justly pertaining to the aforesaid churches ; and one full toft in the town of Perth, which Everard Fleming, formerly held ; and one full toft in Dundee, one full toft in Inveruri, one ploughgate of land in Newtyle, given by Ada, my sister. I grant also to them the tithe of all profits and of my pleas both within and without my land beyond the Mounth, and a tithe of all the property of myself and of my heirs beyond the Mounth, as is contained in the charter of my father aforesaid. Wherefore I will and grant that the aforesaid church of Lundors and the monks there serving God should have, hold, and possess all things aforesaid with all their pertinents ; and their court wholly free, and the dignity of the peace, and all free customs which any abbey in the realm of Scotland ought to have, without any secular service, custom, or exaction, in free, pure, and perpetual alms. So that neither I nor any of my successors may exact anything from them, save only prayers pertaining to the weal of the soul, as the charter of my

XVI

Carta Comitis Johannis de quadam terra in territorio de Lundors.

OMNIBVS hoc scriptum uisuris uel audituris Johannes de Scocia, Comes Huntedun, salutem. Sciatis me dedisse et concessisse et hac presenti carta mea confirmasse deo et monasterio de Lundors et monachis ibidem deo servientibus quandam partem terre mee de Lundors quam eis perambulavi in propria persona coram probis hominibus meis ultra divisas suas versus orientem ad dilatandum gardinum corum. Quare volo ut predictam terram ita libere habeant et teneant sicut alias terras suas, quas de me tenent, liberius tenent et melius. Concedo eciam eis et confirmo excambium factum inter ipsos et Galfridum Maupetit, sicut inter eos convenit. Hiis testibus, Henrico de Strivelin fratre meo, Roberto de Campaniis, Johanne de Brus, Normanno constabulario, Henrico Tuschet, Henrico de Dundemor, Thoma de Lindeseia, Henrico de Boyvilla, Nicholao de Inuerpeffin, Nicholao Meueral, et multis aliis.

(marginalia: a in / ɔ de / s quam / s de / er- / it.)

(*Abstract*)

'CHARTER of EARL JOHN concerning certain land in the TERRITORY of LUNDORES.'

EARL JOHN grants to the monks of Lundors ' a certain part of my land of Lundors which I have in person perambulated, in the presence of my good men, beyond their marches towards the east, for enlarging their garden.' The earl also confirms the exchange of lands (*excambium*) between the monks and Geoffrey Maupetit. Witnesses . . .

XVII

Carta Comitis Johannis de xx^{ti}. solidis in Inueruri.

de terra quam burgenses mei de Inueruri tenent de me
ad firmam, que jacet inter burgum de Inueruri et pontem de
Balhagerdyn, donec illos eisdem in loco certo assignavero:
Tenendos et habendos de me et heredibus meis in puram et
perpetuam elemosinam pro salute anime domini Hugonis de
Roppel, ad pietanciam dictorum monachorum die anniversario
eiusdem Hugonis. Et ego et heredes mei dictos xx. solidos
dictis abbati et conventui contra omnes homines Warrantizabimus. Hiis testibus, dominis Henrico de Striuelyn, B. de
Paunton, H. Phyton, Galfredo de Appelby, Simone de Garen-
tuly, Henrico de Boyvilla, David de | Audereye, et aliis.   [foɩ

(*Abstract*)

'CHARTER of EARL JOHN concerning xx. SHILLINGS in INVERURI.'

EARL JOHN grants to the monks of Lundors twenty shillings sterling
to be received annually 'from the land which my burgesses of Inveruri
hold of me at rent (*ad firmam*) which lies between the burgh of Inveruri
and the Bridge of Balhagerdyn, until I shall assign them [the twenty
shillings] to the same monks in an appointed place.' This sum of
money is to be held in pure and perpetual alms for the weal of the soul
of Sir Hugh de Roppel 'for the pittance of the monks on the day of
the anniversary of the same Hugh.' 'And I and my heirs will warrant
(*warrantizabimus*) the said xx. shillings to the said abbot and convent
against all men.' Witnesses

XVIII

Carta Comitis Johannis de toftis de Inuerbervyn et Inuerrury.

OMNIBVS Sancte Matris ecclesie filiis ad quos presens scriptum
peruenit J. de Scocia, comes Cestre et Huntedon, salutem in
domino. Noueritis me pro salute anime mee, patris mei, et
matris mee, et omnium antecessorum meorum et successorum,
dedisse, concessisse et hac presenti carta mea confirmasse deo et
ecclesie beate Marie de Lundors et monachis ibidem deo ser-

ejusdem uille et capellanorum ibidem serviencium, Illud scilicet dimidium toftum qui fuit Roberti de Bouerdyn, et unam rodam que fuit Bernardi, et aliam rodam que fuit utting Ruffi; Tenenda et habenda de me et heredibus meis in perpetuum, libere, quiete, integre, pacifice, et honorifice cum omnibus pertinenciis, libertatibus, et aisiamentis ad predicta tofta pertinentibus, in liberam puram et perpetuam elemosinam. In cujus rei testimonium huic scripto feci apponere sigillum meum. Hiis testibus, dominis Henrico de Strivelyn, Simone de Garentuli, Willelmode Lacu, Walone de Burg, Girardo de Lindeseye, Ada de Audideleger, Nicholao de Inuerpephin, Roberto de Wrth clerico, et aliis.

(Abstract)

'CHARTER of EARL JOHN concerning the TOFTS of INVERBERVYN and INVERURIE.'

'J[OHN] of Scotland, Earl of Chester and Huntingdon, greeting in the Lord.' He gives, grants, and confirms to the monks of Lundors, for the weal of the soul of himself, his father, and mother, and of all his ancestors and successors, one toft in the vill of Inverbervyn, that, namely, which belonged to Utting Cachepol, near the castle on the south side, in exchange for the toft which Earl David, his father, had given them; and one toft in the vill of Inveruri for the use of the church of the same vill and of the chaplains there serving, namely the half toft which belonged to Robert of Boverdyn, and one rood which belonged to Bernard, and another rood which belonged to Utting Ruffus. To be held of the earl and his heirs, with all pertinents, liberties, and easements, in frankalmoign. Seal. Witnesses

XIX

Carta Comitis Johannis de tofto in Dunde et de perambulacione de Durnach et de libertate molendini.

OMNIBVS hoc scriptum visuris vel audituris Johannes de Scocia, Comes Cestre et Huntendun, Salutem. Sciatis me dedisse et

piscarie quam dedi domino Henrico de Brechyn, uersus portencrag : Tenendam sibi et babendam in liberam, puram, et perpetuam elemosinam. Concessi eciam eis ut terra illa que perambulata fuit inter magnam Durnach et logindurnach coram me et Domino J. abbate de Lundors et aliis probis hominibus sit in communi in perpetuum, sicut recognitum fuit per sacramenta illorum qui terram illam perambulauerunt, et quod de cetero non fiat aliqua perambulacio inter terras meas et terras illorum, sed teneant ipsas diuisas quas habuerunt tempore patris mei et tempore meo, sine molestia et sine grauamine. Volo etiam et concedo ut quando uoluerint uel potuerint facere molendina in terris suis, nullus successorum meorum impediat homines manentes in terris ipsorum ire libere et quiete ad molendina illa cum omni secta sua et multura, quamuis solebant sequi molendina mea quamdiu fuerunt sine molendinis propriis. Testibus, Domino H. de Striuelin fratre meo, domino Roberto de campaniis, domino Hugone Phyton, domino Galfrido de Appelby, domino Anketill de Foleuille, Petro et Rogero clericis, Hugone de Panton, Baldewino de anuers, Petro pincerna, apud Berewic.

(Abstract)

'CHARTER of EARL JOHN concerning a TOFT in DUNDEE, and concerning the PERAMBULATION of DURNACH, and concerning the LIBERTY of the MILL.'

XX

Littere Comitis Johannis de Solucione secundarum decimarum.

J. DE SCOCIA, comes Cestre et huntendun, Balliuis suis de Garuiach, Salutem. Mando uobis quatinus a termino Sancti Martini anno gracie. m°. cc°. xxx°. quarto reddatis abbati de Lundors et humili eiusdem loci couentui decimas tocius terre mee de Garuiach ad ecclesiam suam de Lundors spectantes, sicut solui consueuerunt tempore patris mei et meo, secundum tenorem carte sue quam inde babent; et non dimittatis quin hoc faciatis, valete.

(Abstract)

' LETTER of EARL JOHN concerning the PAYMENT of SECOND TITHES.'

' J[OHN] of Scotland, Earl of Chester and Huntingdon, to his bailiffs of Garviach.'

He commands the bailiffs to pay to the abbot of Lundors and ' to the humble convent of the same place' ' the tithes of my whole land of Garviach pertaining to their church of Lundors' from Martinmas in the year of grace 1234, as they were accustomed to be paid in the time of his father, and in his own time.

XXI

Littere Comitis Johannis de Solucione secundarum decimarum de Garuiach.

OMNIBVS presentes litteras inspecturis uel audituris Johannes de|Scocia, Comes Cester et huntendun, Salutem: Nouerit vniuersitas vestra me teneri Johanni abbati de Lundors et eiusdem loci humili conuentui in quinquaginta et sex libris et tribus obolis sterlingorum pro decimis terre mce de Garuiach ad

(*Abstract*).

'LETTER of EARL JOHN concerning the PAYMENT of the SECOND TITHES of GARRIOCH.'

'EARL JOHN . . . to all who shall see or hear these present letters, greeting. Let all of you know that I am bound to John, abbot of Lundors, and the humble convent of the same place in fifty-six pounds and three half-pence sterling for the tithes of my land of Garviach . . . computed from the time when Simon of Garentulli received from me his bailiffship up to Martinmas 1234 ; the tithe of the rents of that term being counted in the sum named, together with sixty-four shillings and sevenpence of a loan made to me. In testimony of which I have caused my present letters patent to be sealed with my seal. Farewell.'

XXII

Carta Domini Regis Alexandri de Westere fedale.

A. DEI GRACIA Rex Scottorum omnibus probis hominibus tocius terre sue, salutem : Sciant presentes et futuri nos in excambium terre quam monachi de Lundors habuerunt apud Perth que uocatur insula, et in excambium terre de Dunmernoch quam eis contulimus in straththay, dedisse, concessisse, et hac carta nostra confirmasse eisdem monachis terram de fedal in theynagio de ouchyrardour : Tenendam et habendam eisdem monachis per rectas diuisas suas, et cum omnibus iustis pertinenciis suis in liberam, puram, et perpetuam elemosinam libere, quiete, plenarie, et honorifice ab omni seruicio, auxilio, consuetudine, et exaccione seculari : Reddendo annuatim xx. solidos, medietatem ad pentecosten, et aliam medietatem ad festum Sancti Martini : Saluis elemosinis nostris. Testibus, P. Comite de Dunbar, W. Comnyn Comite de menetheth, R. de quency, constabulario Scocie, W. filio alani, senescallo, Justiciario Scocie, Johanne Byset; apud Are vicesimo die aprilis, anno Regni Domini Regis, vicesimo secundo.

'CHARTER of our LORD, KING ALEXANDER, concerning WESTERE FEDALE.'

A[LEXANDER] by the grace of God, King of Scots, to all good men of his whole land, greeting. Let those present and to come know that

Thanage of Ouchyrardour, to be had and held by the same monks, by
its right marches, and with all its just pertinents, in free, pure, and
perpetual alms, freely, quietly, fully and honourably, without any
secular service, aid, custom, and exaction ; on rendering annually xx.
shillings—one half at Whitsunday, and the other half at the feast of
St. Martin ; excepting our alms.   Witnesses, P. Earl of Dunbar; W.
Comyn, Earl of Menteith ; R. de Quency, Constable of Scotland ; W.
Fitz-Alan, Steward, Justiciar of Scotland; John Byset.   At Ayr ; the
twentieth day of April in the twenty-second year of the reign of the
Lord the King. [1]

XXIII

Recognicio diuisarum de Westere fedale.

ANNO gracie m⁰. cc⁰. xlvj⁰. tempore vicecomitatus Domini
Johannis de Haya, Isti iurati recognouerunt secundum rectas
diuisas de Westere fedale sicut Dominus Rex eas tenuit, et
dictis monachis de Lundors per easdem dedit; scilicet, per
aldendoneche usque in aldnecrage, et per aldnecrage usque in
lonbohthe quorum nomina sunt hec, Patricius Ker, Simon
de fedale, et Gillemury filius dicti Simonis, et Simon Derech,
Gillebride, et gillefalyn filius dicti Gillebride, Gillecrist mac
hatheny, et Gillecrist mac moreherthach, Gille ethueny, et
Gillecostentyn, coram dicto Domino J. de Haya, et dicto
Domino abbate et monachis suis de Lundors, et hominibus
quamplurimis Domini Joachim, et hominibus Domini Episcopi
Dumblanensis, Kessy Mackedny et aliis et Burgensibus de
Outerardour, et hominibus Domini Comitis de Strathern, et
hominibus Domini fergusii filij Comitis, Wilellmo de luuetot,
Thoma clerico, Willelmo clerico, et multis aliis.   In cuius, rei
testimonio, ex precepto Domini Justiciarii A. hostiarii per
litteras suas patentes huic scripto sigillum suum apposuit.

(Abstract)

'INQUIRY as to the MARCHES of WESTERE FEDALE.'

IN the year of grace MCCXLVI., in the time when Sir John de Haya was
sheriff, certain persons whose names are given below were sworn to try

These marches were declared to be by Aldendoneche as far as Aldnecrage, and by Aldnecrage as far as Lonbohthe. The names are Patrick Ker ; Simon of Fedale ; and Gillemury, son of the said Simon ; Simon Derech ; Gillebride ; Gillefalyn, son of the said Gillebride ; Gillecrist Mac Hatheny ; Gillecrist Mac Moreherthach ; Gille Ethueny ; Gille-costentyn ; before the said Sir John de Haya, and the said Lord Abbot and his monks of Lundors, and very many men of Sir Joachim, and men of the Lord Bishop of Dunblane, Kessy Mackedny, and others, and burgesses of Outerardour, and men of the Lord Earl of Strathern ; and men of Sir Fergus, son of the earl ; William de Luvetot ; Thomas, clerk ; William, clerk, and many others. In testimony of which thing, at command of the Lord Justiciar, A. Durward (*Hostiarii*) by his letters patent, his seal was affixed to this writ.

XXIV

Carta Domini fergusii de fedal pro secundis decimis.

Omnibvs ad quos presens scriptum peruenerit fergus filius Comitis Gilberti, Salutem : Sciatis me dedisse, concessisse, et hac presenti carta mea confirmasse deo et ecclesie Sancte Marie et Sancti Andree de Lundors et monachis ibidem deo seruientibus et seruituris in perpetuum, fedal que est in Kathermothel, pro decimis quas habere solebant annuatim de cano et redditibus meis tam de Strathern quam de hure ex donacione Domini Malisii patrui mei ; Tenendam de me et heredibus meis, in liberam, puram et perpetuam elemosinam, per suas rectas diuisas et cum omnibus pertinenciis suis in bosco et plano, in terris et aquis, | in stagnis et molendinis, In moris et maresiis, in pratis et pasturis, sine aliquo retinemento, et cum communi aisiamento et libertate capiendi materiem in bosco meo ubi melius et proprius ipsis fuerit ad edificandum et sustentandum edificia necessaria et racionabilia in predicta terra, et ea que pertinent ad agriculturam. Ego autem et heredes mei warentizabimus eis predictam terram cum predictis asiamentis uersus Dominum Regem et uersus omnes homines, et liberam eam faciemus de

[*f*

de mauerunt omnes decimas quas habere solebant de dono[a]
predicti Malisii patrui mei, et cartas quas inde habebant resignauerunt. Testibus, Domino Roberto Comite de Strathern
fratre meo, Waltero Oliphard, Waltero de Rotheuen, Henrico
de Aschirche, Alexandro de Striuelyn, Willelmo de Bayllol,
Rogero de leuuethot, Gilberto fratre meo, fergusio senescaldo
meo, Rogero dispensatore meo.

Ista carta duplatur.

(Abstract)

'CHARTER of SIR FERGUS, of FEDAL, for SECOND TITHES.'

FERGUS, son of Earl Gilbert, gives, grants, and confirms to Lundors
'Fedal, which is in Kathermothel, for the tithes which they were accustomed to have annually of my cane and rents, as well of Strathern as
of Hure, of the gift of my paternal uncle (*patrui*) Sir Malise,' to be
held 'of me and my heirs' in frankalmoign, 'by its right marches
with all its pertinents, in wood and plain, lands and waters, stanks
and mills, moors and marshes, meadows and pastures, without any
reservation, and with the common easement and liberty of taking
material from my wood, where it shall be best and most suitable for
them, for building and keeping up necessary and reasonable buildings in the aforesaid land, and for those things which pertain to
agriculture.'

He grants warrandice of the land and aforesaid easements, 'against
the lord, the king, and against all men.' 'And we will make it [the land]
free of military service (*exercitu*), of aids, and of all service and exaction,
as well in regard to clerks as laymen.' Nothing to be exacted in return
save prayers for the weal of the soul. They (the monks) have quitclaimed all the tithes which they were accustomed to have by gift of the
aforesaid Malise, his uncle, and have resigned the charters which they
had from him. Witnesses   This Charter is doubled.

XXV

Confirmacio Comitis Roberti de fedale, etc.

VNIVERSIS hoc scriptum visuris uel audituris Robertus Comes
de Stratherne, salutem: Sciatis me concessisse et hac presenti
carta mea confirmasse donacionem illam quam dominus fer-

dono domini Malisii patrui mei quas ipsi quietas clamauerunt ;
et cartas quas inde habebant resignauerunt. Quare uolo et
concedo ut predicti monachi habeant et possideant prenominatam terram de fedal per suas Rectas diuisas et cum omnibus
pertinenciis suis, sine aliquo retinemento, et cum communi
asiamento et libertate capiendi necessaria tam ad edificia
quam ad agriculturam in bosco ipsius fergusii et heredum
suorum, in liberam, puram et perpetuam elemosinam, ita libere
et quiete ut ipsi nulli hominum inde respondeant de aliqua
seculari exaccione, sicut carta ipsius fergusii testatur. Testibus
Domino Innocencio abbate de insula missarum, Domino
Gilberto archidiacono Dumblanensi, Magistro christiano
fratre ipsius, Domino Thoma capellano Domini fergusii,
Domino Ricardo de Kinbuch, Bricio de Dunyn, Gilescop de
Cletheueys.

(Abstract)

' EARL ROBERT'S CONFIRMATION of FEDALE, etc.'

ROBERT, Earl of Strathern, grants and confirms 'that gift which Sir
Fergus, my brother, made to God and the monastery of Lundors
of Fedale which is in Kathermothel in exchange for the tithes which they
had annually of the gift of Sir Malise, my paternal uncle, which tithes
they have quitclaimed ; and they have resigned the charters [confirming
the donation of tithes] which they had. . . . Fedale is confirmed with
the rights and privileges named in Charter xxiv. Witnesses

XXVI

Carta domini fergusii de Beny et concrag.

VNIVERSIS hoc scriptum visuris uel audituris fergusius, filius
Gilberti quondam Comitis de Strathern, salutem in domino.
Noueritis me dedisse, concessisse, et hac carta mea confirmasse
deo et ecclesie Sancte Marie et Sancti Andree de Lundors, et
monachis ibidem deo seruientibus et seruituris, pro salute
anime mee et murielis sponse mee, et animarum omnium parentum meorum totam terram meam de Beny cum omnibus
pertinenciis suis, sine aliquo retinemento, per suas rectas diuisas

perpetuam elemosinam, quietas ab omni consuetudine et
seruicio, et excercitu, et auxilio, et omnibus aliis exaccionibus et
consuetudinibus. Et ego et heredes mei warentizabimus eis
predictas terras contra omnes homines, et adquietabimus de
omnibus demandis in mundo. Testibus, Domino Clemente Dun-
40.] blanensi episcopo, Domino Roberto Comite de Stratherne |
fratre meo, Waltero filio Alani de Rotheuen, Willelmo filio
Duncani Comitis de Mar, Rogero de luuetoth, Adam filio
Alani, et multis aliis.

(Abstract)

' CHARTER of SIR FERGUS concerning BENY and CONCRAG.'

' FERGUS, son of Gilbert, late Earl of Strathern,' grants to Lundors,
' for the weal of my soul and of the soul of my spouse Muriel, and of all
my relations,' my whole land of Beny with all its pertinents, and that
land pertaining to Beny, which lies close to the land of Roger de
Luvethot, ' my knight.' To be held in frankalmoign, quit of all
custom and service, and military service and aid, and all other exactions and customs. He and his heirs give warrandice against all men.
Witnesses

XXVII

Confirmacio Comitis Roberti de terra de Beny et concrage.

OMNIБVS ad quos presens scriptum peruenerit, Robertus
Comes de Strathern, Salutem in domino. Sciatis me concessisse,
et hac presenti carta mea confirmasse donacionem illam quam
Dominus fergus frater meus fecit deo et ecclesie beate Marie et
Sancti Andree de lundors, et monachis ibidem deo seruientibus
et seruituris de terra de Beny, et de terra illa pertinente ad
Beny, que iacet iuxta terram Rogeri de Luuethot militis
ipsius, cum suis diuisis et omnibus pertinenciis sine aliquo
retinemento. Quare uolo ut iidem monachi predictas terras
habeant et possideant in liberam puram et perpetuam elemosinam, quietas ab omni consuetudine et seruicio et excercitu et

fratre meo persona de Gasch, Malisio senescaldo meo, Malisio filio meo, Gilberto fratre meo, Malisio persona de Crefe Magistro Cristino et Bricio clericis meis, Gibun de Munfichet.

(*Abstract*)

'Charter of Confirmation of Earl Robert concerning the land of Beny and Concrage.'

Robert, Earl of Strathern, confirms the gift 'which Sir Fergus, my brother, made' to Lundors, of Beny and the land pertaining to Beny near the land of Roger de Luvethot, 'his knight,' in terms of the preceding charter. Witnesses

XXVIII

Carta Domini fergusii de Cotken, etc.

Omnibvs ad quos presens scriptum peruenerit fergus filius G. quondam Comitis de Strathern, salutem : Noueritis vniuersi terram que dicitur Cotken, in Kather mothel, fuisse liberam et communem pasturam, tempore omnium antecessorum meorum, omnibus hominibus circa predictam pasturam manentibus : Ita quod nullus in ipsa pastura aliquam domum faceret uel araret uel aliquid aliud faceret vnde alij possent impediri ab usu ipsius pasture. Quare uolo et concedo ut predicta terra in perpetuum ita sit libera et communis ut nec ego nec aliquis successorum meorum, per aliquam donacionem uel concessionem, communiam illam possimus auferre, et in huius rei perpetuum testimonium, huic carte mee sigillum meum apposui. Testibus, Domino Clemente Dumblanensi episcopo, Dompnis J. et N. de lundors et de Incheaffray abbatibus, Domino M. comite de Strathern, Malisio fratre meo, Magistro luca Decano Dumblanensi, magistro Duncano archidiacono de Strathern, Domino W. de Rotheuen, G. filio suo, Joachym de Kenbuc, Malisio senescaldo, militibus, Willelmo de luuetofte, Brice de Ardros, Brice de Donyn, Malisio fratre suo, et multis aliis.

(*Abstract*)

ancestors free and common pasture to all the men residing around the
said pasture, so that none might build a house in the pasture, or plough
any part of it, or do anything that would interfere with the use of the
pasture.' He declares that it shall be common pasture for ever, and
neither he nor his heirs shall have power by any gift to take away that
common. He causes his seal to be affixed. Witnesses

XXIX

Carta de Rathengoten de malisio filio ferteth.

OMNIBVS sancte matris ecclesie filiis et fidelibus tam presentibus quam futuris, Malisius filius Comitis fertheth, frater Comitis
Gilberti de Strathern, Salutem : Sciatis me dedisse et presenti
carta mea confirmasse deo et ecclesie Sancte Marie et Sancti
Andree de Lundors et monachis ibidem deo seruientibus, in
puram et perpetuam elemosinam, pro salute anime patris mei
et anime matris mee, et animarum antecessorum et parentum meorum, et pro salute anime mee, et anime ade
uxoris mee, filie Comitis Dauid, Rathangothen per rectas
diuisas suas in bosco et plano, in pratis et pascuis, in moris et
marasiis, in aquis, et in omnibus aliis aisiamentis, et cum
omnibus pertinenciis suis, excepto Molendino et aqua stagni
ipsius molendini, volo tamen et concedo quod monachi predicti,
et homines eorum, qui predictam terram tenent de predictis
monachis, molant bladum suum ad molendinum meum, libere,
quiete, et pacifice, sine omni multura, et quieti sint | ab omni
seruicio seculari et consuetudine et exaccione. Quare uolo
quod predicti monachi habeant et possideant predictam terram
ita libere et quiete, plenarie et honorifice sicut aliqua abbacia
in toto regno Scocie aliquam elemosinam liberius, quiecius,
plenius, et honorificencius tenet et possidet. Et ego et
heredes mei predictam terram adquietabimus predictis monachis
uersus Dominum Regem et heredes suos, et uersus omnes
homines de omnibus secularibus seruiciis, et exaccionibus.
Hiis testibus, Waltero olifard, Dauid de lindeseia, Henrico

41.]

(*Abstract*)

' CHARTER of MALISE, son of FERTETH concerning RATHEGOTEN.'

' MALISE, son of Earl Fertheth, and brother of Earl Gilbert,' grants to Lundors, for the weal of the souls of his father, mother, ancestors, and relations, for the weal of the souls of himself and his wife, Ada, daughter of Earl David, Rathengothen . . . in wood and plain . . . with all its pertinents, 'except the mill and the water of the stank of that mill.' The monks and their men, who hold the aforesaid land of the monks, are entitled to grind their corn at the mill without any multure, and shall be free from any secular service. He and his heirs will answer to the king and all men for all secular service and exactions. Witnesses   '

XXX

Confirmacio Comitis Gilberti de Ratengothen.

OMNIBVS sancte matris ecclesie filiis tam presentibus quam futuris, Gilbertus Comes de Strathern, salutem : Sciant tam presentes quam futuri me concessisse, et hoc presenti scripto meo confirmasse, deo et ecclesie Sancte Marie et Sancti Andree de Lundors, et monachis ibidem deo seruientibus, in puram et perpetuam elemosinam, Rathargothen, per omnes rectas suas diuisas, et cum omnibus iustis pertinenciis suis et asiamentis, ita libere, quiete, et honorifice sicut carta Malisii fratris mei, quam ipsi monachi habent de predicta terra, testatur et confirmat. Et ego et heredes mei adquietabimus predictam terram predictis monachis uersus Dominum Regem et heredes suos, et uersus omnes homines de omnibus seruiciis secularibus et exaccionibus. Testibus hiis, Abraham Dumblanensi episcopo, Johanne priore de Incheaffray, Gilberto archidiacono de Dumblayn, Roberto et fergus filiis meis, Malisio senescallo meo, Ricardo de Kinboch, Bricio persona de Crefe, et pluribus aliis.

(*Abstract*)

' CONFIRMATION of EARL GILBERT concerning RATENGOTHEN.'

XXXI

Confirmacio Comitis Roberti de Rathengothen.

Omnibvs sancte matris ecclesie filiis tam presentibus quam futuris Robertus filius Comitis de Strathern, Salutem : Sciant tam presentes quam futuri me concessisse et hoc presenti scripto meo confirmasse deo et ecclesie sancte Marie et sancti andree de lundors, et monachis ibidem deo seruientibus et seruituris, in puram et perpetuam elemosinam, Rathangothen, per omnes rectas suas diuisas cum omnibus iustis pertinenciis suis et asiamentis ita libere, quiete, plenarie et honorifice, sicut carta Malisii auunculi mei, quam ipsi monachi habent de predicta terra, testatur et confirmat. Et ego et heredes mei adquieta-bimus predictis monachis predictam terram uersus Dominum Regem et heredes suos, et uersus omnes homines de omnibus seruiciis et exaccionibus secularibus. Testibus hiis, Domino A. Dumblanensi episcopo, Domino G. Comite patre meo. J. priore de Inchaffrau, G. archidiacono de Strathern, Bricio persona de Crefe, Malisio senescallo, Ricardo de Kinbuch, Willelmo clerico Comitis, et multis aliis.

(*Abstract*)

' Confir) ation of Earl Robert concerning Rathengothen.'

Robert, Earl of Strathern, confirms the grant as it was expressed in ' the charter of Malise, my uncle.' Witnesses

XXXII

Confirmacio fergusii de Ratengothen.

Omnibvs sancte matris ecclesie filiis tam presentibus quam futuris, fergus filius Comitis de Strathern, Salutem : Sciant tam presentes quam futuri etc. ut prius in carta Roberti usque testatur et confirmat. Testibus, Domino G. Comite patre meo, Domino A. Dumblanensi episcopo, Domino Roberto fratre meo, J. priore de Inchaffray, G. Dumblanensi archidiacono, Malisio

(Abstract)

[' Confirmation of Fergus concerning Ratengothen.'
' Fergus, son of the Earl of Strathern,' confirms the grant as in the charter of Robert.   Among the witnesses are 'G. the earl, my father,' and ' Robert, my brother.']

XXXIII
Capitulum Dunkeldense de Rathengothen.

Omnibvs sancte matris ecclesie filiis hoc scriptum uisuris uel audituris capitulum ecclesie Dunkeldensis, Salutem: Nouerit uniuersitas uestra nos, assensu et auctoritate Domini nostri Episcopi H. dunkeldensis et communi consilio tocius capituli ecclesie nostre de Dunkeld, remisisse et quietum clamasse in perpetuum ecclesie sancte marie et sancti andree de Lundors, et monachis | ibidem deo seruientibus et seruituris coneuetum et redditum quem percipere solebamus ad opus Macleins et Scoloccorum in dimidia dauach terre de Rathengoten pro quatuor solidos quos Malisius, filius Comitis ferthet de Strathern, et heredes sui nobis et successoribus nostris et ecclesie nostre in perpetuum persoluent sicut carta eiusdem Malisij inde facta et confirmacio Domini Alexandri Regis Scottorum, et Domini Gilberti comitis de Strathern, et Domini Roberti heredis sui testantur.   Quare uolumus ut predicti monachi de Lundors tam presentes quam futuri predictam dimidiam Dauacatam terre de Rathengoten liberam teneant in perpetuum, et quietam ab omni exaccione que a nobis et successoribus nostris de cetero possit exigi, et ut haec nostra quieta clamacio robur perpetue firmitatis optineat presens scriptum sigilli nostri apposicione Roberauimus.   Hiis testibus, H. archidiacono Dunkeldensi, Matheo Decano, Magistro Matheo, Eugenio clerico, Johanne de hetun, Magistro Roberto de Rapellis, Michaele persona de Kinrossyn, Willelmo capellano Dunkeldensi, Nazaro capellano, B. capellano de Kergille, B. clerico Domini H. Episcopi, Thoma capellano, Magistro alano, et multis aliis.

(Abstract)

'The Chapter of Dunkeld concerning Rathengothen.'

assent and authority of our lord, H[ugh], Bishop of Dunkeld, and by the common counsel of the whole Chapter of our Church of Dunkeld, have surrendered and quitclaimed for ever to the Church of St. Mary and St. Andrew of Lundors . . . the conveth and rent (*redditum*) which we were accustomed to receive for the use of the macleins and scoloccs in a half davach of the land of Rathengoten, in consideration of four shillings which Malise, son of Ferthet, Earl of Strathern, and his heirs shall pay to us and our successors and our Church for ever.   'Our seal' attached.   Witnesses

XXXIV

Confirmacio H. Episcopi Dunkeldensis de Rathengothen.

H. DEI gracia episcopus Dunkeldensis Omnibus sancte matris ecclesie filiis, Salutem in domino.   Nouerit uniuersitas uestra capitulum nostrum de Dunkeld de assensu et auctoritate nostra remisisse, et quietum clamasse, deo et ecclesie sancte marie et sancti andree de lundors et monachis ibidem deo seruientibus et seruituris, redditum et Coneuetum quod ecclesia de Dunkeld percipere solebat annuatim de Ratengothen ad opus Macleins et Scollocorum pro quatuor solidos quos prefata ecclesia de Dunkelden in terra de Hure de cetero percipere debet ab heredibus Malisij filij Comitis fertheth, sicut in eorum auctenticis scriptis continetur, et per confirmacionem carte Domini Regis Alexandri corroboratur, ut autem hec rata et inconcussa futuris temporibus permanere ualeant, scriptum istud sigilli nostri munimine Roborauimus: Hiis testibus, H. archidiacono de Dunkeld, Matheo Decano, Magistro Matheo, Egenio clerico, Johanne de Hetun, Magistro Roberto de Rapellis, Michaele persona de Kinrossin, Willelmo capellano Dunkeldensi, Nazaro capellano, Bernardo capellano de Kergylle, B. clerico Domini H. episcopi, thoma capellano, magistro Alano, et multis aliis.

XXXV

Confirmacio Comitis Malisij generalis de Strathern et Hure.

OMNIBVS Christi fidelibus presentes litteras uisuris uel audituris Malisius Comes de Strathern, salutem eternam in domino : Nouerit vniuersitas vestra nos pro salute anime nostre et pro salute animarum omnium antecessorum et successorum nostrorum concessisse et hac presenti carta nostra confirmasse deo et ecclesie Sancte Marie et Sancti Andree de lundors et monachis ibidem deo seruientibus et seruituris omnes terras, possessiones, et libertates quas habent ex donacionibus et concessionibus Domini Malisii fratris Inclite recordacionis Domini Gilberti quondam Comitis de Strathern, et Domini fergusii auunculi nostri. Quare uolumus ut dicti monachi habeant, teneant, et possideant in liberam puram et perpetuam elemo sinam omnes dictas terras, possessiones, et libertates cum omni bus aisiamentis suis et iustis pertinenciis, et cum aisiamentis siluarum dicti Domini fergusii et heredum suorum adeo libere, quiete, pacifice, integre, et plenarie, sicut in cartis ipsorum super hiis confectis liberius et plenius continetur. In cuius rei testimonium presenti scripto sigillum nostrum fecimus apponi. Hiis testibus, venerabili patre Domino C. tunc Dumblanensi episcopo, Domino Gileberto de Haya, domino Gilberto de Glencarny, Domino Joachim, militibus, Domino Nicholao Canonico de Incheaffray, Domino Ni|cholao camerario   [*fo* Comitis, Gilberto de Kenbuc, et multis aliis.

(*Abstract*)

'EARL MALISE's general Confirmation of STRATHERN and HURE.'

MALISE, Earl of Strathern, grants and confirms 'for the weal of our soul and of the souls of all our ancestors and successors' to God and the church of St. Mary and St. Andrew of Lundors, etc., . . . all the lands, possessions, and liberties 'which they have by the gifts and

XXXVI
Carta Ade filie Comitis de Balemagh.

Vniversis Sancte matris ecclesie filiis et fidelibus, Ada filia Comitis Dauid, vxor Malisii filij Comitis fertheth, Salutem · Sciant tam presentes quam futuri me dedisse et concessisse, et hac carta mea confirmasse deo et ecclesie Sancte Marie et Sancti Andree de Lundors et monachis ibidem deo seruientibus in liberam et perpetuam elemosinam unam carucatam terre cum corpore meo in uilla de Balemagh, cum communi pastura eiusdem uille, liberam et quietam ab omni seruicio et exaccione seculari.   Quare uolo ut predicti monachi predictam terram habeant et possideant ita libere, et quiete, plenarie, et honorifice, sicut aliqua abbacia in regno Scocie aliquam elemosinam liberius et quiecius, plenius et honorificencius, tenet et possidet : Hiis testibus, Henrico capellano, Petro capellano, Malcolmo filio Bertulfi, Willelmo Wascelino, Hugone Malerbe, Kyneth, Anegus fratre eius, Winemero, Radulfo filio eudonis, Kilegirge filio Malisii, Iuone, Rainaldo.

(Abstract)

'CHARTER of ADA, Daughter of the Earl, concerning BALMAGH.'

'ADA, daughter of Earl David, wife of Malise, son of Earl Fertheth,' gives, grants, and confirms to the monks of Lundors in frankalmoign 'one ploughgate of land, with my body, in the vill of Balemagh, with common pasture of the same vill,' free from all secular service.   Witnesses

XXXVII
Carta Willelmi Wascelyn de terra de Newetyl.

Omnibvs Sancte matris ecclesie filiis et fidelibus Willelmus Wascelyn et mabilia uxor eius, salutem : Sciatis nos dedisse et concessisse et hac carta nostra confirmasse pro salute animarum

que iacet proxima terre ecclesie eiusdem uille, scilicet, inter superiorem uiam et collem, et communem pasturam, cum hominibus nostris, in eadem uilla ad decem auerias et xxx^{ta} oues, et unum equum, libere, quiete, plenarie et honorifice, sine omni seruicio et auxilio et consuetudine et exaccione seculari. Volumus eciam ut predicti monachi et eorum homines, qui predictam terram de eis tenuerint, quieti sint de opere molendini nostri, non de multura, et quia concessimus predictis monachis, ut ubicunque in regno Scocie moriamur apud predictum monasterium de Lundors corpora nostra sepeliantur, Volumus ut sepenominati monachi habeant et possideant predictam terram cum prenominata pastura, ita libere, quiete, plenarie, et honorifice, sicut aliqua abbacia in toto regno Scottorum aliquam elemosinam liberius, quiecius, plenius, et honorificencius tenet et possidet. Et nos et heredes nostri predictam terram adquietabimus cum pastura iam dicta antedictis monachis uersus Dominum nostrum Comitem Dauid et eius heredes, et uersus omnes homines de omnibus secularibus seruiciis et auxiliis, et consuetudinibus et exaccionibus, excepta multura molendini nostri. Hiis testibus, Henrico filio Comitis Dauid, Dauid de Haya, et eius fratre Thoma, Adam de Nesh, Roberto de Haya persona de Erole, Philippo senescallo et clerico Comitis Dauid, Willelmo persona de Dunde, Henrico clerico filio ylvf de Neutyl, Dauid de Audre, et Willelmo nepote eius, et Hugone fratre Willelmi, et Dauid oiselario, et multis aliis.

(Abstract)

'WILLIAM WASCELYN'S CHARTER of the LAND of NEWTYLE.'

WILLIAM WASCELYN and Mabel, his wife, give . . . 'for the weal of our souls and of the souls of our ancestors and successors and of our heirs' to the monks of Lundors, in frankalmoign, 'an oxgate of land in the vill of Newtyle, namely between the high way (*superiorem viam*)[1] and the hill, and common pasture with our men in the same vill for ten beasts of burden (*averias*), thirty sheep, and one horse, free of all service, aid, etc. 'And we will that the aforesaid monks, and their men, who hold the said land of them, shall be quit of the work of our mill, [but] not of multure.

have and possess the aforesaid land with the forenamed pasture' as freely, etc. Wascelyn and his wife will be responsible for all secular service due to 'our Lord, Earl David, and his heirs,' or to any other, except the multure of the mill. Witnesses . . .

XXXVIII

Dauid de Sancto Michaele de tofto in munros.

OMNIBVS ad quos presens scriptum peruenerit Dauid de Sancto Michaele, Salutem in domino. Nouerit vniuersitas vestra me dedisse, concessisse, et hac presenti carta mea confirmasse deo et ecclesie Sancte Marie et Sancti Andree de Lundors, et monachis ibidem deo seruientibus pro salute anime mee et anime patris mei, et animarum omnium antecessorum et successorum meorum, in liberam puram et perpetuam elemosi nam, redditum quem solebam annuatim percipere de tofto illo in munros quem bone memorie Rex Willelmus dedit | Willelmo de Saneto Michaele patri meo et heredibus suis, quem videlicet toftum Henricus Griser quondam tenuit de predicto Willelmo patre meo et postea de me. Quare uolo ut predicti monachi habeant et possideant omne ius et dominium quod habui uel habere debui in predicto tofto die quo feci eis hanc donacionem, liberum et quietum de me et heredibus meis in perpetuum sine omni consuetudine, seruicio, et exaccione seculari, ita libere, quiete, plenarie, et honorifice sicut aliquam elemosinam liberius et quiecius in toto regno Scocie tenent et possident. Hiis testibus, Philippo clerico senescallo Comitis Dauid, Domino Johanne Giffard, Waltero de Cungertune, Thoma de Maleuile, Michaele de Inchethor, Waltero de maleuile, Willelmo de munfort, et aliis.

44.]

(Abstract)

'DAVID OF ST. MICHAEL'S [CHARTER] of a TOFT in MUNROS.'

DAVID of St. Michael gives to the monks of Lundors 'for the weal of my soul, and of the souls of my father, and of all my ancestors and successors,' in frankalmoign, 'the rent (redditum) which I used to receive annually from that toft in Munros which King William, of good memory, gave

possess all the right and lordship which I had, or ought to have, in the aforesaid toft on the day when I made this donation.' Without any service, custom, etc. Witnesses

XXXIX

Confirmacio Roberti Griffyn de terra de Newtil.

Omnibvs ad quos presens scriptum peruenerit Robertus Griffin et Mabilia uxor sua, Salutem. Nouerit vniuersitas vestra nos concessisse et hac carta nostra confirmasse deo et ecclesie sancte Marie et sancti Andree de Lundors, et monachis ibidem deo seruientibus illam bouatam terre in Neutyl, quam Willelmus Wascelyn eis dedit, et carta sua confirmauit: vt autem predictam terram libere, quiete, et pacifice in puram et perpetuam elemosinam teneant et possideant, dedimus eisdem unum toftum in uilla nostra de Neutyl et unam acram terre in augmentum subtus predictam bouatam. Et concedimus ut ipsi et homines eorum, qui terram prenominatam de eis tenuerint, quieti sint a multura et opere molendini et omnibus aliis consuetudinibus, et seruiciis et exaccionibus secularibus. Testibus, Domino G. abbate et conuentu de Aberbrothoc, Willelmo de la Karnayll, Roberto filio eius, Domino Wyot capellano, Elya seruiente nostro, et aliis.

(Abstract)

'Robert Griffyn's Confirmation of the Land of Newtyle.'

Robert Griffin and Mabel, his wife, grant and confirm to the monks of Lundors the oxgate of land in Newtyle which William Wascelyn gave to them. Griffin and his wife give the monks in addition a toft in the vill of Newtyle, and an acre of land, below the aforesaid oxgate. 'And we grant that they and their men, who hold of them the aforesaid land, shall be quit of multure, and of the work of the mill, and of all other secular services, customs, and exactions.' Witnesses . . .

XL

Carta Domine Ysabelle de Cragyn.

Omnibvs hoc scriptum uisuris uel audituris, Ysabella de Brus,

sancti Andree de lundors, et monachis ibidem deo seruientibus et seruituris, totum mesuagium meum de Cragyn iuxta Dunde, cum tota terra mea ad me uel heredes meos pertinente in eadem Cragyn, et in uilla que dicitur Mylnetoun, et in uilla Abrahe, sine aliquo retinemento. Tenendum sibi de me [et] heredibus meis in puram et perpetuam elemosinam ad sustentacionem unius monachi qui in predicto monasterio celebrabit missam pro anima mea et pro animabus antecessorum et successorum meorum in perpetuum, quod ipsi michi ad peticionem meam caritatiue concesserunt. Et ego et heredes mei omnia predicta predictis monachis Warentizabimus et adquietabimus de omni seruicio seculari et exaccione. Testibus, Dominis Willelmo de Brechyn, Willelmo de Lacu, Hugone de Beaumys, Michaele de muncur, militibus, Alberto de Dunde, Nicholao filio Roberti, heruino Koks, Normanno de castello Burgensibus, et multis aliis.

(*Abstract*)

'THE LADY YSABELLA'S CHARTER of CRAGYN.'

YSABELLA DE BRUS gives to the monks of Lundors 'my whole messuage of Cragyn near Dundee, with all my land, pertaining to me and my heirs, in the same Cragyn and in the vill which is called Mylnetoun, and in the vill of Abraham, without any reservation. To be held by them of me and my heirs in pure and perpetual alms for the support of one monk, who in the aforesaid monastery will celebrate for ever a mass for my soul, and for the souls of my ancestors and successors; which they [the monks] at my petition have charitably granted.' She and her heirs will answer for all secular service and exaction. Witnesses

XLI

Confirmacio Domini Roberti de Brus de Cragyn.

OMNIBVS hoc scriptum uisuris uel audituris, Robertus de Brus, eternam in domino salutem : Noueritis me diuine pietatis intuitu concessisse, et presenti carta mea confirmasse donaciouem illam quam domina Ysabella de Brus mater mea fecit deo et beate Marie et sancto Andree de lundors et monachis

Mylnetoun, et in uilla Abrahe, sine aliquo retinemento;
Te | nendis et habendis sibi de dicta Domina Ysabella et here-   [*fo*
dibus suis, in puram et perpetuam elemosinam, ad sustentacionem unius monachi, qui in predicto monasterio celebrabit
missam pro anima ipsius Ysabelle, et pro animabus antecessorum et successorum suorum in perpetuum, Ita libere et
quiete, sicut carta eiusdem Ysabelle dictis monachis inde
plenius confecta testatur. Hiis testibus, domino Alexandro
Cumyn, Comite de Buchan, Domino Willelmo de Brechyn,
Dominis Thoma de lascelis, Gilberto de haya, Humfrido
de Kirkepatrik, Ingeramo de Monceus, Hugone Mauleuerer,
Hugone de Berkelay, Hugone de Beaumys, militibus, Domino
Henrico capellano meo, Adam clerico meo, et multis aliis;
Apud Edenburg, anno gracie M° cc° xlviij°, quinto ydus
Augusti.

(Abstract)

' SIR ROBERT DE BRUS'S CONFIRMATION of CRAGYN.'

ROBERT DE BRUS grants and confirms 'that donation which Lady
Ysabella de Brus, my mother, made to God,' etc., 'of her whole
messuage of Cragyn,' etc. [all as in Charter XL.]. Witnesses   At
Edinburgh, 9th Aug. 1248.

XLII

Carta principalis de terra de Eglesmagril, et de ecclesia eiusdem uille et de decimis de Cletheueis.

CVM auctoritate Domini pape Innocencii iij, coram iudicibus
delegatis, scilicet, Simone et Johanne, prioribus de Sancto
Andrea et de May, et magistro laurencio archidiacono Sancti
Andree, super ecclesia de Mothel questio mouetur inter
Dominum Abraham episcopum Dumblanensem ex vna parte,
et Guidonem abbatem et conuentum de lundors ex alia, Post
multas hinc inde altercaciones predictus episcopus de assensu
Nobilis uiri Gilberti Comitis de Strathern, et Roberti heredis
eius, et Gilberti archidiaconi episcopi, et Elphini prioris de
Incheaffran et cleri eiusdem diocesis ex vna parte, et predictus
Guido abbas de Lundors de assensu conuentus sui ex alia

terium de lundors super ecclesia de mothel, pacem perpetuam
prouideret. Ipse uero, assumptis secum uiris prudentibus et
discretis, sub hac forma, inter predictas † pacem formauit,
scilicet, quod predictus episcopus, de assensu predictorum,
concessit deo et ecclesie sancte Marie et sancti Andree de
lundors, et abbati et monachis ibidem deo seruientibus et
seruituris, annuum redditum decem marcarum arbitrio boni
uiri, ita assignatarum, scilicet, uillam que dicitur Eglesmagril
per rectas diuisas suas cum omnibus iustis pertinenciis suis in
bosco et plano, in pratis et pascuis, in moris et stagnis, et
aquis et molendinis, et omnibus aliis asiamentis pro annuo
redditu sex Marcarum, liberam et quietam ab auxiliis et
excercitibus, et canis et coneuetibus, et omni seruicio et exaccione, et consuetudine seculari, Ita quod predictus Gilbertus
Comes de Strathern pro se et heredibus suis in perpetuum
suscepit onus exercitus, et Dominus Episcopus Abraham Dumblanensis et successores sui omnia alia onera sustinebunt, et
insuper ecclesiam eiusdem uille, cum omnibus iustis pertinenciis
suis in assignacionem redditus duarum marcarum liberam et
quietam ab hospiciis et procuracionibus et auxiliis, et ceteris
episcopalibus, preter cathedradicum et canonicam iusticiam, et
omnes decimas et decimaciones de Cletheues, tam de blado
quam de omnibus aliis que decimari possunt, in assignacionem
duarum marcarum liberas et quietas ab omni oneri. Hunc
autem redditum decem marcarum ita libere et quiete, in
perpetuum a predicto monasterio possidendum, predictus
episcopus et successores sui contra omnes homines warenti-
zabunt. Dominus uero Guido, abbas de lundors, pro se et
conuentu suo, et successoribus suis, quietum clamauit in
perpetuum deo et ecclesie Dumblanensi et Domino Abraham
eiusdem loci episcopo et successoribus suis ius quod petebat in
ecclesiam de Mothel ex donacione nobilis viri malisij fratris
46.] predicti Comitis Gilberti | et cartas quas super ecclesia eadem
habuerunt Resignauerunt, et ne idem episcopus uel aliquis
successorum suorum a predicta concessione et donacione possit
resilire, uel predicti abbas et conuentus uel eorum successores

possint in perpetuum compellere stare predictis concessioni et quiete clamacioni. Et in huius rei testimonium haec signa sunt apposita, scilicet, signum Domini Willelmi episcopi sancti Andree, et signa iudicum delegatorum, scilicet, Simonis et Johannis, priorum de sancto andrea et de May, et Magistri laurencii archidiaconi sancti andree, et abrahe episcopi Dumblanensis, et Gilberti Comitis de Stratherne, et Gilberti archidiaconi Dunblanensis, et cleri eiusdem diocesis, et signum prioris et conuentus de Incheaffray, et signa filiorum Comitis G., Roberti scilicet et fergusii.

PRINCIPAL CHARTER concerning the LAND of EGLESMAGRIL, and the CHURCH of the same VILL, and concerning the TITHES of CLETHEUEIS.

WITH the authority of the Lord Pope, Innocent III., a question as to the church of Mothel is raised between the Lord Abraham, Bishop of Dunblane, of the one part, and Guido, the abbot and the convent of Lundors, of the other, before the judges delegate, namely, Simon and John, Priors of St. Andrews and the May, and Master Laurence, Archdeacon of St. Andrews. After many discussions on the one side and the other, the bishop aforesaid (with the assent of the noble man, Gilbert, Earl of Strathern, and of Robert, his heir, and of Gilbert, Archdeacon of the Bishop, and of Elphin, Prior of Inchaffran, and of the clergy of the same diocese) of the one part, and the aforesaid Guido, Abbot of Lundors (with the assent of his convent), of the other part, took an oath to submit themselves to the authority of the Bishop of St. Andrews, William, of good memory, to the end that he, no appeal being allowed, should arrange a lasting agreement between the bishopric of Dunblane and the monastery of Lundors in respect to the church of Mothel. He [the Bishop of St. Andrews] having conjoined with himself prudent and discreet men, made peace between the aforesaid in the following form : ' The bishop aforesaid [the Bishop of Dunblane], with the assent of the aforesaid, has conceded to God and the church of St. Mary and St. Andrew of Lundors, and to the monks who now serve and shall hereafter serve God in that place, an annual payment of ten marks, according to the decree-arbitral of a good man, to be assigned as follows, that the vill which is called Eglesmagril, by its right marches with all its just pertinents, in wood and plain, in meadows and pastures, in moors and stanks, in waters and mills, and all other easements, shall for the payment of six marks be free and quit of aids and military service (hostings), and canes and conveths, and all service and exaction and secular custom. The aforesaid Gilbert, Earl of Strathern, has for himself and his heirs, undertaken for ever the burden of military service

And moreover [it was pronounced] that the church of the same vill, with all its just pertinents, for a payment of two marks should be free and quit of *hospitia* and procurations, and aids and other episcopal dues, excepting the *cathedraticum* and canonical justice. And [it was pronounced] that all the tithes and tithings of Cletheues, as well in corn as in all other things which can be tithed, shall be free and quit of all burdens for the payment of two marks. And that this payment of ten marks shall be possessed free and quit for ever, by the monastery aforesaid, the aforesaid bishop and his successors give warrandice against all men. And the Lord Guido, Abbot of Lundors, for himself, his convent, and their successors, has quitclaimed for ever to God and the church of Dunblane, and to the Lord Abraham, bishop of the same place, and his successors, the right which he sought over the church of Mothel, as granted by the noble man, Malise, brother of the aforesaid Earl Gilbert. And the charters which they had in regard to the same church they have resigned. And lest the same bishop or any of his successors might resile from the aforesaid grant and gift, or lest the aforesaid abbot and convent, and their successors, might act contrary to their quitclaim, they have severally subjected themselves to the power of the aforesaid William, Bishop of St. Andrews, and his successors, so that they [the Bishops of St. Andrews] may be able (no appeal being allowed) to compel them to stand to the aforesaid grant and quitclaim.' And in testimony of this these seals are affixed, namely, the seal of the Lord William, Bishop of St. Andrews ; and the seals of the judges delegate, namely, of Simon and John, Priors of St. Andrews and the May ; and of Master Laurence, Archdeacon of St. Andrews ; and of Abraham, Bishop of Dunblane ; and of Gilbert, Earl of Strathern ; and of Gilbert, Archdeacon of Dunblane ; and of the clergy of the same diocese ; and the seal of the prior and convent of Inchaffray ; and the seals of the sons of Earl Gilbert, namely Robert and Fergus.

XLIII

Carta Comitis Gilberti de excercitu faciendo pro Eglesmagril.

Omnibvs has litteras uisuris uel audituris, Gilbertus Comes de Strathern, Salutem : Nouerit uniuersitas vestra de assensu et uoluntate mea et Roberti heredis mei per virum venerabilem Willelmum episcopum Sancti Andree causam, que uertebatur inter uenerabilem patrem nostrum Abraham episcopum Dum-

amicabiliter esse terminatam iuxta quod in auctentico instrumento inter eosdem super predicta pace confecto continetur; Ita quod ego pro me et heredibus meis in me et heredes meos suscepi onus excercitus que debetur de terra de Eglesmagril que eisdem abbati et monachis est assignata pro annuo redditu sex marcarum in perpetuum, et ne hoc factum meum aliquem possit latere in posterum ipsum presentis pagine testimonio et sigilli mei apposicione dignum duxi declarandum. Hiis testibus, Willelmo episcopo Sancti Andree, Abraham episcopo Dumblanensi, Bricio persona de Crefe, et eius filio malisio, Rogero de Mortimero, Reginaldo de Dunbernyn, Gillenem et malisio senescallis Comitis, anecol et Gillemor filio eius, cum multis aliis.

CHARTER of EARL GILBERT concerning rendering MILITARY SERVICE (*exercitu*) for EGLESMAGRIL.

To all who shall see or hear these letters, Gilbert, Earl of Strathern, greeting. Let all of you know that, with the assent and approval of me and of Robert, my heir, the cause which was in dispute between our venerable father, Abraham, Bishop of Dunblane, of the one part, and Guido, the abbot, and the monks of Lundors, of the other part, concerning the church of Mothel, has been amicably settled by the venerable man, William, Bishop of St. Andrews, according to the terms contained in the authentic instrument executed between them in reference to the agreement aforesaid. In accordance with which I, on behalf of myself and my heirs, have taken upon me and my heirs the burden of the military service which is due from the land of Eglesmagril, which has been assigned to the said abbot and monks, for an annual payment, for ever, of six marks. And lest this my act might in the future be unknown to any, I have thought fit that it should be declared by the testimony of this present writ and by the affixing of my seal: these being witnesses, William, Bishop of St. Andrews; Abraham, Bishop of Dunblane; Brice, Parson of Crefe, and his son, Malise; Roger de Mortimer; Reginald de Dunbernyn; Gillenem and Malise, seneschals of the earl; Anecol, and Gillemor, his son; with many others.

XLIV

Confirmacio Comitis Roberti de exercitu pro eglesmagril.

quod bone memorie Gilbertus Comes pater meus suscepit in se
et heredes suos facere excercitum Domini Regis pro terra de
Eglesmagril in perpetuum.   Quare uolo ut nullus de cetero
aliquod grauamen faciat predicte terre uel alieui manenti in ea
pro tali exaccione, de qua ego et heredes mei illam adquietabimus.   Et in huius rei testimonium huic scripto sigillum
meum apponere feci.   Testibus, Domino C. episcopo nostro,
Domino fergus fratre meo, Domino malisio senescaldo meo,
Domino Rogero de luuetoth, Malisio persona fratre meo,
Magistro Cristiano, Malisio filio meo, Gilberto et Bricio de
Morauia.

'CONFIRMATION of EARL ROBERT concerning MILITARY SERVICE
for EGLESMAGRIL.'

ROBERT, Earl of Strathern, declares that he holds good the undertaking of his father, Earl Gilbert, to 'make the hosting of the Lord
King' for the land of Eglesmagril.   'Wherefore I will that in future no
one put any burden on the said land or on any one residing on it for such
exaction, for which I and my heirs will be responsible.'   Seal affixed.
Witnesses

XLV

De ecclesia de eglesmagril.

ABRAHAM miseracione diuina Dumblanensis ecclesie minister
humilis omnibus has litteras uisuris uel audituris, eternam in
domino Salutem : Sciatis nos de assensu Gilberti, archidiaconi,
et cleri ecclesie nostre, concessisse abbati et conuentui de lundors
annuum redditum duarum marcarum de camera nostra et
successorum nostrorum, die Natiuitatis sancti Johannis Baptiste
et die natalis Domini percipiendarum in uita patricij persone
de Eglesmagril, qui eandem ecclesiam in tota uita sua pacifice
possidebit.   Eo autem cedente uel decedente, predicta ecclesia
libera et quieta cum omni integritate sua redibit ad predictum

Roberto et fergoso filiis Comitis Gilberti, Gilberto archidiacono Dunblanensi, Bricio persona de Crefe, Gillenem et Malisio senescallis Comitis Gilberti, Malisio filio Bricij persone de Crefe cum multis aliis.

'CONCERNING the CHURCH of EGLESMAGRIL.'

ABRAHAƷ, by the divine mercy humble minister of the church of Dunblane, to all who shall see or hear these letters, health everlasting in the Lord.   Know ye that with the assent of Gilbert, the archdeacon, and the clergy of our church, we have granted to the abbot and convent of Lundors an annual payment of two marks from the treasury (*camera*) of ourselves and our successors, to be received on the day of the Nativity of St. John the Baptist [June 24] and on Christmas Day during the life of Patrick, parson of Eglesmagril, who shall peaceably possess the same church during the whole of his life.   But, on his resigning or dying, the aforesaid church shall return in all its completeness to the aforesaid convent, according to what is contained in the authentic instrument of agreement made between us.   But in the future we and our successors shall be free and quit of the payment of the two marks aforesaid.   These are the witnesses : William, Bishop of St. Andrews ; Gilbert, Earl of Strathern ; Elpin, Prior of Inchaffran ; Robert and Fergus, sons of Earl Gilbert ; Gilbert, Archdeacon of Dunblane ; Brice, Parson of Crefe ; Gillenem and Malise, seneschals of Earl Gilbert ; Malise, son of Brice, Parson of Crefe ; with many others.

XLVI

Quieta clamacio Coneueti de Eglesmagril.

OMNIBVS ad quos presens scriptum peruenerit Macbeth, Rex scolarum de Dumblayn, et eiusdem loci scolastici, Salutem : Noueritis nos communi consilio et assensu quietum clamasse in perpetuum deo et ecclesie Sancte Marie et Sancti Andree de Lundors et abbati et monachis ibidem deo seruientibus et

Willelmus episcopus sancti Andree sigillum suum huic scripto apposuit in testimonium.

QUITCLAIN of CONVETH from EGLESMAGRIL.

To all whom the present writ shall come, Macbeth, King (*Rex*) of the schools of Dunblane, and the scholastics of the same place, greeting. Know ye that we, by common counsel and consent, have, for ourselves and our successors, quitclaimed for ever to God and the church of St. Mary and St. Andrew of Lundors and the abbot and monks there serving, or who shall hereafter serve God in that place, the conveth which we were accustomed to receive annually in the vill of Eglesmagril, in return for the payment of two shillings, which the Lord A[braham], Bishop of Dunblane and his successors will give us annually out of his rent from Drumendufelis, as is contained in the deed executed between the bishop, the monks, and us. And because we have no seal, the Lord William, Bishop of St. Andrews, has, at our request, affixed, in testimony, his seal to this writ.

XLVII

Quieta Clamacio Coneueti de Eglesmagril.

OMNIBVS ad quos presens scriptum peruenerit Malduueny, Rex scolarum de Mothel, et eiusdem loci scolastici, salutem. Nouerit vniuersitas vestra nos communi consilio et cetera de uerbo ad uerbum ut in precedenti proxima.

QUITCLAIN of CONVETH from EGLESMAGRIL.

To all to whom the present writ shall come, Malduveny, King (*Rex*) of the schools of Mothel, and the scholastics of the same place, greeting. Let all of you know that we, by common counsel : and the rest, word for word as in the next preceding.

XLVIII

Quieta clamacio Coneueti de Eglesmagril.

quod solebamus percipere annuatim in uilla de Eglesmagril, pro redditu duorum solidorum quos Dominus A. Dumblanensis episcopus et eius successores nobis dabunt annuatim, ad pentecosten, de camera sua. Et quia sigillum non habuimus, ad peticionem nostram Dominus W. episcopus Sancti Andree huic scripto apposuit in testimonium sigillum suum.

(*Abstract*)

QUITCLAIM of CONVETH from EGLESMAGRIL.

THE Clerks of Methfyn quitclaim for ever the annual conveth which they were accustomed to receive in the vill of Eglesmagril, for the payment of two shillings which Abraham and his successors, Bishops of Dunblane, will give to them at Whitsunday from his treasury. 'And because we have no seal,' etc. [As in Charter XLVI.]

XLIX

Confirmacio E. prioris de Incheaffran de Cletheueys.

VNIVERSIS sancte matris ecclesie filiis et fidelibus has litteras uisuris uel audituris, Elphinus dei gracia prior de Incheaffran, et eiusdem loci conuentus, eternam in Domino salutem: Noueritis nos concessisse et hac carta nostra confirmasse deo et ecclesie Sancte Marie et Sancti Andree de lundors et eiusdem loci conuentui omnes decimas de Clethues tam de blado quam de omnibus aliis rebus que decimari debent; Ita libere et quiete, plene et honorifice, sicut vir venerabilis Abraham episcopus Dumblanensis eas cum assensu et auctoritate clericorum suorum, tam archidiaconi quam aliorum, eisdem monachis de lundors dedit et carta sua confirmauit. Et quia sigillum commune tempore huius confirmacionis non habuimus, in rei facte testimonium Domini nostri Gilberti, Comitis de Strathern, huic presenti pagine fecimus apponi sigillum. Hiis testibus, Abraham episcopo Dumblanensi, Gilberto archidiacono eiusdem, Bricio persona de Crefe, et Malisio [filio] eius, duobus filiis Comitis Gilberti Roberto et Fergusio, Malisio senescallo Comitis, et quoad amplius, Teste capitulo nostro.

as well in grain as in all other things which are liable to tithe, as freely
. . . as the Bishop of Dunblane, Abraham, gave them to the same monks,
with the assent and authority of the clergy, the archdeacon, and others.
And because at the time of this confirmation we had not the common
seal . . . we have caused the seal of our lord, Gilbert, Earl of
Strathern, to be affixed to this writ in testimony of what has been
done. Witnesses

L

Sentencia Judicum Delegatorum Auctoritate Domini Pape super Eglesmagril.

OMNIBVS hoc scriptum uisuris uel audituris Willelmus dei
gracia episcopus, Hugo Decanus, et Robertus thesaurarius |
Glasguenses, eternam in domino salutem. Mandatum domini
pape suscepimus in hec uerba. Gregorius Episcopus, seruus
seruorum dei, venerabili fratri . . Episcopo, et dilectis filiis,
Decano et Thesaurario Glasguensibus, Salutem et apostolicam
benediccionem : venerabili fratre nostro, Dumblanensi episcopo,
accepimus intimante, quod cum inter bone memorie A. pre-
decessorem suum ex parte vna, et Abbatem et conuentum de
lundors Sancti Andree diocesis ex altera, super ecclesia de
Mothel coram . . priore Sancti Andree suisque Collegis
auctoritate apostolica questio uerteretur ; Demum hine inde
fuit iuramento prestito in uenerabilem fratrem nostrum Episcopum Sancti Andree tanquam in arbitrum compromissum,
qui equitate postposita iniquum arbitrium promulgauit, in
enormes ecclesie dumblanensis lesiones. Quare idem episcopus
ecclesie predicte subueniri per beneficium restitucionis in
integrum postulauit. Ideoque discrecioni vestre per apostolica
scripta mandamus, quatinus si per arbitrium ipsum inueneritis
Dumblanensem ecclesiam enormiter esse lesam, ad restitu-
cionem ipsius sicut iustum fuerit procedatis, facientes quod
super hoc statueritis per censuram ecclesiasticam firmiter
obseruari : Testes autem qui fuerint nominati, si se gracia,
odio, uel timore subtraxerint, censura simili, appellacione

48.]

Octauo. Huius igitur auctoritate mandati partibus in nostra presencia constitutis, et auditis hincinde propositis, Nos diligenter causam examinantes, licet arbitrium a venerabili uiro Episcopo Sancti Andree prolatum inuenissemus equum rite et bona fide prolatum, Inuenimus tamen ecclesiam Dumblanensem per predictum episcopum Sancti Andree in taxacione redditus Decem marcharum lesam extitisse. Quapropter uolentes ea, que legitime acta sunt, in sua firmitate persistere, et ea que forte per errorem minus licite facta sunt, ad statum debitum reuocare, auctoritate qua fungebamur, in recompensacionem illius lesionis, abbatem et conuentum nomine monasterij de Lundors, Episcopo Dumblanensi et eius successoribus, nomine ecclesie Dumblanensis, in annua prestacione redditus Quinque marcarum sentencialiter condempnauimus; arbitrio viri venerabilis Episcopi Sancti Andree in suo robore perdurante. Quod quidem ratum habemus et illud sicut prouide factum est, et in instrumento super hoc confecto continetur, auctoritate apostolica qua fungebamur confirmauimus. Actum apud Lyston xvj°. Kal. Maij anno gracie m°. cc°. xxx°. v^{to}., et ut haec nostra sentencia robur perpetue firmitatis obtineat huic scripto sigilla nostra apposuimus.

Sentence of the Judges Delegate by authority of our Lord the Pope, on Eglesmagril.

To all who shall see or hear this writ, William, by the grace of God Bishop, Hugh, Dean, and Robert, Treasurer, of Glasgow, health everlasting in the Lord. We have received a mandate of our Lord the Pope in these words: 'Gregory, bishop, servant of the servants of God, to our venerable brother, the bishop, and to our beloved sons, the dean and the treasurer of Glasgow, health and apostolic benediction. We have learned on the information of our venerable brother, the Bishop of Dunblane, that when a question about the church of Mothel was debated between his predecessor, A[braham], of the one part, and the abbot and convent of Lundors in the diocese of St. Andrews, of the second part, before the Prior of St. Andrews and his colleagues appointed by apostolic authority, at length it was agreed by both parties on oath to submit to

greatly injured by that judgment arbitral, ye shall proceed, as shall be just, to effect restitution, and shall cause what ye shall determine upon the matter to be strictly observed, under the pain of canonical censure. And if the witnesses who shall be named fail to appear through favour, hatred, or fear, ye shall compel them by like censure to give testimony to the truth, not permitting any appeal on their part. If ye all shall not be able to take part in executing this mandate, do thou, nevertheless, Brother Bishop, together with one other of those appointed, give execution to this mandate.   Given at Perugia, iii. Non. November [Nov. 3] in the eighth year of our pontificate [1234].'

On the authority, therefore, of this mandate, after the parties had appeared in our presence, and what was put forward on each side had been heard, we diligently examined the cause.   And although we have found that the decree-arbitral pronounced by the venerable man, the Bishop of St. Andrews, was just, and pronounced in due form and in good faith, yet we have found that the church of Dunblane was injured by the aforesaid Bishop of St. Andrews in the estimate of the payment of the ten marks.   Wherefore wishing that those things which were lawfully done should remain firmly established, and that those things which perchance through error were not quite lawfully done should be recalled to their due state, we, by the authority which we possess, have pronounced sentence condemning the abbot and convent of Lundors, as representing the monastery of Lundors, to pay annually to the Bishop of Dunblane and his successors, as representing the church of Dunblane, the sum of five marks, the decree-arbitral of the venerable man, the Bishop of St. Andrews, still remaining in force.   Which decree-arbitral we ratify, and as having been wisely made (as contained in the instrument dealing with matter) we have confirmed it.   Done at Lyston, xvi. Kalends of May [April 16] in the year of grace mccxxxv.   And that this our sentence may be firmly established we have affixed our seals to this writ.

LI

Confirmacio Clementis episcopi Dumblanensis de Eglesmagril.

Vniversis Christi fidelibus ad quos presens scriptum peruenerit, Clemens dei gracia Dumblanensis Episcopus, eternam in domino Salutem: Ea que iudicio uel concordia terminata sunt, ne aliquorum improbitate uel astucia in recidiue conten-

habere sentenciam uirorum uenerabilium Domini Willelmi Episcopi, Hugonis Decani, et Roberti thesaurarij ecclesie Glasguensis, quam auctoritate Domini pape Gregorii Noni tulerunt super arbitrio Domini Willelmi Episcopi Sancti Andree, quondam prolato super controuersia mota inter A. bone memorie, predecessorem nostrum, et abbatem et conuentum de lundors super ecclesia de Mothel; per quod arbitrium causati sumus ecclesiam Dumblanensem fuisse lesam : Qui equitate[a] [a] MS. *e* pensata arbitrium equum et rite prolatum pronunciaverunt; et excessum factum in taxacione redditus | Decem marcarum [*f* vnde dictam ecclesiam lesam perpenderunt corrigentes, condempnauerunt dictos abbatem et monachos, nomine monasterij sui, nobis et successoribus nostris, nomine predicte ecclesie Dumblanensis, in Quinque marcis argenti annuatim soluendis. Quam sentenciam quia in commodum predicte ecclesie nostre lata est, acceptamus et Ratam habemus, bona fide, in periculo anime nostre et animarum successorum nostrorum, promittentes quod super predicto arbitrio nullam de cetero mouebimus questionem : set sicut a predecessore nostro susceptum est, et in instrumento super hoc confecto plenius expressum, et auctoritate Domini pape a iudicibus prenominatis confirmatum, illud sine cauilacione et dolo obseruabimus in perpetuum. Et ut hoc futuris temporibus robur firmitatis obtineat, huic scripto sigillum nostrum apposuimus; actum in sinodo nostra in ecclesia de Outerardouer coram prelatis et clero nostre diocesis, Non. Maij, anno gracie m°. cc°. xxx°. Quinto. Ego Clemens Episcopus consencio et subscribo. Ego R. abbas subscribo. Ego J. abbas subscribo. Ego P. abbas subscribo. Ego Hugo, abbas de sancto Seruano subscribo. Ego Gilbertus archidiaconus Dumblanensis, subscribo. Ego lucas vicarius ecclesie de Methel subscribo. Ego Martinus Decanus de Menethet subscribo. Ego Henricus subscribo. Ego Mauricius prior Keledeorum de Mothel subscribo. Ego Andreas prior Keledeorum de Abernethyn subscribo.

It is meet that those things which have been terminated by judicial sentence or by agreement should be made lasting by the muniment of an authentic writ, lest, by the dishonesty or craft of any, they might relapse into disputes of renewed contention. Wherefore we will that it should be known to all of you that we, with the assent of the clergy of our diocese, hold as established the sentence of the venerable men, the Lord William, Bishop, Hugh, Dean, and Robert, Treasurer, of the church of Glasgow, which, by the authority of our Lord, Pope Gregory ix., they pronounced upon the decree-arbitral of Lord William, Bishop of St. Andrews, formerly pronounced upon the controversy between A[braham], of good memory, our predecessor, and the abbot and convent of Lundors, in respect to the church of Mothel, by which decree-arbitral we pleaded that the church of Dunblane had been injured. Who [the Bishop, Dean, and Treasurer of Glasgow], taking equity into consideration, pronounced and duly promulgated a just decree-arbitral, and corrected the excess in the estimate of the payment of ten marks by reason of which they judged the said church was injured, condemning the said abbot and monks, on the part of the monastery, to pay annually to us and our successors, as representing the aforesaid church of Dunblane, five silver marks.[1] Which sentence, because it was pronounced to the advantage of our church aforesaid, we accept and hold good ; and we promise in good faith, on the peril of our soul and of the souls of our successors, that in the future we will raise no question as to the aforesaid decree-arbitral ; but, as was undertaken by our predecessor, and as is more fully expressed in the instrument executed upon this matter, and on the authority of our Lord the Pope confirmed by the judges aforenamed, we will observe it for all time without cavil. And that this in times to come may hold good, we have placed our seal to this writ. Done in our synod in the church of Outerardouer, in the presence of the prelates and clergy of our diocese, on the Nones [7th] of May, in the year of grace, mccxxxv.

I, Clement, Bishop, consent and subscribe. I, R., Abbot, subscribe. I, J., Abbot, subscribe. I, P., Abbot, subscribe. I, Hugh, Abbot of St. Serf, subscribe. I, Gilbert, Archdeacon of Dunblane, subscribe. I, Luke, Vicar of the church of Methel, subscribe. I, Martin, Dean of Menethet, subscribe. I, Henry, subscribe. I, Maurice, Prior of the Keledei of Mothel, subscribe. I, Andrew, Prior of the Keledei of Abernethyn, subscribe.

LII

Confirmacio Cleri Dumblanensis de Eglesmagril.

P. de Ka[m]buskinel, dei gracia abbates, G. archidiaconus, et uniuersus clerus Dumblanensis diocesis, Salutem in Domino. Noueritis nos ratam habere concordiam quondam prouisam et factam inter ecclesiam Dumblanensem et monasterium de lundors per arbitrium Domini Willelmi Episcopi Sancti Andree super controuersia mota inter partes de ecclesia de Mothel. Ipsumque arbitrium prout in autentico continetur uerbo ad uerbum, et a domino W. Glasguensi Episcopo et suis collegis, auctoritate Domini pape, est declaratum et confirmatum, et a nostro diocesano Domino C. Episcopo Dumblanensi sponte susceptum et obseruatum, communi assensu et consilio acceptamus et in perpetuum bona fide obseruandum decernimus. Et in huius nostre approbacionis testimonium unacum sigillis predictorum abbatum, nomine cleri tocius, quia sigillum commune non habemus, sigillum patroni nostri Domini R. comitis de Strathern huic scripto apponi procurauimus.

CONFIRMATION by the CLERGY of DUNBLANE, of EGLESMAGRIL.

To all the faithful of Christ to whom these presents shall come, R. of Aberbrothoc, Hugh of St. Serf, J. of Inchaffray, P. of Cambuskinel, by the grace of God Abbots,—G. Archdeacon, and all the clergy of the diocese of Dunblane, health in the Lord. Know ye that we hold as ratified the agreement formerly provided and made, between the church of Dunblane and the monastery of Lundors, by the decree-arbitral of the Lord William, Bishop of St. Andrews, upon the controversy between the parties concerning the church of Mothel. And that decree-arbitral we accept, and decree that it be in good faith observed for ever, as it is contained in the authentic instrument, word for word, and declared and confirmed, on the authority of our Lord the Pope, by W. Bishop of Glasgow and his colleagues, and as it was of his own accord accepted and observed by our diocesan, the Lord C., Bishop of Dunblane. And in testimony of our approval we have procured that the seal of our patron (*patroni nostri*), the Sir R., Earl of Strathern, should be attached to this writ, in the name of the whole clergy, together with the seals of the abbots aforesaid, because we have no common seal.

uniuersitas uestra nos ratam et gratam habere sentenciam auctoritate Domini Pape latam uiris uenerabilibus Domino W. Episcopo, Domino H. decano, et Domino R. Thesaurario Glasguensibus, super perpetua pace ordinata inter ecclesiam nostram cathedralem ex una parte, et monasterium de lundors ex altera, per arbitrium bone memorie W. episcopi sancti Andree super ecclesia de Mothel, sicut, in scripto sentenciam illam continente, uerbo ad uerbum continetur. Approbamus insuper et Ratam habemus amicabilem composicionem de assensu nostro factam inter uenerabilem patrem Dominum C. Episcopum nostrum nomine ecclesie sue de Mothel, ex parte vna, et Dominum J. abbatem et conuentum de lundors nomine monasterij sui, ex altera, super decimis de fedale, Beny, et Cuncrag, sicut in scripto inter partes confecto plenius continetur. Et ut hec perpetue firmitatis robur obtineant, maxime cum ad comodum nostre spectant ecclesie, presenti scripto commune sigillum nostrum vnanimi assensu apposuimus in testimonium. Testibus, Domino C. | Episcopo, Domino fergus filio comitis, magistro luca archidiacono, Malisio persona de Gasc, Gillebaran et Padyn, capellanis.

50.]

CONFIRMATION of EGLESMAGRIL by the CHAPTER of DUNBLANE.

To all the faithful of Christ who shall see or hear this writ the Chapter of Dunblane, health everlasting in the Lord. Let all of you know that we hold as ratified and established the sentence pronounced, on the authority of our Lord the Pope, by the venerable men, Lord W., Bishop, Sir [1] H., Dean, and Sir R., Treasurer, of Glasgow, on the perpetual peace established between our cathedral church of the one part and the monastery of Lundors of the other, by the decree-arbitral of W., Bishop of St. Andrews, of good memory, on the church of Mothel, as is contained, word for word, in the writ containing that sentence. We approve, moreover, and hold established the amicable agreement made, with our consent, between the venerable father, Lord C., our bishop, in the name of his church of Mothel of the one part, and Lord J., the abbot, and the convent of Lundors, in name of the monastery, of the other part, as to the tithes of Fedale, Beny, and Cuncrag, as is more fully contained in the instrument executed between the parties. And that these things may be firmly established for ever, especially since they concern the advantage of our church, we have in testimony, with unanimous assent, placed our common seal to this present writ. Witnesses, Lord C., Bishop ; Sir Fergus, son of the Earl ; Master Luke, Archdeacon ; Malise, Parson of Gasc ; Gillebaran and Padyn, chaplains.

LIV
Composicio super decimis de fedal, Beny et Concragh.

Cvm monasterium de lundors haberet quasdam terras sibi in perpetuam elemosinam collatas in parochia de Mothel, scilicet, fedale, Beny et Cunecrach, et idem monasterium immune sit a prestacione decimarum de noualibus suis et de nutrimentis animalium suorum per priuilegium sibi a sede apostolica indultum, et ecclesia de Mothel ad mensam pertineat Domini Dumblanensis episcopi, ne occasione dicti priuilegij ipsam ecclesiam contingeret enormiter ledi, mediantibus uiris Discretis et juris peritis, inter Dominum Clementem Dumblanensem episcopum de assensu capituli Dumblanensis, nomine ecclesie de Mothel ex una parte, et Dominum Johannem abbatem et Conuentum de Lundors nomine monasterij sui ex altera, ita est amicabiliter compositum, quod iidem abbas et conuentus in perpetuum habebunt omnimodas decimas predictarum terrarum quocunque nomine censeantur, a quibuscunque terre ipse fuerint inhabitate, liberas et quietas ab omni exaccione et consuetudine, et persoluent annuatim eidem ecclesie de Mothel sex marcas sterlingorum ad duos terminos, scilicet, tres marcas ad festum sancti Michaelis, et tres marcas ad pasca. De secularibus autem in dictis terris manentibus habebit dicta ecclesia obuenciones debitas, tam pro uiuis quam pro defunctis. Et in huius rei testimonium perpetuum huic scripto inter partes confecto signa partium sunt apposita ; signum, scilicet, partis unius scripto partis alterius. Testibus, Domino H. abbate de insula missarum. Dompno W. Decano Dumblanensi, Domino

AGREEMENT concerning the TITHES of FEDALE, BENY, and CONCRAG.

INASMUCH as the monastery of Lundors had certain lands in the parish of Mothel, namely, Fedale, Beny, and Concrag, conferred on them in perpetual alms, and inasmuch as the same monastery is free from the payment of tithes from their fallow-lands and the young of their flocks, by reason of a privilege granted to them by the Apostolic See, and inasmuch as the church of Mothel pertains to the table (*ad mensam*) of the Lord Bishop of Dunblane, to the end that serious injury might not be inflicted on that church by reason of the said privilege, on the intervention of discreet men, learned in the law, an amicable agreement was made between Lord Clement, Bishop of Dunblane, acting with the assent of the chapter of Dunblane, on behalf of the church of Mothel, of the one part, and the Lord John, the abbot, and convent of Lundors on behalf of their monastery, of the other part, to the effect that the same abbot and convent shall always have all manner of tithes from the lands aforesaid, under whatsoever denomination they are reckoned, by whomsoever those lands shall be inhabited, free and exempt from all exaction and custom, and they shall pay yearly to the same church of Mothel six marks sterling at the two terms, namely, three marks at the feast of St. Michael, and three marks at Easter. But from the seculars residing on the same lands the said church shall have the due obventions as well for the living as the dead. And in perpetual testimony of this thing, to this writ, executed between the parties, the seals of the parties are affixed, namely the seal of the one party to the writ of the other party. Witnesses Lord H., Abbot of Inchaffray; Sir W., Dean of Dunblane; Sir Fergus, son of the Earl; Master Luke, Archdeacon; Sir Adam, Prior of Aberbrothoc; Sir Andrew, Prior of Abernethyn; Master Christian; Gillebaran, Chaplain; Padin, Presbyter of Mothel. Done in the Synod of Gask crist, vij. of the Ides [7th] of April in the year of grace MCCXXXIX.

LV

De terra resignata quam Willelmus de Brechin perambulavit de terra ecclesie de Rathmuriel.

OMNIBVS christi fidelibus hoc scriptum visuris uel audituris Willelmus de Brechyn, salutem: Sciatis me pro amore dei, et anime mee salute dedisse et quietam clamasse deo et

occasione illius perambulacionis. Et ut terra illa remaneat quieta et libera predicte ecclesie de Rathmuriel per easdem diuisas quas habuit ante dictam perambulacionem, Scilicet, per altam viam que vadit de vado de vry uersus Lascelyn. Et in huius rei testimonium huic scripto sigillum meum apposui. Testibus, Dominis Johanne de Haya, Gilberto de Haya, Willelmo de Haya de Balcolmi, Willelmo de Haya fratre Domini Gilberti de Haya, Hugone de Beumys, Henrico de Dundemor, Johanne Wischard, Michaele de Munchur, Dauid de Lochore, militibus meis, et aliis. Apud Lundors, In crastino Decollacionis Sancti Johannis Baptiste, anno gracie M°. cc° xl°. quinto.

(Abstract)

'Of Land resigned, which William of Brechin perambulated, belonging to the Land of the Church of Rathmuriel.'

William of Brechin declares that 'for the love of God and the weal of my soul' he had given and quitclaimed 'to God and the monastery of Lundors that land which was perambulated from the church land of Rathmuriel to the other Rathmuriel which is my land,' and that he had resigned for ever for himself and his heirs all right and claim which could arise by reason of that perambulation. The land was to be free and exempt, by the marches which it had before the perambulation, namely, by the highway which goes from the ford of Ury towards Lescelyn. Seal. Witnesses. At Lundors, on the morrow of the Decollation of St. John Baptist [Aug. 29], mccxlv.

LVI

De terra de Ederlarg.

Vniversis ad quos presens scriptum peruenerit Simon de Garentuly, salutem eternam in domino. Sciatis me dedisse, concessisse, et hac presenti carta mea confirmasse Deo et ecclesie Sancte marie et Sancti Andree de lundors, et monachis ibidem deo seruientibus et seruituris totam terram meam

omnes homines. Testibus, Domino Henrico de Boyuille, Dauid de Andrea, Malcolmo fratre constabularij, Normanno filio Normanni, Jacobo de Vuen, Simone de Boyuille, Simone de tendal, ferhare iudice, Thoma filio eius, Ricardo fratre meo, Ricardo clerico meo, et multis aliis.

(Abstract).

'Of the LAND of EDERLARG.'

SIMON of Garentuly declares that he gives to God and the monks of Lundors 'my land of Ederlarg by the same marches and with the same easements with which I held it.' To be held in frankalmoign of him and his heirs, without any service or secular exaction. Warrandice against all men. Witnesses

LVII

De tholachkere et de secundis decimis, S. de Garentuly.

OMNIBVS christi fidelibus presentes litteras uisuris uel audituris, Simon de Garentuly, miles, eternam in domino salutem, Nouerit uniuersitas uestra quod cum esset causa mota inter uiros religiosos abbatem et conuentum de lundors, ex vna parte, et me ex altera, super secundis decimis terre mee de Creymund et de edengerroke quam habui ex collacione nobilis uiri Comitis Johannis, coram uiris uenerabilibus magistro Abel, archidiacono Sancti Andree, et . . . priore de May, in dicta causa auctoritate apostolica judicibus delegatis et eorundem subdelegatis diucius uentilata : tandem, amicis mediantibus, ut omnis discordie et dissensionis mote et mouende usque in diem confeccionis presencium litterarum materia omnino et Radicitus in perpetuum tolleretur, quam ego uel heredes mei habebamus uel aliquo modo habere poteramus ex quacunque causa contra predictos abbatem et conuentum, dedi et concessi et presenti scripto confirmaui eisdem et monasterio suo de Lundors, pro dictis secundis decimis, octo solidos Sterlingorum

Renuncians omni excepçioni iuris et facti michi competenti uel competiture qua posset predicta solucio predictorum solidorum aliquatenus impediri uel differri. Insuper pro bono pacis, pro remedio, et pro salute anime mee et antecessorum meorum et heredum meorum, renunciaui pro me et heredibus meis in perpetuum omni iuri et clamio quod habebam uel habere poteram, uel habere credebam in terra dictorum abbatis et conuentus et monasterij de lundors, que uocatur tolaukery, et pertinenciis suis ; et predictam terram cum suis pertinenciis dictis abbati et conuentui in perpetuum pro me et heredibus meis quietam clamaui : Renuncians in hac parte omni accioni et iuris beneficio que mihi uel heredibus meis super premissis omnibus et singulis possent uel poterint prodesse, et predictis abbati et conuentui obesse. Et ad hec omnia . et singula sine fraude, cauillacione, et malo ingenio firmiter et fideliter in perpetuum observanda, pro me et heredibus meis, affidavi. Et ad maiorem securitatem et robur perpetue firmitatis presentibus litteris sigillum meum apposui. Testibus, Thoma de Perth et Thoma de Benuer monachis de Lundors, Ricardo tunc vicario de fintreth, Michaele Prath, Alano le larderer, laicis, et multis aliis. Actum apud fintreth, anno gracie M° cc° l° secundo, die Jouis proxima post festum sancti Johannis Baptiste.

(Abstract)

'SIꝹON of GARENTULY concerning THOLACHKERE, and concerning SECOND TITHES.'

SIꝹON of Garentuly, knight, recounts that litigation had been carried on between the abbot and convent of Lundors, of the one part, and himself, of the other part, as to the second tithes of his land of Creymund and of Edengerroke (which land he had of the collation of Earl John) before the judges delegate in the said cause, by the authority of the Apostolic See, namely Master Abel, Archdeacon of St. Andrews and . . . Prior of May. The cause was long discussed by the subdelegates of the judges delegate. At length, on the intervention of friends, with a view to the removal of all cause of dispute, he gives and confirms to

of his soul and of the souls of his ancestors and his heirs, he renounces
for himself and his heirs for ever 'all right and claim which I had, or
could have, or was believed to have in the land of the aforesaid abbot
and convent and monastery of Lundors, which is called Tolaukery, and
its pertinents,' and quitclaims the said land.   He further renounces
his right to action at law in this respect.   And he gives his pledge that
these things, all and singular, shall be observed firmly and faithfully
for ever, without fraud, cavil, or evil design.   Seal.   Witnesses.   Done
at Fintreth, on the second Thursday next after the feast of St. John
Baptist,[1] ᴅ ᴄᴄʟ.

LVIII

De Capella de Cremond.

Nᴏᴛᴠᴍ sit omnibus hoc scriptum uisuris uel audituris quod
dompnus Johannes abbas et conuentus de lundors concesserunt domino Simoni de Garentuly ut faciat sibi capellam
intra septa curie sue, ubi ipse et priuata familia sua tantum
audiant diuinum officium.   Ita tamen quod in diebus precipue
festiuitatis eant ad matricem ecclesiam, et homines de eo
tenentes more debito ueniant ad matricem ecclesiam. | Idem
autem Simon et heredes sui inuenient de suo omnia necessaria
predicte capelle, et facient fidelitatem ecclesie de Inuerhuri,
ipsi et capellani ministrantes in capella; Quod si aliqua
obuencio ibi facta fuerit integre persoluetur eidem ecclesie et
quod occasione illius nichil amittet ecclesia.   Et si aliter
fecerint tamdiu suspendetur capella donec plene satisfecerint.
In recognicionem autem huius concessionis dabunt annuatim
idem Simon et heredes sui matrici ecclesie duas libras cere ad
festum assumpcionis beate Marie.   In huius rei testimonium
hoc scriptum est conscriptum.

52.] (margin)

Oғ the Cʜᴀᴘᴇʟ of Cʀᴇᴍᴏɴᴅ.

Bᴇ it known to all who shall see or hear this writ that Lord John,
the abbot, and the convent of Lundors have granted to Sir Simon of
Garentuly to make for himself a chapel within the enclosure of his

Yet so that on the principal festivals they and the tenants holding of him should come, in the accustomed manner, to the mother-church. The same Simon and his heirs shall at their own cost find all things necessary for the aforesaid chapel, and shall do fealty to the church of Inverhuri, they themselves and the chaplains ministering in the chapel. If there be any obvention there made, it shall be paid in full to the same church, so that by reason of it [the chapel] the church may lose nothing. And if they shall act otherwise the chapel shall be suspended until full satisfaction shall have been made. And in recognition of this grant the same Simon and his heirs shall give annually to the mother-church two pounds of wax at the feast of the Assumption of St. Mary [Aug. 15]. In testimony of this thing this writ has been drawn up.

LIX

De Capella de Weredors.

OMNIBVS hoc scriptum uisuris uel audituris Bartholomeus flandrensis, salutem ; Sciatis me dedisse et hac carta mea confirmasse deo et ecclesie sancti Drostani de Inchemabani vnum toftum et duas acras terre arabilis iuxta eundem toftum, in Rauengille uilla mea inter magnam uiam et morum uersus Gillandreston, cum communi asiamento eiusdem uille, et cum communi pastura ad sex animalia et vnum equum et quadraginta oues ; Tenendum et habendum eidem ecclesie et rectoribus ipsius de me et heredibus meis ita libere et quiete, sine omni consuetudine et exaccione seculari, sicut aliqua terra ecclesie liberius tenetur et quiecius : feci eciam fidelitatem et per cartam istam obligo me et heredes meos quod predicta ecclesia de Inchemabany sine dampno erit nec aliquid amittet de iure suo occasione capelle mee, quam feci michi et priuate familie mee tantum per licenciam domini abbatis et conuentus de lundors, sicut in eorum carta quam inde habeo continetur. Testibus, Domino G. episcopo, Domino Malcolmo archidiacono Aberdonensi, Normanno constabulario, Simone de Garentuly, Henrico de Boyuilla, Simone filio eius, et multis aliis.

of Ravengille between the great road and the moor towards Gillandreston, with the common easement of the same vill, with common
pasture for six 'animals,' one horse, and forty sheep : to be held of him
and his heirs by the same church and the rectors of it, as freely, etc.

He declares that he has given his faith and bound himself and
his heirs that the church of Inchemabani shall suffer no injury and lose
none of its rights by reason of his chapel, which he had made by leave
of the abbot and convent of Lundors (as contained in the charter in
his possession) for the use of himself and his private family only.
Witnesses

LX

De firma [1]

OMNIBVS ad quos presens scriptum peruenerit Henricus de
Brechyn, filius Comitis Dauid, eternam in domino salutem ·
Sciatis me dedisse, concessisse, et hac presenti carta mea con
firmasse, pro salute anime mee, et Juliane sponse mee, et
Willelmi filij mei, et pro animabus omnium antecessorum et
successorum meorum deo et ecclesie sancte Marie et sancti
Andree de lundors et monachis ibidem deo seruientibus et
seruituris, in liberam et puram et perpetuam elemosinam,
viginti solidos sterlingorum annuatim percipiendos de me et
heredibus meis in perpetuum, ad festum sancti martini, apud
Brechyn.   Volumus autem et concedimus tam ego quam
predicta Juliana uxor mea ut ad obitum nostrum corpora
nostra portentur ad lundors sepelienda, quia ibidem locum
sepulture nobis elegimus, sicut illi qui recepti sumus in pleno
capitulo in fraternitatem domus et participacionem omnium
oracionum et beneficiorum que in ea fient.   Et ut hec donacio
et concessio perpetuam obtineat firmitatem presenti scripto
sigillum meum apposui.   Testibus, Domino G. Brechinensi
episcopo, Domino Henrico de Striuelin fratre meo, Domino
Ricardo filio Thome, Willelmo filio meo, Henrico de Edeneburg, Willelmo, Waltero, seruientibus meis.

(*Abstract*)
[*Title only partially legible.*]

shillings sterling, to be received yearly from him and his heirs for ever, on the feast of St. Martin, at Brechin. He and his aforesaid wife, Juliana, desire and grant that on their decease their bodies should be carried to Lundors there to be buried, 'because there we have chosen a place of sepulture, as being persons received, in full chapter, into the brotherhood of the house and into participation of all the prayers and benefits which are to be had therein.' In confirmation he seals the writ with his seal. 'Witnesses; the Lord G., Bishop of Brechin; Sir Henry of Stirling, my brother; Sir Richard, son of Thomas; William, my son; Henry of Edeneburg; William and Walter, my servants.'

LXI

Confirmacio domini Willelmi de Brechyn [1] . .

OMNIBVS christi fidelibus presens scriptum visuris uel audituris Willelmus de Brechyn, eternam salutem in domino. Nouerit vniuersitas vestra me concessisse et hac presenti carta mea confirmasse deo et ecclesie sancte marie et sancti Andree de Lundors et monachis ibidem deo seruientibus et seruituris illum annuum redditum xx solidorum quem inclite recordacionis Henricus pater meus pro salute anime sue et Juliane sponse sue, et pro salute anime mee, et successorum suorum eisdem pie contulit | et concessit in liberam, puram, et perpetuam elemosinam, sicut carta ipsius super hoc confecta plenius testatur. Assignaui eciam eis predictum annuum redditum xx solidorum percipiendum perpetuo de firma mea et heredum meorum de Lundors per manus Balliui mei et heredum meorum quicunque ibidem pro tempore fuerit, ad duos terminos, videlicet Decem solidos ad festum penthecostes, et Decem solidos ad festum sancti martini in hyeme. Et ad maiorem huius rei securitatem concessi eisdem quod si in solucione predictorum denariorum prenominatis terminis aliquando cessatum fuerit, liceat eisdem, elapsa quindena post terminum, non petita ab aliquo licencia, sine aliqua calumpnia, cauillacione, uel contradiccione capere namos meos et heredum meorum in predicta

[*fo*

Testibus, Dominis Petro de Haya, Roberto de Rossith, et Hugone de Beumys, militibus, Magistro Hugone de Striuelyn rectore ecclesie de forgrund, Gilberto clerico Rectore ecclesie de Adel, Johanne de Kinkel capellano, Laurencio clerico Rectore ecclesie de Kinetles, Roberto filio Mabilie, tunc seruiente meo de Lundors, et multis aliis.

(*Abstract*)

'SIR WILLIAꝰ of BRECHIN'S CONFIRꝰATION.   '

WILLIAꝰ of Brechin confirms to Lundors the annual payment of twenty shillings, which Henry, his father, had granted for the weal of his soul and of the soul of Juliana, his spouse, ' and for the weal of my soul' and of his successors, as the charter made by him more fully declares. He assigns the payment to be made from his rents (*firma*) of Lundors by the hands of the bailiff, ten shillings at Whitsunday and ten shillings at Martinmas. ' And for the greater security of this thing I have granted to the same, the monks of Lundors, that if at any time the payment of the money aforesaid at the forenamed terms should cease, it shall be lawful for them after the lapse of fifteen days from the term, without asking leave of any and without charge, cavil, or dispute, to take poinds from me and my heirs in the aforesaid land of Lundors, and to detain them and not give them up to any on pledge or security, until full payment has been made to them for the portion due at the past term.' Seal. Witnesses . . .

LXII

De Capella domini Willelmi de Brechyn de Lundors.

OMNIBVS christi fidelibus presens scriptum visuris uel audituris Willelmus de Brechyn, eternam in Domino Salutem : Nouerit vniuersitas uestra nos obligasse nos et heredes nostros ad in- ueniendum omnia necessaria cuidam capellano nostro qui in capella castri nostri de lundors celebrabit divina, quando nos uel heredes nostri uoluerimus quod ibidem diuina celebrentur. Dictus autem capellanus canonicam obedienciam faciet matrici ecclesie de Ebedyn, et omnes oblaciones ad dictam capellam uenientes eidem matrici ecclesie fideliter persoluet. Nos autem

dictam capellam nullum predicte ecclesie matrici in aliquo stat preiudicium. In recognicione autem iuris matricis ecclesie nos et heredes nostri dabimus annuatim prefate ecclesie de Ebedyn vnam libram thuris infra septimanam penthecostes. In cuius rei testimonium sigillum nostrum presentibus litteris apponi fecimus. Datum apud Inchemurthach, dominica qua cantatur oculi mei, in quadragesima anno gracie m° cc° xl° octauo.

(Abstract)

'OF SIR WILLIAꝰ of BRECHIN'S CHAPEL at LUNDORS.'

WILLIAꝰ of Brechin takes the obligation, for himself and his heirs, to find all things necessary for the chaplain who will celebrate divine service in the chapel of his castle at Lundors, whenever he or his heirs may desire divine service to be celebrated there. But the said chaplain shall make canonical obedience to the mother-church of Ebedyn, and will faithfully pay to the mother-church all oblations coming to the chapel. William and his heirs will in all things repair, whenever there is need, the said chapel, which he had built at the will of David, Bishop of St. Andrews, and with the assent of the abbot and convent of Lundors, so that the chapel should in no way be prejudicial to the mother-church. In recognition of the rights of the mother-church he and his heirs will annually give to the said church of Ebedyn one pound of incense within the week of Whitsunday. Seal. 'Given at Inchemurthach on the Sunday in Lent on which is sung *Oculi mei*,[1] in the year of grace ꟾccxlviii.'

LXIII

Ordinacio Episcopi Sancti Andree super capella de Dundemor.

OMNIBVS hoc scriptum uisuris uel audituris Dauid dei gracia episcopus Sancti Andree, eternam in domino salutem. Noueritis quod cum mota esset controuersia inter abbatem et conuentum de lundors ex una parte, et Dominum Henricum de Dundemor militem, ex altera, super seruicio capelle de Dundemor; Tandem partibus coram nobis constitutis in sinodo nostra celebrata

de Dundemor et heredibus suis viginti et quinque solidos ad sustentandum][1] vnum capellanum ministrantem in capella de Dundemor percipiendos per manum capellani qui pro tempore ministrabit in matrici ecclesia de Ebedyn, ad duos terminos anni, scilicet, duodecim solidos et sex denarios ad festum Sancti Martini in hyeme, et duodecim solidos et sex denarios *54.]* ad Penthe | costen, saluo iure matricis ecclesie de Ebedyn in omnibus; Ita, uidelicet, quod omnes parochiani de Dundemor, excepta propria familia domus domini H. de Dundemor et heredum suorum, uenient ter in anno ad matricem ecclesiam de Ebedyn, scilicet, die Natalis Domini, et die Pasce, et die Sancti Andree apostoli, et percipient in matrice ecclesia omnia sacramenta sua. Dictus uero H. et heredes sui honeste facient deseruiri dicte capelle, et capellano, qui in eadem celebrabit diuina, in omnibus necessaria inuenient. Nec unquam de cetero aliquid exigent a dictis abbate et conuentu nisi predictos xx et v solidos. Capellani uero qui in dicta capella ministrabunt iuramentum prestabunt quod fideles erunt matrici ecclesie de Ebedyn, et omnes oblaciones que in dicta capella fient eidem ecclesie de Ebedyn fideliter persoluent. Dictus uero abbas ornatum per visum proborum hominum sufficientem tam in libris quam in uestimentis et calice dicte capelle semel inuenient, et dictus H. et heredes sui dictum ornatum sumptibus suis in per- petuum sustentabunt. Et ad hec fideliter obseruanda, dictus abbas pro se et conuentu, et dictus Henricus pro se et heredibus suis in manu magistri Andree de Aberdon, tunc officialis Sancti Andree, affidauerunt. Nos, uero, ad maioris roboris firmitatem, predictam ordinationem in modum cirographi confectam, Cuius ordinacionis una pars penes abbatem et conuentum, alia penes Henricum et heredes suos residet, sigilli nostri munimine, vna cum sigillorum Domini A. archidiaconi Sancti Andree, et magistri A. de Aberden, Officialis nostri, et parcium apposicione communimus.

(*Abstract*)

'ORDINANCE of the BISHOP of ST. ANDREWS on the CHAPEL of DUNDEMOR.'

vent of Lundors, of the one part, and Sir Henry of Dundemor, of the other, concerning the service of the chapel of Dundemor.   At length the parties appeared before the bishop in his synod at Perth on the fourth of the Nones of June [June 2] in the year of grace MCCXLVIII., and by consent submitted themselves to his determination of the dispute, which determination took the form of the following ordinance : The abbot and convent will every year give five and twenty shillings to Sir Henry and his heirs for the maintenance of a chaplain ministering in the chapel of Dundemor.   This money was to be paid through the hand of the chaplain, for the time being, of the mother-church of Ebedyn, at the two terms of the year : twelve shillings and six pence at the feast of St. Martin in winter, and twelve shillings and six pence at Whitsunday, saving the rights of the mother-church of Ebedyn in all things.   Thus, all the parishioners of Dundemor, except the family of the house of Sir Henry and his heirs, were to go to the mother-church of Ebedyn three times a year, namely, on Christmas Day, Easter Day, and the feast of St. Andrew the Apostle, and in the mother-church they were to receive all their sacraments.   The said Henry and his heirs were to cause the chapel to be decently (*honeste*) served, and were to find all things necessary for the chaplain who would celebrate service there.   For the future Henry and his heirs were not to demand anything from the abbot and convent except the five and twenty shillings aforesaid.   The chaplains ministering in the chapel were to take an oath that they would be faithful to the mother-church of Ebedyn, and would faithfully pay to the mother-church all the oblations made in the chapel.   The abbot and convent were in the first instance to provide for the chapel sufficient furnishing (*ornatus*), 'at the sight of good men,' both in books, vestments, and chalice, and Henry and his heirs were ever after at their own expense to maintain the furnishing.   That they would faithfully observe this ordinance, the abbot, for himself and his convent, and Henry, for himself and his heirs, pledged themselves ' in the hand of Master Andrew of Aberdeen, then Official of St. Andrews.' The ordinance of the Bishop of St. Andrews was written in the form of an indenture (*in modum cirographi*), one part of which was to be kept by Henry and his heirs, and the other part by the abbot and convent.   It was sealed with the seals of the bishop, of A., Archdeacon of St. Andrews, and of Master A. of Aberdeen, the Official of St. Andrews, and with the seals of the parties.

LXIV

Ornamenta capelle de Dundemor.

ympnarium, legenda, et antiphonarium, et gradale, et totum
plenarium seruicium tocius anni, et uestimentum plenarium ad
missam celebrandam, coram Magistro Adam de Malkarueston,
Domino Willelmo de Balcolmy, Mauricio de Abernythyn
senescaldo, Ricardo Palmero de Kingore, et Thoma capellano
de Dunbulg, Johanne capellano de Cullessy, Thoma capellano
de Ebedyn, et multis aliis.   In cuius rei testimonium magister
Adam de Malkarueston, ad instanciam predicti Domini
Johannis, huic scripto sigillum suum apposuit.

(Abstract)

MEᴊORANDUᴊ : On Sunday next after the feast of St. John before
the Latin Gate [May 6], ᴊCCLIII., at Ebedyn, John de Dundemor,
knight, received a silver chalice, and a Missal in which were contained
Psalter, Hymnary, Legenda, Antiphonary, and Gradual, and the whole
full service for the entire year, also a complete vestment for celebrating
mass; in the presence of . . . In testimony of which Master Adam of
Malkarueston, at the instance of Sir John, put his seal to this writ.

LXV

De tofto in Munorgrund.

OMNIBVS ad quos presens scriptum peruenerit Magnus de
Morgrund, salutem : Noueritis me dedisse et hac presenti carta
mea confirmasse monasterio de Lundors et monachis ibidem
deo seruientibus et seruituris unum toftum et unam acram
terre que iacet proxima terre domini Henrici de Striuelyn in
Monorgrund : Tenendum sibi de me et heredibus meis, in
liberam et puram et perpetuam elemosinam, sine omni seruicio
et consuetudine et exaccione seculari.   Vnde ego et heredes
mei ipsam terram in perpetuum adquietabimus et waranti-
zabimus contra omnes homines.   Testibus, domino Henrico de
Striuelyn, Nicholao de Inverpefrin, Michaele de Muncur,
Roberto de Fodinrey, Gilberto et Randolfo de Polgauelyn,
Adam homine meo, et multis aliis.

(Abstract)

Stirling, in Monorgrund. To be held of Magnus and his heirs in free, pure, and perpetual alms, without any service, custom, and secular exaction. Warrandice against all men. Witnesses

LXVI
De tofto theodorici quondam tinctoris de Perth.

OMNIBVS hoc scriptum uisuris uel audituris Johannes de Haya et uxor eius Juliana, Salutem. Sciatis nos, pro animabus nostris et liberorum nostrorum et pro animabus antecessorum et successorum nostrorum, Dedisse et concessisse et hac presenti carta nostra confirmasse deo et ecclesie Sancte Marie et Sancti Andree de Lundors et monachis ibidem deo seruientibus, in puram et perpetuam | elemosinam omne ius quod habemus uel   [ƒ habere poterimus in tofto illo quem Alanus de Lasceles uendidit Teoderico tinctori de Perth : Tenendum sibi de nobis et heredibus nostris in perpetuum. Quare uolumus ut predicti monachi habeant et possideant predictum ᵃ ius prefati tofti ita •ᴹˢ. libere, quiete, plenarie, et honorifice sicut aliqua abbacia in toto regno Scocie aliquod ius in aliquo tofto liberius, quiecius, plenius, et honorificencius tenet aut possidet. Et ut donacio nostra rata et illibata permaneat sigillorum nostrorum munimine corroborauimus. Hiis testibus, Domino Dauid de Haya, Roberto fratre eius, Simone de Camera, Serlo talliatore, Henrico filio Galfridi, Arnaldo tinctore, Roberto et Patricio ᴵde insula, et multis aliis.

(Abstract)
'OF the toft of THEODORIC, late dyer of PERTH.'

JOHN DE HAYA and his wife, Juliana, grant to Lundors, for the souls of themselves, their children, their ancestors and successors, in free and perpetual alms, all right which they had in the toft which Alan de Lasceles sold to Theodoric, the dyer of Perth ; to be held as freely, etc. Their seals attached. Witnesses

LXVII

presenti carta mea confirmasse, deo et ecclesie Sancte Marie et
Sancti Andree de Lundors et monachis ibidem deo seruientibus
et seruituris, celarium meum in Perth, quod est sub domo que
quondam fuit Johannis Norreys : Tenendum et habendum sibi
post mortem meam, in liberam et perpetuam elemosinam, saluo
seruicio Domini Regis.   Ego autem Ricardus eisdem monachis
annuatim sex denarios de eodem celario ad festum Sancti
Johannis Baptiste in uita mea persoluam, et de dicto celario
predictis monachis plenam feci saisinam.   Et ad maiorem
securitatem huic scripto sigillum commune de Perth vnacum
sigillo meo feci apponi.   Testibus, Henrico filio Galfridi,
Johanne de la batayle, Osberto Redberd, Johanne filio leue,
Michaele filio serlonis, Johanne Cokyn, Waltero filio Roberti
de Perth, et Roberto fratre eius, et multis aliis.

(Abstract)

' OF a CELLAR in PERTH.'

RICHARD DE LEYCESTRE grants to Lundors his cellar in Perth which was
under the house of the late John Norreys, to be held after the death of
Richard in free and perpetual alms, saving the service of the king.
During his life Richard will pay yearly to the monks of Lundors six
pence out of the said cellar at the feast of St. John the Baptist [June
24] and 'to the aforesaid monks I have made full sasine of the said
cellar.   And for greater security I have caused the common seal of
Perth to be put to this writ, together with my seal.'   Witnesses

LXVIII

[De Terra in Forgrund.] [1]

OMNIBVS hoc scriptum uisuris uel audituris Rogerus de
Berkeley, salutem in domino.   Sciatis me dedisse, concessisse,
et hac presenti carta mea confirmasse, deo et monasterio
Sancte Marie et Sancti Andree de Lundors et monachis ibidem
deo seruientibus et seruituris pro salute anime mee, et Mar-
garete uxoris mee, et animarum omnium antecessorum et
successorum meorum, vnam bouatam terre in manerio meo de

pinquiores illis uersus aquilonem : Tenendam sibi de me et heredibus meis in puram et perpetuam elemosinam, liberam et
quietam ab omni seruicio et omni consuetudine et omni exaccione
seculari. Vnde ego et heredes mei predictam terram adquietabimus et warentizabimus contra omnes homines. Testibus.
Domino Henrico de Striuelyn, Domino Reginaldo de Warenne,
Domino Adam Oliphard, Domino Alexandro de Striuelin,
Archebaldo fratre eius, Radulfo senescaldo meo, Postoyle,
maro meo, Alwino seruiente meo, et multis aliis.

(Abstract)
[' OF LAND in FORGRUND.']

ROGER DE BERKELEY grants to Lundors, for the weal of his soul and
of the soul of Margaret, his wife, and the souls of his ancestors and
successors, one oxgate of land in his manor of Forgrund, namely the
whole of the land which he had at that part of his land which was
formerly in dispute between Forgrund and Eglesmagrille, 'for nine
acres,' and four acres which lie next them towards the north. To
be held of him and his heirs in frankalmoign. He grants warrandice
against all men. Witnesses

LXIX

De dimidia petra cere firmitatis Rogeri de Berkeley.

OMNIBVS hoc scriptum visuris uel audituris Rogerus de
Berkeley, salutem in domino. Noueritis me diuine pietatis
intuitu dedisse, concessisse et hac presenti carta mea confirmasse
deo et abbacie de Lundors vnam dimidiam petram cere in perpetuum annuatim percipiendam de firma terre quam Robertus
Herneys de me tenuit in forgrund : et predictam ceram
recipient annuatim de me et heredibus meis ad assumpcionem
beate Marie, in liberam puram et perpetuam elemosinam.
Hiis testibus, Domino Patricio vicario de forgrund, Hugone,
Doven|aldo, Waltero filiis meis, Radulpho senescaldo, Poys-
toyl maro meo, Alewin seruiente meo, et multis aliis.

[<i>fo</i>

in Forgrund, to be delivered as free, pure, and perpetual alms at the Assumption of Blessed Mary [Aug. 15]. Witnesses

LXX

De Warenna.

Omnibvs christi fidelibus ad quos presens scriptum peruenerit, Reginaldus de Warenna, Salutem in domino. Nouerit vniuersitas vestra me quietum clamasse pro me et heredibus meis omne ius quod habui uel habere potui in uilla de Eglesmagril, deo et ecclesie sancte marie et sancti andree de lundors et monachis ibidem deo seruientibus et seruituris, pro dimidia marca argenti quam dominus Abraham episcopus Dumblanensis et eius successores michi et heredibus meis ad duos terminos soluent annuatim de camera sua, medietatem, scilicet, ad penthecosten, et medietatem ad festum sancti martini. Ego, eciam, pro me et heredibus meis firmiter promisi, et me et heredes meos presenti carta obligaui quod Domino abbati et conuentui de Lundors nullam de predicta terra inferam molestiam aliquando, licet predictum Episcopum uel successores eius in solucione predicte dimidie marce cessare contingeret. Hiis testibus, Domino W. episcopo Sancti Andree, Laurencio eius archidiacono, Gilberto archidiacono Dumblanensi, Willelmo decano de Perth, Edwardo capellano Episcopi Sancti Andree, magistris Michaele et Ricardo eiusdem episcopi clericis, Willelmo de Golin, Adam fratre Reginaldi de Warenna, Henrico de Wincestre, cum multis aliis.

(Abstract)

'De Warrenne.'

Reginald de Warrenne quitclaims to Lundors all right which he had in the vill of Eglesmagril, in return for a half mark of silver, which Abraham, Bishop of Dunblane, and his successors should pay to him and his heirs from their treasury (camera), half at Whitsunday and half

LXXI

Warenna de tribus acris iuxta Eglesmagrill.

OMNIBVS ad quos presens scriptum peruenerit, R. de Warrene, salutem in domino. Nouerit vniuersitas vestra, Adam nepotem meum de uoluntate et consilio omnium parentum et amicorum suorum, Dedisse et concessisse deo et ecclesie sancte marie et sancti andree de Lundors, et monachis eiusdem loci, tres acras terre arabilis mensuratas, proximas terre illi quam dedi eisdem monachis versus aquilonem : Tenendas sibi in per-petuum, in liberam et puram elemosinam, de ipso A. et heredi-bus suis libere et quiete ab omnibus seruiciis et consuetudini bus, et exaccionibus secularibus. Et quoniam ipse A. sigillum non habuit, ad peticionem suam et suorum predictas tres acras terre predictis monachis sicut dominus principalis con firmaui ; Ita quod ego et heredes mei predictam terram eis contra Dominum Regem, et contra omnes homines in omnibus auxiliis et seruiciis adquietabimus et warentizabimus per illas diuisas que facte sunt coram me et aliis probis hominibus, scilicet, Hugone Sax, Patricio persona de Eglesmagril, Adam et Thoma fratre eius de Pethkathilin, Dauid fratre predicti ade nepotis mei, Johanne nepote ipsius, et Roberto Herneys de forgrund, et pluribus aliis probis hominibus, scilicet, sicut torrens aque currit inter terram meam et ipsorum mona-chorum. Et in huius donacionis et confirmacionis testimonium presenti carte sigillum meum apposui. Testibus predictis probis hominibus, et aliis multis.

Ista carta duplata est.

(Abstract)

' WARENNE, of three acres near EGLESMAGRIL.'

R. DE WARENNE makes known that his nephew Adam, with the consent and advice of all his relations and friends, had given to Lundors three

will answer for all the aids and services due from the said land according
to the marches which were assigned in the presence of him and other
good men, and grants warrandice 'against the king and all men.'   The
names of the 'good men' in the presence of whom the marches were
fixed are given.   He affixes his seal.   Witnesses, the 'good men' already
named, 'and many others.'

This charter is doubled.

LXXII

De Warenna.

VNIVERSIS Sancte matris ecclesie filiis et fidelibus, ad quos
presens scriptum peruenerit, Reginaldus de Warenna, Salu
tem : Nouerit vniuersitas vestra me dedisse, concessisse,
et hac presenti carta mea confirmasse deo et ecclesie
sancte marie et sancti andree de Lundors et monachis
ibidem deo seruientibus, in liberam et puram et perpetuam
elemosinam, pro salute anime patris mei et matris mee, et pro
salute anime mee et uxoris mee, et omnium antecessorum et
successorum meorum, totam terram illam que mea fuit que
iacet inter duos riuulos, scilicet, inter illum riuulum qui
currit inter Eglesmagril et Dunbernyn uersus occidentalem
plagam ex una parte et inter alium riuulum qui currit
inter Eglesmagril et petcathelin uersus orientalem plagam
ex alia parte.   Quare uolo et concedo ut predicti monachi totam terram predictam ita libere et quiete, plenarie
et honorifice, sine omni seruicio et auxilio et consue-
57.]   tudine, et exaccione seculari, iure | perpetuo habeant et possi-
deant sicut aliqua abbacia uel aliqua domus religionis in toto
regno Scocie aliquam terram uel aliquam elemosinam liberius,
quiecius, plenius, et honorificencius habet et possidet.   Hanc
autem terram prefato monasterio de lundors et monachis
ibidem deo seruientibus ita libere et quiete in perpetuum
possidendam dedi et concessi, et hac carta mea confirmaui, ut

(*Abstract*)

' DE WARENNE.'

REGINALD DE WARENNE gives to Lundores for the weal of the souls of his father and mother, himself and his wife, his ancestors and successors, in frankalmoign, all his land which lay between the two burns, namely, between the burn which runs between Eglesmagril and Dunbernyn towards the west, on the one side, and the burn which runs between Eglesmagril and Petcathelin towards the east, on the other side. It was to be held as freely, etc., as any abbey or house of religion in the kingdom of Scotland had or possessed any land or any alms, etc.   None of his heirs or successors were to presume to require anything from the monks except their prayers. Witnesses

LXXIII

Conan de Bosco.

OMNIBVS hoc scriptum uisuris uel audituris Conanus filius henrici quondam Comitis de Athoyle, Salutem. Sciatis me dedisse, concessisse, et hac presenti carta mea confirmasse deo et abbacie de Lundors et Domino Johanni tunc abbati, et monachis ipsius abbacie deo seruientibus et seruituris, pro salute anime mee et uxoris mee, et puerorum meorum, et omnium antecessorum et successorum meorum, lignum siccum quod dicitur mortuum boscum ad ardendum quantum uoluerint, et ligna que dicuntur Wrawes de bule et de auhne, quantum opus habuerint: Et centum tractus uirgarum de corilo ad trabas suas faciendas, et centum longas uirgas ad circulos faciendos ; Capiendas annuatim de Bosco meo Tulyhen, vbi melius et propius eis fuerit, et habenda sibi et successoribus suis de me et heredibus meis in perpetuum, et unum messuagium in terra mea ubi manere possint homines illorum qui predicta ligna secabunt, et ad aquam trahent, cum pastura ad v. uaccas et ad unum equum, in puram liberam et perpetuam elemosinam, scilicet, vbicunque uacce mee pascunt, sine omni exaccione seruicio et demanda

(Abstract)

' Conan, of wood.'

Conan, son of Henry, late Earl of Atholl, grants to Lundors and to Lord John, then abbot, and the monks, for the weal of the souls of himself, his wife, his children, his ancestors and successors, dry timber (*lignum siccum*), which is called dead wood (*mortuum boscum*), for fuel, as much as they need, and the wood which is called ' wrawes of bule and of auhne,' also one hundred loads (*tractus*) of hazel rods for making their sleds (*trahas*), and one hundred long rods for making hoops (? *circulos*), to be taken yearly from his wood of Tulyhen, where it shall be best and nearest to them, and also one house (*messuagium*) on his land where the men of the monks may stay who will cut the aforesaid wood and draw it to the water, with pasture for five cows and one horse, in pure and perpetual alms, wherever his cows were pastured, free of all service, etc. He and his heirs grant warrandice.   Witnesses

LXXIV

Kinespinedyn de terra in Perth.

Omnibvs hoc scriptum uisuris uel audituris Malcolmus de Kinspinithin et Margeria uxor eius, Salutem in domino. Noueritis nos de assensu et uoluntate Willelmi filij nostri primogeniti dedisse, concessisse, et hac presenti carta nostra confirmasse Deo et ecclesie sancte marie et sancti andree de Lundors et monachis ibidem Deo Seruientibus, terciam partem tofti illius in Perth, quod quondam fuit Willelmi filij Lambyn, proximum tofto Johannis filii Leue, cum omni iure quod in ea habuimus uel habere potuimus sine aliquo retinemento.   Et ut hec nostra Donacio stabilis sit in perpetuum huic scripto sigilla nostra apposuimus. Testibus, Domino Elya Decano de Perth, Johanne de Dunbernyn capellano, Arnaldo rupe, Alexandro Wlfe, Willelmo filio nostro, Michaele seruiente nostro.

(Abstract)

' Kinespinedyn, of land in Perth.'

have in it, without any reservation. The seals of Malcolm and his wife are affixed. Witnesses

LXXV

Willelmus de Munford de sicco alleci.

Vniversis Sancte matris ecclesie filiis, Willelmus de Muntfort, salutem. Sciant omnes tam posteri quam presentes, me dedisse et concessisse, et hac carta mea confirmasse deo et ecclesie sancte marie et sancti andree de Lundors et monachis ibidem deo seruientibus, in liberam et puram et perpetuam elemosinam, vnum dimidium miliarium de sicco allec singulis annis inperpetuum: quod ego et heredes mei reddemus ipsis monachis in perpetuum singulis annis ad purificacionem sancte marie, ad Karel de mea carucata terre in Karel. Quare uolo et concedo ut predicti monachi predictam elemosinam ita libere et quiete habeant et possideant in perpetuum, sicut aliquam aliam elemosinam in regno Scocie liberius et quiecius habent et possident. | Testibus, Willelmo persona de Aberden, Matheo   [fc clerico fratre eius, Philippo clerico Comitis Dauid, Walkelino filio Stephani, Malcolmo filio Bartolfi, Willelmo Wascelyn, Gilberto filio Gocelin, Willelmo filio Hugonis, Henrico de tindale, Dauid de furthrit.

(Abstract)

' WILLIAⱸ DE MUNFORD, OF DRIED HERRING.'

WILLIAⱸ DE MUNFORD grants to Lundors, in free, pure, and perpetual alms, five hundred-weight of dried herring every year, to be rendered by him and his heirs annually at the feast of the Purification of St. Mary [Feb. 2], at Karel, from his ploughgate of land at Karel. Witnesses . . .

LXXVI

De piscaria de Glasbani et Rugesablyn.

Omnibvs Sancte matris ecclesie filiis et fidelibus presentibus

anime patris mei et matris mee, et pro salute anime mee et pro
salute animarum uxorum mearum Ethne et Eue, et pro salute
animarum fratrum et sororum mearum, antecessorum et successorum meorum, terciam partem piscarie recium meorum
trahencium super sabulum de Glesbanin, et terciam partem
piscarie recium meorum trahencium super rugesablun contra
Colcric, saluis piscariis meis stantibus cum palo et sepi.
Quare, uolo et concedo ut predicti monachi de Lundors habeant
et possideant terciam partem prenominate piscarie recium
meorum trahencium super sabulum de Glesbanyn, et terciam
partem predicte piscarie recium meorum trahencium super
Rugesablun contra Colcric, in perpetuam et puram elemosinam,
ita libere, et quiete, plenarie, et honorifice sicut aliqua abbacia
in toto regno Scocie aliquam elemosinam liberius, quiecius,
plenius, et honorificencius tenet et possidet.   Ita ut michi succedencium nullus aliquid ab eis nisi solas oraciones ad anime
salutem exigere presumat.   Hiis testibus, Gilberto filio meo,
Roberto de Haya fratre meo, Malcolmo de Haya fratre meo,
Thoma Gigan, Patricio capellano, Baldewino de Lornyn, Ada
Walensi tunc temporis senescallo, Oliuero de Graham, et
multis aliis.

(Abstract)

'OF the FISHERY of GLASBANI and RUGESABLYN.'

DAVID DE HAYA grants to Lundors in pure and perpetual alms, for the
weal of the souls of his father and mother, and for the weal of his soul
and of the souls of his wives, Ethna and Eva, and for the weal of the
souls of his brothers and sisters, and of his ancestors and successors, a
third part of his draw-net fishery on the sands of Glesbaniu and a third
part of his draw-net fishery at Rugesablyn, opposite Colcric. His fishery
of stake nets was excepted from the grant. Witnesses

LXXVII

De decima piscarie de Glasbani et de Rugesablun.

OMNIBVS sancte matris ecclesie filiis et fidelibus, presentibus et

trarum et pro salute animarum antecessorum nostrorum, in puram elemosinam, totam decimam recium ipsorum mona-chorum trahencium super sabulum de Glesbanin, et super sabulum de Rugesablun contra colcric, que ex dono domini Dauid fratris nostri tenent et possident, sicut carta ipsius Dauid testatur; Reddendo nobis inde annuatim duos salmones ad festum, scilicet, sancti Johannis Baptiste. Quare uolumus ut predicti monachi teneant et possideant predictam decimam recium ipsorum trahencium super prenominata sabula ita libere et quiete, ut nullus ex nostris in uita nostra nisi solas oraciones ab eis aliquid exigere presumat. Hiis testibus, Domino Dauid de Haya, Gilberto filio ipsius, Dauid, Thoma Gygan, Patricio capellano, Baldewino de Lornyn, Ada Walensi, Oliuero de Graham, et multis aliis.

(Abstract)

' OF the TITHE of the FISHERY of GLASBANI and of RUGESABLUN.'

ROBERT DE HAYA and Malcolm, his brother, grant to Lundors, for the weal of their souls, and for the weal of the souls of their ancestors, in pure alms, a whole tithe of the monks' draw-nets on the sands of Glesbanin and on the sands of Rugesablun, over against Colcric, which the monks hold and possess by the gift of David, their brother. The monks were to hold the tithe aforesaid on rendering to Robert and Malcolm two salmons at the feast of St. John the Baptist [June 24]. During their lifetime, neither of them would exact anything from the monks, save only their prayers. Witnesses

LXXVIII

De tercia parte piscarie.

OMNIBVS christi fidelibus presens scriptum visuris uel audi-turis, Gilbertus de Haya, eternam in domino Salutem. Nouerit vniuersitas vestra me concessisse et presenti carta mea con firmasse deo et ecclesie sancte marie et sancti andree de Lundors, et monachis ibidem deo seruientibus et seruituris, donacionem illam quam bone memorie Dauid de Haya, pater

ecclesie sancte marie et sancti andree de lundors et monachis eiusdem monasterij deo seruientibus et seruituris pro salute anime dicti Dauid patris mei, et matris mee, et pro salute anime mee, et anime Edoyne uxoris mee, et pro salute | animarum omnium fratrum et sororum, antecessorum et successorum meorum totam terciam partem piscarie recium meorum trahencium super Joymersandes, in puram liberam et perpetuam elemosinam. Quare uolo et concedo ut predicti monachi de lundors teneant et possideant omnia prenominata de me et heredibus meis, ita libere et quiete, plenarie et honorifice in omnibus, sicut aliqua abbacia in toto regno scocie aliquam elemosinam liberius, quiecius, plenius et honorificencius tenet et possidet; Ita, uidelicet, ut michi succedencium nullus aliquid ab eis nisi solas oraciones ad anime salutem exigere audeat uel presumat. In cuius rei testimonium presenti scripto sigillum meum apposui. Hiis testibus, Dominis Rogero de Berkeley, Ricardo Cumyn filio Ricardi Cumyn, militibus, Nicholao filio meo, Willelmo tunc capellano meo, Roberto de Haya nepote meo, Malisio de Strathern consanguineo meo, Galfrido de Keldelech, et multis aliis.

(Abstract)

' OF the THIRD PART of the FISHERY.'

GILBERT DE HAYA confirms to Lundors the donation which David de Haya, his father, had made to the monks, namely, a third part of the fishery of his draw-nets on the sands of Glesbanyn and on the sands of Rugesablun, over against Colcric. He also grants to Lundors, for the weal of the souls of David, his father, and his mother, and of himself and his wife, Edoyna, and for the weal of the souls of all his brothers and sisters, ancestors and successors, a third part of his draw-net fishery at Joymersandes, in free, pure, and perpetual alms. He promises that none of his successors should demand anything of the monks but prayers only. His seal attached. Witnesses . . .

LXXIX
De decima recium.

de Erole, uestigiis inherentem, concessisse et presenti carta mea confirmasse donacionem illam quam ipsi fecerunt abbati et conuentui de Lundors, videlicet, de decima recium ipsorum monachorum trahencium super sabulum de Glesbanyn et super Rugesablun contra Colcrike. Dedi eciam eisdem abbati et conuentui decimam recium ipsorum trahencium super Joymersandes : Tenendas et habendas eisdem in tota uita mea ; Reddendo inde annuatim michi uel actornato meo duos salmones ad Natiuitatem sancti Johannis Baptiste. In cuius rei testimonium presenti scripto sigillum meum apposui.

(Abstract)

'OF the TITHE of NETS.'

DAVID DE HAYA, rector of the church of Erole, declares that following the example of Robert de Haya and Malcolm, his brother, formerly rectors of the church of Erole, he confirms the grant which they had made to Lundors of the tithe of the monks' draw-nets on the sands of Glesbanyn and of Rugesablun. He also grants to the monks a tithe of their draw-nets at Joymersandes. Those gifts were to be had and held during the whole of his life on the monks rendering to him annually at the Nativity of St. John the Baptist [June 24] two salmons. His seal attached.

LXXX

De Logydurnach.

VNIVERSIS christi fidelibus presens scriptum visuris uel audituris Alanus Ostiarius, Justiciarius Scocie, eternam in domino salutem : Nouerit vniuersitas uestra me anno gracie m° cc°. l°, primo, Die martis, infra octavas apostolorum Petri et pauli, pro anima pie recordacionis domini mei Alexandri quondam illustris regis scocie, et pro salute anime mee, et Margerie uxoris mee, et omnium antecessorum et successorum meorum, de consensu et uoluntate venerabilis Patris, Domini P. dei

residebit, et de licencia dictorum Domini Episcopi Aberdonensis et abbatis et conuentus de Lundors in perpetuum de
gloriosa uirgine maria diuina celebrabit, soluendas annuatim
uicario ecclesie de Logindurnach qui pro tempore fuerit, ad
duos terminos anni, scilicet, duas marcas et dimidiam ad
Penthecosten, et duas marcas et dimidiam ad festum sancti
martini in hyeme, de terra mea de Kinnerny per me et heredes
meos, uel per ipsum quicunque dictam terram tenuerit : Ita,
uidelicet, quod non liceat michi uel heredibus meis prefatam
terram uel aliquam ipsius partem aliquo genere alienacionis
alienare, quin predicte quinque marce prefate capelle ad
sustentacionem vnius capellani, ut dictum est, integre reseruen-
tur, dicto vicario singulis annis fideliter persoluende. Ipse
autem uicarius dictam capellam et prenominatum capellanum
in omnibus decenter sustentabit, et omnia ornamenta ipsius
capelle honeste inueniet. Quod quidem Ricardus tempore
donacionis huius perpetuus uicarius ecclesie de Logindurnach
existens nomine uicarie sue de consensu et uoluntate dicti
domini Episcopi Aberdonensis pro se et successoribus suis
60.] fideliter promisit, | et in se nomine uicarie sue onus suscepit.
Et sciendum quod si aliquo tempore a solucione dicte pecunie
seu administracione capellani, quod absit, cessatum fuerit,
liceat episcopo aberdonensi qui pro tempore fuerit tam me et
heredes meos, quam predictum uicarium ad omnia premissa et
singula fideliter obseruanda per censuram ecclesiasticam compellere; Renunciato hincinde omni iuris beneficio, et omni
excepcione sublata que michi et heredibus meis uel prefato
uicario poterit competere, uel que executionem dicte censure
aliquatenus poterit impedire uel differre. In cuius rei testimonium duo super hoc in modum cirograffi confecta sunt
instrumenta; vnum sigillo dicti domini episcopi aberdonensis
et sigillo meo sigillatum, quod penes se habere debent dicti
abbas et conuentus de Lundors, et alterum communi sigillo
ipsorum abbatis et conuentus, et sigillo prenominati vicarij de
Logindurnach sigillatum penes me et heredes meos semper

Of Logydurnach.

To all the faithful of Christ who shall see or hear the present writ, Alan Durward, Justiciar of Scotland, health everlasting in the Lord. Know all of you that on Tuesday within the octave of the Apostles Peter and Paul, in the year of grace, MCCLI.,[1] for the soul of my Lord, Alexander, of pious memory, late illustrious King of Scotland, and for the weal of my soul, and of Margery, my wife, and of all my ancestors and successors, I have, with the will and consent of the venerable father, P[eter], by the grace of God, Lord Bishop of Aberdeen, and of the religious men [i.e. men bound by monastic vows] the abbot and convent of Lundors, given, granted, and by this present writ confirmed to God and the chapel of Blessed Mary, situated in the parish of Login-durnach, five marks sterling a year, for the maintenance of a chaplain who in the said chapel will reside continually, and with the leave of the said Lord Bishop of Aberdeen and of the abbot and convent of Lundors will for ever celebrate divine services in honour of the Glorious Virgin Mary, [the five marks] to be paid annually to the vicar of the church of Logindurnach at the two terms of the year, namely, two marks and a half at Whitsunday and two marks and a half at the feast of St. Martin in winter, by me and my heirs, out of my land of Kinnerny, or by him whosoever shall hold the said land, in such wise that it may not be lawful for me or my heirs to alienate by any kind of alienation the aforesaid land or any part of it without reserving the aforesaid five marks for faithful payment to the said vicar every year in full, as has been said, for the maintenance of the chaplain of the said chapel. But the vicar will maintain the said chapel and the aforenamed chaplain becomingly in all things, and will find all the ecclesiastical fur-nishings of the chapel in honourable wise. Which thing, Richard, being perpetual vicar of the church of Logindurnach at the time of this donation, faithfully promised, with the will and consent of the said Lord Bishop of Aberdeen, for himself and his successors, in the name of his vicarage [i.e. the benefice]; and in the name of his vicarage took the burden upon himself. And let it be known that if at any time the pay-ment of the said money or the service of the chaplain shall cease, which God forbid, it shall be lawful for the Bishop of Aberdeen for the time being to compel by ecclesiastical censure as well me and my heirs as the aforesaid vicar to faithfully observe the premises, all and singular ; all benefit of law being renounced, and all exception [in law] surrendered, which might be competent to me and my heirs, or to the vicar aforesaid, or which might impede or delay the execution of the said censure. In testimony of which two instruments were drawn up on the matter, in the manner of an indenture, one sealed with the seal of the said Lord Bishop of Aberdeen and with my seal, which should remain with the

---

[1] The feast of St. Peter and St. Paul is June 29th. This fell on Thursday in A.D. 1251, so the date of the charter is July 4th.

said abbot and convent of Lundors, and the other, sealed with the common seal of the abbot and convent and with the seal of the aforesaid vicar, always to remain with me and my heirs. Witnesses, Sir Colin Durward, my brother, Sir Thomas de Cunigburch, knights; Master Nicholas de Eddun; James de Oven; excommunicated John; and many others.

LXXXI

Donacio patronatus ecclesie de Lesselyn.

VNIVERSIS sancte matris ecclesie filiis tam presentibus quam *lius,* futuris, Normannus filius[a] malcolmi, salutem: Sciatis me concessisse et hac carta mea confirmasse deo et ecclesie sancte marie et sancti andree de Lundors et monachis ibidem deo seruientibus et seruituris, ecclesiam de Lescelyn cum terris et decimis, obuencionibus et omnibus aliis rectitudinibus ad eandem ecclesiam iuste pertinentibus, pro amore dei et pro salute anime domini mei Comitis Dauid fratris Regis Scottorum, et Matildis Comitisse uxoris sue, et antecessorum et successorum suorum, et pro salute anime mee, et A. uxoris mee et antecessorum et successorum meorum; Tenendam in liberam et puram et perpetuam elemosinam. Quare uolo ut prefati monachi predictam ecclesiam cum omnibus ad ipsam pertinentibus ita libere et quiete, plenarie et honorifice teneant et possideant in perpetuum, sicut aliquod monasterium aliquam ecclesiam uel aliquod ecclesiasticum beneficium ex alicujus concessione in toto regno Scocie liberius, quiecius, plenius et honorificencius tenet et possidet. Hiis testibus, Johanne Aberdonensi episcopo, Domino Comite Dauid, Waldeuo monacho de Kelcho, R. Decano de Aberdene, magistro omero, Johanne et Bricio capellanis de Burgo, Matheo et S. capellanis de Aberdene, Waltero Olifer, Dauid de Lindesei, h. et h. filiis Comitis Dauid, Willelmo Wacelyn, Willelmo persona de Dunde, Kinef iudice, Normanno filio Bertolfi, J. de Stokes senescaldo episcopi de Aberdene, W. de Warte, Jacobo camerario, Matheo filio edrici, Willelmo filio Hugonis, Johanne capellano de Inueruri, Petro Pincerna, et multis aliis.

to the same church, for the love of God, and for the weal 'of the soul of my lord, Earl David, brother of the King of Scots, and of the Countess Matilda, his wife, and of all his ancestors and successors, and for the weal of the soul of me, and of my wife A., and of all my ancestors and successors,' to be held in free, pure, and perpetual alms, as freely, quietly, etc. Witnesses

LXXXII

Confirmacio comitis Dauid super donacione patronatus ecclesie de Lesselyn.

VNIVERSIS sancte matris ecclesie filiis et fidelibus tam presentibus quam futuris, Comes Dauid frater Regis Scottorum, Salutem : Sciatis me concessisse, et hac presenti carta mea confirmasse deo et ecclesie sancte marie et sancti andree de Lundors, et monachis ibidem deo seruientibus, donacionem quam Normannus filius malcolmi predictis monachis dedit, scilicet, ecclesiam de Lescelin, cum terris et decimis et omnibus aliis prouentibus et iustis pertinenciis suis, in perpetuam et puram elemosinam, in proprios usus et sustentaciones ipsorum monachorum libere, quiete, plenarie et honorifice, sicut carta predicti Normanni testatur. Quare uolo et concedo ut prefati monachi predictam ecclesiam habeant et possideant, ita libere, quiete, plenarie, et honorifice sicut aliqua alia abbacia uel domus religionis aliquam elemosinam vel aliquam ecclesiam in toto regno Domini Regis fratris mei, liberius, quiecius, plenius, et honorificencius tenet et possidet. | Hiis testibus, Johanne [*fo* episcopo aberdonensi, Simone archidiacono, Roberto Decano, Ricardo capellano comitis, duobus Henricis filiis Domini Comitis, Willelmo Wascelyn, Henrico et Ricardo clericis Domini Comitis, cum multis aliis.

(*Abstract*)

'EARL DAVID'S CONFIRMATION of the DONATION of the PATRONAGE of the CHURCH of LESSELYN.'

LXXXIII

Ratificacio filij de ecclesia Lesselyn super donacione patris.

Vniversis sancte matris ecclesie filiis hoc scriptum uisuris uel audituris Normannus filius Normanni constabularij, salutem. Nouerit vniuersitas vestra me ratam et gratam habere donacionem quam bone memorie Normannus constabularius, pater meus, fecit abbati et monachis de Lundors ibidem deo seruientibus et in perpetuum seruituris de ecclesia de Lescelyn cum omnibus pertinenciis suis, sieut carta dicti Normanni patris mei super hoc confecta plenius testatur: Et ut hec mea donacio rata et inconcussa maneat in perpetuum, presenti scripto sigillum meum apposui. Hiis testibus, venerabili patre, Radulfo Aberdonensi episcopo, magistris Roberto Decano Aberdonensi, Ricardo officiali, Andrea de Aberdene, Willelmo de Kirketon, Ricardo Veyrement, Reginaldo Buscel, Johann de Soltre, et Dominis Walerano de Normanville, Simone de Garentuli, Johanne de Lamberton, Ada Nappario, Simone de Tyndale, Ricardo de insula, Johanne fratre meo, Willelmo de Blakeburne, Willelmo de Edduy, et multis aliis. Datum in ecclesia sancti Nicholai de Aberdene, anno gracie, m⁰.cc⁰.xl⁰. tercio, in crastino sancti Bartholomei apostoli.

(Abstract)

' RATIFICATION by the son of the gift of the CHURCH of LESSELYN made by the father.'

NORMAN, son of Norman, Constable, ratifies the donation which his father Norman, Constable, made to Lundors, namely of the church of Lescelyn with all its pertinents, as the charter of Norman, his father, more fully contains. His seal attached. Witnesses. . . . Given in the Church of St. Nicholas of Aberdeen on the morrow of St. Bartholomew the Apostle [Aug. 24], in the year of grace MCCXLIII.

LXXXIV

[De Johanne filio Thome de Malind.]

salutem eternam in domino. Nouerit vniuersitas vestra me quietam clamasse abbati et conuentui de Lundors pro me et heredibus meis totum ius ligiacionis quod me habere clamaui in Johannem filium thome de malind, et in omnem sequelam de corpore suo exeuntem in perpetuum. Saluo michi clamio quod habeo in alios de parentela dicti Johannis. Et in huius quiete clamacionis testimonium huic scripto sigillum meum apposui. Datum apud capellam sancti Appolinaris, die sabbati proxima post translacionem sancti Thome Martiris, anno gracie m⁰. cc⁰. l⁰. tercio, presentibus Dominis Bartholomeo flandrensi, Andrea de lescelin, militibus, Willelmo theyno de Kintor, Roberto de tubertyn, clerico, Henrico de Maleuile, Johanne Roberti, Johanne filio Walteri, Burgensibus de Inueruri, Henrico filio Johannis, et aliis.

(*Abstract*)

[Of John, Son of Thomas of Malind.]

To all the faithful of Christ who shall view the present letters, Norman de Lescelin, son of Norman, the Constable, health everlasting in the Lord. Know all of you that I have quitclaimed for ever to the abbot and convent of Lundors, for me and my heirs, all right of bondship (*jus ligiacionis*) which I claimed to have on John, son of Thomas of Malind, and in all the issue of his body (*in omnem sequelam de corpore suo exeuntem*) saving the claim which I have upon others of the kin of the said John. And in testimony of this quitclaim I have put my seal to this writ. Given at the chapel of St. Apollinaris, on Saturday next after the Translation of St. Thomas the Martyr [July 7 ¹], in the year of grace MCCLIII., there being present Sir Bartholomew Fleming and Sir Andrew de Lescelin, knights; William, Thane of Kintore; Robert de Tubertyn, clerk; . . . and others.

LXXXV

[De Tofto in Inuerkaithin.²]

Robertvs de lundoniis, filius Regis Scottorum omnibus amicis

in burgo meo de Inuerkaithin, in liberam et quietam et perpetuam elemosinam.   Quare uolo ut predicti monachi habeant
et possideant predictum toftum ita libere et quiete et pacifice
et honorifice, sicut aliqua ecclesia aliquam elemosinam in toto
regno Scocie liberius, quiecius, plenius et honorificencius tenet
et possidet.   Hiis testibus, Comite Dauid fratre Regis Scotorum,
Comite patricio, Willelmo de Lindesei, Willelmo de Haya,
Ricardo Ridel, Willelmo Sumeruille, Walkelino filio Stephani,
Simone de Seyntliz, Nicholao de Adsles, Hugone de dettauerley.[1]

(Abstract)

[OF a TOFT in INVERKAITHIN.]

' ROBERT of London, son of the King of Scots, to all his friends, greeting.'   He grants to Lundors one full toft in his burgh of Inverkaithin
to be held in frankalmoign, as freely . . .as any church holds any alms
in the kingdom of Scotland.   Witnesses

LXXXVI

De j marca in Hamildun.

VNIVERSIS Christi fidelibus Willelmus de Camera, salutem in
domino.   Nouerit vniuersitas vestra me dedisse, concessisse,
et hac presenti carta mea confirmasse deo et ecclesie sancte
marie et sancti andree de Lundors, et monachis ibidem deo
seruientibus et seruituris, pro salute anime Domini mei Comitis
Dauid et Matilde Comitisse uxoris sue, et antecessorum et
successorum suorum, et pro salute anime mee, et B. uxoris mee,
62.] et patrum nostrorum et matrum nostrarum | et puerorum et
omnium antecessorum et successorum nostrorum, in liberam
puram et perpetuam elemosinam, omne dominium quod
habui in parua hamildune et vnam marcam argenti de firma
ipsius uille, ita quod vna altera marca quam inde solebam percipere remaneat michi, et cui illam uoluero concedere.   Quare
uolo et concedo ut predicti monachi habeant et possideant
dominium predicte uille liberum et quietum de me et heredibus

michi, et cui illam concessero, sine aliquo alio iure uel dominio uel clamio quod habui uel habere potui, uel aliquis heredum meorum, in uilla prenominata, vt autem hec mea donacio et concessio stabilis sit in perpetuum, presenti scripto sigillum meum apposui.   Hiis testibus, Domino meo Comite Dauid, et filiis ipsius Johanne et henrico de Striuelin et henrico de Brechin, Roberto Basset, Roberto filio Roberti, Constantino de Mortemer, militi Domini Comitis, Alexandro de Striuelin, Ricardo filio hugonis, henrico filio Walkelini filij Stephani.

(Abstract)

' OF one MARK in HAMILDUN.'

WILLIAM DE CAMERA grants to Lundors for the weal of the soul ' of my lord, Earl David, and of the Countess Matilda his wife, and the souls of all his ancestors and successors, and for the weal of my soul and of B. my wife, our fathers and our mothers, and our children and all our ancestors and successors,' in frankalmoign, ' all lordship which I have in Little Hamildune and one silver mark out of the rent of that vill, so that one other mark which I was accustomed to receive shall remain with me and him to whom I may will to grant it.' Wherefore he grants that the monks should possess the lordship of the said vill, of him and his heirs, as fully and freely as he possessed it at the date of this gift.   They are to receive their one mark from the vill, and the other mark is to remain with him and the person to whom he might grant it, but without any other right, lordship, or claim.   His seal attached.   Witnesses

LXXXVII

De iij marcis de Stokes in comitatu leycestre.

OMNIBVS hoc scriptum visuris uel audituris Willelmus de campania, salutem.   Nouerit vniuersitas vestra me dedisse, concessisse, et hac presenti carta mea confimasse, deo et ecclesie sancte marie et sancti andree de Lundors et monachis ibidem deo seruientibus et seruituris, pro salute anime patris mei Roberti de campania, qui ibidem sepultus est, et pro animabus

in perpetuum ad altare sancti Nicholai cantetur aliqua missa in eadem ecclesia, in qua fiet commemoracio specialis pro anima patris mei, et pro animabus omnium fidelium defunctorum. Vt autem hec mea donacio rata sit et stabilis in perpetuum presenti scripto sigillum meum apposui. Testibus, Domino Johanne Comite Cestre et Huntendone, Domino henrico de Striuelyn, Domino henrico de Brechyn, Domino Radulfo de Campania, Domino Galfrido de Appelby, Domino Tebaldo de Bellus, Domino Hugone Fitun, Domino Radulfo de Saye, Domino Anketyn, Domino Peleryn, Hugone clerico, Petro clerico, Nichola de Inuerpeffyr, et multis aliis.

(*Abstract*)

' OF three MARKS from STOKES in the COUNTY of LEICESTER.'

WILLIAM DE CAMPANIA grants to Lundors for the weal of the soul of his father Robert de Campania, and of all his ancestors and successors, in pure and perpetual alms, three silver marks to be received annually of him and his heirs at Whitsunday ' in my land of Stokes in the county of Leicester. The monks aforesaid have charitably granted my petition that a mass should be sung every day for ever at the altar of St. Nicholas in the same church [*i.e.* the church of Lundors], in which mass special commemoration shall be made for the soul of my father and for the soul of all the faithful departed.' Seal. Witnesses . . .

LXXXVIII

MEMORANDVM quod dominus Willelmus de Campania in curia sua apud Turleston, die Sancti Botulfi abbatis anno gracie m° cc° quadragesimo octauo, assignauit Willelmum de Estleye ad reddendum annuatim quam diu uixerit apud stoke monachis de Lundors uel eorum nuncio quadraginta solidos argenti infra ebdomodam Penthecostes. Hiis testibus, Domino Alano tunc celarario de Suleby, Hugone de Blaby tunc capellano de Turleston, Willelmo Walkelyn de Leycestre capellano, Rogero de Stoke, Willelmo Vmfrey de Stoke, Thoma de heyham,

appointed William de Estleye to pay yearly, as long as he lived, at Stoke, to the monks of Lundors, or their messenger, forty silver shillings, within the week of Whitsunday.   Witnesses . . .]

LXXXIX

De tofto in Dunde.   [fo

Omnibvs christi fidelibus presens scriptum visuris uel audituris Thomas dei gracia abbas de Lundors et eiusdem loci conuentus, eternam in domino salutem.   Nouerit vniuersitas uestra nos vnanimi consensu et uoluntate dimisisse ad feodamfirmam Laurencio de monte alto clerico totum toftum nostrum integrum in uilla de Dunde quod iacet proximum terre uicarij eiusdem uille, quam habet idem uicarius iuxta ecclesiam sancti Clementis martiris in parte occidentali : Tenendum de nobis et successoribus nostris sibi et assignatis suis et heredibus assignatorum in perpetuum, Integre, plenarie et honorifice cum eisdem libertatibus et asiamentis quibus nos dictum toftum tenuimus uel tenere debuimus.   Prenominatus autem Laurencius, quamdiu uixerit, nobis et successoribus nostris pro predicto tofto reddet annuatim vnam marcam argenti infra nundinas de Dunde.   Assignati, uero, eiusdem Laurencii et eorundem assignatorum heredes qui dictum toftum tenebunt post mortem ipsius Laurencij reddent nobis annuatim duas marcas argenti infra dictas nundinas de Dunde.   Et preterea predictus Laurencius et assignati sui et eorum heredes inuenient nobis et nostris, omnibus et singulis, quociens uoluerimus, honestam domum in dicto tofto vbi nos et nostri decenter hospitari poterimus, pro omni exaccione et demanda. Et sciendum quod predictus Laurencius predictum toftum nullis secularibus personis nobis dicioribus uel potencioribus, nec eciam alieui domui Religiose siue uiris Religiosis assignabit.   Nec idem Laurencius uel sui assignati uel eorum heredes

insuper se et suos assignatos et assignatorum heredes si aliquando, quod absit, contra tenorem huius scripti maliciose uel fraudulenter fecerint, per sepedicti tofti amissionem et omnium bonorum in eo existencium, donec nobis satisfactum fuerit, obligauit. In cuius rei firmitatem, et perpetuam securitatem istud scriptum in modum cirograffi est confectum, Cuius uidelicet scripti vni parti commune sigillum capituli nostri est appensum, quam partem penes se debet habere dictus Laurencius uel aliquis ex parte ipsius. Alteri autem parti huius scripti sigillum predicti Laurencii est appositum, que quidem pars penes nos remanet. Teste Capitulo.

(Abstract)

'Of a Toft in Dundee.'

Thomas, by the grace of God, Abbot of Lundors, grants at fee-farm to Laurence de Montealto, clerk, 'our whole entire toft in the town of Dundee, which lies next the land of the vicar of that town, which the same vicar has near the church of St Clement the Martyr, in the western part, to be held of us and our successors by him and his assignees and the heirs of his assignees for ever,' with all its liberties, easements, etc. Laurence as long as he lives is to pay annually to the abbot and his successors one silver mark during the holding of the fair of Dundee. After the death of Laurence his assignees and the heirs of his assignees are to pay at the aforesaid time each year two silver marks. In addition the said Laurence and his assignees and the heirs of his assignees 'shall find for us and ours, all and singular, a house in the said toft where we and ours may be entertained becomingly as often as we wish, and this in lieu of every exaction and demand.' And let it be known that the aforesaid Laurence will not assign the toft to any secular persons richer or more powerful than we are, nor even to a religious house or to any religious men [*i.e.* to any monks]. Nor shall the said Laurence, his assignees or their heirs sell the toft, or alienate it in any way, unless with the will and permission of the abbots of Lundors. To faithfully observe all these things Laurence for himself, his assignees, and the heirs of his assignees, made oath. And further he bound himself, his assignees and their heirs by the loss of the toft and all good thereupon (till full satisfaction was made) if they ever did any thing maliciously or fraudulently, which God forbid, contrary to the tenor of this writ. The writ was made in the form of an indenture, one part of which, sealed

XC

De Tofto in Dunde, et de perambulacione de Durnach.[1]

Omnibvs hoc scriptum uisuris uel audituris J.de Scocia, comes Cestre et huntendun, salutem. Sciatis me dedisse et hac carta mea confirmasse Deo et ecclesie Sancte marie et sancti andree de Lundors et monachis ibidem Deo seruientibus et seruituris, vnum Toftum in Dunde, proximum tofto Sancti clementis uersus occidentem, et piscariam in tehy proximam piscarie quam dedi domino Henrico de Brehin uersus Portincrag; Tenendum sibi et habendum in liberam puram et perpetuam elemosinam. Concessi eeiam eis ut terra illa que perambulata fuit inter magnam Durnach et logindurnach coram me et Dompno J. abbate de Lundors et aliis probis hominibus, sit in communi inperpetuum, sicut recognitum fuit per sacramenta illorum qui terram illam perambulauerunt, et quod de cetero non fiat aliqua perambulacio inter terras meas et terras illorum, sed teneant ipsas diuisas quas habuerunt tempore patris mei et tempore meo sine molestia et grauamine. Volo eciam et concedo ut quando uoluerint uel potuerint facere molendina in terris suis, nullus successorum meorum impediat homines | manentes in terris ipsorum ire libere et quiete ad molendina illa, cum omni secta sua et multura, quamuis solebant sequi molendina mea quamdiu fuerint sine molendinis propriis. Testibus, Domino H. de Striuelin fratre meo, Domino Roberto de Campaniis, Domino Hugone phiton, Domino Galfrido de Appilby, Domino Anketill de foleuille, Petro et Rogero clericis, Hugone de Pantona, Baldwino de Anuers, Petro Pincerna; apud Berewic.

margin: De percione nach.

margin: [fc

(*Abstract*)

'Of a Toft in Dundee, and of the Perambulation of Durnach.'

that that land which was perambulated between Great Durnach and Logindurnach in the presence of himself, J., Lord Abbot of Lundors, and other good men should be for ever in common, as it was acknowledged to have been on the oaths of those who perambulated it. And further he grants that in future there should be no perambulation between his lands and the lands of the monks of Lundors, but that they should have the same marches which they had in the time of his father and in his time, without trouble or annoyance. He further grants that when the monks are able and willing to make mills upon their lands none of his successors should hinder the men residing on the lands of the monks from going freely and quietly to those mills with all their suit and multure, although they had been accustomed to be thirled to his mills as long as they had been without mills of their own. Witnesses, Henry of Stirling, my brother,

XCI

De manso iuxta ecclesiam de Cullessy.

Omnibvs christi fidelibus ad quos presens scriptum peruenerit, Dominus Serlo de Sancto Andrea, salutem eternam in domino. Nouerit vniuersitas vestra me caritatis intuitu, et ad instanciam precum magistri Ade de Malcharwiston tunc temporis Rectoris ecclesie de Colessy, dedisse et quieteclamasse deo et ecclesie Sancti Andree de Colessy, in puram et perpetuam elemosinam, totum jus quod hahui uel habere potui in edificiis uel in mesuagio personatus ecclesie de Colessy, in libero introitu et exitu ex parte australi usque ad stratam publicam, usque eciam ad illas diuisas inter ipsum mesuagium et terram meam circum-iacentem limitanas ; et incipiunt ille diuise ex parte Aquilonari cuiusdam furni siti infra mesuagium pertinens ad ecclesiam, et

Johanne de Kindeloch, Henrico de Winton, Willelmo de Monimel capellano, et multis aliis.

(*Abstract*)

'OF the MANSE near the CHURCH of CULLESSY.'

SIR SERLO of St. Andrews, out of charity and at the instance of Master Adam of Malcharwiston, at that time rector of the church of Colessy, gives and quitclaims to God and the church of St. Andrew at Colessy, in pure and perpetual alms, all the right which he had or could have in the buildings and messuage of the parsonage of the church of Colessy, with free entrance and exit on the south to the public street, as far also as the boundary marches between that messuage and his surrounding land. The marches begin on the north of a certain oven (*furni*) situated within the messuage pertaining to the church, and extend towards the east as far as a stone placed to mark the boundary, and so across toward the south to another stone similarly placed to mark the boundary, and from that place in a line to a boundary made at the wall of the graveyard. 'To be held and had by God and the aforesaid church free and released, so that neither he nor any of his heirs could exact any right or claim in time to come within the said marches.' Seal. Witnesses

XCII

De vicariis qui molestauerunt locum nostrum.[1]

CANCELLARIVS morauiensis et thesaurarius Dunkeldensis dele-gati perpetui ad infrascripta, una cum tercio collega iam defuncto, cum illa clausula quod si non omnes hiis exequendis poteritis tractare duo vestrum ea nichilominus exequantur, a sede apostolica specialiter deputati, omnibus et singulis decanis, archidiaconis, cantoribus, cancellariis, thesaurariis, et canonicis ecclesiarum cathedralium per totum regnum scocie constitutis, nec non rectoribus et perpetuis vicariis, capellanis, et notariis publicis infra dictum regnum et aliis, ubilibet constitutis, Salutem in domino, et nostris, ymo verius apostolicis, humiliter

conuentus monasterij de L. ordinis beati benedicti Sancti Andree diocesis nobis presentatas, sanas et integras, cum debita reuerencia recepimus et vidimus, tenoris et continencie instrumenti publici presentibus annexati. Post quarum presentacionem nobis fuit expositum conquirendo quod nonnulli vicarij in supradictis literis apostolicis nominati, videlicet, perpetui vicarii ecclesiarum de C. de R. et de K. ipsis abbati et conuentui super augmentacionem suarum vicariarum molestias et iniurias inferunt, faciendo eos citari coram non suo iudice in hoc casu sub grauibus laboribus et expensis, et nichilominus dictus vicarius de K. eisdem subtrahit xxx agnos pacabiles, in quibus eisdem tenetur annuatim, et in ipsorum solucione iam per tres annos cessauit, in ipsorum preiudicium atque dampnum, quare nobis fuit ex parte ipsorum et conuentus de oportuno remedio supplicatum. Nos, igitur, huius modi supplicacionibus annuentes, auctoritate apostolica, quam fungimur in hac parte, vobis et vestrum cuilibet in solidum in uirtute sancte obediencie, et sub pena excommunicacionis precipimus et mandamus quatinus infra sex dies postquam ex parte ipsorum abbatis et conuentus, aliquis vestrum fuerit requisitus, dictos vicarios et eorum quemlibet moneatis, quod a predictis molestacionibus cessent penitus et desistant, et quod vicarius de K. de dictis xxx agnis tam de anno presenti quam de tempore suo preterito ipsis abbati et conuentui satisfaciat, et quod tam ipse quam vicarij de C. et de R. de fabrica cancellarum suarum ecclesiarum, et de omnibus oneribus extraordinariis pro porcione sua respondeant de cetero, et contribuant cum ipsis abbate et conuentu ad premissa, et quod hec omnia faciant et perficiant infra xv dies a tempore monicionum vestrarum computandos: quorum quinque pro prima, v pro secunda, et reliquos v dies pro tercia et peremptoria monicione eis et eorum cuilibet assignamus, sub pena excommunicacionis quam ex nunc prout extunc in hiis scriptis ferimus in rebelles, absolucione nobis et superiori nostro, preterquam in mortis articulo, reseruata. Datum sub sigillis nostris apud

(Abstract)

'OF VICARS who have troubled our PLACE.'

THE Chancellor of Moray and the Treasurer of Dunkeld holding in continuation the office of Papal Delegates in respect to the matters dealt with below (as having been specially deputed, together with a third colleague now deceased, in a writ containing the clause that 'if all of you cannot proceed to the execution of these things, nevertheless let two of you execute them'), to all and singular the deans, archdeacons, chantors, chancellors, treasurers, and canons of the cathedral churches throughout the whole realm of Scotland, also to the rectors, perpetual vicars, chaplains, and notaries public within the said kingdom and others, wheresoever they may happen to be, [wish] health in the Lord 'and obedience to our commands, or, more truly, the commands of the Apostolic See.' They recount that they had received with becoming reverence Letters Apostolic, presented on the part of the abbot and convent of Lundors. These Letters were whole and perfect, and of the tenor and contents of the public instrument annexed to these presents.[1] After the presentation of the Letters Apostolic it was explained to the Delegates on inquiry that some vicars named in the Letters Apostolic, namely, the perpetual vicars of the churches of C., of R., and of K., were causing trouble and injury to the abbot and convent in regard to an augmentation of their vicarages. They had caused the abbot and monks to be cited before a judge, who in this matter had no jurisdiction over them, and by this they caused heavy expense and inconvenience to the abbot and convent. Moreover, the vicar of K. had withdrawn from the convent the payment of thirty marketable (*pacabiles*) lambs which he was bound to render every year. It was now three years since the payment of the lambs had been made, to the harm and loss of the abbot and convent. Wherefore supplication was made to the Delegates on the part of the monks for suitable redress. 'We, therefore, assenting to such supplications, order and command, by the apostolic authority which we exercise in this respect, you and each of you severally, in virtue of holy obedience and under pain of excommunication, that, within six days after any of you shall have been requested on the part of the abbot and convent, ye admonish the said vicars and each of them to wholly cease and desist from the molestations aforesaid, and that the vicar of K. satisfy the abbot and convent for the thirty lambs, as well for the present year as for the time past; and that he [the vicar of K.], as also the vicars of C. and R.,

date of your admonition. Of these fifteen days we assign, to them and
each of them, five days for the first, five days for the second, and the
remaining five days for the third and peremptory monition, under pain
of excommunication, which we pronounce, now as well as then, against
rebels, absolution being reserved to us and our superior, save at the
hour of death (*in mortis articulo*). Given under our seals at Perth on
the twenty-fourth day of the month of June in the year of our Lord
MCCCLXXV.

'Whoever gives the monition is to inform us as to the date, so that
if necessary we may be able to provide further remedy. Given as
above.'

XCIII

65.] Magnum priuilegium Celestini de exempcione.[1]

CELESTINVS Episcopus, seruus seruorum dei, Dilectis filiis
abbati et fratribus monasterij de Lundors, salutem et apostoli
cam benediccionem. Officij nostri debitum et caritas ordinata
requirunt vt eorum deuocionem ad incrementum plenius attenta
sollicitudine prouocemus, qui ampliando creatoris obsequio
diligenter insistunt, et firmum iam propositum assumpserunt
ad idem forcius ac feruencius ipsius fauente gracia intendendi.
Ea propter, Dilecti in domino filij, propensius attendentes quod
Dilectus filius noster Nobilis uir Dauid Comes frater Karissimi
in Christo filij nostri W. illustris Regis Scocie, monasterium
uestrum ea intencione fundauerit, ac dilatauerit plurimis bonis
ut dignus in eo debeat domino sub monastico habitu famulatus
impendi, et affectu habeat possessiones et redditus eius vberius
ampliandi, eius instanti supplicacione deuicti, monasterium
ipsum in quo diuino mancipati estis obsequio a iurisdiccione
quorumlibet eximentes, in ius et proprietatem beati Petri suscipimus, et presentis scripti patrocinio communimus. In primis
siquidem statuentes, ut ordo monasticus, qui secundum Deum
et beati benedicti regulam in eodem monasterio institutus esse
dinoscitur, perpetuis ibidem temporibus inuiolabiliter obseruetur.
Preterea quascunque possessiones quecunque bona idem monas-

cione fidelium seu aliis iustis modis, prestante domino, poterit adipisci, firma vobis uestrisque successoribus et illibata permaneant. In quibus hec propriis duximus exprimenda uocabulis : Locum ipsum, in quo prefatum monasterium situm est, cum omnibus pertinenciis suis per suas rectas diuisas ex dono et concessione eiusdem Comitis, et liberam curiam in terra uestra et firmam pacem infra diuisas ipsius uille de Lundors sicut carta ipsius Comitis protestatur : Ecclesiam quoque eiusdem uille de Lundors, cum omnibus iustis pertinenciis suis, et terram ad predictam ecclesiam pertinentem per rectas diuisas suas, et alias terras in eadem uilla, que terre in carta eiusdem Comitis continentur : Et asiamenta insule que vocatur redinche communia uobis sicut et comiti ad proprios usus vestros, et vnam piscariam in They iuxta prenominatam insulam, et molendinum predicte uille de Lundors, cum omni secta sua et multura : Ecclesiam quoque de Dunde cum omnibus pertinenciis suis, et vnum toftum in burgo de Dunde, liberum et quietum ab omni seruicio et exaccione : Et ultra muneth, fintrith per rectas diuisas suas cum omnibus pertinenciis, et ecclesiam eiusdem uille, cum pertinenciis suis : Et in Garuiach, Ledhgauel et Malind cum omnibus pertinenciis suis et per rectas diuisas suas : Et ecclesiam de Rothket cum capellis suis, scilicet, Inueruryn et Munkegin, et cum aliis pertinenciis suis : Et ecclesiam de Durnach, ecclesiam de Prame, ecclesiam de Radmuriel, ecclesiam de Ingemabanin, ecclesiam de Culsamuel, et in episcopatu Lincolniensi ecclesiam de Cunigton ; ecclesiam de Kelalcmund cum capellis earundem ecclesiarum, terris, et decimis, et omnibus earum pertinenciis, ad proprios usus et sustentaciones vestras : Et vnum toftum in burgo de Inueruryn liberum et quietum ab omni seruicio et exaccione : Decimam eciam omnium lucrorum et placitorum eiusdem Comitis infra terram suam et extra ultra muneth, quam habuit tempore quo fecit donacionem istam : Et Decimam omnium lucrorum ipsius que ei proueniunt de lueris predicti Regis in toto regno suo, et decimam omnium Rerum dicti Comitis et heredum suorum ultra moneth : Ex donacione quoque memorati regis, vnum plenarium toftum

Perth : Et vnum plenarium toftum in burgo suo de forfar, et
vnum plenarium toftum in burgo suo de Munros, et vnum
plenarium toftum in burgo suo de Aberden : Ex donacione
uero Roberto de Lundres filij prefati regis, vnum plenarium
toftum in burgo de Inuerkeythyn, sicut hec que prediximus iuste
ac pacifice possidetis ut[a] in donatorum earum scriptis auctenticis continetur, Vobis et per uos monasterio uestro auctoritate apostolica confirmamus.   Sane Noualium uestrorum que
propriis manibus aut sumptibus colitis, siue de nutrimentis
animalium uestrorum nullus a uobis decimas exigere uel extorquere presumat.   Liceat quoque uobis clericos et laicos liberos
et absolutos e seculo fugientes ad conuersionem recipere, et eo
absque contradiccione retinere.   Prohibemus insuper ut nulli
fratrum uestrorum post factam in eodem loco professionem fas
sit absque abbatis sui licencia de eodem loco nisi arcioris
religionis obtentu discedere.   Discedentem uero absque com-
munium litterarum caucione nullus audeat retinere.   Cum
autem generale interdictum terre fuerit, liceat uobis, clausis
ianuis, exclusis excommunicatis et interdictis, non pulsatis cam
panis, suppressa uoce diuina officia celebrare.   In parochialibus
uero ecclesiis quas habetis, liceat uobis sacerdotes eligere, et
diocesanis episcopis presentare, quibus si idonei fuerint episcopi
curam animarum committant, ut eis de spiritualibus, vobis uero
de temporalibus, debeant respondere.   Crisma, uero, oleum
sanctum, Consecraciones altarium seu basilicarum, ordinaciones
clericorum qui ad sacros ordines fuerint promouendi a diocesano
suscipietis episcopo si quidem catholicus fuerit, et graciam et
communionem apostolice sedis habuerit, et ea uobis uoluerit
sine prauitate qualibet exhibere.   Alioquin liceat uobis quemcunque malueritis catholicum adire antistitem, graciam et
communionem apostolice sedis habentem, qui nostra fretus
ndo   auctoritate vobis quod postulatur impendat.   Obeunte uero te
nunc eiusdem loci abbate, uel tuorum quolibet successorum,
nullus ibi qualibet surrepcionis astucia seu uiolencia preponatur,
nisi quem fratres communi consensu uel fratrum maior pars
consilij sanioris secundum dei timorem et Beati benedicti regu-

mulgare presumat. Interdicimus, autem, ut nulli licitum sit
infra terminos parochiarum vestrarum ecclesiam, cimiterium,
oratorium uel xenodochium de nouo construere, seu constructa
alij subdere, absque vestro et diocesani episcopi assensu, saluis
priuilegiis romanorum pontificum. Sepulturam, preterea,
ipsius loci liberam esse decernimus, ut eorum deuocioni et
extreme uoluntati qui se illic sepelliri deliberauerint, nisi forte
excommunicati uel interdicti sint, nullus obsistat, salua tamen
iusticia illarum ecclesiarum a quibus mortuorum corpora
assumuntur. Decernimus ergo ut nullis ᵃ omnino hominum fas ᵃ MS.ʎ
sit personas vestras seu monasterium ipsum temere perturbare,
uel nouis et indebitis exaccionibus fatigare ; aut hanc nostre
paginam confirmacionis, exempcionis et constitutionis infringere, uel ei ausu temerario contraire : Si quis autem hoc
attemptare presumpserit, indignacionem omnipotentis dei et
beatorum Petri et Pauli apostolorum eius se nouerit incur
surum. Ad indicium, autem, huius a sede apostolica libertatis
percepte duos bisancios nobis et successoribus nostris annis
singulis persoluetis. Datum Lateran., viij Id. Marcij, Pontificatus nostri anno quarto.

(Abstract)

'CELESTINE'S GREAT CHARTER of EXEMPTION.'

CELESTINE, bishop, servant of the servants of God, to the abbot and
brethren of the monastery of Lundors, etc. Having learned of the
foundation and endowment of the monastery by 'Earl David, brother of
our dearest son in Christ, William, the illustrious King of Scotland,'
the Pope desires to promote his pious intentions; and therefore he
exempts the monastery from the jurisdiction of all whomsoever, and
takes it 'into the jurisdiction and possession of Blessed Peter.' He first
decrees that the monastic order there instituted 'according to God and
the rule of Blessed Benedict' should there for ever be inviolably observed.
Further, all the possessions and goods which the monastery then

church of Lundors and its pertinents, and the land pertaining to the church, and the other lands in the same vill which are contained in the earl's charter; the easements of the island which is called Redinche, for their use as for the use of the earl; a fishery in the Tay near the aforesaid island; the mill of the vill of Lundors with all its suit and multure; the church of Dundee; a toft in the burgh of Dundee, free of all service and exaction; beyond the Mounth, Fintrith, and the church of the same vill; and in Garviach, Ledhgavel, and Malind; and the church of Rothket with its chapels of Inveruryn and Munkegin, and with its other pertinents; the church of Durnach; the church of Prame; the church of Radmuriel; the church of Ingemabanin; the church of Culsamuel; and in the bishopric of Lincoln the church of Cunigton; the church of Kelalcmund; with the chapels of the same churches, their lands, tithes, and all their pertinents 'for your own use and maintenance'; and a toft in the burgh of Inveruryn, free and quit of all service and exaction; the tithe of all profits and issues of the earl's courts, both within and without his lands beyond the Mounth, which he had in the time when he made this gift; and a tithe of all the profits which come to the earl from the profits of the king throughout his whole kingdom; and a tithe of all the property of the earl and his heirs beyond the Mounth.

Further, of the gift of the king, a full toft in his burgh of Berwick; a full toft in his burgh of Stirling; a full toft in his burgh of Carel; a full toft in his burgh of Perth; a full toft in his burgh of Forfar; a full toft in his burgh of Munros, and a full toft in his burgh of Aberdeen.

Further, of the gift of Robert of London, son of the said king, a full toft in the burgh of Inverkeythyn.

All these things are to be possessed as in the charters of the donors is contained, and are confirmed to the monks of Lundors by apostolic authority.

'Let no one presume to exact or extort tithes from the fallow-lands (*novaliis*) which ye have brought under cultivation by your own hands or at your own cost, or tithes of the increase of your animals.'

It is lawful for the monks of Lundors to receive and retain without gainsaying clerks and laymen, if they be free and released, who fly from the world to the monastic life (*ad conversionem*). It shall not be lawful for any of the brethren, after having made his profession at Lundors, to leave that place without the permission of the abbot, unless it be with a view to enter a monastic order of stricter rule. Let no one dare to retain any one leaving the monastery without the precaution of common letters.

When the land is subjected to a general interdict, it shall be lawful for the monks to celebrate the divine offices in a low voice (*suppressa*

dioceses, to which priests, if they shall be fit, the bishops may commit the cure of souls, ' so that these parish clergy may answer to the bishops in spirituals, and to you in temporals.'

Chrism, holy oil, consecrations of altars and of churches, and the ordinations of clerks who should be advanced to holy orders are to be obtained by the monastery from the bishop of the diocese, if he be Catholic and possess the favour and fellowship of the Apostolic See, and is willing to grant these things without any pravity. Failing the diocesan bishop they might go to any bishop whom they preferred, who was Catholic and possessed the favour and fellowship of the Apostolic See, who, relying on the Pope's authority, would grant them what they sought.

On the death of the abbot that now is, or of any of his successors, no one may be advanced to that office by deceit or violence. The brethren by common consent, or else the majority of the brethren, of saner counsel, shall provide that the abbot be elected in accordance with the fear of God and the rule of Blessed Benedict.

The Pope prohibits any one from presuming to promulgate a sentence of excommunication, suspension, or interdict, against the brethren or their monastery without manifest and reasonable cause.

It shall not be lawful for any to make a church, burying-ground, hospice (*xenodochium*), or oratory within the bounds of the parishes of the monastery, or to subject those already made to another, without the assent of the monks and that of the bishop of the diocese, saving the privileges of the Roman pontiffs. Sepulture in the place itself shall be free, so that none may oppose the devotion and last will of those who shall choose to be buried there, unless they happen to be excommunicated or under interdict, saving always the just claim (*justicia*) of those churches from which the bodies of the dead are taken.

It shall not be lawful for any one to rashly disturb the monks or the monastery, or to harass them with new and undue exactions, or to infringe or rashly contravene this writ of the Pope's confirmation, exemption, and constitution. ' But if any one shall presume to attempt this, let him know that he will incur the indignation of Almighty God and of Blessed Peter and Paul, His Apostles.' In token of this liberty received from the Apostolic See the monks are to pay yearly to the Pope and his successors two bezants.

Given at the Lateran, viij. Ides of March [March 8] in the fourth year of our pontificate [*i.e.* A.D. 1195].[1]

XCIV

Magnum priuilegium Innocencii tercij. |

[*fo*

fratribus tam presentibus quam futuris regularem uitam professis in perpetuum. Religiosam uitam eligentibus apostolicum conuenit adesse presidium, ne forte cuiuslibet temeritatis incursus aut eos a proposito reuocet, aut robur, quod absit, sacre religionis infringat. Ea propter, Dilecti in domino filij, uestris iustis postulacionibus clementer annuimus, et prefatum monasterium sancte marie de Lundors in quo diuino estis obsequio mancipati sub beati petri et nostra proteccione suscipimus, et presentis scripti priuilegio communimus. In primis siquidem statuentes ut ordo monasticus, qui secundum deum et beati benedicti regulam in eodem monasterio institutus esse dinoscitur, perpetuis ibidem temporibus inuiolabiliter obseruetur. Preterea quascunque possessiones, quecunque bona idem monasterium in presenciarum iuste et canonice possidet, aut in futurum concessione pontificum, largicione regum uel principum, oblacione fidelium, seu aliis iustis modis, prestante domino, poterit adipisci, firma uobis vestrisque successoribus, et illibata permaneant. In quibus hec propriis duximus exprimenda uocabulis: Locum ipsum in quo prefatum monasterium a dilecto filio nobili uiro Dauid Comite, fratre Karissimi in Christo filij nostri W. illustris Scocie Regis, constructum est cum omnibus pertinenciis suis per suas rectas diuisas, et liberam curiam in terra uestra et firmam pacem infra diuisas ipsius uille de Lundors, sicut carta predicti Comitis protestatur : Ecclesiam quoque eiusdem uille de Lundors cum omnibus pertinenciis suis, scilicet, capellas de Dundemor, et terram ad predictam ecclesiam pertinentem per suas rectas diuisas, et alias terras in eadem uilla, sicut in carta eiusdem Comitis continetur : Insulam que uocatur Redinche, et piscarias in they iuxta prenominatam insulam : Molendinum de Lundors cum omni secta sua et multura : Ecclesiam quoque de Dunde cum omnibus pertinenciis suis, et terram ad eandem ecclesiam pertinentem, et vnum toftum in burgo de Dunde liberum et quietum ab omni seruicio et exaccione, et vuam karucatam terre in uilla de Newtile, et in uilla de Perth terram que 'uocatur Insula : Ultra Moneth, fintreth per suas rectas diuisas, cum omnibus pertinenciis suis, ecclesiam eiusdem uille, cum omnibus pertinenciis suis : In Garuiach,

... Progedn̄ dilectis filiis Gu... ...
nasty scē marie de luuedoƀ· eiusƀ frib; tam psentibƺ
regularem uictū pfessis In ꝑpetuum· Religiosam uitam
gentibƺ apłicum conuenit ... psidari ne ferte cuilibᷓ testimt...
itur sꝰ aut eos a ꝓposito reuocet aut id ƀꝺ qꝺ ab stō facere relīgīs
msꝰ ... Eapꝑ ōdilm dꝺs filii uꝰo uotis postulacōibꝵ clemē̄
annuim̄ e pfatū moastium scē marie de ... ... Tꝙ diuino estis
obsequio mancipati sub bꝰ ꝓt ē mꝺa ꝓtectōe sustipim̄· eꝑsentis
sčpti priulegio cōmunim̄? In ꝓmis siqdē statuentes ut ordo mo-
nasticꝰ quī secꝺm deū e beati biꝺti regulā in eadem monꝰ ... ꝑstī
tucꝰ ꝑꝺ dm̄oscit ꝑpetuis ibiꝺm temꝑibƺ inuiolabilitr obsuetur
... guastiꝵ posse ... ... q ... ... bonꝰ ... monꝺ ... in psentī
... ... canonīe posse ... ... aut ut ... futurū ... cōcessione ꝓtinū?
... ... largictōe regum uel ꝓncipū oblacōe fidelium seu alus iustis
modis ꝓstante dno poterit adipisci· Fina uobis uł isꝙ suꝺ sectꝰ
allibata ... ... ꝑ hec ꝓpis duxim expmēda uocłƀ·
locum iꝑm in quo ꝓfatū moastium a dilecto filio Nobilibꝰ ꝺo
comite ste Kꝰini in ꝺo filii nr̄i W· ... Scōe ꝺcie ... cōstat
ꝫ tū ... ꝑnacio suo ꝑ sua ... terciꝰ diuisas· ꝫ filiꝺm ... ...
ꝫ ꝺula· ꝫ finam partem iꝰfra diuisas ipsiꝰ uille de luuedꝺ ꝫ ...
... ꝑ comitis ꝑstatur· Eccłiam quoqƺ eiusꝺe uille de luuꝺ
... cū omniƺ ꝑti ... scilicet capellas de Gundemiꝰ ꝫ ꝺc
ad ꝓdcam ecłiam ꝑtinente ꝑ ... ꝺerīs diuersis· ꝫ aliaꝵ eiusꝺe
eadem uilla sꝺcut uꝵ carta eiusdem comitis continet· Iꝺ eꝺ langꝰ
uocat ... ... ꝫ ꝺei iuxta ꝓnotatam n... ꝺlata·

rectas diuisas : Ecclesiam de Rothketh cum capellis suis
scilicet Inuerurin et munkegin, et aliis pertinenciis suis:
Ecclesiam de Durnach, ecclesiam de prame, ecclesiam de Rathmuriel, ecclesiam de Inchemabanin, ecclesiam de Culsamuel:
In episcopatu lincolniensi ecclesiam de Cunigtone, ecclesiam de
Wissindene : In episcopatu de Stratheren, ecclesiam de Mothel ·
ecclesiam de Kelalcmund, cum capellis predictarum ecclesiarum
et terris et decimis, ac omnibus earum pertinenciis ad proprios
usus monachorum concessis, et vnum plenarium toftum in burgo
de Inuerurin, liberum et quietum ab omni seruicio et exaccione :
Decimas omnes quas habetis in terra predicti Comitis et
extra : Ex donacione quoque Regis Scocie, vnum plenarium
toftum in burgo de Berewic, et aliud plenarium toftum in
burgo de Striuelin, plenarium toftum in burgo de Karel,
plenarium toftum in burgo de Perth, plenarium toftum in
burgo de forfare, plenarium toftum in burgo de Munros, et
vnum plenarium toftum in burgo de Aberden, et terram unam
in uilla de Perth, in libero burgagio. Sane noualium vestrorum, que propriis manibus et sumptibus colitis, siue de
nutrimentis animalium vestrorum, nullus a uobis decimas
exigere uel extorquere presumat. Liceat quoque vobis clericos
uel laicos liberos et absolutos e | seculo fugientes, ad conver-   [ʃɩ
sionem recipere, et eos absque contradiccione aliqua retinere.
Prohibemus insuper ut nulli fratrum uestrorum post factam
in eodem loco professionem fas sit absque abbatis sui licencia
de eodem loco, nisi arcioris religionis obtentu, discedere. Discedentem uero absque communi litterarum caucione nullus
audeat retinere. Cum autem generale interdictum terre fuerit,
liceat uobis clausis ianuis, exclusis excommunicatis et interdictis, non pulsatis campanis, suppressa uoce diuina officia celebrare. Crisma, uero, oleum sanctum, consecraciones altarium
seu Basilicarum, ordinaciones Monachorum seu clericorum

ut infra fines parochie vestre nullus sine assensu diocesani episcopi et vestro Capellam seu oratorium de nouo construere audeat, saluis priuilegiis romanorum pontificum.   Ad hec eciam inhibemus ne quis in uos uel monasterium vestrum excommunicacionis, suspensionis, uel interdicti sentenciam absque manifesta et racionabili causa promulgare presumat.   Obeunte uero te nunc eiusdem loci abbate uel tuorum quolibet successorum, nullus ibi qualibet surrepcionis astucia seu uiolencia preponatur, nisi quem fratres communi consensu uel fratrum maior pars consilij sanioris secundum dei timorem et beati benedicti regulam prouiderint eligendum.   Decernimus ergo ut nullis omnino hominum liceat prefatum monasterium temere perturbare, aut eius possessiones auferre uel ablatas retinere, minuere, seu quibuscunque uexacionibus fatigare, set omnia integra conseruentur eorum pro quorum gubernacione ac sustentacione concessa sunt usibus omnimodis profutura, salua sedis apostolice auctoritate, et diocesani episcopi canonica iusticia.   Si qua igitur in futurum ecclesiastica secularisue persona hanc nostre constitucionis paginam sciens contra eam temere uenire temptauerit secundo tercioue commonita, nisi reatum suum congrua satisfaccione correxerit, potestatis honorisque sui dignitate careat, reamque se diuino iudicio existere de perpetrata iniquitate cognoscat et a sacratissimo corpore ac sanguine dei et domini Redemptoris nostri ihesu Christi aliena fiat, atque in extremo examine districte ulcioni subiaciat.   Cunctis autem eidem loco sua iura seruantibus sit pax domini nostri ihesu Christi, quatinus et hic fructum bone accionis percipiant, et apud districtum iudicem premia eterne pacis inueniant, Amen.

rip-
dina-
   ❡ Ego Innocencius Catholice ecclesie episcopus subscribo.
Ego ottavianus hostiensis et velletrensis Episcopus subscribo.
   ❡ Ego Petrus portuensis et sancte rufine episcopus subscribo.

et tuscan. episcopus subscribo.   Ego Guido sancte marie transtiberim, tt. calixti presbyter cardinalis subscribo.   ⁋ Ego hugo presbyter cardinalis sancti martini tt. equicij subscribo. Ego sosfredus tt. sancte praxedis presbyter cardinalis subscribo.

⁋ Ego Johannes tt. sancte prisce presbyter cardinalis subscribo.   Ego Gracianus sanctorum Cosme et Damiani diaconus cardinalis subscribo.   ⁋ Ego Gregorius sancte marie in aquiro diaconus cardinalis subscribo.   Ego Gregorius sancti georgij ad velum aureum Diaconus Cardinalis subscribo.   ⁋ Ego Nicholàus sancte marie Incosmidyn Diaconus Cardinalis subscribo.   Ego Bobo sancti theodorij Diaconus Cardinalis subscribo.   Dat. Lateran. per manum Raynaldi, domini pape Notarij, Cancellarij vicem agentis : xiij. kl. aprilis ; Indiccione prima ; Incarnacionis dominice anno M.C.XC.VIII, Pontificatus vero Domini Innocencii pape tercii anno secundo.

(Abstract)

'THE GREAT PRIVILEGE of INNOCENT III.'[1]

INNOCENT, bishop, servant of the servants of God, etc., to Guido, Abbot of the monastery of St. Mary of Lundors, and the brethren, etc.   The Pope takes the monastery 'under the protection of Blessed Peter and of us.'   He first decrees that the Benedictine rule should be inviolably observed [in the language of XCIII.].   The possessions of the monastery are to remain inviolate [in the language of XCIII.].   After specifying Lundors and its church, we find the addition of 'the chapels of Dundemor,' as pertinents of the church of Lundors.   Further additions are a ploughgate of land in the vill of Newtile, and in Perth the land which is called Inch (insula).   The property beyond the Mounth and in Garviach remain as specified in XCIII.   The church of Wissendene is added to the church of Cunigtone, both in the diocese of Lincoln.   'In the bishopric of Strathern, the church of Mothel ; and the church of Kelalcmund, with the chapels of the aforesaid churches.'   To the donations of King William, as given in XCIII., is added 'one land in the town of Perth, in free burgage.'   Other variations of language from XCIII. are as follows : 'We prohibit any one daring to erect a chapel or oratory within the bounds of your parish without the assent of the bishop of the diocese and your assent ; saving the privileges of the Roman Pontiffs.'

Chrism, holy oil, consecrations of churches, and ordinations of monks and clerks to holy orders 'we command to be supplied to you by the bishop of the diocese without any pravity.'   In the clause dealing with the erection of churches or oratories within the bounds of their parishes the word 'hospice' (*xenodochium*) is omitted.   After the passage threatening punishment here and hereafter to those who would infringe this papal constitution, there is added : 'But may the peace of our Lord Jesus Christ be to all who preserve its rights to the same place [*i.e.* the monastery of Lundors], to the end that here they may receive the fruit of their good deed, and in the presence of the strict Judge may find the reward of peace.   Amen.'

I, Innocent, Bishop of the Catholic Church, subscribe.   I, Octavian, Bishop of Ostia and Velletri, subscribe.

I, Peter, Bishop of Porto and St. Rufina, subscribe.   I, Pandulf, cardinal priest of the basilica of the Twelve Apostles, subscribe.

I, Peter, cardinal priest of the title of St. Cecilia, subscribe.   I, Jordan, cardinal priest of St. Pudentiana, of the title of Pastor, subscribe.

I, John, cardinal, of the title of St. Clement, Bishop of Viterbo and Tuscana [Toscanella], subscribe.   I, Guido, of St. Maria Transtyberim, of the title of Calixtus, cardinal priest, subscribe.

I, Hugo, cardinal priest of St. Martin, of the title of Equitius, subscribe.   I, Sosfred, of the title of St. Praxedis, cardinal priest, subscribe.

I, John, of the title of St. Prisca, cardinal priest, subscribe.   I, Gracian, of SS. Cosmas and Damian, cardinal deacon, subscribe.

I, Gregory, of St. Maria in aquiro, cardinal deacon, subscribe.   I, Gregory, of St. George ad Velum Aureum, cardinal deacon, subscribe.

I, Nicholas, of St. Maria in Cosmedin, cardinal deacon, subscribe.   I, Bobó, of St. Theodorius, cardinal deacon, subscribe.

Given at the Lateran, by the hand of Raynald, notary of our Lord the Pope, acting for the Chancellor ; xiij. Kalends of April [March 20] first indiction ; in the year of our Lord's Incarnation ᴊcxcviii., the second year of the pontificate of our Lord, Pope Innocent iii. [1]

XCV

De Bonis in Strathern Innocencius tercius.

INNOCENCIVS episcopus, seruus seruorum dei, Dilectis filiis abbati et conuentui monasterij de Lundors, Salutem et apostolicam benediccionem.   Cum a nobis petitur quod iustum est et

ut id per sollicitudinem officij nostri ad debitum perducatur effectum. Ea propter, Dilecti in domino filij, uestris iustis postulacionibus grato concurrentes assensu personas vestras[a] et monasterium in quo diuino estis obsequio mancipati, cum omnibus bonis que in presenciarum racionabiliter possidetis, aut in futurum iustis modis, prestante domino, poteritis adipisci, sub petri beati et nostra proteccione suscipimus, specialiter autem uillam et ecclesiam de Eglesmagrille cum decimis de cletheueys, quas venerabilis frater noster Abraham episcopus ac dilecti filij capitulum Dumblanense uestro monasterio concesserunt; Et ecclesiam cum pertinenciis suis, terras de Ratengoden, Neutile, hameldune, et mernes, cum piscaria in Sabulo, et pertinenciis earundem; Farinam quoque Braseum, caseos et porcos annuos, que M. quondam frater Nobilis uiri G. Comitis de Strathern pia uobis liberalitate concessit, sicut ea omnia iuste ac pacifice possidetis, uobis et per uos dicto monasterio vestro auctoritate apostolica confirmamus, et presentis scripti patrocinio communimus. Nulli ergo omnino hominum liceat hanc paginam nostre proteccionis et confirmacionis infringere uel ei ausu temerario contraire. Si quis autem hoc attemptare presumpserit, indignacionem omnipotentis dei et beatorum petri et pauli apostolorum eius se nouerit incursurum. Datum Lateran. x Kalend. februarij, Pontificatus nostri anno septimo decimo.

[a] MS. *vestras.*

(*Abstract*)

INNOCENT III., of possessions in STRATHERN.

INNOCENT, to the abbot and convent of the monastery of Lundors. Assenting to their just requests, he takes 'under the protection of Blessed Peter and of us' the persons of the abbot and monks, and the monastery in which they were bound to the service of God, and all their possessions, as well those now reasonably held by them as those which in future they might with God's assistance be able to obtain by

by year, which M., late brother of the noble man, G., Earl of Strathern, granted to you with pious liberality.   As all these things are now justly and peaceably possessed by you, we by apostolic authority confirm to you, and, through you, to your monastery aforesaid, and make secure by the protection of the present writ.   It is not lawful for any man to infringe, etc.   But if any one shall presume, etc.   'Given at the Lateran, on x Kal. February [Jan. 23], in the seventeenth year of our pontificate.'[1]

XCVI

Confirmacio composicionis super ecclesiis de Garuiach.

HONORIVS episcopus, seruus seruorum dei, Dilectis filiis Abbati et conuentui monasterij de Lundors, salutem et apostolicam benediccionem.   Ea que iudicio uel concordia statuuntur, firma debent et illibata consistere, et ne in recidiue contencionis scrupulum relabantur, apostolico conuenit presidio communiri. Ea propter, Dilecti in domini filij, uestris iustis postulacionibus grato concurrentes assensu composicionem que inter uos, ex parte una, et uenerabilem fratrem nostrum episcopum Sancti Andree ex altera, super quarundem terrarum redditibus in loco qui Garuihac dicitur positarum, mediantibus . . abbate de Aberbrothoc et magistro Laurencio Sancti Andree, et W. Laudonie, archidiaconis, amicabiliter interuenit, sicut rite sine prauitate prouide facta est, et ab utraque parte recepta et hactenus pacifice obseruata, et in litteris inde confectis plenius continetur, auctoritate apostolica confirmamus, et presentis scripti patrocinio communimus.   Nulli ergo omnino hominum liceat hanc paginam nostre confirmacionis infringere, uel ei ausu temerario contraire.   Si quis autem hoc attemptare presumpserit, indignacionem omnipotentis dei et Beatorum Petri et Pauli apostolorum eius se nouerit incursurum.   Datum Lateran. xij Kal. Marcij, Pontificatus nostri anno xj°.

(Abstract)

CONFIRMATION of an AGREEMENT as to the CHURCHES of GARVIACH.

St. Andrews, of the other part, as to the revenues of certain lands 'situated in the place which is called Garviach,' an agreement arrived at through the friendly intervention of . . . Abbot of Aberbrothoc, Master Laurence, Archdeacon of St. Andrews, and W., Archdeacon of Lothian, as it was duly made 'without pravity,' and was received and observed up to the present by both parties. 'It shall not be lawful for any man,' etc. 'Given at the Lateran, xii. Kalends of March [Feb. 18], in the eleventh year of our pontificate.' [1]

XCVII

De composicione terrarum ecclesiarum de Garuiach.

GREGORIVS episcopus, seruus seruorum dei, Dilectis filiis abbati et conuentui Monasterij de Lundors, salutem et apostolicam Benediccionem. Justis petencium desideriis dignum est nos facilem prebere consensum, et uota que a racionis tramite non discordant effectu prosequente complere. Ea propter, Dilecti in Domino filij, nostris iustis | postulacionibus grato concurrentes assensu, composicionem que inter uos ex parte vna et venerabilem fratrem nostrum Episcopum Sancti Andree ex altera, super redditibus quarundem terrarum in loco qui Garuiach dicitur positarum, mediantibus abbate de Aberbrothoc, et magistro Laurencio Sancti Andree et Willelmo Laudonie, archidiaconis, amicabiliter interuenit, sicut sine prauitate provide facta est, et sponte ab utraque parte recepta, et in litteris inde confectis plenius continetur, auctoritate apostolica confirmamus, et presentis scripti patrocinio communimus. Nulli ergo omnino hominum liceat hanc paginam nostre confirmacionis infringere, uel ei ausu temerario contraire. Si quis autem hoc attemptare presumpserit, indignacionem omnipotentis dei et Beatorum Petri et Pauli apostolorum eius se nouerit incursurum. Datum Lateran. vij Kalend. Junii, Pontificatus nostri anno Primo.

[fo

(Abstract)

OF the AGREEMENT as to the CHURCHLANDS of GARVIACH.

XCVIII

De ecclesia de Dunde et aliis bonis.

GREGORIVS episcopus, seruus seruorum dei, Dilectis abbati et conuentui monasterij de Lundors ordinis sancti Benedicti, sancti andree diocesis, Salutem et apostolicam Benediccionem. Justis petencium desideriis Dignum est nos facilem prebere consensum, et uota que a racionis tramite non discordant effectu prosequente complere. Ea propter, Dilecti in domino filij, uestris iustis postulacionibus grato concurrentes assensu, personas uestras et monasterium de Lundors in quo diuino uacatis obsequio, cum omnibus bonis que in presenciarum racionabiliter possidet, aut in futurum iustis modis, prestante domino, poterit adipisci, sub Beati Petri et nostra proteccione suscipimus ; Specialiter, autem, ecclesiam de Dunde, quam venerabilis frater noster Episcopus Brechinensis, spectantem ad eum, capituli sui accedente consensu, dicto monasterio pia et prouida liberalitate donauit, prout in ipsorum litteris confectis exinde dicitur contineri, necnon libertates et immunitates secularium exaccionum a Regibus, Comitibus, et Baronibus Scocie, aliisque Christi fidelibus pia uobis liberalitate concessas ; Terras quoque possessiones et alia bona uestra sicut ea omnia iuste ac pacifice obtinetis, Vobis et eidem monasterio per uos auctoritate apostolica confirmamus, et presentis scripti patrocinio communimus. Prouiso ut de predicte ecclesie prouentibus sacerdoti perpetuo in ea domino seruituro congrua porcio assignetur, ex qua comode sustentari ualeat, ac episcopalia et alia onera ecclesie supportare. Nulli ergo hominum omnino liceat hanc paginam nostre proteccionis et confirmacionis infringere uel ei ausu temerario contraire. Si quis autem hoc attemptare presumpserit, indignacionem omnipotentis dei et Beatorum Petri et Pauli [apostolorum] eius se nouerit incursurum. Datum Lateran. xvj° Kalendas Marcij, Pontificatus nostri anno Duodecimo.

(*Abstract*)

protection of St. Peter and himself: and specially the church of Dundee, which the Bishop of Brechin, with the consent of his chapter, granted to the monastery of Lundors, as is said to be contained in letters drawn up thereupon. Likewise, the Pope confirms to them the liberties and immunities from secular exactions, which, with pious liberality, had been granted by the kings, earls, and barons of Scotland, and by others of the faithful of Christ. Provided that out of the revenues of the aforesaid church of Dundee a fitting portion should be assigned to a priest who would continue to serve the Lord in it. Out of which portion he might be conveniently maintained, and be able to support the burden of bishop's dues (*episcopalia*) and other burdens of the church. 'It is not lawful to any man to infringe, etc. But if any shall presume, etc. Given at the Lateran, xvi. Kalends of March [Feb. 14], in the twelfth year of our pontificate.' 1]

XCIX

Super ecclesia de Dunde de mutacione Keledeorum.

INNOCENCIVS episcopus, seruus seruorum dei, Dilectis filiis abbati et conuentui Monasterij de Lundors, ordinis sancti Benedicti, Sancti Andree diocesis, Salutem et apostolicam Benediccionem. Officij nostri sollicitudo requirit ut uiros religiosos qui, relictis seculi uanitatibus, se diuinis obsequiis deuouerunt, quantum cum deo possimus, in omnibus foueamus. Cum igitur, sicut ex parte uestra fuit propositum coram nobis quondam Dauid comite huntindone, monasterij uestri fundatore, ius patronatus quod habebat in ecclesia de Dunde, Brechinensis diocesis, vobis et per uos monasterio uestro liberaliter conferente, loci diocesanus, capituli sui accedente consensu, eandem ecclesiam in proprios usus uestros duxerit concedendam, et quod per eundem episcopum taliter factum extitit in hac parte per apostolicam sedem fuerit postmodum confirmatum, deuocionis | uestre supplicacionibus inclinati, presencium vobis auctoritate [*fo* concedimus, ut ex eo quod fratres, qui consueuerunt esse in ecclesia Brechinensi, Keledei uocati fuerunt, nunc, mutato

uel ei ausu temerario contraire. Si quis, autem, hoc attemp-
tare presumpserit, indignacionem omnipotentis dei et Beatorum
Petri et Pauli apostolorum eius se nouerit incursurum. Datum
Lugdun. xij Kalend. Marcij, Pontificatus nostri anno septimo.

(*Abstract*)

' ON the CHURCH of DUNDEE, concerning the changing of the KELEDEI.'

INNOCENT [IV.], bishop, servant of the servants, etc., to the abbot
and convent, etc. Since, as was stated before us on your behalf, the
late David, Earl of Huntingdon, founder of your monastery, liberally
conferred on you, and, through you, on your monastery, the right of
patronage which he had in the church of Dundee, in the diocese of
Brechin, and the diocesan of the place, with the consent of his chapter,
considered that the same church should be granted to you for your own
uses (*in proprios usus*), and what was done by the same bishop in this respect
was presently confirmed by the Apostolic See, we, inclined by your devout
supplications, grant by the authority of these presents that no prejudice
shall be created to you and your monastery in respect to the aforesaid
from the fact that the brethren who have been accustomed to be in the
church of Brechin were called Keledei and now by change of name are
styled canons. This notwithstanding, what has been duly done in regard
to the aforesaid shall remain firm and established for ever. It is not
lawful for any man to infringe, etc. But if any one presume, etc.
Given at Lyons, xij. Kalends of March [Feb. 18], in the seventh year of
our pontificate. [1]

C

Super ecclesia de Dunde de mutacione Keledeorum.

INNOCENCIVS episcopus, seruus seruorum dei, Dilectis filiis
abbati de Dunfermelyn, et Priori de May sancti andree diocesis
Salutem et apostolicam Benediccionem. Officij nostri sollicitudo
requirit ut uiros religiosos qui relictis seculi uanitatibus se
diuinis obsequiis deuouerunt, quantum cum deo possuimus, in
omnibus foueamus. Cum igitur sieut ex parte dilectorum
filiorum abbatis et conuentus monasterij de Lundors ordinis
sancti Benedicti, Sancti Andree diocesis, fuit propositum coram

liter conferente, loci diocesanus, capituli sui accedente consensu, eandem ecclesiam in proprios eorum usus duxerit concedendam, et quod per eundem episcopum taliter factum extitit in hac parte, per apostolicam fuerit sedem postmodum confirmatum, eorundem abbatis et conuentus supplicacionibus inclinati per nostras eis litteras duximus concedendum, ut ex eo quod fratres, qui consueuerunt esse in ecclesia Brechinensi, Keledei uocati fuerunt, nunc mutato uocabulo sunt canonici nuncupati, nullum super premissis sibi et monasterio memorato possit preiudicium generari, et hoc eciam non obstante quod super hiis rite factum est, firmum et stabile in perpetuum perseu[er]et. Ideoque discrecioni uestre per apostolica scripta mandamus quatinus prefatos abbatem et conuentum non permittatis contra concessionis nostre tenorem super hiis ab aliquibus indebite molestari, molestatores huiusmodi per censuram ecclesiasticam, apellacione postposita, compescendo. Quod si non ambo hiis exequendis potueritis interesse, alter uestrum ea nichillominus exequatur. Datum Lugdun. xij kalend. Maij, Pontificatus nostri anno septimo.

(*Abstract*)

'On the CHURCH of DUNDEE, concerning the changing of the KELEDEI.'

INNOCENT [IV.], bishop, servant of the servants of God, to our beloved sons, the Abbot of Dunfermline and the Prior of the May of the diocese of St. Andrews, etc. [The facts are recited in the language of XCIX. down to the words 'firm and established for ever.'] 'Wherefore we enjoin on your discretion by apostolic writ that ye do not permit the aforesaid abbot and convent to be troubled without just cause, contrary to the tenor of our concession in this respect, by restraining those who give such trouble by means of the censure of the Church, appeal being postponed. Which if both of you cannot engage in executing, let the other, nevertheless, execute the same. Given at Lyons, xii. Kalends of May [April 20], in the seventh year of our pontificate.' [1]

CI

Confirmacio generalis Innocencij quarti.

ouem.   Sacrosancta romana ecclesia deuotos et humiles filios
ex assuete pietatis officio propensius diligere consueuit, et, ne
prauorum hominum molestiis agitantur, eos tanquam pia mater
sua proteccionis munimine confouere.   Ea propter, Dilecti in
domino filij, uestris iustis postulacionibus grato concurrentes
assensu, personas uestras et locum in quo diuino estis obsequio
mancipati cum omnibus Bonis que in presenciarum racionabiliter possidet aut in futurum, iustis modis, prestante domino,
poterit adipisci, sub Beati Petri et nostra proteccione suscipimus.   Specialiter autem, terras, possessiones, redditus et alia
bona uestra, sicut ea omnia iuste ac pacifice possidetis, uobis
et per uos monasterio vestro auctoritate apostolica confirmamus, et presentis scripti patrocinio communimus.   Nulli ergo
omnino hominum liceat hanc paginam nostre proteccionis et
confirmacionis infringere, uel ei ausu temerario contraire.   Si
72.] quis | autem hoc attemptare presumpserit indignacionem omni-
potentis dei et Beatorum Petri et Pauli apostolorum eius se
nouerit incursurum.   Datum Lugdun. ij Nonas Decembris,
Pontificatus nostri anno Sexto.

(Abstract)

'GENERAL CONFIRMATION of INNOCENT IV.'

INNOCENT [IV.], bishop, etc., to the abbot and convent of the monastery
of Lundors.   The Pope, concurring in their just requests, takes under
the protection of Blessed Peter and himself the persons of the monks,
and the place in which they are bound to the service of God, with all
their possessions, etc.   He confirms these possessions and protects them
by the present writ.   It is not lawful, etc.   But if any, etc.   'Given at
Lyons, ii. Nones of December [Dec. 4], in the sixth year of our pontificate.' [1]

CII
De Pensione de Wissindene.

INNOCENCIVS Episcopus, seruus seruorum dei, Dilectis filiis

catum ut cum uos annuam pensionem Decem marcarum per venerabilem fratrem nostrum episcopum Lincolniensem in ecclesia de Wissindene, Lincolniensis diocesis, in qua ius patronatus uos habere proponitis uobis concessam prout in ipsius episcopi litteris dicitur plenius contineri, Dilecto filio magistro Rolandino, Capellano nostro, rectori eiusdem ecclesie pro reuerencia nostra duxeritis personaliter remittendam, prouidere ne per huiusmodi remissionem uobis et monasterio uestro in posterum generetur preiudicium paterna sollicitudine curaremus. Nos igitur vestris supplicacionibus inclinati quod per predictam remissionem nullum uobis uel monasterio uestro super pensione prefata, cedente uel decedente memorato capellano, preiudicium generetur, Deuocioni uestre auctoritate presencium indulgemus. Nulli ergo omnino liceat hanc paginam nostre concessionis infringere uel ei ausu temerario contraire. Si quis, autem, hoc attemptare presumpserit, indignacionem omnipotentis dei et Beatorum Petri et Pauli apostolorum eius se nouerit incursurum. Datum Lugdun. viij Idus Decembris, Pontificatus nostri anno Sexto.

(Abstract)
' OF a PENSION from WISSINDENE.'

INNOCENT [IV.], bishop, servant, etc., to the abbot and convent of the monastery of Lundors, etc. A humble supplication had been made by the monastery to the Pope that with fatherly care he would provide that no prejudice to the rights of the monastery should be created through the fact that out of reverence to the Pope they had thought fit to remit to Master Rolandin, the Pope's chaplain, then rector of the church of Wissindene, in the diocese of Lincoln, a pension of ten marks out of the church of Wissindene, which pension had been granted to them by the Bishop of Lincoln, as was more fully contained in the bishop's letters; the right of patronage in the church of Wissindene being, as was stated by the monks, in their hands. The Pope, yielding to their supplications, grants that by reason of the aforesaid remission of the ten marks to Rolandin no prejudice should be created to the monastery, on his resignation or death. It shall not be lawful to any man, etc. But if

CIII

Contra inuasores et detentores bonorum.

Innocencivs Episcopus, seruus seruorum dei, Dilectis filiis abbati et conuentui monasterij de Lundors ordinis Sancti Benedicti, Sancti Andree diocesis, salutem et apostolicam Benediccionem. Ex parte uestra fuit propositum coram nobis, quod non [n]ulli clerici et laici asserentes contra uos aliquid questionis habere, aliquando monachos, interdum conuersos, et nonnumquam animalia et alia bona monasterij uestri, pretextu cuiusdam praue consuetudinis, temeritate propria uadiare, inuadere, et tam diu detinere presumunt donec sit eis de huiusmodi questionibus iuxta ipsorum Beneplacitum satisfactum, quamquam in uos iurisdiccionem non habeant qua hoc possint, ordinariam seu ceiam delegatam. Cum igitur iudicialis ordo ideo sit constitutus in medio ut nemo sibi audeat presumere ulcionem, et ob hoc id, tanquam nullo iure subnixum, non sit aliquatenus tollerandum, Nos uolentes quieti uestre consulere ac predic torum maliciis obuiare, auctoritate presencium districcius inhibemus, ne quis occasione predicte consuetudinis uobis memoratas inferre molestias ac bona predicti monasterij absque iure[a] occupare, uadiare, inuadere, seu quolibet modo detinere presumat. Nulli ergo omnino hominum liceat hanc paginam nostre inhibicionis infringere, uel ei ausu temerario contraire. Si quis autem hoc attemptare presumpserit, indignacionem omnipotentis dei et Beatorum Petri et Pauli apostolorum eius se noverit incursurum. Datum Lugdun. v. Kalendas Maij, Pontificatus nostri anno septimo.

ris.

(Abstract)

'Against those who invade and detain Property [of the Monastery]'

Innocent [iv.], bishop, servant, etc., to the abbot and convent of the monastery of Lundors, etc. On your part it was alleged in our presence that some clerks and laymen, professing to have some question against

to be tolerated ; for the office of judge is exercised in a public tribunal, so that no man may venture to presume to avenge himself. The Pope, desirous to consult for the peace of the monastery, and to prevent the evil practices of the aforesaid persons, strictly forbids any one on the plea of the aforesaid custom to molest the monastery, or to seize, take in pledge, or detain in any way the goods of the monastery. It shall not be lawful, etc. But if any one shall presume, etc. Given at Lyons, v. Kalends of May [April 27], in the seventh year of our pontificate.[1]

CIV

Conseruatorium de Londors.

INNOCENCIVS episcopus, seruus seruorum dei, Dilectis filiis abbati de Dunfermelyn et priori de May, Sancti Andree diocesis, Salutem et apostolicam Benediccionem. Ex parte dilectorum filiorum abbatis et conuentus monasterij de Lundors, ordinis Sancti Benedicti, Sancti Andree diocesis, fuit propositum coram nobis quod non [n]ulli clerici et laici asserentes contra eos aliquid questionis habere, aliquando monachos, interdum conuersos, et non nuncquam animalia et alia Bona dicti monasterij pretextu cuiusdam praue consuetudinis | temeritate propria uadiare,   [fo inuadere et tam diu detinere presumat donec sit eis de huius- modi questionibus iuxta ipsorum beneplacitum satisfactum ; quamquam in eos non habeant qua hoc possint iurisdiccionem ordinariam uel eciam delegatam. Cum itaque iudicialis ordo ideo sit constitutus in medio ut nemo sibi audeat presumere ulcionem, et ob hoc id, tanquam nullo iure subnixum, non sit aliquatenus tollerandum, Nos uolentes quieti ipsorum consulere, ac predictorum maliciis obuiare, auctoritate apostolica duximus districcius inhibendum, ne quis occasione predicte consuetu- dinis eis memoratas inferre molestias, ac bona predicti monas-

(Abstract)

' WRIT of PROTECTION (*conservatorium*) of LUNDORS.'

INNOCENT [IV.], bishop, servant, etc., to the Abbot of Dunfermline and the Prior of May, in the diocese of St. Andrews, etc.   The account of the seizure and holding in pledge of monks, converts, animals, and other goods of the monastery is recited as in CIII.   After which follows: ' Wherefore we commit to your discretion by apostolic writ that ye do not permit them to be improperly molested by any contrary to the tenor of our inhibition, restraining offenders of this kind by the censure of the Church, appeal being postponed.   Given at Lyons, v. Kal. of May [April 27], in the seventh year of our pontificate.[1]

CV

De episcopis Abirdonensis ecclesie qui molestauerunt locum nostrum.

INNOCENCIVS episcopus, seruus seruorum dei, Dilectis filiis, Cancellario Morauiensi, Thesaurario, et magistro Johanni de Euerley Canonico Dunkeldensi, Salutem et apostolicam Benediccionem.   Presentata nobis Dilectorum filiorum de Kelchou, de Aberbrodoch, et de Lundors, abbatum, sancti andree diocesis, sancti Benedicti, ac prioris cathedralis ecclesie sancti Andree sancti Augustini ordinum, conuentuumque suorum peticio, continebat quod cum bone memorie aberdonenses Episcopi, capituli sui accedente consensu, quasdam ecclesias aberdonensis diocesis in quibus abbates, prior, et conuentus iidem ius obtinent patronatus, in proprios usus eorum sibi duxerint concedendas, et quod per eosdem episcopos taliter factum extitit in hac parte per apostolicam sedem fuerit postmodum confirmatum ; Venerabilis frater noster Aberdonensis Episcopus, episcoporum illorum successor, vicariis ecclesiarum ipsarum sub pena suspensionis pro sua inhibuit uoluntate ne ultra pensiones antiquas de dictis ecclesiis aliquid de cetero soluerent abbati-

set in proprios usus canonice deputatas, inhibicionem episcopi prelibati, auctoritate nostra, reuocare curetis. Nec ullatenus permittatis abbates, priorem, et conuentus eosdem super hiis ulterius ab aliquibus indebite molestari; Molestatores huiusmodi per censuram ecclesiasticam, sublato appellacionis obsta culo, compescendo : Non obstantibus aliquibus litteris ueritati et iusticie prejudicantibus, per quas execucio mandati presentis impediri ualeat uel differri, et de quibus specialem oporteat in presentibus fieri mencionem. Quod si non omnes hiis exequendis potueritis interesse, duo vestrum ea nichilominus exequantur. Datum Lugdun. xij. Kalendas Maij, Pontificatus nostri anno Septimo.

(*Abstract*)

' Of Bishops of the Church of Aberdeen who have molested our place.'

Innocent [iv.], bishop, servant, etc., to the Chancellor of Moray, the Treasurer, and Master John of Everley, Canon of Dunkeld, etc. A petition presented to the Pope by the abbots of Kelchou, Aberbrothoc, and Lundors, in the diocese of St. Andrews, of the order of St. Benedict, and the prior of the cathedral church of St. Andrews, of the order of St. Augustine, and their convents, contained that Bishops of Aberdeen, of good memory, with the consent of their chapters, had thought fit to grant to them for their own uses (*in proprios usus*) certain churches in the diocese of Aberdeen, in which their abbots, the prior, and convents have the right of patronage ; and what was done in this respect by the bishops was presently confirmed by the Apostolic See. Further, the petition went on to state that the Bishop of Aberdeen, successor of those bishops, had of his own will inhibited, under pain of suspension, the vicars of those churches from paying anything in future to the abbots, prior, and convents aforesaid, beyond the old pensions from those churches. Wherefore it is committed to the Chancellor of Moray, the Treasurer, and John of Everley, canon of Dunkeld, that they should carefully examine the documentary evidence (*instrumentis*) on the matter ; and if they found that the said churches were not pensionary [that is, liable for payment of a fixed pension], but had been made over to the abbots, prior, and convents for their own uses, they were to revoke, by the Pope's authority, the inhibition of the Bishop of Aberdeen. They were further to prevent the abbots, prior, and convents being molested, by restraining those who molest them by the censure of the Church, appeal being disallowed (*sublato appellationis obstaculo*), and this, notwithstanding any letters prejudicial to truth and justice by which the execu-

of you cannot take part in the execution of these things, nevertheless let two of you execute them.   Given at Lyons, xij. of the Kalends of May [April 20], in the seventh year of our pontificate.[1]

CVI

Item de eisdem episcopis Abirdonensibus.

INNOCENCIVS episcopus, seruus seruorum dei, Dilectis filiis Cancellario Morauiensi, Thesaurario, et magistro Johanni de Euerley, canonico Dunkeldensi, salutem et apostolicam Benediccionem.   Presentata nobis Dilectorum filiorum de Kelchou, de Aberbrodoch, et de Lundors, Abbatum, Sancti Andree diocesis, Sancti Benedicti, ac prioris cathedralis ecclesie Sancti Andree, Sancti Augustini ordinum, Conuentuumque suorum peticio continebat quod cum bone memorie Aberdonenses Episcopi, Capituli sui acce|dente consensu, quasdam ecclesias Aberdonensis diocesis in quibus Abbates, prior, et conuentus iidem ius obtinent patronatus in proprios usus eorum sibi duxerint concedendas, et quod per eosdem episcopos taliter factum extitit in hac parte per apostolicam sedem fuerit postmodum confirmatum, Venerabilis frater noster Aberdonensis Episcopus, episcoporum illorum successor, pro sua nobis suggerens uoluntate, quod nonnulli abbates, priores, aliique prelati, tam religiosi quam eciam seculares, in ciuitate Aberdonensi et Diocesi constituti vicariis quarundam ecclesiarum quas in proprios usus tenent imponentes nouas contra Lateranensis statuta concilij pensiones, terras et alias possessiones, ad uicarias spectantes easdem, ipsis subtrahunt vicariis, eas in usus proprios conuertendo; Quidam uero prelatorum ipsorum tantum de prouentibus ecclesiarum percipiunt predictarum quod earum vicarij nequeunt de residuo comode sustentari, a nobis obtinuit [litteras] continentes ut super hiis auctoritate nostra statueret prout utilitati ecclesiarum ipsarum secundum deum expedire

idem episcopus ordinare, fines tenoris earum perperam exce-
dendo, quod prefati abbates, prior,[a] et conuentus de pro- • MS.
uentibus dictarum ecclesiarum certam annuatim reciperent *prior e*
conuen
porcionem, et omnes reliqui prouentus ipsarum assignarentur
vicariis earundem, Jam dicti abbates, prior, et conuentus se ac
ecclesias suas seu monasteria sua per ordinacionem huiusmodi
sencientes indebite aggrauari, per apellacionis remedium
nostram audienciam inuocarunt, cui dictus episcopus detulit
reuerenter sicut in eius litteris perspeximus contineri. Quo-
circa discrecioni uestre per apostolica scripta mandamus,
quatinus facultatibus ipsarum ecclesiarum diligenter solicite-
que pensatis in eis prout discrecio uestra secundum deum
uideret expedire, certas et determinatas curetis statuere ui-
carias, et de prouentibus ecclesiarum illarum porcionem ipsis
congruam assignantes, nominatos abbates, priorem, et con
uentus postea contra ordinacionem vestram super hiis nullatenus permittatis ab aliquibus indebite molestari, molestatores
huiusmodi per censuram ecclesiasticam, sublato appellacioni
obstaculo, compescendo ; Non obstantibus aliquibus litteris
ueritati et iusticie preiudicantibus, per quas execucio mandati
presentis impediri ualeat uel differri, et de quibus specialem
oporteat in presentibus fieri mencionem. Quod si non omnes
hiis exequendis potueritis interesse, duo uestrum ea nichilominus exequantur. Datum Lugdun. xij. Kalend. Maij, Pontificatus nostri anno Septimo.

(*Abstract*)

'Concerning the same Bishops of Aberdeen.'

the said churches that the vicars cannot be properly maintained out of the residue. The Bishop of Aberdeen obtained from us letters to the effect that he might by our authority make enactments on these matters, as might, in the sight of God, seem to him expedient, for the advantage of those churches, notwithstanding all concessions and confirmations whatsoever which had been obtained from the Apostolic See, restraining opponents by the censure of the Church, appeal being postponed. And since, under pretence of these letters, the limits of the tenor of which he has much exceeded, the bishop endeavours to ordain that the aforesaid abbots, prior, and convents should receive yearly a fixed portion from the revenues of the said churches, all the remaining revenues of the same being assigned to the vicars of the same, the aforesaid abbots, prior, and convents, feeling themselves and their churches, or monasteries, to be aggrieved, have appealed for remedy to our judgment, to which the aforesaid bishop reverently submitted himself, as appears from his letters. Wherefore we commit to your discretion by our apostolic writ to weigh diligently and carefully the capabilities (*facultatibus*) of these churches, as may seem expedient to your discretion in the sight of God, and then to fix and determine the values of the vicarages [*i.e.* the benefices], and to assign a fitting portion to the vicars of the same, and after that to prevent the abbots, prior, and convents suffering molestation in this matter, restraining those who would molest them by the censure of the Church, appeal being disallowed. And this, notwithstanding any letters prejudicial to truth and justice, by which the execution of this mandate could be hindered or delayed, and of which letters special mention should be made in these presents. Which, if not all of you, etc. Given at Lyons, xij. Kalends of May [April 20], in the seventh year of our pontificate.[1]

CVII

De confirmacione Ecclesie de Lundoris.

VNIVERSIS sancte matris ecclesie filiis et fidelibus, Rogerus dei gracia Episcopus Sancti Andree, perpetuam in Domino Salutem. Nouerint omnes, tam posteri quam presentes, Dominum Dauid comitem, fratrem domini Willelmi Regis Scotorum, fundasse abbaciam quandam de ordine Kelkoensi apud Lundors, pro salute Domini Willelmi Regis fratris sui, et pro salute anime sue et matildis comitisse coniugis sue, et

Lundors cum omnibus iustis pertinenciis suis abbati et monachis ibidem Deo seruientibus in liberam et puram et perpetuam
elemosinam concessisse. Nos igitur diuini amoris intuitu, ad
peticionem domini Dauid comitis iam dicti, auctoritate nostra,
damus et concedimus et hac carta nostra confirmamus abbati
et monachis ibidem Deo serui|entibus ipsam ecclesiam de   [*fol*
Lundors et personatum eiusdem ecclesie cum omnibus iustis
pertinenciis suis ad sedem abbacie, in liberam et puram et
perpetuam elemosinam ad proprios usus et sustentationes
eorundem monachorum, vt iam dicta ecclesia de Lundors
libera sit et quieta a conrediis et hospiciis, et sinodalibus, et Nota
can, et conueth ; concedimus eciam et confirmamus eis digni tatem
tatem pacis et omnes alias libertates quas abbacia habere debet,
ita libere, quiete, plenarie et honorifice, sicut aliqua abbacia in
regno Scocie liberius, quiecius, plenius, et honorificiencius tenet
et possidet. Hiis Testibus, Domino Rege Willelmo, Comite
Dauid fratre eius, Johanne Episcopo Aberdonensi, Ricardo
Episcopo Morauiensi, Reginaldo Episcopo Rossensi, Jonatha
episcopo Dunblanensi, Johanne episcopo Dunkeldensi, Radulpho episcopo Brechinensi, O. abbate de Kalkov, Henrico
abbate de Abirbrothoc, Ranulfo archidiacono, Johanne
archidiacono Laodonie, A. Comite de Fyfe, M. filio eius,
Willelmo de Lyndeseya, A. A. filio eius, Philippo de Valoniis, Dauid de Haya, Walkelino filio Stephani, Malcolmo filio
Bertulphi, Roberto Basset, Wilelmo de Wiuile, Malcolmo de
Keth, Wilellmo de Swatham, cum multis aliis.

(Abstract)

'Of the Confirmation of the Church of Lundors.'

Roger, by the grace of God, Bishop of St. Andrews, to all the sons of
Holy Mother Church, etc.   Let all, as well those to come as those
present, know that the Lord David, earl, brother of the Lord William,
King of Scots, founded an abbey at Lundors of the order of Kelko, for
the weal of the king his brother, and for the weal of his own soul and of
the soul of the Countess Matilda, his wife, and of all his heirs, and for

by this present charter confirm, to the abbot and monks there serving
God, the church itself of Lundors and the rights of rector (*personatum*),
with all its just pertinents at the seat of the abbey, in free, pure, and
perpetual alms, for their own uses and the maintenance of the same monks,
so that the aforesaid church of Lundors may be free and exempt from
corrodies and claims for entertainment (*hospiciis*), and synodals, and
cane, and conveth. We grant and confirm to them also the dignity of
the peace, and all other liberties which an abbey ought to have, as
freely, etc. Witnesses,

CVIII

Item de eadem ecclesia.

Vniversis sancte matris ecclesie filiis et fidelibus Willelmus
dei gracia episcopus Sancti Andree, perpetuam in domino Salu
tem.   Nouerint omnes tam posteri quam presentes dominum
Dauid comitem, fratrem domini Willelmi Regis Scottorum,
fundasse abbaciam quandam de ordine Kelkoensi apud
Lundors, pro salute domini Regis Willelmi fratris sui, et pro
salute anime sue et matildis comitisse coniugis sue, et omnium
heredum ipsorum, et pro salute anime Dauid regis aui sui, et
comitis Henrici patris sui, et Ade Comitisse matris sue, et
omnium antecessorum suorum, et ipsam ecclesiam de Lundors
cum omnibus iustis pertinenciis suis abbati et monachis ibidem
deo seruientibus in liberam et puram et perpetuam elemosinam
concessisse.   Nos igitur diuini amoris intuitu, auctoritate
nostra, concedimus et hac carta nostra confirmamus abbati et
monachis ibidem deo seruientibus ipsam ecclesiam de Lundors
et personatum eiusdem ecclesie, cum omnibus iustis pertinenciis suis, in liberam et puram et perpetuam elemosinam, ad
proprios usus et sustentaciones eorundem monachorum, vt
iam dicta ecclesia parochialis de Lundors libera sit et quieta a
conrediis et hospiciis et synodalibus.   Concedimus eciam et

Petro Baillard, Johanne de Haut thuysille, Radulpho nigro, clericis nostris, Magistro Symone Sancti Andree, Stephano de Perth, Magistro Ysaac, Willelmo Decano de Carel, et multis aliis.

(Abstract)

' Of the same Church.'

To all the sons of Holy Mother Church, etc. William, by the grace of God, Bishop of St. Andrews, etc.

The language of the preceding charter [cvii.] is repeated with the following alterations : the bishop's confirmation is not said to be at the request of Earl David ; the church of Lundors is spoken of as 'the parish church of Lundors'; and the exemption from 'cane and conveth' is omitted. Witnesses

CIX

De Eadem Ecclesia.

David, permissione Diuina Ecclesie Sancti Andree minister humilis, omnibus christi fidelibus presens scriptum visuris uel audituris, eternam in Domino salutem. Nouerint, tam posteri quam presentes, Dominum Dauid Co | mitem, fratrem Domini [ƒo. Willelmi Regis Scotorum, fundasse abbaciam quamdam de ordine Kelkoensi apud Lundors, pro salute domini Regis W. fratris sui, et pro salute anime sue, et Matildis Comitisse coniugis sue, et omnium heredum ipsorum, et pro salute anime Regis Dauid aui sui, et comitis Henrici patris sui, et Ade Comitisse matris sue, et omnium antecessorum suorum, Et ipsam ecclesiam de Lundors,[a] cum omnibus iustis pertinenciis suis, abbati et monachis ibidem Deo seruientibus in liberam, et puram et perpetuam elemosinam concessisse. Nos igitur diuini amoris intuitu, auctoritate nostra, damus et concedimus et hac carta nostra confirmamus abbati et monachis ibidem deo

a ms.
ecclesia Lundo
ipsam e
de Lun

ngno. et honorifice sicut aliqua abbacia in regno[a] Scocie liberius, quiecius, plenius, et honorificencius tenet et possidet. Hiis testibus, et cetera.

(*Abstract*)

' OF the same CHURCH.'

DAVID, by divine permission, humble minister of the church of St. Andrews to all the faithful of Christ, etc.

The language of the preceding charter [cviii.] is repeated, but ' cane and conveth ' appear again, as in the charter of Bishop Roger [cvii.].

CX

Item de eadem ecclesia.

GAMELINVS, miseracione diuina ecclesie Sancti Andree Minister humilis, omnibus christi fidelibus presens scriptum visuris uel audituris, eternam in domino Salutem. Nouerint tam presentes quam futuri dominum Dauid comitem, fratrem domini Willelmi Regis Scotorum, fundasse abbaciam quamdam de ordine Kelkoensi apud Lundors, pro salute anime sue, et Matildis coniugis sue, et omnium heredum ipsorum, et pro salute animarum omnium antecessorum et successorum suorum, et parochialem ecclesiam de Lundors, cum omnibus iustis pertinenciis suis, abbati et monachis ibidem deo seruientibus, in liberam et puram et perpetuam elemosinam, concessisse. Nos igitur diuini amoris intuitu, auctoritate nostra, damus et concedimus et hac carta nostra confirmamus abbati et monachis ibidem deo seruientibus, ipsam parochialem ecclesiam de Lundors et personatum eiusdem ecclesie, cum omnibus iustis pertinenciis suis, ad sedem abbacie, in liberam et puram et perpetuam elemosinam, ad proprios usus et sustentaciones eorundem monachorum, vt iam dicta ecclesia de Lundors sit libera et quieta a conrediis, et hospiciis, et Synodalibus, et Can, et Conueth. Concedimus eeiam ét confirmamus eis dignitatem pacis, et omnes alias libertates quas abbacia

domini, Anno gracie M°. Ducentesimo quinquagesimo nono.

(*Abstract*)

' OF the same CHURCH.'

GAMELIN, by divine mercy, humble minister of the church of St. Andrews, to all the faithful of Christ, etc.

The language of the preceding charter [CIX.] is repeated. Witnesses . . . Given at Lundors on Saturday next before Christmas, in the year of grace MCCLIX.

CXI

❡ De bosco capiendo in Glenlithere in Stratherne.

OMNIBVS christi fidelibus presens scriptum uisuris uel audituris Robertus dictus frater senescalli de Stratherne, eternam in do mino Salutem. Nouerit uniuersitas uestra quod cum auctoritate apostolica mota esset causa coram archidiacono Dunkeldensi et commissariis suis, videlicet priore et sacrista de Abirbrothoc, inter viros religiosos abbatem et conuentum de Lundores actores, ex vna parte, et me reum ex altera ; Ac ex parte dictorum abbatis et conuentus mihi esset | editum sub hac [*fo* forma, Dicunt abbas et conuentus de Lundores contra Robertum fratrem senescalli de Stratherne quod cum ipsi et homines eorum essent in pacifica possessione capiendi materiem in Bosco de Glenlicherne in Stratherne ad edificia sustinenda et reparanda in terra sua de fedal que est in Kater mothel, et similiter ea que pertinent ad agriculturam, dictus Robertus prefatos abbatem et Conuentum prefata sua pacifica posses- sione contra iusticiam spoliauit. Quare dicti abbas et conuentus petunt ad possessionem suam pristinam restitui, et predictum Robertum ad possessionem candem eisdem abbati et conuentui plenarie faciendam per censuram ecclesiasticam compelli. Hec dicunt et petunt, saluo sibi iuris beneficio in omnibus, protestantes se uelle petere expensas in lite factas et de cetero faciendas. Tandem ego Robertus pro mea contumacia per dictos commissarios ab ingressu ecclesie, auctoritate apostolica, suspensus, ac postmodum, multiplicata contumacia, excommuni- catus, lesamque in hac parte habens conscienciam liti cedere pocius quam contendere existimavi. Vnde prestito super hoc corporali iuramento pro me et meis omnibus et singulis, fideliter promisi quod prefatos abbatem et conuentum ac homines eorundem prefata possessione sua capiendi materiem in pre dicto bosco libere gaudere permittam. Nec eos uel successores suos uel homines eorum aliquatenus super premissis in posterum uexabo,inquietabo, perturbabo,nec perturbacionem aliquam per me uel per alios procurabo. Ita tamen quod homines dictorum abbatis et conuentus, vnus uel plures, quandocunque uoluerint *dere.* caedere[a] in dicto bosco, me uel seruientem meum tantummodo premunient. Volo eeiam et concedo, si ego, contra prefatam litis cessionem, prestiti iuramenti obseruacionem et promissionem contrauenire presumpsero, uel aliquis meorum contra premissa attemptare presumpserit, quod archidiaconus Sancti Andree uel eius Officialis, qui pro tempore fuerint, quorum iurisdiccioni me et meos subieci sub alternacione in hac parte, ex tunc me et meos omnes et singulos ad omnia premissa et singula firmiter obseruanda, terna tantum monicione premissa, absque omni strepitu iudiciali per suspensionis, excommunicacionis, et interdicti sentencias in personam meam et meorum libere ualeat compellere. In cuius rei testimonium presenti scripto sigillum meum apposui et sigillis dictorum Commissariorum, vna cum sigillo dicti Archidiaconi, Judicis principalis, apponi procuravi. Datum apud Lundors in Crastino purificacionis beate virginis, Anno gracie millesimo ducentesimo L° sexto.

(Abstract)

'OF TAKING WOOD in GLENLITHERE in STRATHERNE.'

To all the faithful of Christ, etc. 'Robert, called the brother of Steward (*senescalli*) of Stratherne,' etc. Inasmuch as a suit has been carried on before the Archdeacon of Dunkeld and his commissaries, to wit, the Prior and the Sacrist of Aberbrothoc, acting under apostolic authority, between the religious, the Abbot and Convent of Lundors, pursuers (*actores*), of the one part, and me, defender (*reum*), of the other part; and on the part of the said abbot and convent, an indictment was served on me in the following terms, 'The Abbot and Convent of Lundors affirm

of justice deprived the aforesaid abbot and convent of the aforesaid peaceable possession. Wherefore the said abbot and convent seek to be restored to their former possession, and crave that the said Robert should be compelled by the censure of the Church to give full possession of the same to the same abbot and convent. These things they affirm and seek, reserving their right to all benefit of the law, and publicly declaring that they desire to seek the costs incurred, or hereafter to be incurred, in litigation.' At length I, Robert, having been suspended, for my contumacy, from entering the church, by the said commissaries acting on apostolic authority, and afterwards having been excommunicated for repeated contumacy, and having as regards this matter a troubled conscience, have thought it better to withdraw from the suit than to carry on the contention. Accordingly I have taken my corporal oath and faithfully promised for me and mine, all and singular, that I will permit the aforesaid abbot and convent and their men to freely enjoy their aforesaid possession of taking timber in the aforesaid wood. Nor will I in future vex, annoy, or disturb them or their successors or their men in respect to the aforesaid, nor will I procure that they should be in any way disturbed by myself or by others. Provided that whenever the men of the said abbot and convent, one or more, shall desire to cut [timber] in the said wood they shall give previous notice to me or my officer (*servientem*). If I, contrary to my withdrawal from this suit, shall presume to contravene my promise and the observance of my oath which I have taken, or if any of mine shall presume to attempt anything contrary to the premises, I consent and allow that the Archdeacon of St. Andrews, or his official, for the time being, to whose jurisdiction, whether of the one or the other, I subject me and mine, may thereupon freely compel me and mine, all and singular, to strictly observe the premisses, all and singular, after three monitions only and without any judicial proceedings, by sentences of suspension, excommunication, and interdict against the persons of me and mine. In testimony of which thing I have affixed my seal to the present writ, and procured the seals of the said commissaries, together with the seal of the archdeacon, judge principal, to be affixed.

Given at Lundors, on the morrow of the Purification of the Blessed Virgin [Feb. 2], in the year of grace ᴊCCLVI.

CXII
Joachim de Kynbuc super bosco capiendo in Curelundyn.

mota esset causa coram archidiacono Dunkeldensi inter uiros religiosos abbatem et conuentum de Lundors actores ex vna parte, et me reum ex altera, ac ex parte dictorum abbatis et conuentus mihi esset editum sub hac forma, Dicunt abbas et conuentus de Lundors contra dictum Joachym de Kynbuc militem, quod cum ipsi et homines eorum essent in pacifica possessione capiendi materiem in bosco de Curelundyn in Stratherne ad edificia sustinenda et reparanda in terra sua de fedale que est in Cather Mothyl, et similiter ea que pertinent ad agriculturam, dictus Joachim prefatos abbatem et conuentum prefata sua pacifica possessione contra iusticiam spoliauit. Quare dictus Abbas et conuentus petunt ad possessionem suam pristinam restitui, et predictum Joachim ad possessionem eandem eisdem abbati et conuentui faciendam plenarie per censuram ecclesiasticam compelli. Hec dicunt et petunt, saluo sibi iuris beneficio in omnibus, Protestantes se uelle petere expensas in lite factas et de cetero faciendas. Tandem ego Joachim pro contumacia a dicto archiadiacono ab ingressu ecclesie auctoritate apostolica suspensus, lesamque in hac parte habens consciencian liti pocius cedere quam contendere existimaui. Vnde prestito super hoc corporali iuramento pro me et successoribus meis omnibus et singulis fideliter promissi quod prefatos abbatem et conuentum prefata possessione sua capiendi materiem in predicto bosco libere gaudere permittam. Nec eos uel successores suos uel homines eorum aliquatenus super premissis in posterum vexabo, | inquietabo, perturbabo, nec perturbacionem aliquam per me uel per alios procurabo. Volo eciam et concedo, si ego contra prefatam litis cessionem, prestiti iuramenti obseruacionem et promissionem contrauenire presumpsero, uel aliquis successorum meorum contra premissa attemptare presumpserit, quod ex tunc ad omnia premissa et singula fideliter in perpetuum obseruanda, me et successores meos omnes et singulos obligando jurisdiccioni archidiaconi Sancti Andree qui pro tempore fuerit subieci. Videlicet ut dictus archidiaconus me et successores meos omnes et singulos ad omnia premissa et singula,

78.]

ualeat compellere. In cuius rei testimonium presenti scripto sigillum meum apposui Et sigillum dicti archidiaconi Dunkeldensis apponi procuraui. Datum in crastino sancti Vincencii anni gracie m^i cc^i L vj^i.

(Abstract)

'JOACHIM of KYNBUC upon taking WOOD in CURELUNDYN.'

To all the faithful of Christ, etc., Joachim of Kynbuc, knight, etc. The writ recites in language similar to that of CXI., that litigation had been raised before the Archdeacon of Dunkeld, acting under 'apostolic authority,' between the abbot and convent of Lundors, pursuers, and Joachim of Kynbuc, defender. The indictment on behalf of the abbot and convent is precisely in the same form, *mutatis mutandis*, as in the preceding writ. The wood of Curelundyn is said to be in Stratherne. Joachim subjects himself and his successors to the jurisdiction of the Archdeacon of St. Andrews (whose official is not mentioned, as in the preceding writ). The promise of Joachim is made on behalf of himself and his successors. 'In testimony of which thing I have affixed my seal to the present writ and procured the seal of the Archdeacon of Dunkeld to be affixed. Given on the morrow of St. Vincent [Jan. 22] of the year of grace ᴅ CCLXI.'

CXIII

Carta domini Roberti de Campaniis.

OMNIBVS Christi fidelibus presens scriptum visuris vel audituris Robertus de Campaniis, Salutem in domino sempiternam. Noverit universitas vestra quod cum auctoritate domini pape coram judicibus delegatis esset mota controversia inter religiosos viros, abbatem et conventum de Lundors, ex parte una, et me ex altera, super quodam annuo redditu trium marcarum eisdem abbati et conventui per dominum Willielmum de Campanis, cui ego jure hereditario succedo, in puram et perpetuam elimosinam pro se et heredibus suis collatarum, et in terra sua de Stokes in Comitatu Leycestre assignatarum, monachis ibidem Deo servientibus et servituris, pro salute anime patris mei Roberti de Campaniis qui ibidem sepultus est, et pro animabus omnium antecessorum et successorum meorum, in puram et perpetuam elimosinam, tres marcas argenti annuatim percipiendas de me et heredibus meis ad Penthecosten, in terra mea de Stokes in Comitatu Leycestre. Predicti vero monachi ad peticionem meam caritative concesserunt quod singulis diebus in perpetuum ad altare Sancti Nicholai cantetur aliqua missa in eadem ecclesia in qua fiet commemoracio specialis pro anima patris mei et pro animabus omnium fidelium defunctorum ; ut autem hec mea donacio rata sit et stabilis in perpetuum, presenti scripto sigillum meum apposui. Testibus, domino J. Comite Cestre et Huntendun, domino Henrico de Strivelin, domino Radulpho de Campaniis, domino Galfrido de Appelby, domino Theobaldo de Bellus, domino Hugone Fitun, domino Radulpho de Sayer, domino Anketino, domino Peleryn, Hugone clerico, Petro clerico, Nicholao de Innerpeffyr, et multis aliis. Tandem ego Robertus in judicio constitutus, inspecto tenore predicte carte non cancellate, non abolite, nec in aliqua parte sui viciate, confessus sum me et heredes meos teneri in perpetuum singulis annis predictis abbati et conventui in tribus marcis sterlingorum solvendis annuatim in festo Penthecostes juxta tenorem predicte carte, ac post hujusmodi confessionem in judicio factam, mediantibus eisdem judicibus delegatis et aliis viris fidedignis, predicta contro-versia conquievit sub hac forma, videlicet quod predicti abbas et conventus ad peticionem meam remiserunt michi omnia arreragia, dampna, et expensas, que vel quas petebant a me in judicio, occasione dictarum trium marcarum detentarum a tempore obitus dicti domini W. de Campaniis usque in diem veneris proximam post festum Sancti Mathie apostoli, Anno gracie m°. cc°. L°. nono, et preterea assignacioni eisdem abbati et conventui faete in terra de Stokes de predictis tribus marcis renunciaverunt, propter quod ego Robertus de Campaniis pre-fatis religiosis predictas tres marcas assignavi in terra mea de Castelton de Borg in Galwythia, percipiendas in perpetuum

torum, vel tenencium meorum quicunque dictam terram pro tempore tenuerint. Volo eciam et concedo et hac presen|ti carta mea confirmo pro me et heredibus meis et assignatis, ut predicti religiosi predictas tres marcas sine aliqua molestia, gravamine, vel contradiccione annuatim percipiant, et in puram, liberam et perpetuam elimosinam habeant et possideant. Et ne in posterum predicti religiosi in percepcione dictarum trium marcarum aliquam molestiam paciantur, obligo me et heredes meos et assignatos, corporali super hoc in presencia dictorum judicum prestito juramento, quod predictam terram in qua eisdem assignavi dictas tres marcas nunquam ego vel heredes mei, sive assignati alienabimus per quod impediantur easdem tres marcas statuto termino percipere. Suppono eciam me et heredes meos et assignatos ac tenentes meos dicte terre juris-diccioni venerabilium patrum Sancti Andree et Candide case episcoporum qui pro tempore fuerint; Ita quod si aliquando cessatum fuerit termino statuto a dictarum trium marcarum solucione, vel prefati religiosi aliquod impedimentum incur-rerint in perceptione dictarum trium marcarum per me uel per heredes meos uel assignatos siue per dicte terre tenentes meos seu per quemcunque alium de meis vel meorum nomine, dicti episcopi vel eorum alter, qui fuerit ex parte dictorum abbatis et conventus requisitus, me et heredes meos et assignatos ac dicte terre tenentes meos, ac quoscunque alios meo vel meorum nomine impedientes quo minus dicti religiosi dictas tres marcas sine molestia et gravamine possint libere percipere, tantum unica monicione premissa, possint vel possit vinculo excommunicacionis innodare, nuncquam relaxande quousque dictis religiosis de totali prefato redditu trium marcarum, dampnis, expensis, et interesse, plenarie fuerit satisfactum, nisi generalis guerra fuerit in terra. Super cessacione vero solucionis dictarum trium marcarum ad terminum statutum, expensis,

[*fol.*

juxta tenorem dicte carte domini Willelmi de Campaniis, quamquidem cartam michi post confeccionem presentis scripti resignaverunt.   Et ut hec omnia rata et inconcussa permaneant in perpetuum presenti scripto sigillum meum apposui : Et ad majorem securitatem et testimonium, predicti domini episcopi et dominus Rogerus de Queney Comes Wynton et Constabularius Scocie ad peticionem meam eidem Scripto sigilla sua pariter apposuerunt.   Datum apud Borg sabbato proximo ante dominicam in ramis palmarum, anno domini M⁰. cc⁰. lx⁰

(Abstract)

'Charter of Sir Robert de Campaniis.'

To all Christ's faithful, etc., Robert de Campaniis, etc. He relates that with the authority of the Pope a suit was instituted before judges delegate between the Abbot and Convent of Lundors, of the one part, and him of the other part, in respect to the annual payment of three marks, granted in pure and perpetual alms to the abbot and convent by Sir William de Campaniis (to whom Sir Robert succeeded by right of heirship), for himself and his heirs, and assigned to be paid in his land of Stokes in the county of Leicester, as was more fully contained in the charter of the said Sir William, signed with his seal, the tenor of which was as follows : 'To all who shall see or hear this writ William de Campaniis, greeting.   Let all of you know that I have given, granted, and by this my present charter confirmed, to God and the Church of St. Mary and St. Andrew of Lundors, and the monks now serving God, or who shall hereafter serve God, in that place, for the weal of the soul of my father, Robert de Campaniis, who is buried there, and for the souls of all my ancestors and successors, in pure and perpetual alms, three marks of silver to be yearly received of me and my heirs at Whitsunday, in my land of Stokes in the county of Leicester.   And the monks aforesaid have charitably granted, at my petition, that there should be sung every day for ever a mass at the altar of St. Nicholas in the same church, in which mass special commemoration would be made for the soul of my father and for the souls of all the faithful departed. And that this my gift may be established and secure for ever I have affixed my seal to the present writ. Witnesses, ... At length I, Robert, having appeared before the judges, and having examined the contents of the charter aforesaid, not being cancelled, abrogated, or in any part vitiated, acknowledged that I and my heirs were bound for ever to pay yearly to the aforesaid abbot and convent three marks

abbot and convent at my petition have remitted to me all the arrears, damages, and costs which they sought from me in court by reason of my not having paid the said three marks from the time of the death of the said Sir William de Campaniis up to the Friday next after the feast of St. Matthias the Apostle,[1] in the year of grace MCCLIX; and, moreover, they have renounced the assigning of the payment of the three marks in the land of Stokes, as was made to the said abbot and convent.   On account of which I, Robert de Campaniis, have assigned to the aforesaid religious the aforesaid three marks in my land of Castelton of Borg, in Galwythia, to be received each year, for ever, out of my said land of Castelton, on the day of the Holy Trinity,[2] by them and their successors, through their certified agent (*per certum nuncium*), at the hands of me, and my heirs, or assignees, or my tenants, who for the time shall hold the said land.   I also will and grant for me, my heirs and assignees, that the aforesaid religious should yearly receive the aforesaid three marks, without any annoyance, trouble, or objection, and should have and possess them in free, pure, and perpetual alms.   And to the end that in future the aforesaid religious should not suffer any annoyance in receiving the said three marks, I oblige myself, my heirs and assignees, by my corporal oath thereupon taken in the presence of the said judges, that I, my heirs and assignees, will never alienate the said land in which I have assigned to them the said three marks, by which alienation they might be hindered in receiving the same three marks at the appointed term.   And I subject myself, my heirs and assignees, and my tenants of the same land to the jurisdiction of the venerable fathers, the Bishops of St. Andrews and Galloway (*Candida Casa*) from time to time, so that if there be any stoppage in the payment of the said three marks at the appointed term, or if the aforesaid religious are hindered in any way from receiving the said three marks by me or my heirs, or my assignees, or by my tenants of the said land, or by any other of mine, or in the name of mine, the said bishops, or either of them, who shall be so requested on the part of the said abbot and convent, may, after one monition only, place under the bond of excommunication me, my heirs, assignees, tenants of the said land, and any others whomsoever, who in my name or the name of mine, hinder the said religious from freely receiving the said three marks without trouble or annoyance, such excommunication to be never relaxed until full satisfaction be made to the said religious for the whole of the three marks, damages, costs, and interest, unless in the case of there being a general war in the country.

As regards the stoppage of the payment of the three marks aforesaid at the appointed term, and as regards costs, damages, and interest, full credence is to be given to the simple statement of the proctor of the

said abbot and convent, whoever shall happen to be appointed to that
office, without putting on him any burden of proof. The aforesaid
monks, at my request, have, of their charity, granted to me that they
will make every day, for ever, special commemoration in one mass for the
souls of my father and of Sir Robert de Campaniis, and of all the faithful
departed, according to the tenor of the charter of Sir William de Campaniis, which charter they resigned to me after the execution of the
present writ. And that all these things may be established and secure
for ever, I have put my seal to the present writ. And for the greater
security, and for testimony, the aforesaid lords, the bishops, and Lord
Roger de Quency, Earl of Wynton and Constable of Scotland, have
likewise at my request put their seals to the present writ. Given at
Borg, on the Saturday next before Palm Sunday, in the year of our Lord
MCCLX.[1]

CXIV

De conuencione facta inter abbatem et conuentum de Lundores et Willelmum de Brechyn.

ANNO gracie millesimo ducentesimo sexagesimo primo | die
sabbati proxima post festum Sancti Martini in hyeme. Apud
Lundors facta est hec Convencio inter Abbatem et conventum
monasterii de Lundors ex una parte et dominum Willelmum
de Brechynch ex altera, videlicet, quod cum terra ejusdem
domini Willelmi, de Lundors, de Bondington, de Kyndeloich, et
terra quondam Galfridi Maupetyt, tenerentur molendino
dictorum abbatis et conventus ad sectam et multuram tanquam
ad molendinum seyre de Lundors, quod est ipsorum abbatis et
conventus ex donacione inclite recordacionis Comitis David,
iidem abbas et conventus pro se et suis successoribus in perpetuum quietam clamaverunt dicto domino Willelmo et suis
heredibus et eorum hominibus in dictis terris manentibus
dictam sectam et multuram de dictis terris de Lundors, de
Bondyngton, et de Kyndeloich, et de terra quondam Galfridi
Maupetyt. Ita ut nec dictus dominus Willelmus nec heredes
sui nec eorum homines in dictis terris manentes de cetero com-
80.] pelli | possint racione alicujus juris vel consuetudinis ad dictam

terio de Lundors in perpetuum triginta tres solidos et quatuor denarios sterlingorum annuos, in liberam, puram et perpetuam elimosinam, percipiendos annuatim de terra sua et heredum suorum de Lundors per manus ballivi sui, vel firmarii, seu fir- mariorum suorum de Lundors, vel quorumcumque aliorum, q uo- cumque nomine censeantur, qui dictam terram tenuerint: medietatem uidelicet ad Pentecosten et aliam medietatem ad festum Sancti Martini in hyeme. Ita ut si infra octo dies cujus- cunque termini de porcione ejusdem termini non fuerit eisdem abbati et conventui satisfactum, liceat eisdem abbati et conventui namos dicti domini Willelmi, vel heredum suorum, seu hominum suorum, vel firmariorum suorum in dictis terris manencium, nulla alia licencia petita, capere, et tam diu detinere nulli replegiandos, vel ad vadium dandos, seu aliquo alio modo libe- randos, quousque eisdem abbati et conventui de porcione non soluta fuerit plenarie satisfactum. Concessit eciam dictus dominus Willelmus pro se et heredibus suis quod dicte terre nulli darentur nec alienarentur quin eedem [a] terre ad dictum an- [a] MS. uuum redditum triginta trium solidorum et quatuor denariorum eisdem abbati et conventui sub convencionibus predictis annuatim persolvendum remaneant obligate. Concessit insuper dictus dominus Willelmus pro se et heredibus suis et suis assignatis in perpetuum dictis abbati et conventui ut cursus aque que descendit de magno lacu de Lundors ad molendinum eorundem abbatis et conventus nullo modo impediatur pei molendinum ipsius domini Willelmi vel heredum suorum, set ipsam aquam ita liberam habeant prout illam habere consue- verunt et debuerunt ex donacione Comitis David: In cujus rei testimonium uni parti istius scripti, in modum cirograffi con- fecti, residenti penes dictum dominum Willelmum appositum est sigillum commune monasterii de Lundors, et alii parti remanenti penes dictos abbatem et conventum sigillum domini Willelmi de Brechynch est appensum, ad majorem securitatem omnium predictorum.

(Abstract)

Abbot and Convent of the monastery of Lundors of the one part, and
Sir William of Brechyn, of the other part, to wit, that, since the lands
of Lundors, Bondington, and Kyndeloich, and the land of the late
Geoffrey Maupetyt, all of them belonging to the same William of
Brechin, are thirled to the mill of the said abbot and convent in suit
and multure, as if to the mill of the shire (*scyre*) of Lundors, which
belongs to the abbot and convent by the gift of Earl David, of illustrious
memory, the same abbot and convent for themselves and their successors
have quitclaimed for ever to the said Sir William and his heirs, and to
their men residing in the said lands, the said suit and multure from the
lands of Lundors, Bondyngton, Kyndeloich, and from the land which was
held by the late Geoffrey Maupetit, so that in future neither the said
Sir William, nor his heirs, nor their men residing in the said lands,
can be compelled to render the said suit and multure by reason of any
right or custom.   But in return for the said quitclaim, in consideration
of the said suit and multure [thus surrendered], William of Brechin
gives and grants to the said abbot and convent for ever thirty-three
shillings and fourpence sterling, in free, pure, and perpetual alms, to be
received yearly out of his land of Lundors by the hands of his bailiff, or his
farmer or farmers, or by those whomsoever, by whatever name they may
be called, who shall hold the said land.   Half of this money shall be paid
at Whitsunday, and the other half at the feast of St. Martin in winter.
If within eight days after each term the abbot and convent have not
received full satisfaction for the portion due at that term, the abbot and
convent may, without seeking leave from any, take poinds (*namos*) from
the said Sir William, or his heirs, or his men, or his farmers, residing
in those lands.   Such poinds were not to be repledged, or given at wad
(*ad vadium*), or delivered up in any other manner, until full satisfaction
has been given to the abbot and convent for the portion not paid.   The
said Sir William also grants for himself and his heirs that the said lands
shall not be given or alienated to any, but that they shall remain under
obligation for the yearly payment of the thirty-three shillings and fourpence to the abbot and convent, under the agreement aforesaid.   Moreover, the said Sir William has granted to the abbot and convent for
himself, his heirs, and assignees, that the flow of water which comes
down from the great lake of Lundors to the mill of the abbot and convent shall in no way be obstructed by the mill of the said Sir William
or his heirs, but that they shall have that water as free as they were
accustomed and were entitled to have it by the gift of Eärl David.   In
testimony of which this writ is executed in the form of an indenture,
one part of which, sealed with the common seal of the monastery, shall
be kept by William of Brechin, and the other part, sealed with the seal

CXV
De Inirberwyn.

Omnibvs Christi fidelibus presentes literas visuris vel audituris Alanus Hostiarius, Salutem eternam in domino. Noverit univer sitas vestra nos dedisse, concessisse, et hac presenti carta nostra confirmasse deo et ecclesie Sancte Marie de Lundors et Monachis ibidem Deo servientibus et inperpetuum servituris, in liberam, puram et perpetuam elemosinam, totum illud toftum quod fuit quondam Ade clerici in Inirbervyn; Ita quod nec nos nec aliquis heredum nostrorum vel successorum aliquid ab eis de dicto tofto inposterum exigamus vel exigere possimus, nisi omnimodo oraciones ad salutem animarum. In cujus rei testimonium eisdem super hoc has literas nostras fieri fecimus patentes, et sigillo nostro muniri. His testibus, dominis Roberto Byseth, Thoma Hostiario, David de Cambrun rectore ecclesie de Lundyn rothery. Apud Sconam, die dominica proxima post festum Sancti Barnabe apostoli, anno gracie M° CC° Lx° vj^{to}.

(*Abstract*)

'Of Inirberwyn.'

To all the faithful of Christ, etc., Alan Durward (*Hostiarius*), etc. He grants to Lundors in frankalmoign the whole of that toft which was held by the late Adam, clerk[1] in Inirbervyn, so that neither he [Durward] nor his heirs or successors might exact anything in future because of the said toft, save only prayers for the weal of souls. 'In testimony of which thing we have caused our letters to be made patent to the same, and to be fortified with our seal.' Witnesses, . . . At Scone, on the Sunday next after the feast of St. Barnabas the Apostle [June 11],[2] in the year of grace mcclxvi.

CXVI
De Villa Willelmi in Garuiach. Nota eciam de secundis decimis.

[fo

Omnibvs Christi fidelibus presentes litteras visuris vel audituris Robertus de Brus dominus Vallis Anandie, eternam in domino Salutem. Noverit universitas vestra nos, pro salute anime nostre cessisse,et presenti carta nostra confirmasse viris religiosis,abbati et conventui de Lundors, terram nostram que dicitur villa Willelmi in Garviach, que jacet inter terras eorum de Lethgaven et Wrangham, Et terram nostram de Bondes juxta Caskyben in parochia de Inverury, in escambium secundarum decimarum quas idem abbas et conventus consueverunt percipere annuatim de terris nostris, lucris, placitis, et eschaetis, et omnibus aliis rebus nostris infra terram nostram et extra, ultra Moneth, in Garviach ex dono Comitis David avi nostri, sic quod in carta dicti Comitis David plenius continetur. Quare volumus et concedimus ut predicti abbas et conventus et eorum successores in perpetuum habeant, teneant,et possideant predictas terras per rectas divisas suas cum omnibus communis libertatibus, liberis consuetudinibus, aisiamentis, et omnibus pertinenciis ad dictas terras spectantibus, in liberam, puram et perpetuam elemosinam, adeo libere, quiete, plenarie, et honorifice sicut aliqua abbacia vel domus religionis in toto regno Scocie aliquam elemosinam liberius, quiecius, plenius, et honorificencius tenet et possidet. Ita quod nobis succedencium nullus aliquid ab eis racione predictarum terrarum, nisi solas oraciones ad salutem animarum, exigere possit. Nos vero et heredes nostri predictas terras cum omnibus communis libertatibus, liberis consuetudinibus, et asiamentis suis, et omnibus pertinenciis suis ad easdem terras spectantibus, prefatis abbati et conventui ac corum successoribus contra omnes homines et feminas warentizabimus, defendemus, et adquietabimus in perpetuum ab omni seculari auxilio et exercitu, et ab omni alio servicio, servitute, exactione, et demanda seculari. In cujus rei testimonium presens scriptum sigilli nostri apposicione roboravimus. Hiis testibus, venerabili patre domino Ricardo Episcopo Aberdonensi, Dominis Bartholome Flandrensi, Andrea de Garviach, Ada de Cartres, Willelmo de Sancto Michaele, militibus, Johanne de Sancto Michaele, Jacobo de Ouen, Ada de Ran, Roberto Russel, Henrico Engleys, Andrea de Porteriston, Roberto de Brechyn, et multis aliis.

(*Abstract*)

our children, and of all our ancestors and successors' he grants to Lundors his land which is called the vill of William in Garviach, which lies between their [the monks'] lands of Lethgaven and Wrangham, and his land of Bondes near Caskyben, in the parish of Inverury, 'in exchange for the second tithes which the abbot and convent were accustomed to receive annually from our lands, gains, pleas, and escheats, and all our other property, both within and without our land, beyond the Mounth in Garviach, of the gift of Earl David, our grandfather, as in the charter of the said Earl David is more fully contained.' The abbot and convent and their successors are to have, hold, and possess the said lands by their right marches, with all liberties of commonage, free customs, easements, and other pertinents in free, pure and perpetual alms, as freely, fully, etc., as any abbey or house of religion in the whole kingdom of Scotland, etc.   None of his successors were to demand anything by reason of the said lands save only prayers for the weal of souls.   He grants for himself and his heirs warrandice 'against all men and women,' and promises to be answerable for all secular service, aid, and military service (*exercitu*), etc.   His seal attached.   Witnesses

CXVII

Item de eadem terra Willelmi, de Letgauen, de Wrangham, et de terra de Bondes.   Item nota de secundis decimis.

ALEXANDER dei gracia rex Scottorum Omnibus probis hominibus tocius terre sue, salutem.   Sciatis nos concessisse et hac presenti carta nostra confirmasse donacionem illam quam Robertus de Brus fecit religiosis viris abbati et conventui de Lundors, de terra sua que dicitur villa Willelmi in Garviach, que jacet inter terras eorundem abbatis et conventus de Lethgaven et de Wrangham, et de terra sua de Bondes juxta Caskyben in parrochia de Inverury, in escambium secundarum decimarum quas idem abbas et conventus consueverunt percipere annuatim de terris eiusdem Roberti, et lucris, placitis, eschaetis, et omnibus aliis rebus dicti Roberti infra terram suam et extra, ultra Moneth, in Garviach, ex

servicio nostro. Testibus, Willelmo Archidiacono Sancti Andree Cancellario, Johanne de Dundemor, Johanne de Parco, et Willelmo de Sancto Claro. Apud Kynros, vicesimo nono die Augusti, Anno Regni nostri tercio decimo.

(Abstract)

'LIKEWISE concerning the same land of WILLIAI, concerning LETH-GAVEN, concerning WRANGHAM, and concerning the land of BONDES. Likewise a NOTE concerning SECOND TITHES.'

'ALEXANDER, by the grace of God, King of Scots, to all good men of his whole land, greeting.' The king confirms the donation of Robert de Brus as recorded in the preceding charter, 'saving our service.' Witnesses, William, Archdeacon of St. Andrews, chancellor ; John of Dundemor ; John of Park ; William of St. Clair. At Kynros, 29th day of August, in the thirteenth year of our reign.[1]

CXVIII

De donacione Henrici de Hastinges de Flandres.

OMNIBVS Christi fidelibus presens scriptum visuris vel audituris Henricus de Hastinges, eternam in domino salutem. Noverit universitas vestra me pro salute anime mee et omnium ante-cessorum et successorum meorum dedisse, concessisse, et presenti carta meo confirmasse deo et ecclesie sancte Marie et sancti Andree de Lundors et monachis ibidem Deo servientibus et in perpetuum servituris totam villam meam de Flandres in Garviach per rectas divisas suas, quas habuit tempore hujus donacionis mee, in escambium secundarum decimarum quas consueverunt percipere de terris meis ultra moneth, de dono Comitis David avi mei, sic quod plenius continetur in carta ejusdem Comitis David ; Tenendam et babendam de me et heredibus meis eisdem monachis et eorum successoribus in perpetuum cum omnibus justis pertinenciis suis, juribus, et asiamentis ad dictam villam juste pertinentibus, ut predictum est, in liberam, puram et perpetuam elemosinam, libere, quiete,

aliis pertinenciis suis sicut superius dictum est. Ego vero Henricus et heredes mei seu successores mei, quicumque pro tempore fuerint, predictam villam[1] cum omnibus pertinenciis suis, sicut dictum est, tanquam liberam, puram, et perpetuam elemosinam predictis monachis et eorum successoribus contra omnes homines et feminas warentizabimus, defendemus, et ab omnibus auxiliis, exercitibus, et aliis omnimodis forinsecis serviciis adquietabimus. Volo itaque et concedo ut predicti monachi predictam villam, ut dictum est, teneant et habeant quietam et liberam ab omni exaccione, consuetudine, et demanda, et ab omnibus aliis secularibus serviciis que per me vel heredes meos seu successores aliquo tempore exigi poterunt vel extorqueri, Ita quod nec ego nec aliquis michi succedencium aliquid ab eis exigere presumamus nisi tantummodo oraciones ad animarum salutem. In cujus rei testimonium presens scriptum sigilli mei apposicione roboravi. Hiis testibus etc.

(Abstract)

' Of the GIFT of FLANDRES made by HENRY of HASTINGES.'

To all Christ's faithful, etc., Henry of Hastinges, etc. For the weal of his soul, and of the souls of all his ancestors and successors, he grants to Lundors 'my whole vill of Flandres in Garviach, by its right marches which it had at the time of this grant in exchange for the second tithes which the monks of Lundors were accustomed to receive' from his lands beyond the Mounth 'by the gift of Earl David, my grandfather, as in the charter of the said Earl David is more fully contained.' Flandres was to be held by the monks of Henry and his successors for ever with all the just pertinents, rights, and easements pertaining to the said vill, in free, pure, and perpetual alms . . . 'in wood and plain, meadows and pastures, moors, marshes, and petaries, waters and mills, stanks, livepools (vivariis), and fisheries, in roads and paths, and all other pertinents. He and his successors give warrandice 'against all men and women.' Further, he promises for himself and his successors to be answerable for all aids, hostings (exercitibus), and for all forinsec services, and from all exactions, demands, and other secular services which could be exacted from him, his heirs, or successors at any time. Neither he nor his successors will presume to exact anything from the monks save only prayers for the weal of souls. In testimony his seal is affixed. These being witnesses, etc.[2]

---

[1] Before the word *predictam* the word *ad* appears in the MS., but it is sub-

CXIX

De Confirmacione de Flandris.

ALEXANDER dei gratia Rex Scottorum Omnibus probis hominibus tocius terre sue, salutem. Sciatis nos concessisse et hac presenti carta nostra confirmasse donacionem illam quam Henricus de Hastinges, miles, fecit deo et ecclesie sancte marie et sancti andre[e] de Lundors et Monachis ibidem Deo servientibus et in perpetuum servituris de tota villa sua de Flandres in Garviach per rectas divisas suas, quas habuit tempore ejusdem donacionis sue, in escambium secundarum decimarum quas consueverunt percipere de terris suis ultra le Moneth, de dono Comitis David avi sui : Tenenda et habenda eisdem monachis et eorum successoribus in perpetuum de dicto Henrico et heredibus suis, cum omnibus juribus, aisiamentis et pertinenciis ad ipsam | villam juste spectantibus, adeo libere, quiete, plenarie, et honorifice sicut carta ipsius Henrici eisdem monachis exinde confecta plenius juste testatur ; Salvo servicio nostro. Testibus, &c.

83.] (in margin)

(Abstract)

' OF the CONFIRMATION of FLANDRES.'

' ALEXANDER, by the grace of God, King of Scots, to all good men of his whole land, greeting.' He confirms that gift which Henry of Hastinges, knight, made, as in his charter is more fully contained, ' saving our service.' Witnesses, etc.[1]

CXX

De confirmacione a prima fundacione.

ALEXANDER dei gratia Rex Scottorum Omnibus probis hominibus tocius terre sue, salutem. Sciant presentes et futuri nos abbati et conventui de Lundors concessisse ut habeant et teneant, in liberam, puram et perpetuam elemosinam, omnes

hibemus ne quis eos contra hanc concessionem nostram injuste vexare presumat super nostram plenariam forisfacturam. Testibus, etc.

(Abstract)

'OF the CONFIRMATION of lands of LUNDORS from the FIRST FOUNDATION.'

ALEXANDER, by the grace of God, King of Scots, to all good men of his whole land, etc.   Let those present and to come know that we have granted to the Abbot and Convent of Lundors that they should have and hold in free, pure, and perpetual alms, all their lands which they have had and held from the first foundation of their house of Lundors with all liberties which they have been accustomed to use, and that they should be quit of aids, hostings, and other forinsec services due from the aforesaid lands.   Wherefore 'on [pain of] our full forfeiture' we strictly prohibit any one from presuming to trouble them unjustly, contrary to this our grant.   Witnesses, etc.[1]

CXXI

Item de confirmacione.

ALEXANDER dei gracia Rex Scottorum Omnibus probis hominibus tocius terre sue, salutem. Sciant presentes et futuri nos concessisse et hac carta nostra confirmasse abbati et conventui de Lundors concessionem illam quam dominus A. bone memorie illustris rex, pater noster, fecit eisdem, videlicet, ut habeant et teneant, in liberam, puram et perpetuam elemosinam, omnes terras suas quas habuerunt et tenuerunt a prima fundacione domus sue de Lundors, cum omnibus libertatibus quibus uti consueverunt, et quod quieti sint de auxiliis, exercitibus, et aliis forinsecis serviciis de predictis terris. Quare firmiter prohibemus ne quis contra hanc concessionem nostram eos injuste vexare presumat super nostram plenariam forisfacturam. Testibus, etc.

(Abstract)

' LIKEWISE of the CONFIRMATION.'

CXXII

De mandato Regis Alexandri.

ALEXANDER dei gratia rex Scottorum Justiciariis, vicecomitibus, et omnibus aliis ballivis tocius terre sue ad quos presentes
littere pervenerint, salutem. Mandamus vobis et precipimus
Quatinus permittatis abbatem et conventum de Lundors
gaudere eisdem libertatibus quibus tempore inclite recordacionis domini regis Alexandri, patris nostri, et nostro hactenus
juste gavisi sunt et pacifice. Nec ipsos super eisdem libertatibus aliquo modo vexetis injuste, per quod ab eis justam
querimoniam audiamus. Testibus, etc.

(Abstract)

'OF the MANDATE of KING ALEXANDER.'

ALEXANDER, by the grace of God, King of Scots, to the justiciars,
sheriffs, and all other the bailiffs of his whole land, etc. We command
you and enjoin that ye permit the Abbot and Convent of Lundors to
enjoy the same liberties which they have justly and peaceably enjoyed
in the time of our father King Alexander [II.] of famous memory. Nor
shall ye in any way trouble them unjustly upon these liberties, by
reason of which a just complaint on their part might come to our hearing. Witnesses, etc.[1]

CXXIII

De conuencione facta inter abbatem conuentum de Lundores et Gocelinum de Balliolo.

ANNO ab incarnacione domini M° cc° sexagesimo, facta fuit
hec convencio inter abbatem et conventum de Lundors, ex una
parte, et dominum Gocelinum de Balliolo ex altera, videlicet,
quod dicti abbas et conventus pro se et successoribus suis
remiserunt et quietum clamaverunt in perpetuum dicto domino
Gocelino omnimodas decimas, exceptis decimis garbarum quas
consueverunt percipere de firmis et omnibus aliis lucris et

dicto Domino Johanne de balliolo tempore quo facta fuit ista composicio, Pro qua quidem quieta clamacione et remissione dictus dominus Gocelinus pro se et heredibus suis dedit et concessit in escambium dictarum decimarum prefatis abbati et conventui et successoribus suis inperpetuum, in liberam, puram et perpetuam elemosinam, octo | marcas sex solidos et octo   [fo denarios sterlingorum singulis annis percipiendas in molendino suo de Inveralmeslei, uel in terra sua de balhagerdi si dictum molendinum deficiat, per manus firmariorum dicti molendini, vel dicte terre de balhagardi quicunque pro tempore fuerint, ad duos terminos anni, scilicet, medietatem ad festum Sancti Martini in bieme et alteram medietatem ad Pentecosten. Preterea predictus dominus Gocelinus pro se et heredibus suis dictis abbati et conventui et successoribus suis, in liberam et perpetuam elemosinam, dedit et concessit liberum cursum aque de Ouri, continentem quatuor pedes et dimidium in latitudine usque ad molendinum de Inchemabani, per medium terre sue quam habuit ex orientali parte Castri sui de Donidor, ubicunque dicti abbas et conventus voluerint : Ita tamen quod locum quem semel elegerint postmodum mutare non possint nisi de voluntate eius processerit. Et sciendum quod si processu temporis per inundacionem aque predictus cursus aque excreverit vel ampliatus fuerit ultra predictos quatuor pedes et dimidium, illud predictis abbati et conventui nullo modo imputabitur, nec aliquam propter hoc sustinebunt jacturam sive molestiam, dum tamen ipsi abbas et conventus predictum cursum suo artificio non ampliaverint. In recognicione autem predicti cursus aque dabunt predicti abbas et conventus singulis annis predicto domino Gocelino et heredibus suis unum par cirotecarum albarum ad Penthecosten apud Castrum suum de Donidor pro omni servicio, exactione, secta, et demanda seculari; Ita quod occasione predicti cursus aque prefatus dominus Gocelinus vel heredes sui nichil possint aliquo tem-

octo denarios impediantur annuatim, ut dictum est, percipere. In cujus rei testimonium presens scriptum in modum cirograffi est confectum, cuius una pars sigillo predicti domini Gocelini signata penes sepenominatos abbatem et conventum remanet, et altera pars communi sigillo capituli de Lundors penes prefatum dominum Gocelinum et heredes suos residet.

'OF an AGREEMENT made between the ABBOT and CONVENT of LUNDORS and GOCELIN DE BALLIOL.'

IN the year MCCLX. from the Incarnation of our Lord this agreement was made between the Abbot and Convent of Lundors, of the one part, and Sir Gocelin de Balliol, of the other part, to wit, that the abbot and convent for themselves and their successors have remitted and quitclaimed for ever to the said Sir Gocelin the tithes of all kinds, saving garbal tithes, which they have been accustomed to receive from the rents (*firmis*), and all other profits and escheats of his lands in Garviach, which he had of the gift of Sir John de Balliol, his brother, and likewise those of all the other lands which the noble man, the Earl of Mar, held of the said Sir John de Balliol at the time when this agreement was made. For which quitclaim and remission the said Sir Gocelin, for himself and his heirs has given and granted for ever to the aforesaid abbot and convent and their successors, in free, pure, and perpetual alms, in exchange for the said tithes, eight marks, six shillings, and eight pence, sterling, to be received by them each year in the mill of Inveralmeslei, or in his land of Balhagerdi, if the said mill should be lacking [in the sum named] by the hands of the farmers of the said mill or of the said land of Balhagerdi, whoever they may be at the time, at the two terms of the year, to wit, half at the feast of St. Martin in winter, and the other half at Whitsunday.

Moreover, the aforesaid Sir Gocelin, for himself and his heirs, has given and granted in free and perpetual alms a free water-course from the Ouri, measuring four feet and a half in breadth, as far as the mill of Inchmabani, by the middle of the land which he has on the east of his castle of Bondor, wherever the said abbot and convent shall choose ; yet so that the place which they have once chosen they cannot afterwards change without his will. And let it be known that if in process of time the [size of the] aforesaid water-course shall be increased or enlarged by floods, beyond the aforesaid four feet and a half, this shall in no wise be imputed to the aforesaid abbot and convent, nor shall they on that account sustain any risk or trouble, so long as the abbot and convent themselves have not artificially enlarged the aforesaid

that on account of the aforesaid water-course the aforesaid Sir Gocelin and his heirs may not at any time exact or extort anything from the aforesaid abbot and convent, save only the aforesaid gloves.

Moreover, the aforesaid Sir Gocelin has granted for himself and his heirs that neither he nor his heirs will at any time alienate the aforesaid mill or the aforesaid land of Balhagerdi by any kind of alienation, by reason of which the aforesaid abbot and convent might be hindered in receiving annually (as has been said) the aforesaid eight marks, six shillings, and eight pence. In testimony of which thing the present writ has been executed in the form of an indenture (*cirograffi*), of which one part, signed with the seal of the aforesaid Sir Gocelin, remains in possession of the often-named abbot and convent, and the other part, signed with the common seal of the chapter of Lundors, remains in the possession of the aforesaid Sir Gocelin and his heirs.

CXXIV

De x marcis in Kelle in Buchan.

Omnibvs Christi fidelibus ad quos presens scriptum pervenerit Alexander Cumyn Comes de Buchan, salutem in domino sempiternam. Noverit universitas vestra nos dedisse, concessisse, et hac presenti carta nostra confirmasse deo et ecclesie Sancte Marie et Sancti Andree de Lundors et monachis ibidem Deo servientibus et inperpetuum servituris decem Marcas sterlingorum annuas in tenemento nostro de Kelly in Buchan, pro salute anime pie recordacionis domini Alexandri quondam regis Scotorum illustris, et pro salute anime nostre, et pro animabus omnium antecessorum et successorum nostrorum, in escambium terre de Kyncardinbegg, quam nobis dimiserunt et quietam clamaverunt in perpetuum. Quare volumus quod predicti monachi predictas decem marcas annuas in perpetuum percipiant et habeant de predicto tenemento nostro de Kelly in liberam, puram, et perpetuam elemosinam, adeo | libere et quiete, sicut aliqua elemosina in toto regno Scotie liberius datur vel ab aliquo possidetur. Et propter ipsorum comodum et quietem, et in augmentum elemosine nostre, obligamus nos et heredes nostros et quoslibet alios successores nostros ad solvendum predictas decem marcas singulis annis apud Wrangham, infra octabas festi nativitatis Sancti Johannis baptiste, Abbati de Lund rs vel monacho seu all'vo   ne illuc

[*fo*

deficere in solucione predicte elemosine predictis loco et
termino aliqua vice, quod absit, volumus et concedimus pro
nobis et heredibus nostris ac successoribus quod liceat ballivo
et hominibus predictorum monachorum post octabas prefatas
namare predictum tenementum de Kelly, absque aliqua requisi-
cione licencie, et namos captos absque aliqua replegiacione
detinere usque ad octo dies post predictas octabas. Et si tunc
dicta elemosina non fuerit soluta, liceat eis dictam compulsionem
vendere usque ad valorem elemosine predicte, et quod nullum
impedimentum eis faciemus per nos vel nostros in capcione,
detencione, seu vendicione dictorum namorum, dummodo dictum
tenementum non fuerit ita devastatum guerra quod non
remaneat in illo redditus decem marcarum, et si idem ibi
remaneat illud habeant sine impedimento, ut predictum est.
Subjicimus eciam nos et heredes nostros et quosque alios
successores nostros et homines nostros dicti tenementi juris-
diccioni Episcopi et archidiaconi Aberdonensium, vel eorum
officialium, qui pro tempore fuerint, quod ipsi vel eorum alter,
qui super hoc fuerit requisitus ex parte dictorum monachorum,
possint vel possit, unica tantum monicione premissa, nos
compellere per sentencias excommunicacionis in personas, et
interdicti in dictum tenementum, sive fuerit in warda sive extra
wardam, nullo modo relaxandas vel suspendendas donec prefatis
monachis de prefata elemosina plenarie fuerit satisfactum.
Promittimus eciam et obligamus nos et heredes nostros quod
nullo modo alienabimus predictum tenementum de Kelly nisi
salva predictis monachis elemosina, compulsione, et submissione
memoratis; Renunciantes plene et expresse pro nobis, heredibus et successoribus nostris, regie prohibicioni, omni appellacioni, privilegio crucesignatis vel crucesignandis indulto vel
indulgendo, omnibus litteris, privilegiis, et graciis, inpetratis vel
inpetrandis a quacumque curia seculari vel ecclesiastica, omni
legi et statuto, omni exceptione, et defensioni reali et personali
juris et statuti, que pro parte nostra poterunt opponi contra
hoc instrumentum vel factum. Et nos et heredes nostri
predictas decem marcas annuas prefatis monachis contra omnes

domini episcopi Aberdonensis, Dominus W. episcopus Sancti Andree ad preces nostras sigillum suum apposuit huic scripto. Hiis testibus, domino Willelmo Dei gracia episcopo Sancti Andree, domino Andrea Abbate de Cupro, dominis Willelmo de Montealto, Willelmo Cumyn, Fergus Cumyn, Johanne Wyschard, Gilberto Scot, militibus, Waldeuo rectore ecclesie de fovern, Roberto de Lech rectore ecclesie de Slanys, Ricardo rectore ecclesie de essy, Et Rogero pater noster, clericis nostris, Duncano judice, dauit filio Kyneth de Neuticbyr[1] et multis aliis.

Of ten marks in Kelle in Buchan.

To all Christ's faithful to whom the present writ shall come, Alexander Cumyn, Earl of Buchan, health everlasting in the Lord. Let all of you know that we have given, and granted, and by this present charter have confirmed to God and the church of St. Mary and St. Andrew of Lundors and the monks who are there serving God, or who shall serve Him in all time coming, ten marks sterling each year in our holding (*tenemento*) of Kelle in Buchan, for the weal of the soul of our lord, Alexander, late illustrious King of the Scots, of pious memory, and for the weal of our soul, and for the souls of all our ancestors and successors, in exchange for the land of Kyncardinbegg, which they have surrendered to us and quitclaimed to us for ever. Wherefore we will that the aforesaid monks shall receive and have the aforesaid ten marks yearly for ever from our aforesaid holding of Kelly in free, pure, and perpetual alms as freely and quietly as any alms in the whole kingdom of Scotland is most freely given and possessed by any one. And with a view to their convenience and quiet, and as enhancement of our alms, we oblige ourselves and our heirs, and any others, our successors, to pay the aforesaid ten marks every year at Wrangham within the octave of the feast of the Nativity of St. John the Baptist [June 24] to the Abbot of Lundors, or to a monk, or to his bailiff, whomsoever shall come thither in the name of the same monks. And if on any occasion we fail, which God forbid, in the payment of the aforesaid alms at the aforesaid place and term, we will and grant for ourselves, our heirs, and successors, that it shall be lawful for the bailiff and men of the aforesaid monks after the octave before named to poind (*namare*) the aforesaid holding of Kelly, without any request for leave, and to detain the goods seized (*namos*) without any replegiation, until eight days after the aforesaid octave. And if then the said alms shall not have been paid, it shall be lawful for them to sell the said distress (*compulsionem*) up to the value of the afore-

---

[1] The reading of this word is very doubtful. It may possibly be read 'Neuticlyr.' There is also a doubt whether the third letter of the word is 'n' or 'u.'

said alms ; and we shall cause no hindrance by ourselves or by ours in the seizure, detention, or sale of the aforesaid poinds, so long as the said holding shall not have been so devastated by war that there does not remain in it a return of ten marks ; and if the same does remain in it, they may have it without hindrance, as has been said.

We also subject ourselves and our heirs and our other successors, whosoever they may be, and our men of the same holding (*tenementi*) to the jurisdiction of the Bishop and Archdeacon of Aberdeen, or their officials, for the time being, so that they, or any one of them, who shall be required on the part of the said monks, can after only one monition previously given, compel us, by sentences of excommunication against persons, and interdict against the said holding, whether it be in ward or out of ward ; such sentences to be in no wise relaxed or suspended until full satisfaction shall have been made to the aforesaid monks for the aforesaid alms.

Moreover, we promise and oblige ourselves and our heirs that we will not alienate in any way the aforesaid holding of Kelly, unless the alms is secured to the aforesaid monks by the compulsion and submission which have been mentioned. We renounce fully and expressly for ourselves, our heirs, and our successors, any royal prohibition, appeal, privilege granted, or to be granted, as indulgence to those who either now or hereafter be Crusaders; all letters, privileges, and graces, procured, or hereafter to be procured, from any secular or ecclesiastical court whatsoever ; every law and statute, every exception and plea (*defensioni*), real and personal, of law and statute, which on our part could be opposed to this instrument or deed. And we and our heirs will for ever warrant, secure (*acquietabimus*), and defend the aforesaid ten marks yearly to the aforesaid monks against all men and women. In testimony of which we have caused the present writ to be fortified with our seal. And because of the absence of the Lord Bishop of Aberdeen, William, Lord Bishop of St. Andrews, has at our request affixed his seal to this writ. These being the witnesses : William, by the grace of God, Lord Bishop of St. Andrews; Andrew, Lord Abbot of Cupar ; Sirs William de Montealto, William Cumyn, Fergus Cumyn, John Wyschard, Gilbert Scot, knights ; Waldeve, rector of the church of Fovern ; Robert de Leth, rector of the church of Slanys; Richard, rector of the church of Essy ; and Roger Paternoster, our clerks ; Duncan, judge ; David, son of Kyneth of Neuticbyr ; and many others.

CXXV

De Multura de Kynard.

5.]

OMNIBVS Christi fidelibus hoc scriptum visuris vel audituris

vestra quod cum auctoritate apostolica coram discreto viro domino N. Abbate de Dunfermelyn, vnico judice delegato, eiusque commissario, decano scilicet christianitatis de Abirden et Magistro Scolarum eiusdem loci, mota esset controuersia inter religiosos viros dominos N. abbatem et conuentum de Lundors actores, ex parte vna, et nos reas ex altera, super multura terre nostre de Kynhard soluenda, et secta facienda molendino dictorum abbatis et conuentus tanquam molendino syre de Lundors, quod est ipsorum abbatis et conuentus ex donacione inclite recordacionis comitis Dauid, nobis quia ex parte dictorum Abbatis et conuentus esset editum sub hac forma.   Dicunt et proponunt in iure coram vobis, Domine N. magister scolarum Abirden, Commissari Domini N. abbatis de Dunfermelyn, vnici iudicis a sede apostolica delegati, abbas et conuentus monasterii de Lundors contra priorissam et conuentum de Elyoch quod cum felicis recordacionis nobilis vir comes Dauid, pro salute anime sue et predecessorum et successorum suorum, molendinum de Lundors cum tota secta sua et multura eisdem et monasterio suo dedisset et concessisset, in puram et perpetuam elemosinam, de cuius secta molendini villa de Kynhard extitit et existit, iidem priorissa et conuentus, sectam et multuram eiusdem ville ad predictum molendinum spectantes, subtrahentes homines qui ad predictam sectam tenentur ne ad predictum molendinum accedant, sicut tenentur et consueuerunt, presumunt et diucius presumpserunt contra iusticiam impedire, in eorum abbatis et conuentus preiudicium et grauamen non modicum vnde dictos abbatem et conuentum predictis secta et multura iam per triginta et quatuor annos elapsos defraudarunt.   Quare petunt dicti abbas et conuentus dictas priorissam et conuentum a predicto impedimento coherceri, et predictos homines ad predictam sectam faciendam auctoritate apostolica compelli.   Petunt eciam dicti abbas et conuentus arreragia multure prouenientis ex dicta secta sibi cum integritate reddi, qui estimant valere centum et viginti mercas sterlingorum.   Hec dicunt et petunt dicti abbas et conuentus, saluo sibi iuris beneficio in omnibus addendi, minuendi, mutandi, et omnia alia faciendi que sibi poterunt
rodesse e   arti aduerse obesse.

maiores persone conuentus nostre pro nostra contumacia a
predictis iudicibus ab ingressu ecclesie suspense, lesamque in
hac parte habentes conscienciam, liti pocius cedere quam
contendere existimauimus. Vnde cum prefatis monachis super
prefatis secta et multura de Kynhard conuenimus in hunc
modum, videlicet, quod quamdiu contigerit. nos non habere
proprium molendinum infra dictam terram nostram de Kynhard constructum, firmarii nostri de eadem terra seu homines
nostri in ipsa manentes, uel quicunque alii ipsam terram
colentes, quocunque nomine censeantur, facient sectam, et
multuram debitam soluent molendino dictorum abbatis et
conuentus. Postquam autem molendinum infra limites dicte
terre, nostre de Kyn | hard construxerimus, ad quod constru-
endum dicti Abbas et conuentus nobis plenariam licenciam
dederunt, a die ipsius molendini totaliter constructi solvemus
singulis annis prefatis abbati et conventui per nos, vel per
manus firmariorum nostrorum, seu quorumcunque aliorum
dictam terram de Kynhard colencium pro dictis secta et
multura tres marcas argenti ad duos terminos anni, videlicet,
viginti solidos ad penthecosten et alios viginti solidos ad
festum Sancti Martini in hyeme; Ita quod si infra octo dies
cujuscunque termini de porcione ejusdem termini non fuerit
eisdem abbati et conventui satisfactum, liceat eisdem ex tunc
namos nostros et firmariorum hominumque nostrorum in dicta
terra manencium, nullius requisito consensu, nec ab aliquo
aliqua petita licencia, capere et tam diu nulli replegiandos, nec
ad vadium dandos, neque aliquo alio modo liberandos, detinere
quousque eisdem abbati et conventui de porcione suo termino
non soluta plenarie fuerit satisfactum. Ut autem ista convencio
firma sit et stabilis inperpetuum, Nicholaus dei gratia tunc
abbas de Lundors pro se et conventu suo et successoribus suis,
et ego prefata, Agnes priorissa de Elyoch pro me et conventu
mea et nobis succedentibus ad premissa omnia fideliter et sine
diminucione futuris temporibus observanda invicem affidavimus.
Si vero contigerit, quod absit, nos moniales vol nobis succedentes

87.]

convencionis, ita tamen quod non audiamur in judicio nec aliqua fides dictis nostris vel procuratoris nostri adhibeatur donec de centum et viginti marcis in dicta edicione petitis racione arreragiorum dictarum secte et multure non solutarum, nec non de dampnis et expensis, que vel quas dicti abbas et conventus incurrerint aut fecerint, occasione dicte convencionis non observate, super quibus simplici eorum verbo vel procuratoris sui credi volumus, ipsis abbati et conventui integre et totaliter satisfecerimus. In cujus rei testimonium uni parti istius scripti in modum cirograffi confecti, residenti penes prefatos abbatem et conventum, sigilla venerabilis patris domini Willelmi dei gracia Episcopi Sancti Andree et predicti abbatis de Dunfermelyn una cum communi sigillo capituli nostri sunt appensa, Alteri vero parti penes nos remanenti commune sigillum capituli monasterii de Lundors est appositum. Datum apud Lundors, die conversionis Sancti Pauli apostoli, anno domini milesimo ducentesimo octogesimo primo.

Of the Multure of Kynard.

To all Christ's faithful who shall see or hear this writ Agnes of Arroch, Prioress of Elyoch [Elcho], and the convent of the same place, health everlasting in the Lord. Let all of you know that a question was raised in debate before the discreet man, N., Lord Abbot of Dunfermline, sole judge delegate by apostolic authority, and his commissary, namely, the Dean of Christianity, of Aberdeen, and master of the schools of the same place, between the religious men [the monks], N., Lord Abbot and the convent of Lundors, pursuers, of the one part, and us, defenders, of the other part, on the multure to be paid from our land of Kynhard, and on the suit to be made to the mill of the said abbot and convent, as if to the mill of the shire of Lundors, which belonged to the said abbot and convent of the gift of Earl David, of famous memory. And on the part of the said abbot and convent the ground of action was put forth to us in the following terms : ' The Abbot and Convent of the monastery of Lundors state and declare in legal process (in jure) before you, Sir, (domine) N., master of the schools of Aberdeen, commissary of N., Lord Abbot of Dunfermline, sole judge delegated by the Apostolic See, against the Prioress and Convent of Elyoch that the noble man, of happy memory, Earl David, for the weal of his soul and of his predecessors and successors, gave and granted in pure and perpetual alms, to the

from the same vill [of Kynhard] by withdrawing the men who are bound
to the aforesaid suit, so that they should not come to the aforesaid mill,
to the prejudice and no small grievance of the abbot and convent.
Whence it has come to pass that they have defrauded the said abbot and
convent of the aforesaid suit and multure now for thirty and four
years past.   Wherefore the said abbot and convent seek that the said
prioress and convent should be restrained from causing this hindrance,
and that the men aforesaid should be compelled by apostolic authority
to make the aforesaid suit.   The said abbot and convent also seek
the arrears of multure arising from the aforesaid suit to be paid to
them in full; and they estimate those arrears at the value of one
hundred and twenty marks sterling.   These things the said abbot and
convent allege and seek, reserving to themselves in all things the benefit
of law to add to, take from, and change, and to do all other things
which can be of advantage to them, and of disadvantage to the opposite
party, declaring that they wish to seek the costs incurred or hereafter to
be incurred in litigation.'

At length the higher members (*majores persone*) of our convent were
suspended by the aforesaid judges from entering the church; and,
having a wounded conscience in regard to this, we have thought it
better to retire from the litigation than to further contest the matter.
Wherefore we came to an agreement with the aforesaid monks upon the
aforesaid suit and multure of Kynhard in this manner, to wit, that so
long as it happened that we have no mill of our own built within our own
land of Kynhard, the farmers of our said land, or our men residing in it,
or any others, whosoever, that cultivate that land, under whatever name
they are reckoned, shall make suit and pay due multure to the mill of
the said abbot and convent.   But after we shall have constructed a mill
within the bounds of our said land of Kynhard, for the construction of
which the said abbot and convent have given full permission, we shall,
from the day on which the mill has been completed, pay every year to
the said abbot and convent, in lieu of the said suit and multure, three
marks of silver, at the two terms of the year, namely, twenty shillings
at Whitsunday and the other twenty shillings at the feast of St. Martin
in winter, by our own hands, or those of our farmers, or of the others,
whoever they may be, who cultivate the said land of Kynhard.   So that
if within eight days after each term the abbot and convent shall not have

his convent, and his successors, and I, the aforesaid Agnes, Prioress of Elyoch, for myself and my convent and those who shall succeed us, have given our mutual faith to observe all the premises faithfully and without diminution in time to come. But if it shall happen, which God forbid, that we, the nuns, or those who succeed us, or any one in our name, or in the name of our church, shall at any time attempt anything contrary to the aforesaid agreement to the prejudice of the said abbot and convent, we will that the said question in dispute [between the monks and us] now settled should be regarded as in the same state in which it was on the day when this agreement was made, yet in such wise that we may not be heard in judgment, nor any credence be given to our words or the words of our proctor, until we shall have fully and completely satisfied the abbot and convent for the hundred and twenty marks claimed in the said formal charge (*editione*) on the ground of arrears of the said suit and multure not yet paid, and also shall have satisfied for the damages and costs which the said abbot and convent shall have incurred or expended by reason of this agreement not having been observed, with regard to which [damages and costs] we will that credence should be given to their bare word, or to the word of their proctor.

In testimony of which thing the seals of the venerable father, William, by the grace of God Lord Bishop of St. Andrews, and of the aforesaid Abbot of Dunfermline, together with the common seal of our chapter, have been appended to that part of this writ, executed in the manner of an indenture, which remains in the possession of the aforesaid abbot and convent. To the other part, remaining in our possession, the common seal of the chapter of the monastery of Lundors is affixed.

Given at Lundors, on the day of the Conversion of St. Paul the Apostle [Jan. 25], in the year of our Lord MCCLXXXI.

CXXVI

De Kynmuk de Balbuthan, et de Hathirwych.

ROBERTVS dei gracia Rex Scottorum Omnibus probis homini- bus tocius terre sue, clericis et laicis, Salutem. Sciatis nos pro salute anime nostre et pro salute animarum omnium anteces- sorum et successorum nostrorum, regum Scocie, dedisse, conces- sisse, et hac presenti carta nostra confirmasse deo, et beate Marie | Virgini, Sancto Andree, et Monasterio de Lundors, [fo

de Brus; Tenendas et habendas dictis monachis et corum successoribus in perpetuum per omnes rectas metas et divisas suas, in bosco et plano, pratis, pascuis et pasturis, viis, semitis, moris, maresiis, aquis, stangnis, vivariis, et multuris, in aucupacionibus et venacionibus, et cum omnibus aliis libertatibus, comoditatibus, aisiamentis, consuetudinibus, et ceteris pertinenciis ad dictam terram spectantibus, seu alio modo spectare valentibus in futurum, in liberam puram et perpetuam elemosinam, adeo libere et quiete, pacifice, integre, et honorifice, cum omnibus libertatibus et comoditatibus suis, tam non nominatis quam nominatis, sieut aliqua terra alicui monasterio seu pio loco per nos aut predecessores nostros infra regnum nostrum Scocie in liberam, puram, et perpetuam elemosinam data, et concessa liberius, quiecius, plenius, aut honorificencius tenetur aut possidetur, ita quod de dictis terris cum pertinenciis aut de monachis supradictis uel eorum hominibus dictas terras inhabitantibus nichil omnino exigi aut demandari poterit in futurum preter oracionum tantummodo suffragia deuotarum. In cuius.

Of Kynmuk, of Balbuthan, and of Hathirwych.

Robert [I.], by the grace of God, King of Scots, to all good men of his whole land, clerical and lay, greeting. Know ye that we, for the weal of our soul and for the weal of the souls of all our ancestors and successors, Kings of Scotland, have given, granted, and by this our present charter confirmed, to God, the Blessed Virgin Mary, St. Andrew, and the Monastery of Lundors, the religious men, the abbot and monks, who serve or shall for ever serve God there, the lands of Kynmuk, of Balbuthan, and of Hathirwych, with the multure of the same lands, in exchange for the land of Bernes in the Garviauch (*in le Garviauch*), which the said religious had of the gift and infeftment (*infeodacione*) of our beloved brother, Sir Edward de Brus; to be held and had by the said monks and their successors, by all their right meiths and marches, in wood and plain, meadows, pastures, and grazings, roads, paths, moors, marshes, waters, stanks, live-pools, and multures, in hawkings and huntings, and with all other liberties, conveniences, easements, customs, and other pertinents which belong to the said land or can in any wise belong to it in the future, in free, pure, and perpetual alms, as freely and

in future nothing whatsoever cau be exacted or demanded from the said lands with their pertinents, or from the monks aforesaid, or their men, save only the suffrages of devout prayers.   In [testimony] of which.

CXXVII
[De ecclesia de Moethel.]

VNIVERSIS Sancte Matris ecclesie filiis et fidelibus Malis filius comitis Ferteht, salutem.   Sciant tam presentes quam futuri me dedisse et concessisse et hac carta mea confirmasse deo et ecclesie Sancte Marie et Sancti Andree de Lundors, et monachis ibidem deo seruientibus, In puram et perpetuam elemosinam, ecclesiam de Moethel cum terra ad eandem ecclesiam perti- nente, cum decimis et obuencionibus, et omnibus ad eandem ecclesiam iuste pertinentibus.   Quare volo ut predicti monachi prenominatam ecclesiam liberam et quietam ab omni seruicio et seculari exaccione teneant et possideant, ita libere et quiete et plenarie et honorifice sieut aliqua abbacia in regno Scocie aliquam ecclesiam liberius, quiecius, plenarius, et honorificencius tenet et possidet.   Hiis testibus, Henrico abbate de Aber- brothoc, Johanne archidiacono de Dumblane, et ceteris.

(*Abstract*)
[OF the CHURCH of MOETHEL.][1]

To all the sons of Holy Mother Church and the faithful, Malise, son of Earl Ferteht, greeting.   He gives, grants, and confirms to Lundors, in pure and perpetual alms, the church of Moethel with its land, tithes, oblations, and all other pertinents, to be held free and quit of all service and secular exaction, as freely as any abbey in Scotland holds any church.   Witnesses, Henry, Abbot of Aberbrothoc; John, Archdeacon of Dunblane, and others.

CXXVIII
De una marca quam dedit nobis Radulphus de   L*fo* Lascellis.

heredum suorum, necnon pro salute anime mee et anime
quondam matildis sponse mee, et animarum omnium antecessorum et successorum meorum dedisse, concessisse, et hac presenti carta mea confirmasse, Religiosis viris Abbati et conuentui
de Lundors vnam marcam argenti ad sustentacionem duorum
cereorum coram magno altari in Monasterio suo ardencium ad
omnes missas, vesperas, et matutinas que de beata virgine Maria
celebrantur in dicto monasterio, et in omnibus festis que
sint in cappis.   Volo eciam et concedo quod dicti abbas et
conuentus et eorum successores percipiant dictam marcam
singulis annis de terra mea de Huchannane Locherton, quam
teneo de comite de Buchan, per manus meas vel firmarii mei
de dicta terra quicunque fuerit, vel per manus heredum meorum
ad vnum terminum anni, Scilicet, ad pentecosten, pro qua
quidem marca singulis annis in perpetuum percipienda, vt
dictum est, dicti Abbas et conuentus sustentacionem dictorum
duorum cereorum in se susceperint, et ad hoc fideliter faciendum
dicti Abbas et conuentus se et successores suos, et ego me et
heredes meos per hoc scriptum firmiter obligamus, ita videlicet
quod liceat eisdem Abbati et conuentui namos meos vel
heredum meorum siue successorum meorum vel firmarii nostri,
si firmarium habuerimus, nec non et omnia mea vel heredum
meorum bona siue successorum meorum vel firmarii nostri, vt
dictum est, in dicta terra inuenta capere, et si in solucione dicte
marce statuto termino defecerimus, tam diu nulli replegianda
detinere, donec dicta marca eisdem plenarie fuerit satisfacta
vna cum arreragiis, si que fuerint.   Ego vero et heredes mei
nunquam aliquo modo dictam terram alienabimus nisi salva
dictis Abbati et conuentui marca predicta.   Si vero contingat,
quod absit, quod dicti Abbas et conuentus aliquo tempore
dictos duos cereos sustentare recusauerint, ex tunc liceat michi
et heredibus meis dictam marcam tam diu detinere donec ipsi
ad sustentacionem eorum redire voluerint.   In cuius rei testimonium istud scriptum in modo cirograffi est confectum, cuius
vna pars signata sigillo meo penes dictos Abbatem et conuen-

(Abstract)

'OF one MARK which RALPH DE LASCELLIS gave us.'

To all Christ's faithful, etc., Ralph de Lascellis, knight, etc. For the weal of the soul of the late Sir Alexander Comyn, Earl of Buchan, 'my lord,' and his heirs, 'and for the weal of my soul and for the soul of the late Matilda, my spouse, and for the souls of all my ancestors and successors,' he grants to Lundors one mark of silver for sustaining two wax tapers before the great altar in the monastery, to be lighted at all masses, vespers, and matins of the Blessed Virgin Mary, and on all festivals when copes are worn. The mark is to be received every year from his land of Huchannane Locherton, which he held of the Earl of Buchan, by his hands or the hands of the farmers of the said land, or by the hands of his heirs, at the term of Whitsunday. The abbot and convent take on themselves in return for the one mark to maintain the two wax tapers. The abbot and convent shall have the right, in the event of the mark not being duly paid, to take poinds from him, or his heirs, or the farmer of the said land, if there be a farmer, and to seize all the goods of him, his heirs, or his farmer, which might be found on the said land, and to detain them, without repledging them to any, until the payment of the mark, and of arrears, if any, shall have been fully made. For himself and his heirs he engages not to alienate the land in any way without securing the mark to Lundors. If the abbot and convent at any time refuse, which God forbid, to maintain the two wax tapers, it shall be lawful for him and his heirs to retain the mark until the monks will revert to fulfilling the engagement.

The writ was executed in the form of an indenture, of which one part, sealed with his seal, remained in the possession of the abbot and convent, and the other part, sealed with the common seal of the convent, remained with him. Given at Lundors on Thursday next after the feast of St. Mathias the Apostle [Feb. 24], MCCXC.

CXXIX

De flandres.

me et heredibus meis, predicto comiti Dauid et heredibus suis totum ius et clamium quod ego vel successores mei unquam habuimus, vel quod successores mei unquam habere poterint in predicta terra de coninton cum pertinenciis suis, pro predictis escambiis, et id iuraui et affidaui eis tenendum pro me et heredibus meis, coram Willelmo Rege Scocie, in manu Dauid de Lindesey, tunc Justiciarii Regis Scotorum, et quod quandocunque idem comes Dauid per consilium hominum suorum a me exegerit securitatem, inde ei faciam in Anglia. Hiis testibus, Galtero olifard, Dauid de Lindesey, Henrico de Scocia et multis aliis.

(*Abstract*)

'OF FLANDRES.'

HUGH BRITON makes known to all that he has received from Earl David, brother of the King of Scotland, by exchange of Coninton with its pertinents, the land which belonged to Gillandres Buch in Garviach, and in the same place a half ploughgate of land in Flandres, and seven acres of land 'on account (*propter*) of Loeinge and Drocion,' and the land which Abraham Mare[1] and Eyncus held. He quitclaims for ever to Earl David and his heirs all right and claim which he or his ancestors ever had, or which his successors ever could have, in the aforesaid land of Coninton with its pertinents. He swears and gives his faith to this effect before William, King of Scotland, 'in the hand of David de Lindesay, then justiciar of the King of Scots,' and engages that whenever. Earl David 'on the advice of his men' shall require security from him [Briton] he will give it to him [Earl David] in England. Witnesses . . .

5.]   CXXX

OMNIBVS christi fidelibus hoc scriptum visuris vel audituris, Reginaldus de Chen pater, salutem eternam in domino. Nouerit vniuersitas vestra me pro salute anime mee et antecessorum et

Doesblare, nec aliqua impetracio perambulacionis fiat ex parte nostra inter predictas terras; Et quod nobis non ualeat si impetratur. Quoniam totum ius et clamium quod habebamus in illis uel aliqua parte earum uel ulla^a perambulacione procuranda illud eis dono et quietum clamo inperpetuum. In cuius rei testimonium presenti scripto sigillum meum vna cum sigillo domini Reginaldi filii et heredis mei est appositum. Datum apud sconam, die iouis proxima post festum Sancti Johannis ante portam latinam, anno gracie millesimo ducentesimo septuagesimo octauo.

ᵃ MS. ι

De tho de cre de doe Et quo peram fiat int

(Abstract)

[OF the LAND of THOLAUKERY.]¹

REGINALD DE CHEN, senior (*pater*), for the weal of his soul, and for the souls of his ancestors and successors resigns and quitclaims to Lundors, for himself, his heirs, and successors, all right and claim which he had, or believed that he had, in the land of Tholaukery. He engages that in future there shall be no perambulation between his land of Cremund and the monks' lands of Tholaukery and of Doesblare, and that no demand for a perambulation between the aforesaid lands shall be made on his part; and that if such demand be made it shall be of no avail. Inasmuch as he gave and quitclaimed for ever all right and claim which he had in those lands or in any part of them, or in what might be obtained by any perambulation. In testimony the writ is sealed with his seal, and the seal of Reginald, his son and heir. Given at Scone on the Thursday next after the feast of St. John before the Latin Gate [May 6], MCCLXXVIII.

CXXXI

Carta ecclesie de Cullessy.

OMNIBVS presens scriptum visuris vel audituris Rogerus de Quency Comes Wyntone, Constabularius Scocie, eternam in domino salutem. Nouerit vniuersitas vestra nos caritatis

cum omnibus suis pertinenciis ; Habendam et tenendam dicto abbati et conventui, et eorum successoribus, in liberam, puram et perpetuam elemosinam, libere, quiete, bene, et in pace in perpetuum ; Sieut aliqua ecclesia melius, liberius, et quiecius in Regno Scocie dari poterit et concedi, videlicet, quod cedente vel decedente magistro Adam de Malcarreston Rectore dicte ecclesie, liceat predictis abbati et conuentui et eorum successoribus, pro nobis et heredibus nostris, in dictam ecclesiam pacifice intrare et possidere et in vsus proprios conuertere, si eandem in vsus proprios aliquatenus possint impetrare. Et si eandem ecclesiam in vsus proprios conuertendam possint impetrare et optinere, nos vel heredes nostri nichil juris seu clamium in dicta ecclesia de cetero exigemus seu vendicabimus, nec contra suam impetracionem in aliquo veniemus. Et nos et heredes nostri dictam donacionem, concessionem, et confirmacionem dicte ecclesie de Culessyn cum omnibus suis pertinenciis, vt prenominatum est, dictis abbati et conuentui et eorum successoribus contra omnes gentes in perpetuum warantizabimus. Set si dictam ecclesiam in vsus proprios conuertendam non possint inpetrare, jus aduocacionis in dicta ecclesia ad nos et heredes nostros expresse et sine alicuius contradiccione reuertetur. In cuius rei testimonium et securitatem presentem cartam sigilli nostri impressione duximus |

6.] Roborandam. Hiis testibus, Dominis Willelmo de Oyly, Johanne becard, militibus, Magistro Adam de Malcarreston, Magistro Eustacio de Scelford, domino Ricardo de Radeswelle, Magistro Roberto tunc phisico nostro, domino Willelmo de Sancto Edwardo capellano, Saero de Setun, Rogero Raboc, Alexandro de Seton, Rogero Bourc clerico, et aliis.

(Abstract)

' CHARTER of the CHURCH of CULLESSY.'

ROGER DE QUENCY, Earl of Wyntone, Constable of Scotland, for the weal of his soul, and for the souls of his ancestors and successors gives, grants, and confirms to Lundors the church of Culessin with all its

are able to obtain it to any extent for their own uses.[1] If they are able to convert the church to their own uses, he and his heirs will raise no obstacle grounded on any right or claim. This gift, grant, and confirmation of the church of Culessyn to the monks of Lundors he and his heirs will warrant for ever 'against all people' (*contra omnes gentes*). But if the monks are not able to secure the church for conversion to their own uses, the right of advowson (*jus advocationis*) is to revert to him and his heirs. De Quency's seal. Witnesses

CXXXII
De confirmacione regis Alexandri.

ALEXANDER dei gracia Rex Scottorum, Omnibus probis hominibus tocius terre sue, Salutem. Sciatis nos concessisse et hac presenti carta nostra confirmasse Donacionem illam quam Rogerus de Quency Comes Wintoun, Constabularius Scocie, fecit caritatis intuitu, pro salute anime sue et pro animabus antecessorum et successorum suorum, deo et beate Marie et ecclesie sancti Andree de Lundors et abbati et conuentui ibidem deo seruientibus et in perpetuum seruituris, de ecclesia de Cullessin, cum omnibus suis pertinenciis; Tenenda et habenda eisdem abbati et conuentui et eorum successoribus in perpetuum in liberam, puram, et perpetuam elemosinam, adeo libere, quiete, plenarie et honorifice, sicut carta dicti Comitis eis inde confecta plenius iuste testatur. Testibus, Gamelino episcopo sancti Andree, Ricardo episcopo Dunkeldensi, Roberto episcopo Dunblanensi, Willelmo Comite de Marre Camerario, Johanne Cumyn, Hugone de Abirnethin, Hugone de Berklay Justiciario Laodonie, Johanne de Lamberton, apud Linlithgov, vicesimo quinto die decembris, anno regni nostri Quintodecimo.

(Abstract)

'OF KING ALEXANDER'S CONFIRMATION.'

ALEXANDER, King of Scots, confirms that gift which Roger de Quency, Earl of Wintoun, Constable of Scotland, made to Lundors at the prompt-

Witnesses . . . At Linlithgow, the 25th of December, in the fifteenth year of our reign.[1]

CXXXIII

De amicabili composicione inter Abraham Episcopum Dunblanensem et Guidonem abbatem [de Lundors].

OMNIBVS christi fidelibus hoc scriptum visuris vel audituris. Johannes de Mubray, miles, dominus de Methfen, salutem eternam in Domino. Nouerit vniuersitas vestra quod cum predecessores mei, pro salute animarum suarum et suorum successorum, dederunt, concesserunt et per cartas suas specialiter confirmaverunt deo et ecclesie Dunblanensi terram de Eglis magril cum pertinenciis suis ; Ac ipsa terra de Eglismagril per amicabilem composicionem inter dominum quondam Abraham episcopum Dunblanensem nomine ecclesie sue, et dominum *de.* Guidonem quondam abbatem de[a] Lundors et conuentum suum nomine monasterij sui super ecclesia de Mothel, ex arbitrio domini Willelmi sancti andree episcopi, ad ipsos abbatem et conuentum de Lundors et suos successores fuerit deuoluta, et in processu temporis dictam terram de Eglismagril ecclesie predicte Dunblanensi a predictis collatam, pro salute anime mee et predictorum omnium, liberam et quietam ab omni auxilio, exercitu, et forinseco seruicio, per cartam meam specialiter de gracia mea eidem ecclesie concessero et confirmauero : Volo et] concedo pro me et heredi | bus meis et meis successoribus, quod dicti abbas et conuentus teneant et possideant predictam terram de Eglismagril, cum pertinenciis suis, in liberam, puram, et perpetuam elemosinam, liberam et quietam ab omni secta cuiuscunque curie, exactione, citacione, recognicione, namacione, et omnimodo exercitu, omnique genere auxilii vel seculari demanda facienda uel prestanda, necnon et ab omni forinseco seruicio, onere et seruitute, quocunque casu uel causa contingente, quorum omnium onus in me et heredes meos ac meos

heredibus ac successoribus meis quod nunquam grauamen, molestiam, uel inquietudinem super dicta terra, occasione pre- missorum uel alicuius de premissis, prefatis abbati et conuentui futuris temporibus inferemus,[a] nec districcionem aliquam per capcionem bonorum in ipsa terra de Eglismagril existencium uel alio aliquo[b] modo super eisdem faciemus, neque fieri per- mittemus nec ab aliis fieri procurabimus. In cuius rei testi- monium presenti scripto sigillum meum apposui. Data apud Methfen, in festo Sancti Vincencii martiris, Anno gracie M° C° C° C°

[a] MS. *inus.*
[b] MS.

(Abstract)

'OF a FRIENDLY AGREEMENT between ABRAHAM, BISHOP of DUNBLANE, and GUIDO, ABBOT [of LUNDORS].'

JOHN DE MUBRAY, knight, Lord of Methfen, makes known to all that his predecessors, for the weal of their own souls and the souls of their successors, had given and by their charters specially confirmed to the [cathedral] church of Dunblane the land of Eglismagril with its perti- nents. He further narrates that the said land had been made over to Lundors by a friendly agreement between Abraham, former Bishop of Dunblane, and Guido, former Abbot of Lundors, as to the church of Mothel, in consequence of the decree arbitral of William, Bishop of St. Andrews. He purposes, of his favour, to grant and confirm by charter to Lundors this land which had been conferred on the church of Dunblane by his predecessors for the weal of souls, and to grant that it should be free and quit of all aid, hosting (*exercitu*), and forinsec service. Wherefore he wills and concedes, for himself, his heirs, and his successors, that the monks of Lundors should hold and possess the land of Eglismagril with its pertinents in free, pure, and perpetual alms, quit of all suit of any court whatsoever, of exaction, citation, recognition, poinding (*namacione*), all hosting, all kinds of aids and secular demands, all forinsec service, burden, and subjection, which might arise by any chance or from any cause. The burden of all such he takes on himself, his heirs, and successors, and faithfully promises that neither he nor his heirs nor successors will in future give any trouble or annoyance to the monks of Lundors, nor make any distraint by the seizure of goods upon the land of Eglismagril, nor permit nor procure such to be made by others. His seal. 'Given at Methfen, on the feast of St. Vincent the Martyr [Jan. 22], in the year of grace MCCC.'

Lundors a predecessoribus nostris fundetur, et per quam plura
guerrarum discrimina, pensiones intollerabiles, necnon assedaciones terrarum per quosdam abbates ipsius monasterij, non
immerito dispositas quandoque concessas, in dampnum non
modicum monasterij eiusdem et lesionem elemosine nostre, ac in
iacturam bonorum dicti monasterij vehemencius debilitetur ;
Ita quod redditus eiusdem monasterij ad sustentacionem monachorum ibidem seruiencium vix poterunt sufficere ; Et quia
vt intelleximus per bone memorie dominum, patrem nostrum,
dudum Regem Scottorum et quondam Thomam Ranulphi
Comitem Morauie, dilectum nepotem nostrum, tunc locum
nostrum tenentem, de consensu diocesani, videlicet, quondam
Jacobi dei gracia tunc Episcopi Sancti Andree, in cuius Episcopatu dictum monasterium situm est, et per plenum consilium
in pleno parliamento, tento apud Sconam, omnia huiusmodi
facta dictorum Abbatum reprobata, reuocata, et omnino de
iure fuerunt adnihillata ; Nos omnes huiusmodi pensiones,
donaciones, et assedaciones per quemcunque dictorum Abbatum
vsque in diem confeccionis presencium, qualitercunque factas et
concessas, reuocantes : vobis firmiter precipiendo mandamus
quatinus probos viros religiosos | super hac reuocacione nostra
vnam litteram magno sigillo nostro sigillatam, in debita forma
capelle nostre confectam, Justiciarijs, vicecomitibus, prepositis,
et ceteris ministris nostris quibuscunque qui pro tempore
fuerint, et quorum interest, visis presentibus, habere faciatis, vt
ipsi predictos viros religiosos secundum propositum nostrum
in premissis sustineant, manuteneant, et defendant.   Datum
apud monasterium de Kynlosse, vicesimo nono die marcij, anno
regni nostri Tercio decimo.

8.]

[Of the maintenance of the MONKS' of LUNDORS.]¹

DAVID, by the grace of God, King of Scots, to Thomas de Carnot,
knight, our Chancellor of Scotland, greeting. Inasmuch as the monastery
of Lundors was founded by our predecessors, and is exceedingly enfeebled
both by the very many perils of the wars, unbearable pensions, and
leases of the lands granted, not unjustly at the time, by certain abbots

suffice for the maintenance of the monks serving there ; and because, as we have understood, all acts of this kind done by the said abbots were rejected, revoked, and made wholly null in law, by our father of good memory, late King of Scots, and the late Thomas Randolph, Earl of Moray, our dear cousin, then holding our place, with the consent of the diocesan, to wit, the late James, by the grace of God then Bishop of St. Andrews, in whose bishopric the said monastery is situated, and by the full council in full parliament held at Scone; we revoking all pensions, gifts, and leases of this kind by whomsoever of the said abbots, or howsoever made and granted up to the day of the making of these presents, strictly command and enjoin that you on sight of these presents should cause the good men, the monks, to have a letter upon this our revocation, sealed with our Great Seal in the due form of our chapel, addressed to the justiciars, sheriffs, provosts, and other officers of ours, whosoever they may be for the time, and to whom it is of concern, and that they in accordance with our purpose in the premises should support, aid, and defend the religious aforesaid. Given at the monastery of Kynlosse, the twenty-ninth day of March, in the thirteenth year of our reign.[1]

CXXXV

Liberum chymnachium per totam terram Domini R. de Quincy.

OMNIBVS Christi fidelibus presens scriptum visuris vel audituris Rogerus de Quency Comes Wynton et constabularius Scocie, Salutem in domino. Noueritis nos diuine caritatis intuitu dedisse, concessisse, et hac presenti carta nostra confirmasse deo et Monachis de Lundors vt tam ipsi quam eorum homines cum suis bobus, equis, et carris liberum Cheminagium habeant per medium Boscum nostrum de Kyndelohc, si sibi viderint expedire, Et per totam terram nostram ubi melius et proprius sibi visum fuerit, usque ad moram de Edyn pro Bruera, et per ipsam moram mediam usque ad pethariam que[2] Monagrey pro Pethys, Ac abinde ad Monasterium suum eundo et redeundo, Sine impedimento vel contradiccione alicujus ballivi nostri vel heredum seu successorum nostrorum inper-

presens scriptum sigilli nostri munimine roboravimus. Hiis
testibus, Magistro W. Wyscard Archidiacono Sancti Andree,
tunc Cancellario Scocie, Magistro A. de Malcarueston preposito Sancti Andree, Dominis Willelmo de Holy, Johanne
Bekard, Roberto de Sancto Andrea, Malcolmo Butyler, Hugone
de Bevmys et Rogero de Forfar, militibus. Willelmo capellano
nostro, domino Ricardo de Redwelle clerico, et Magistro
Roberto medico nostro, et multis aliis.

(Abstract)

' FREE ROAD through the whole land of SIR R. DE QUINCY.'

ROGER DE QUENCY, Earl of Wynton, and Constable of Scotland, at the
prompting of divine love, gives, grants, and confirms by the present
charter to God and the monks of Lundors, that they and their men
with their oxen, horses, and carts should have a free road (cheminagium)
through the middle of his wood of Kyndeloch, if they think it an advantage to them, and through the whole of his land, wherever it might
seem to them best and most suitable, as far as to the moor of Edyn for
heather ; and through the middle of the moor itself as far as the peat-
moss, which is called Monagrey, for peats, and thence to the monastery,
both going and returning, without hindrance or opposition from his
bailiff, or the bailiff of his heirs and successors. He and his heirs will
warrant and defend to the monks and their successors the aforesaid
right of way against all people and women (contra omnes gentes et feminas).
Seal of De Quincy. Witnesses

CXXXVI

Carta Elene de Brechyn de loco concesso pro petis
Abbatis | de ij porciunculis terre de Kyndloch.

9.]

VNIVERSIS Christi fidelibus presentes literas visuris vel audituris, Elena relicta quondam domini · Willelmi de Brechin,
domina de Kyndeloch, Salutem in salutis auctore. Noverit
universitas vestra me in viduitate mea dedisse, concessisse, et hac
presenti carta mea confirmasse deo et Monasterio Sancte Marie
et Sancti Andree de Lundors et Monachis ibidem Deo ser-

.

Omnib̅s x̅ fidelib̅ p̅sentes litt̅as inspic̅t ut audit̅
... Alena relicta q̅ond̅am dn̅i Willm̅i de Bret...
dn̅a de kynueloch. Salut̅m in salutis auctore. Nouerit uniuisitas ur̅a me in viduitate mea dedisse.
co̅cesse et hac p̅senti carta mea c̅firmasse do et
Monastio sc̅e Marie ⁊ sc̅i Andr̅ de Lud̅or. et mo-
chis ibid̅ d̅o seruient̅b⁊ ⁊ imp̅petuu̅ seruituris
p̅ salute ai̅e mee ⁊ ai̅ar̅ o̅mium anecess̅or ⁊ successor meor̅ duas p̅tic̅ulas t̅re Inf̅ venem̅
tu̅ meu̅ de kynueloch. q̅s p̅sonali̅ p̅ambula̅
...a Albert̅ de Lud̅ouis. suo ... q̅iet̅ su̅
noi̅e in possessione p̅stit̅ corporale̅ ad p̅
...di̅ sue ... p̅tas suas sue socal... ⁊
cu̅q̅ eis indebit̅ exp̅die ⁊ ad echis...
sc̅e p̅struend̅a p̅ c̅o ... c̅olu̅ad̅...
p̅ c̅u̅icta̅ t̅re ... ...

ventus sui nomine, in possessionem posui corporalem, ad ponendum sive staccandum petas suas, sive focale, quando-cunque eis videbitur expedire, et ad edificia in eisdem con-struenda pro dicto focali salvando. Quarum porciuncularum terre una vocatur Insula qui jacet ex parte boriali immediate juxta terram dictorum monachorum quam habent et prius habuerunt in villa de Kyndelohc, et circumdata est illa insula ex parte occidentali et boriali quodam Marisio quod anglice dicitur Seggymir, et ex parte orientali quodam Marisio quod vocatur anglice Muchelli; alia vero porciuncula est in parte australi more de Edin, jacens, ex parte boriali, immediate ad Marisium monachorum quod alio nomine dicitur Mungrey. Et illa porciuncula terre unam acram et quartam partem acre continet. Dedi eciam et concessi et hac presenti carta mea confirmavi dictis Monachis licenciam et liberam viam ducendi sive cariandi, sine impedimento, dictum focale suum, per terras meas de Kyndeloch de Marisio suo ad utrumque locum et extra quociescunque opus fuerit et dictis monachis placuerit. Et hanc presentem donacionem meam dictis monachis in puram et perpe|tuam elemosinam per me concessam et factam contra omnes homines et feminas libere et quiete warendizabo Et warendizandum me et heredes meos per presentes obligo. In cujus rei testimonium presentibus sigillum meum apposui. Datum apud Lundors, die veneris in festo Sancti Bartholomei apostoli, Anno gracie m°ccc° secundo; Hiis testibus, domino Johanne decano Dunblanensi, dominis Roberto et Johanne Capellanis meis, Magistris Michaele et Thoma clericis meis, Waltero Byseth, Johanne de Kyndeloch, Roberto Cumyn, et multis aliis.

[_fo_

(Abstract)

'CHARTER of ELENA of BRECHIN concerning a place granted for the ABBOT'S PEATS and concerning two small portions of the land of KYNDELOCH.'

ELENA, relict of the late Sir William of Brechin, Lady of Kynde-

ing buildings for saving the said fuel. Of which small portions of land one is called Inch (*Insula*), which lies to the north, immediately next to the land which the monks have and had in the vill of Kyndeloch. And that Inch is surrounded on the west and north by a marsh, which is called in English Seggymir, and on the east by a marsh which is called in English Muchelli. But the other small portion is in the south part of the moor of Edin lying, on its north part, next adjoining the marsh of the monks, which by another name is called Mungrey. And that small portion of land contains one acre and a quarter. She also gives the monks a free road for drawing and carting (*cariandi*) the said fuel without hindrance through her lands of Kyndeloch from their marsh to each of the two places, and beyond, as often as they please and have need. She will warrant, and by the present charter obliges herself and her heirs to warrant this gift, in pure and perpetual alms, against all men and women. Her seal. Given at Lundors, on Friday, being the feast of St. Bartholomew the Apostle [Aug. 24],[1] MCCCII. Witnesses

CXXXVII

Carta Super brueram in mora de Kyndloche et petera de Monegrey.

UNIVERSIS Sancte Matris ecclesie filiis presens scriptum visuris vel audituris Rogerus de Quency, Comes Winton, Constabularius Scocie, Salutem in domino sempiternam. Noveritis nos caritatis intuitu, pro salute anime nostre et pro salute animarum antecessorum et successorum nostrorum, dedisse, concessisse et hac presenti Carta nostra confirmasse in liberam, puram, et perpetuam elemosinam, deo et ecclesie Sancte Marie de Lundors et Monachis ibidem Deo servientibus et in perpetuum servituris, ducentas Carratas bruere in mora nostra de Kyndoloch annuatim inperpetuum percipiendas in loco nobis et heredibus nostris minus nocivo et dictis Monachis competenciori. Et si ducente Carrate bruere eis non sufficiant volumus, quod ipsi propinquiores sint omnibus aliis ad brueram eandem,[a] quantum necesse habuerint in eadem bruera; Dedimus eciam eisdem

ndam.

que vocatur Monegre quot voluerint ad sufficienciam sustenta-
cionis sue. Ita videlicet quod nullus alius in dicta petera nostra
petas fodiat sine licencia et voluntate dictorum monachorum,
nec ipsi de predicta petera dabunt, nec vendent, nec aliquo
alio modo alienabunt, nec conuertent nisi in usus proprios
predicte domus sue ; concessimus eciam eisdem Monachis longi-
tudinem et latitudinem unius acre in dicta mora eis annuatim
assignande proximo adjacente loco in quo dictas | petas fodient,   [f̸
In cujus quidem acre longitudine et latitudine predictas petas
suas sine alicujus impedimento licite possint desiccare. Dedimus
preterea dictis monachis unum messuagium adjacens proximo
vado quod vocatur Ethyweyn ex parte orientali in campo de
Thoreston continens duas acras terre, ad quod quidem mesuagium attractum suum de bruera et petis facere possunt, et
custos eorum, qui predictum mesuagium et focale custodiet,
quicunque pro tempore fuerit,[a] duas vaccas et decem oves in ᵃ ᴍꜱ.
communi pastura more nostre de Kyndeloch habeat [b] pascentes. ᵇ ᴹꜱ.
Volumus eciam quod predicti monachi et eorum homines cum
suis bobus et carris liberum chiminagium habeant per rectum
usque moram pro bruera, et per mediam moram pro petis et
abinde ad mesuagium suum redeundo, sine alicujus impedimento vel contradiccione. Concedimus eciam eisdem monachis
pro nobis et heredibus nostris quod eorum boves, qui predictum
focale attraxerint, communem pasturam habeant in dicta mora
nostra de Kyndeloch, a tempore quo inceperint ad trahendum
usque ad Nativitatem beate Marie virginis annuatim ; Ita
tamen quod nullatenus causa istius nostre donacionis seu concessionis aliquod de suis averiis nec aliquem de suis bohus in
dicta pastura ponere possint, nisi solummodo boves suos dictum
focale attrahentes per tempus prenotatum : Habendum et
tenendum de nobis et heredibus nostris predictis monachis in
perpetuum libere, quiete, et solute, secundum quod aliqua
elemosina liberius, quiecius, et honorificencius dari potest vel
concedi. Nos vero et heredes nostri predictas ducentas carratas

Wykes, Johanne Berkard, Johanne de Wemes, Roberto de Hereford et Philipo de Chetewind, militibus, Johanne de Kyndeloch, Christephero de Seton, Alexandro filio suo, Roberto et Rogero de Crafford, clericis, et aliis. Datum apud Dysart, prima dominica quadragesime, Anno domini M° Ducentesimo Quadragesimo Septimo.

(Abstract)

'ON HEATHER on the MOOR of KYNDELOCH, and the FEAT-MOSS of MONEGREY.

ROGER DE QUENCY, Earl of Winton, Constable of Scotland, grants to Lundors two hundred cart-loads (*caratas*) of heather, to be taken yearly on his moor of Kyndeloch, at a place which was not injurious to him or his heirs, and was most suitable to the monks. And if the two hundred cart-loads of heather did not suffice, they were to take as much more as was wanted, inasmuch as they were nearer to the moor where the heather was to be had than any others. He also grants to the monks leave to dig and take as many peats in his peat-moss, 'which is called Monegre,' as they need for their wants. No one should without the leave of the monks dig peats in the said peat-moss. But the monks were not to give, or to sell, or in any way to alienate anything from the peat-moss. The peats were to be solely for the use of their monastery (*domus sue*). He also grants to the monks land to the extent of one acre next adjoining the place where they dig the peats, in which acre they can dry their peats without hindrance. He also grants to the monks a messuage adjacent to the nearest ford, 'which is called Ethyweyn, on the eastern side in the field (*in campo*) of Thoreston,' containing two acres of land, to which messuage they can draw their heather and peats; and the keeper who keeps the messuage and fuel is permitted to feed two cows and ten sheep on the common pasture of the moor of Kyndeloch. Further, the monks and their men are permitted to have a free road (*chiminagium*), in a straight line as far as the moor, for heather, and a free road through the middle of the moor for peats, and thence to the messuage in returning. The earl also grants that the monks' oxen which draw the said fuel may have common pasture on the moor of Kyndeloch from the time when they begin to draw up to the Nativity of the Blessed Virgin Mary [Sept. 8]. But this concession does not extend to any of the monks' beasts of burden (*averiis*) or any of their oxen save only the oxen which shall be engaged in drawing the fuel during the space of time already defined. These rights are to be held

CXXXVIII

Carta Willelmi regis Scocie.

WILLELMVS dei gracia Rex Scottorum episcopis, abbatibus, comitibus, baronibus, justiciariis, vicecomitatibus, prepositis, ministris, et omnibus probis hominibus tocius terre sue, clericis et laicis, salutem. Sciant presentes et futuri me concessisse et hac carta mea confirmasse deo et ecclesie sancte marie et sancti andree de Lundors et abbacie quam comes David frater meus ibi fundavit, et monachis ibidem Deo servientibus et servituris, in liberam et puram et perpetuam elemosinam, ecclesiam de Lundors, cum omnibus justis pertinenciis suis, et terram ad predictam ecclesiam pertinentem, per rectas divisas suas in bosco et plano, et totam terram ab occidentali parte rivuli descendentis de magno lacu usque in they preter insulam que vocatur Redinche. Et preterea unam piscariam in they juxta predictam insulam et asiamenta ipsius insule, scilicet, Redinche, ita eis communia ad proprios usus eorum sieut prefato comiti aut heredibus suis, et molendinum de Lundors, scilicet, molendinum ipsius ville de Lundors, cum omni secta sua et molitura; Ita quod homines comitis facient omnia que pertinent ad molendinum sicut facere solebant tempore quo comes illud in manu sua habuit. Si autem molendinum comitis non possit molere, ipse bladum suum proprium molere faciet ad molendinum monachorum sine molitura. Et si molendinum monachorum molere non possit, ipsi molent ad molendinum comitis bladum suum proprium, similiter sine molitura. Concedo eciam eisdem monachis ecclesiam de Dunde cum omnibus pertinenciis suis, et unum thoftum in burgo de Dunde, liberum et quietum ab omni servicio et exaccione. Et ultra moneth Fyntre per rectas divisas suas et cum omnibus justis perti-

et ecclesiam de Inchemabanin, et ecclesiam de Kursamuel, et ecclesiam de Kelabemunt, cum capellis earundem ecclesiarum, et terris et decimis et oblacionibus omnimodis et omnibus justis pertinencns suis, ad proprios usus et sustentaciones eorundem monachorum, et unum toftum in burgo de Inverury, liberum et quietum ab omni servicio et exaccione. Concedo eciam eis decimam omnium lucrorum et placitorum infra terram comitis et extra, ultra moneth, quam habuerit tempore quo fecit donacionem istam, et decimam omnium lucrorum que ei proveniunt de lueris meis in toto regno meo, et decimam omnium rerum comitis et heredum suorum ultra moneth, scilicet, decimacionem bladi et farine, butiri et casei, carnis et venacionis, cibi et potus, et coriorum ferarum cum mota canum captarum, cere et salis, uncti et sepi, et omnium aliarum rerum que decimari possunt, et que dabuntur, vel vendentur, vel ad firmam ponentur, de maneriis comitis ultra moneth, vel eciam que in eis expendentur, preter assisos redditus denariorum quos comes habuerit tempore quo fecit hanc donacionem: Ita ut prenominati monachi omnia supradicta et in terris et in ecclesiis et in omnibus aliis ad proprios vsus et sustentaciones suas habeant et teneant. Concedo eciam eis curiam suam

13.] omnino liberam, et dignitatem pacis | et omnes alias libertates quas abbacia habere debet. Quare volo et precipio ut monachi prefate abbacie de Lundors habeant et possideant omnes predictas terras, tenementa, et possessiones, et ecclesias, cum capellis et terris et decimis et omnibus aliis iustis pertinenciis suis, in bosco et plano, in pratis et pascuis, in aquis et molendinis, in stagnis et viuariis, in piscariis, in viis et semitis, cum omnibus libertatibus et liberis consuetudinibus, sine omni seruicio et consuetudine et auxilio et seculari exaccione, in liberam et puram et perpetuam elemosinam, ita bene et in pace, libere, quiete plenarie, integre, et honorifice sicut aliqua abbacia uel domus religionis in toto regno meo melius et liberius, quiecius, plenius, et honorificencius aliquam elemosinam tenet et possidet Ita

(*Abstract*)

'CHARTER of WILLIAᴍ, KING of SCOTLAND.'

'WILLIAᴍ, by the grace of God, King of Scots, to the bishops, abbots, earls, barons, justiciars, sheriffs, provosts, officers, and all good men of his whole land, clerical and lay, greeting.' He confirms to Lundors the gift of Earl David, his brother, [as contained in Charter II.]. But the following variations have to be noted. He excepts the island which is called Redinche. He grants one fishing on the Tay near the said island, but no express mention is made of the yare. The easements of Redinche, as common to the monks and Earl David, are confirmed, so that there is no real difference in substance between this Charter and Charter II. as regards Redinche. But Inch (*Insula*) at Perth is not mentioned. When confirming the tithe of Earl David's property beyond the Mounth, the present Charter excepts certain payments of rent in money (*preter assisos redditus denariorum*). Again, it is worthy of notice that in the concluding paragraph, where Earl David uses the word 'successors,' King William's confirmation uses the word 'heirs.' On this difference the lawyer who drew up the legal opinion contained in CXLIX. founds an argument. There are differences in the spelling of the names of places, which suggest that the scribe who copied the present Charter adapted the orthography of the names, or of some of them, to the pronunciation of the later time when he wrote; for example, 'Inverurin' of Charter II. becomes 'Inverury.'

CXXXIX

Johannes de Scocia.

OMNIBVS hoc scriptum visuris uel audituris Johannes e Scocia comes de Huntedon, Salutem. Sciatis me concessisse et hac presenti carta mea confirmasse deo et ecclesie sancte marie et sancti andree de Lundors et monachis ibidem deo serui- entibus, donacionem illam quam bone memorie pater meus comes Dauid fecit eisdem, scilicet, totam terram que 'iacet ab occidentali parte riuuli descendentis de magno lacu de Lun-

Dunde, de ffintreth, de Inuerury, de Durnach, de Prameth, de Rathmuriel, de Inchemabanin, de Kilsamuel, de Kilalkmund, et de dono Normanni, constabularij, ecclesiam de Lescelyn, cum terris et decimis et omnibus ad predictas ecclesias iuste pertinentibus, et vnum plenarium toftum in villa de Perth, quem Euerardus flandrensis quondam tenuit, et vnum plenarium toftum in Dunde, vnum plenarium toftum in Inuerury, vnam carucatam terre in Neutyle de dono Ade sororis mee. Concedo eciam eis decimam omnium lucrorum et placitorum meorum, infra terram meam et extra, vltra moneth, et decimam omnium rerum mearum et heredum meorum vltra moneth, sicut in carta predicti patris mei continetur. Quare volo et concedo ut predicta ecclesia de Lundors et monachi ibidem deo seruientes habeant, teneant, et possideant omnia predicta cum omnibus suis pertinenciis, et curiam suam liberam omnino, et dignitatem pacis, et omnes liberas consuetudines quas aliqua abbacia habere debet in regno Scocie, sine omni seruicio et consuetudine et exaccione seculari, in liberam et puram et perpetuam elemosinam, Ita quod nec ego nec aliquis successorum meorum aliquid ab eis exigat, nisi solas oraciones ad anime salutem pertinentes, sicut carta predicti patris mei eisdem facta testatur. Hiis testibus, etc.

(*Abstract*)

['JOHN of SCOTLAND.'

NOTE.—This Charter does not vary from Charter xv. except in the spelling of some of the names of places. These variations can be seen on a comparison of the Latin texts of the two charters, and it has not been thought necessary to reproduce the translation here.]

CXL

Cokeburn super diuisione terre de Collelessy et Cardynside.

presenti Carta mea confirmasse, deo et monasterio de Lundors et monachis ibidem deo seruientibus et seruituris in perpetuum totam terram illam cum pertinenciis | que iacet in latitudine [f inter magnam viam, que ducit de villa mea de Cullessin ad monasterium de Lundors, et terram ipsorum monachorum que dicitur Cardynside; Et in longitudine incipiendo a terra eorundem Monachorum que dicitur Suthleys versus aquilonem vsque ad riuulum qui currit in magnum lacum inter me et ipsos, cum illa particula terre quam eis extendi et limitari ᵃ ᵃ MS. feci ex parte australi predicte magne vie, recta linea, a terra mea que dicitur Wudeknocside versus aquilonem vsque in medium prati eorundem Monachorum quod dicitur pratum magni lacus. Preterea dedi, concessi, et presenti Carta mea confirmaui eisdem Monachis duas acras terre extra villam de Culessin versus aquilonem, ad faciendum eis vnum mesuagium vbi possint petas et alia bona sua attrahere et saluo custodire, si voluerint; Et liberum transitum seu cheminagium per mediam terram meam de Coulessin, videlicet cundo per mediam villam meam de Coulessin cum eorum hominibus, equis, et bobus, plaustris et carrectis, versus petariam suam in mora de Edyne, et redeundo per eandem viam sicut ire consueuerunt, ad trahenda focalia sua, sine perturbacione mei vel meorum seu heredum vel assignatorum meorum, saluo blado nostro et herbagio. Et si contingat quod eorum boues, seu plaustra, Equi, vel carrecte, per negligenciam hominum suorum, vel aliquo alio casu bladum nostrum seu herbagium secus viam calcauerint et dampnum fecerint, dicti Monachi ad visum proborum virorum, sine aliqua inprecacione, namacione, seu perturbacione mei vel meorum vel heredum seu assignatorum meorum, illud dampnum racionabiliter restaurabunt. Volo eciam et concedo vt quicumque predictas duas acras terre de dictis monachis aliquo tempore tenuerint habeant asiamentum pasture vbi homines mei vel heredum seu assignatorum meorum de Culessin pascunt sua animalia, ad unum equum, duas vaccas,

quod nec ego nec heredes mei uel assignati nec aliquis alius aliquid ab eis exigere poterimus, nisi solas oraciones ad animarum salutem. Et ego Johannes et heredes seu assignati mei totam predictam terram cum cheminagio et aliis supra nominatis, in liberam, puram, et perpetuam elemosinam, predictis Monachis contra omnes homines et feminas warentizabimus et defendemus, et ab omnimodis auxiliis, excercitibus, secularibus seruiciis, et demandis, inperpetuum acquietabimus. In cuius Rei testimonium presens scriptum sigilli mei munimine roboraui. Hiis testibus, dominis Hugone de Abirnyhethyn. Fergus Cumyn, Hugone de Beumys, Alano d[e] Harcaris et Edwardo de Pethglassyne, militibus, Johanne de Kyndeloch, Roberto de [1] Mabilie, Roberto de Drumgreue, Nicholaio de Ramesei, Jordano, Willelmo de Fliske, et multis aliis.

(Abstract)

‘ COKEBURN on the DIVISION of the LAND of COLLESSY and CARDYNSIDE.’

JOHN DE KOCBRUN, for the weal of his soul, and of the souls of his ancestors and successors, gives, grants, and by the present charter confirms to Lundors ‘that whole land with its pertinents which lies in breadth between the main road (*magnam viam*), which leads from my vill of Cullessin to the monastery of Lundors, and the land of the monks which is called Cardynside, and in length, beginning from the land of the same monks which is called Suthleys, towards the north as far as the burn (*rivulum*) running into the great lake, between me and them, with that small portion (*particula*) of land which I have caused to be estimated (*extendi*), and bounded for them on the south part of the aforesaid main road, in a right line from my land which is called Wudeknocside northward as far as the middle of the meadow belonging to the same monks, which is called the meadow of the great lake.’ Moreover, he gives to the monks two acres of land outside the vill of Culessin, towards the north, where they may make a messuage for themselves, to which they can draw their peats and other goods, and there, if they wish, keep them safe ; and also a free passage or road by the midst of his land of Coulessin, to wit, in going through the midst of his vill of Coulessin, with their men, horses, oxen, waggons, and carts (*carrectis*), towards their peat-moss in the moor of Edyne, and in returning, by the same way, as they had been accustomed for the purpose of drawing their fuel, without any disturbance on the part of him, his heirs, and assignees, excepting [damage to] their corn and meadow-grass (*herbagio*). And if it happened that the monks’ oxen or waggons, horses or carts, through the negligence of the men, or by any other chance, trampled or damaged his corn or meadow-grass outside the path (*secus viam*) the monks 'at the sight of good men' were to give reasonable restitution without any poinding or other disturbance on the part of him, his heirs, ·or assignees. He also grants that whoever might at any time hold the two acres of the monks should have the easement of pasture for one horse, two cows, and twenty sheep, with their young (*sequela*) up to a year old, where his men of Culessin pasture their animals. He also grants that the monks should have the land, the right of free passage, and the other privileges before named, in free, pure, and perpetual alms, so freely that he, his heirs, or assignees, or any other, could not exact anything from the monks, save only prayers for the weal of souls.   He promises that he and his heirs and assignees will warrant and defend the aforesaid to the monks 'against all men and women,' and will acquit them for ever for all manner of aids, hostings, and secular services and demands. His seal. Witnesses

CXLI

Carta super ecclesia de Cullessi.

OMNIBVS presens scriptum visuris vel audituris, Rogerus de Queney Comes Wynton, Constabularius Scocie, eternam in domino salutem.   Nouerit vniuersitas vestra nos caritatis intuitu, et pro salute anime nostre, et pro animabus ante-cessorum et successorum nostrorum, dedisse, concessisse, et pre-senti carta nostra confirmasse deo et beate marie et ecclesie sancti andree de Lundors et abbati et conuentui ibidem deo seruientibus et in perpetuum seruituris, ecclesiam de Cullessyn cum omnibus suis pertinenciis ; Habendam et tenendam dicto abbati et conuentui et eorum successoribus, in liberam, puram, et | perpetuam elemosinam, libere, quiete, bene, et in pace in   [*fo* perpetuum sieut aliqua ecclesia melius, liberius, et quiecius in Regno Scocie dari poterit et concedi, videlicet, quod cedente vel decedente magistro Ada de Malcariuston, Rectore dicte ecclesie, liceat predictis abbati et conuentui et eorum succes-soribus, pro nobis et heredibus nostris, in dictam ecclesiam pacifice intrare, possidere, et in vsus proprios conuertere, si eandem ecclesiam in vsus   o i   l˙ uatenus   ossint im-

possint impetrare, et optinere, nos vel heredes nostri nichil iuris seu clamium in dicta ecclesia de cetero exigemus seu vendicabimus, nec contra suam impetracionem in aliquo veniemus. Et nos et heredes nostri dictam donacionem, concessionem, et confirmacionem dicte ecclesie de Cullessyn cum omnibus suis pertinenciis, vt prenominatum est, dictis abbati et conuentui et eorum successoribus contra omnes gentes in perpetuum warentizabimus. Set si dictam ecclesiam in vsus proprios conuertendam non possint impetrare, jus aduocacionis in dictam ecclesiam ad nos et heredes nostros expresse et sine alicuius contradiccione reuertetur. In cuius Rei testimonium et securitatem, presentem cartam sigilli nostri impressione duximus roborandam. Hiis testibus, dominis Willelmo de Oylby, Johanne Becard, militibus, magistro Ada de Malcariuston, magistro Eustachio de Sceleford, Domino Ricardo de Radeswel, Magistro Roberto tunc phisico nostro, domino Willelmo de Sancto Edwardo capellano. Saero de Seton, Rogero Raboch, Alexandro de Seton, Rogero Bourc, clerico, et aliis.

(*Abstract*)

' CHARTER on the CHURCH of CULLESSI.'

CXLII

Concessio in husus proprios Ecclesie de Cowlessi per episcopum.

OMNIBVS christi fidelibus audituris has literas vel visuris, Gamelinus miseracione diuina ecclesie Sancti Andree minister humilis, Salutem in domino sempiternam. Nouerit vniuersitas vestra nos, intuitu domini et beate marie virginis, et beati andree apostoli patroni ecclesie de Lundors, Dedisse, concessisse, et nostra episcopali auctoritate confirmasse, prefate ecclesie de Lundors et Religiosis viris abbati et conuentui eiusdem loci deo seruientibus ibidem et in perpetuum seruituris, in vsus suos proprios ecclesiam de Cullessyn cum omnibus iuribus et pertinenciis suis ad instanciam nobilis viri domini Rogeri de Queney, Comitis Wynton, Constabularii Scocie, patroni eiusdem ecclesie, quam ipse, pro salute anime sue et antecessorum et successorum suorum, eisdem Monachis, quantum in ipso fuit, per cartam suam perpetuo possidendam donavit, sicut in eadem carta quam inde habent plenius continetur; Ita videlicet quod, cedente vel decedente Magistro Ada de Malcariuston rectore predicte ecclesie, liceat eisdem Abbati et conventui eandem ecclesiam de Cullessyn tanquam suam propriam, auctore Deo, ingredi ac in perpetuum tenere et in usus proprios pacifice possidere; Ita libere, quiete, plenarie, et honorifice in omnibus sicut alii viri religiosi in diocesi Sancti Andree ecclesias in usus proprios liberius, quiecius, plenius, et honorificencius tenent ac possident; Salva vicario in eadem ecclesia perpetuo servituro sufficienti et honesta sustentacione sua de proventibus et bonis ejusdem ecclesie, et salvis nobis, et successoribus nostris, episcopalibus juribus nostris in omnibus. In cujus rei testimonium sigillum nostrum presentibus duximus apponendum. Hiis testibus, domino Gilberto priore Sancti Andree, Magistro Ada de Malcariuston preposito ecclesie

Anand, Henrico de Newton, Johanne de Eglisfeld et aliis. Datum apud Deruasyn, Nonas Junii, Anno etc. Millesimo cc° sexagesimo secundo.

(Abstract)

'GRANT of the CHURCH of COWLESSI for [our] own uses by the BISHOP.'

'GAMELIN, by divine pity humble servant (<i>minister</i>) of the church of St. Andrews,' grants, and confirms by his episcopal authority, to the monks of Lundors, the church of Cullessyn with all its pertinents for their own uses, at the instance of Sir Roger de Quency, Earl of Wynton, Constable of Scotland, patron of the said church, which he, for the weal of his soul and the soul of his ancestors and successors, gave, as far as he could give, to the monks, by his charter, as in the same charter, which the monks possess, is more fully contained ; to the effect that on the resignation or death of Master Adam de Malcarivston, rector of the said church, it should be lawful for the monks to enter the church as though it were their own through the gift of God (<i>auctore Deo</i>), to hold and possess it peaceably for their own uses, as freely as any other religious in the diocese of St. Andrews most freely hold and possess churches for their own use—saving to the perpetual vicar serving in the church a sufficient and decent maintenance from the revenues and goods of the same church, and 'saving to us and our successors our episcopal rights in all things.' His seal. Witnesses . . . Given at Dervasyn [Dairsie], the Nones of June [June 5], MCCLXII.

CXLIII

16.]

Resignacio ecclesie de Cowlessy per Rectorem.

OMNIBVS Christi fidelibus has literas visuris vel audituris Adam de Malcariuston, prepositus ecclesie sancte Marie civitatis sancti andree, et domini pape capellanus, Salutem in domino. Noveritis me de voluntate et licencia bone memorie domini Gamellini dei gracia episcopi Sancti Andree, prout in instrumento suo super hoc confecto plenius continetur, resignasse ecclesiam Meam de Cullessyn in Manus domini Thome Abbatis de Lundors, et omni juri, quod in eadem ecclesia babui vel habere potui, penitus cessisse, contra quas meas resignacionem

(Abstract)

'RESIGNATION of the CHURCH of COWLESSY by the RECTOR.'

ADAꝰ DE MALCARIVSTON, provost of the church of St. Mary in the city of St. Andrews, and chaplain of the Pope, makes known to all that, with the licence of Gamelin, late Bishop of St. Andrews, as is more fully contained in the instrument of the bishop on the subject, he had resigned his church of Cullessyn into the hands of Thomas, Abbot of Lundors, and had wholly surrendered all right which he had, or could have, in that church ; contrary to which resignation and surrender he now promises that he will never take any action.   His seal attached. 'Given at Lundors, on Saturday next after the feast of St. Barnabas the Apostle' [June 11], MCCLXII.

CXLIV

Confirmacio Capituli S. A. super ecclesia de C.

OMNIBVS Christi fidelibus presentes literas visuris vel audituris Gilbertus Dei gracia Prior cathedralis ecclesie sancti Andree et ejusdem loci Conventus humilis, salutem eternam in Domino. Noverit universitas vestra nos de communi consensu capituli nostri, auctoritate dei et beati andree apostoli, caritatis intuitu, concessisse et hac presenti carta nostra confirmasse ecclesie sancte marie et sancti andree de Lundors et Monachis ibidem deo servientibus et in perpetuum servituris ecclesiam de Cullessyn, Sancti Andree diocesis, cum omnibus juribus et pertinenciis suis, quam nobilis vir, dominus Rogerus de Queney, Comes Wynton, et constabularius Scocie, patronus ejusdem ecclesie de Cullessyn, pro salute anime sue et antecessorum et successorum suorum, eisdem Monachis, quantum in ipso fuit, per cartam suam donavit, Et venerabilis pater Gamelinus divina providencia episcopus noster Sancti Andree eisdem pie contulit et concessit ac per cartam suam confirmavit in usus suos proprios perpetuo possidendam prout in eisdem cartis quas inde habent plenius continetur : Ita, videlicet, quod, cedente vel decedente Magistro Ada de Malcarston rectore predicte ecclesie, liceat eisdem monachis eandem ecclesiam de Cullessyn tanquam suam propriam autore Deo ingredi ac in-

ejusdem ecclesie ; Et salvis dicto domino nostro Episcopo
Sancti Andree et suis successoribus juribus suis episcopalibus in
omnibus.   In cujus rei testimonium presens scriptum apposicione communis sigilli capituli nostri duximus roborandum.
Teste capitulo ipso.   Apud sanctum Andream, die sancti barnabe apostoli, Anno gracie millesimo cc° sexagesimo secundo.

(Abstract)

'CONFIRMATION of the CHARTER of ST. A[NDREWS] on the CHURCH
of C[ULLESSYN].'

'GILBERT, by the grace of God, Prior of the cathedral church of
St. Andrews and the humble convent of the same place,' with the
common consent of the chapter, 'by the authority of God and of
Blessed Andrew, the Apostle,' at the prompting of charity, grant and
by this charter confirm to Lundors the church of Cullessyn in the
diocese of St. Andrews, with all its rights and pertinents, which
Roger de Quency, Earl of Wynton and Constable of Scotland, patron
of the same church, gave, as far as in him lay, to the monks of Lundors,
for the weal of his soul and of his ancestors and successors, and which
'the venerable father, Gamelin, by divine providence our Bishop of St.
Andrews, piously conferred and granted, and by his charter confirmed,
to be possessed by them for ever for their own uses, as in the same
charters, which they have, is more fully contained.'   In such wise
that on the resignation or death of Master Adam de Malcarston, rector
of the said church, it shall be lawful for the same monks to enter, hold
for ever, and peaceably possess for their own uses the same church of
Cullessyn, as if it were their own by the gift of God, as freely, quietly,
fully, and honourably in all things as other religious in the diocese of
St. Andrews hold and possess churches for their own uses—saving to the
perpetual vicar, who will serve in the church, his sufficient and decent
maintenance out of the revenues and goods of the same church, and
saving to the said lord, our Bishop of St. Andrews, and his successors
their episcopal rights in all things.   The common seal of the chapter.
'Witness, the chapter itself.'   At St. Andrews, the day of St. Barnabas
the Apostle [June 11], ɔ CCLXII. [1]

CXLV

Recepcio litere resignacionis ecclesie de Cowlessy
per episcopum Sancti Andree.

humilis, Salutem eternam in domino. Noverit universitas vestra nos literas resignacionis et cessionis Magistri Ade de Malcarston super ecclesia de Cullessyn, non cancellatas non abolitas, nec in aliqua sui parte viciatas, sigillo suo signatas diligenter inspexisse, in forma subscripta. Omnibus Christi fidelibus has literas visuris vel audituris Adam de Malcarston, prepositus ecclesie Sancte Marie civitatis Sancti Andree, et domini pape capellanus, Salutem in domino. Noveritis me de voluntate et licencia bone memorie Domini Gamelini, dei gracia episcopi Sancti Andree, prout, in instrumento suo super hoc confecto, plenius continetur, resignasse ecclesiam meam de Cullessyn in manus domini Thome Abbatis de Lundors, et omni juri quod in eadem ecclesia habui vel habere potui penitus cessisse, contra quas meas resignacionem et cessionem, promitto fideliter me nunquam attemptaturum. In cujus rei testimonium, presentibus literis sigillum meum apposui. Data apud Lundors, Sabbato proximo post festum Sancti Barnabe apostoli, Anno | gracie millesimo ducentesimo sexagesimo [*fo* secundo. Nos vero predictas cessionem et resignacionem, ratas firmasque habentes, ac volentes eas stabiles et inconcussas perpetuo permanere, illas auctoritate nostra episcopali confirmamus et suplemus defectum si quis habitus est in predictis. Et si quid de cetero secus actum fuerit, illud totum irritum decernimus et inane. In cujus rei testimonium, presens scriptum sigilli nostri impressione roboravimus. Data apud Monimel, die veneris proxima post Epiphaniam domini, Anno gracie millesimo ducentesimo septuagesimo septimo.

(Abstract)

'RECEPTION by the BISHOP of ST. ANDREWS of a LETTER of RESIGNATION of the CHURCH of COWLESSY.

'WILLIAM, by the divine pity, humble servant (*minister*) of the church of St. Andrews,' makes known to all that he has diligently inspected

permission of Gamelin, of good memory, [1] by the grace of God, Lord
Bishop of St. Andrews, as in the instrument executed by him on this
matter is more fully contained, I have resigned my church of Cullessyn
into the hands of Thomas, lord abbot of Lundors, and have wholly ceded
all right which I had, or could have, in the same church, in opposition to
which resignation and cession I faithfully promise that I will never raise
any question.   In testimony of which thing I have put my seal to the
present letters.   Given at Lundors, on the Saturday next after the feast
of St Barnabas the Apostle [June 11], in the year of grace one thousand,
two hundred and sixty-two.'   The Bishop of St. Andrews holds this
resignation and cession to be good and valid, and confirms it by his
episcopal authority.   If there be any defect in the resignation, he (the
bishop) supplies anything lacking ; and anything done to the contrary in
the future he decrees to be null and void.   The bishop's seal.   'Given
at Monimel on the Friday next after the Epiphany of our Lord [Jan. 6],
in the year of grace MCCLXXVII.'

CXLVI

Confirmacio alia super ecclesia de Cowlessy.

OMNIBVS Christi fidelibus hoc scriptum visuris vel audituris
Willelmus, permissione divina ecclesie Sancti Andree minister
humilis, salutem eternam in domino.   Noverit universitas
vestra nos confirmacionem bone memorie domini Gamelini dei
gracie predecessoris nostri factam religiosis viris, abbati et
conuentui de Lundors, super ecclesia de Cullessyn sigillo suo
autentico signatam, non cancellatam,[a] non abolitam, nec in aliqua
sui parte viciatam, inspexisse in forma subscripta.   Omnibus
Christi fidelibus audituris has literas vel visuris, Gemelinus,
miseracione diuina ecclesie Sancti Andree minister humilis,
Salutem in domino sempiternam.   Nouerit vniuersitas vestra nos
intuitu dei et beate marie virginis, et beati andree apostoli,
patroni ecclesie de Lundors, dedisse, concessisse, et nostra episcopali auctoritate confirmasse prefate ecclesie de Lundors et religiosis viris, abbati et conuentui eiusdem loci, deo seruientibus
ibidem et in perpetuum seruituris, in vsus suos proprios, ecclesiam
de Cullessyn, cum omnibus iuribus et pertinenciis suis ad instanciam nobilis viri domini Rogeri de Queney comitis Wyntonie,

am.

constabularij Scocie, patroni eiusdem ecclesie, quam ipse pro
salute anime sue, et antecessorum et successorum suorum, eisdem
monachis, quantum in ipso fuit, per cartam suam perpetuo possidendam, donauit ; sieut in eadem carta, quam inde habent,
plenius continetur ; Ita, videlicet, quod cedente vel decedente
magistro adam de malcarstoun, Rectore predicte ecclesie, liceat
eisdem abbati et conuentui eandem ecclesiam de Cullessyn,
tanquam suam propriam auctore deo ingredi ac in perpetuum
tenere, et in vsus proprios pacifice possidere, Ita libere, quiete,
plenarie et honorifice in omnibus sicut alij viri religiosi in diocesi
sancti andree ecclesias suas in vsus proprios liberius, quiecius,
plenius et honorificencius tenent ac possident; Salua vicario,
in eadem ecclesia perpetuo seruituro, sufficienti et honesta
sustentacione sua, de prouentibus et bonis eiusdem ecclesie, et
saluis nobis et successoribus nostris episcopalibus iuribus
nostris in omnibus. In cuius rei testimonium sigillum nostrum
presentibus duximus apponendum: Hiis testibus, domino
Gilberto priore Sancti Andree, Magistro Adam de Malkarstoun, preposito ecclesie Sancte Marie eiusdem ciuitatis,
domino Johanne priore de Aberbrothoch, domino Dauide de
Lochor, domino Thoma de Brad, domino Rogero de Walychop,
magistro Gilberto de Herys, tunc officiali, Johanne de Kyndeloch, dominis Willelmo de Dalgernoch, Bartholomeo tunc
decano de Fyfe, Adam de Anand, Henrico de Neutune,
Johanne de Eglisfeld, et alijs, Datum apud Deruasyn, nonas
Junij, Anno gracie M° cc. Sexagesimo secundo. Nos igitur,
ipsius domini Gamelini, bone memorie, predecessoris nostri,
vestigijs inherentes, damus, concedimus et confirmamus,
nostra episcopali auctoritate, prefate ecclesie de Lundors, et
monachis predictis, predictam ecclesiam de Cullessyn, cum
omnibus iuribus et pertinenciis suis ; Tenendam et perpetuo
possidendam in vsus suos proprios, adeo libere et quiete sicut
dominus quondam Rogerus de Quency, comes Wyntonie, verus

mamus. Decernimus, eciam, irritum et inane, si secus actum fuerit de prefata ecclesia.

(Abstract)

'Another Confirmation upon the Church of Cowlessy.'

William, Bishop of St. Andrews, makes known that he had inspected the Confirmation of Gamelin of good memory, 'our predecessor,' and had found it to be not cancelled, erased, or in any part vitiated, and that it ran in the form following. He then transcribes the Confirmation of Gamelin, which is to be found in Charter cxlii. At the close of the transcript the Charter resumes its course as follows. 'We therefore walking in the footsteps of Lord Gamelin, our predecessor of good memory, give, grant, and confirm, by our episcopal authority, to the aforesaid church of Lundors and the monks aforesaid, the aforesaid church of Cullessyn, with all its rights and pertinents, to be held and possessed for their own uses as freely and quietly as the late Lord Roger de Quency, Earl of Wyntonia, true patron of the same church, gave it, so far as it was in his power, and our aforesaid predecessor gave, granted, and confirmed the same to them.' He further approves and confirms the resignation and concession of Adam de Malcarstoun (see Charter cxlv.), and decrees that any thing that might be done to the contrary should be null and void.[1]

CXLVII

18.]

De protectione regis Dauid.

David dei gracia Rex Scottorum, episcopis, Abbatibus, Comitibus, Baronibus, Justiciariis, Vicecomitibus, ac ceteris regni nostri ministris, clericis et laicis, salutem in domino sempiternam. Cum regiam maiestatem deceat viros religiosos deo deuote seruientes in pace, tranquilitate, et quiete confouere [et] eorum iura, libertates, et priuilegia, a nonnullis progenitoribus nostris, regibus Scocie, predecessoribus nostris concessa, pia deuocione protegere, defendere, et conseruare ; Quia summa racio est que pro religione et religiosis facit ; Hinc est quod

predecessoribus nostris regibus Scocie concessarum, ad plenum intelleximus predictos religiosos, monasterium suum, homines, terras, possessiones vbicumque infra regnum nostrum existentes, bona, ac omnia alia iura sua, ad predictos religiosos et monasterium predictum spectancia, esse sub patronatu et regia maiestate regum Scocie, nullo medio, et pertinere ad eosdem; Nos vestigijs predecessorum nostrorum regum inherentes, predictos religiosos viros, monasterium suum, homines suos, terras et possessiones suas, vbicumque infra regnum nostrum existentes, sub nostra proteccione, patronatu, iurisdiccione, et regia maiestate nullo medio suscepimus, et recognoscimus fore subjectos, nec alium quemquam recognoscere debere, quantum ad superioritatis titulum, clameum, vel exaccionem secularem, preter nos, licet idem monasterium et dicti religiosi ibidem deo seruientes fuerint ab antiquo per Comitem Dauid, fratrem recolende memorie Willelmi regis Scocie predecessoris nostri fundati, et de diuersis terris et possessionibus in diuersis partibus regni nostri dotati. Quare vniuersitati vestre tenore presencium significamus et declaramus quod, licet terram nostram de le Garvyach nobis iure obuientem in consanguineum nostrum Thomam Comitem de Marre transtulimus, et eidem per cartam concessimus, intencionis nostre seu voluntatis nostre non extitit, nec est, dictos religiosos, monasterium suum, homines suos, terras, redditus, vel possessiones suas vbicumque existentes, et immediate ad nos pertinentes, in ipsum comitem de Marre, seu quemcunque alium transferre a nostro patronatu, vel regie maiestatis titulo abdicare, discidere, vel alienare : firmiter inhibentes ne predictus comes de Marre seu quicumque alius racione vel pretextu cuiuscumque donacionis siue concessionis per nos, quouismodo facte seu faciende in futurum, predictos religiosos, monasterium suum, homines suos, terras seu possessiones suas vbicumque infra regnum nostrum existentes, molestare vel inquietare presumant, seu

quibuscunque a nobis [uel] nostris predecessoribus eisdem religiosis indultis et concessis, libere et quiete vti et gaudere permittant.   In cuius rei testimonium sigillum nostrum presentibus literis precepimus apponi, apud Edynburgh quintodecimo die Decembris anno Regni nostri vicesimo nono.

(Abstract)

' OF the PROTECTION of KING DAVID [II.].'

'DAVID, by the grace of God, King of Scots, to the bishops, abbots, earls, barons, justiciars, sheriffs, and other officers of our kingdom clerical and lay, health everlasting in the Lord.'   It behoves the royal majesty[1] to cherish in peace, tranquillity, and quiet the religious who devoutly serve God, and to protect, defend and preserve with pious devotion their rights, liberties, and privileges, which were granted by some of his progenitors, the Kings of Scotland.   After an inspection of the Charters of the Abbot and Convent of Lundors granted by his predecessors, he understood fully that the monks, their monastery, their men, lands and possessions wherever they were throughout the kingdom, their goods, and all other rights possessed by the monks, were under the patronage and royal majesty of the Kings of Scotland, with no intermediary.   Following in the footsteps of his predecessors he took under his protection, patronage, jurisdiction, and royal majesty, with no intermediary, the monastery, men, lands, and possessions of the monks, and declared that they were not subject to, nor ought to recognise, any other so far as related to title of superiority, claim, or secular exaction, although the monastery and the monks were founded of old by Earl David, brother of William, of revered memory, King of Scotland, his [King David's] predecessor, and endowed by him with divers lands and possessions in divers parts of the kingdom.   ' Wherefore we signify and declare to all of you by the tenor of these presents that although we have transferred and granted by charter to our cousin, Thomas, Earl of Mar, our land of Garvyach, coming to us by right, it neither was nor is any part of our intention or will to transfer to the Earl of Mar himself, or to any other, the said religious, their monastery, their lands, rents, or possessions wherever they may be, which pertain to us without an intermediary, or to renounce, separate, or alienate them from the title of the royal majesty.'   Wherefore he strictly forbids the Earl of Mar or any other whomsoever to molest or disturb the monks and their possessions by reason of, or under pretext of, any gift or grant made, or

the king. On the contrary they are to permit the monks to use and enjoy freely and quietly the liberties, privileges, possessions, and other easements of all kinds which had been granted by him or his predecessors.

The King's Seal. 'At Edynburgh, on the 15th of December, in the twenty-ninth year of our reign.'[1]

CXLVIII

De Contrauersia inter nos et dominum Thomam Comitem de Mar.

Omnibvs hoc scriptum visuris vel audituris Thomas | comes de   [*f*° Marre et dominus de Garvyach, salutem in domino sempiter nam. Nouerit vniuersitas vestra quod licet nuper quesiverimus et petiverimus a religiosis viris abbate et monachis monasterii sancte marie et sancti andree apostoli de Lundors, Sancti Andree dyocesis, homagium, fidelitatem, sectas et compariciones ad curias nostras, sicut a ceteris libere tenentibus nostris de le Garvyach, racione terrarum quas predicti religiosi tenent et possident infra le Garviach, nunc vero alio modo de veritate informati et de corum libertatibus ad plenum instructi, predictos religiosos et corum terras ad predicta onera nobis vel successoribus nostris prestanda pro nobis, heredibus nostris[2] vel successoribus nostris recognoscimus in nullo fore obligatos; Et istud omnibus quorum interest vel interesse possit pro nobis, heredibus, et successoribus nostris tenore presencium manifestamus. In cujus rei testimonium hoc presens scriptum sigillo nostro magno autentico muniri fecimus penes predictos religiosos perpetuo remansurum. Datum apud castrum nostrum de Kyldromy, decimo nono die mensis Augusti, Anno domini M° ccc^mo quinquagesimo nono.

(*Abstract*)

' Of the dispute between us and the Lord Thomas, Earl of Mar.'

Thomas Earl of Mar, and Lord of Garvyach, makes known to all that although he had lately sought and claimed from the abbot and monks of Lundors, in the diocese of St. Andrews, homage, fealty, and suits

possessed within the Garviach, yet now, having been informed as to the truth, and being fully instructed as to their liberties, he acknowledges that the aforesaid religious and their lands are in no way under obligation for the burdens aforesaid due to him, his heirs, and successors. By the tenor of these presents he declares this for himself, his heirs, and successors, to all whom it may, or could, concern.

In testimony of this he has caused the present writ to be fortified by his Great Seal. The writ was to be kept in the custody of the said religious. 'Given at our castle of Kyldromy, on the nineteenth day of the month of August, in the year of our Lord MCCCLIX.'

CXLIX
Dauid Comes de Hunthyngton.[1]

DAVID Comes de Huntinetoune [frater] regis Willelmi fundavit Abbathiam de Lundores et dedit et concessit deo et beate marie et monachis ibidem Deo servientibus, in liberam, puram, et perpetuam elemosinam, post certas terras et ecclesias, ultra month Fyntre, et in Garvyach Lethgawyl et Malynd cum pertinenciis suis et concessit eisdem decimam omnium lucrorum et placitorum suorum infra terram suam et extra, ultra month, quam habuit tempore donacionis illius Et decimam omnium rerum suarum et heredum suorum scilicet decimacionem bladi et farine, butiri et casii, carnis et venacionis, cibi et potus, coriorum ferarum cum mota canum captarum, et salis, uncti et cepi, et omnium aliarum rerum que decimari possunt et que dabuntur, vel vendentur, vel ad firmam ponentur, de maneriis suis vltra month. Et voluit et concessit vt predicta ecclesia de Lundors et monachi habeant et teneant omnia predicta in liberam, puram, et perpetuam elemosinam, de se et heredibus suis, cum omnibus libertatibus suis[2] et liberis consuetudinibus

sine omni seruicio et consuetudine et auxilio et seculari
exaccione, bene et in pace, integre et honorifice, sicut aliqua
abbathia in toto regno Scocie melius et liberius, quiecius et
honorificencius aliquam elemosinam tenet et possidet, et ita
libere sicut ipse eas vmquam tenuit et habuit, Et ita libere et
pacifice vt nullus sibi succedencium aliquid ab eis nisi solas
oraciones ad anime salutem exigere presumat. Teste Willelmo
rege Scottorum.

Et Rex Willelmus concessit et confirmauit predicta omnia
et vtitur uerbo concedo eis etc., et sciant presentes et futuri me
dedisse et concessisse et hac carta mea confirmasse, etc. Et
concedo eciam eisdem monachis vltra month fyntreth et
ecclesiam eiusdem ville, et in garvyach Lethgawylle et malynde,
ita vt prenominati monachi predicta omnia in terris et ecclesiis
ad proprios vsus et sustentaciones habeant et teneant: Et
concedo eis cuream suam omnino liberam, et dignitatem pacis,
sine omni seruicio et consuetudine et auxilio et seculari
exaccione, in liberam etc. Et subdit in fine, ita vt nullus
heredum | prefati comitis, fratris mei, a predictis monachis [/ℓ
quicquid nisi solas oraciones ad anime salutem exigere presumat.
Et sic interpretatur verbum succedencium in carta comitis
Dauid. Post istam donacionem religiosi isti possidebant omnia
ista pacifice in libera regalitate, confirmata et priuilegiata per
sedem apostolicam, absque exaccione seculari per tempus et
tempora viuente ipso Dauid comite, et Johanne de Scotia, filio
suo, et tribus sororibus et eorum filiis, quibus demum successit
recolende memorie Rex Dauid Scocie vterinus † iure sanguinis
et propinquitatis qui terram de Garvyach dedit consanguineo
suo Thome, comiti marrie, cum libere tenentibus, bondagiis, et
seruiciis, et ita libere in omnibus et plene, vt dicitur, sicut Dauid
comes de Huntynton ipsam habuit vel tenebat. Qui dominus
comes marrie petiuit ab ipsis religiosis compariciones et sectas,
fidelitatem et homagia, et super istis vexauit: set demum

Rex Anno regni sui xxix° suscepit istos religiosos, monasterium
suum, homines, terras et possessiones vbicumque infra regnum
scocie existentes, sub sua proteccione, patronatu, iure et regia
magestate, [n]ullo medio, et recognoscit fore subiectos, Nolens
quod ipsi alium quemcumque, quo[1] superioritatis titulum,
clameum, vel exaccionem secularem, preter ipsum recognoscerent,
licet ipsi fuerint ab antiquo per comitem Dauid de diuersis terris
et possessionibus dotati, et significat et declarat quod quamuis
ipse terram suam de Garvyach sibi iure obuenientem in[a]
consanguineum suum dominum Thomam, comitem marrie,
transtulit, Intencionis sue seu voluntatis non extitit dictos
religiosos homines, suas terras, vel redditus ab eo abdicare,
Inhibens ne predictus comes de marre vel quicumque alius,
racione cuiuscumque donacionis per ipsum faete quouismodo
seu faciende in futurum, predictos religiosos homines, suas
terras vel possessiones vbicumque infra regnum suum existentes,
molestare vel inquietare presumat super suam plenariam forisfacturam, ac sub pena omnium que erga ipsum amittere quoquo
modo [poterit].   Isti comiti marrie succedit dominus comes de
Duglas, et petit quod isti religiosi recognoscant eum vt patronum
suum, et heredem quondam comitis Dauid, et prestent sibi
obsequia que ipsi comiti Dauid prestare tenebantur, et inter
cetera petit fidelitatem nominatim, et. ostensionem cartarum
suarum in curia sua.   Et processum fecit per tres dies contra
ipsum abbatem sicut contra tenentes alios, quo processu | stante
et valido, promisit abbas die proxima assignanda per dictum
comitem, ut in quarto die processus, comparere et facere que in
quarto die facere tenebatur: quo die comparuit et dictum
dominum comitem disclamauit, et dominum nostrum regem
inuocauit, et de curia comitis sic recessit.   Et comes postea terras
in manu sua fecit recognosci, quas idem abbas a domino nostro
rege infra tempus debitum peciit debite restitui.   Qui ipsum
restitui mandauit plene et integre ad easdem modo queritur, ex
quo dictus comes Dauid eis terras istas et ecclesias in puram et
perpetuam elemosinam etc. et quod sint libere ab omni

ipsique religiosi domino regi inseparabiliter et continue adhesi-
rint, sibi soli et nulli alii fidelitatem facientes per triginta
annos et amplius.   An Comiti fidelitatem facere teneantur, et
videtur quod non, quia vassallus non cogitur pro uno feodo plures
dominos habere : nota Hostien. in summa ; de feu. c° ultimo
v. set numquid tenebitur : et iste terre de **Garviach** in una
carta cum aliis et post alias terras et sub eadem data eis donata [a]   [a] So ir
fuerint, pro quibus omnibus dominum nostrum regem recogno-
verunt per xxx[ta] annos et ultra, et hodie recognoscunt, et sibi
pro eis fidelitatem fecerunt et faciunt, igitur alii pro eis fidelitatem facere non debent, nec pro aliis terris ab eis per xxx[ta]
annos pacifice possessis, quia pro eis domino nostro regi
servicium debitum exhibuerunt in cujus manu tanto tempore
fuerunt : nam in li. feu[orum]ti. si de feu. de defunct. fuerit, c.
si quis coll. x., dicitur si quis per xxx annos rem aliquam
in feudum possedit et servicium domino exhibuit, quamvis de ea
re nuncquam investitus sit, prescriptione tamen xxx annorum
poterit se tueri.   Si enim prescriptus† libertatis contra dominum in libertate sua tuendus erit. C. de episcopis et cleri. li. 1.
et sufficit in talibus prescripcio xxx annorum : habetur eciam in
libro feudorum de feu. dato invicem legis commissor. c. quid
obligavit.   Cum enim libertas favorabilis sit, de facili prescripsit
contra servitutem, de privilegiis c. cum olim, § per, et c. ex ore,
§ fi. non sit e contra c. de prescrip. contra libertatem et non
adversus libertatem, l. fi. et pretores fovent libertatem, ff. de
alienacione, iuii. mdi. ca. facta, l. iij. § i.   Rex eciam Willelmus hoc videtur voluisse quia ubi comes **David** dixit Quare
volo et concedo ut predicta ecclesia de **Lundoris** et monachi
ibidem deo servientes habeant et teneant in liberam etc. de
me et heredibus meis prenominatas terras ita libere etc, Idem
rex **Willelmus** omittit, <u>ut videtur</u> scienter, hec verba de me et

remissa, quia feodum invenitur sine fidelitate in libro feu. quantum fiat investitura, c. nulla, et invenitur feodum liberum et immune unde communiter dicitur, Ego teneo hoc castrum in feodum liberum et de tali non tenetur quis facere nisi simplicem recognicionem, nota Hostien. in summa de[1] . . . etc. generaliter in quartum versum, set contra, versus finem versus. Set comes et rex concedit terras sine omni servicio et exaccione seculari in liberam etc. ut[1]   modo fidelitas est servicium quo videtur esse remissa quia subdit quod nullus michi succedencium etc.   Item quia dominus sine voluntate vassalli feodum alienare non possit, nec vassali in generali alienacione concurrent, nisi hoc nominatim dictum sit. Azo. cujus fuit hoc quoad decimam quod sicut vassallus invito domino feodum alienare quomodo tales alienatas cadit a feodo[2]

per fredericum c. inperialem §. Preterea ducatus, et ita t₃ pe. de bel. per. quemadmodum, nec jus filiacionis transferri possit invito filio, ff. de adop. l. ij. idem Hostiensis de ma. et obe. dilecti, in locutura†, et in summa de feu. ult. vers. set nequit, et spe. ti. de feu § i. vers. xxix ; et hoc verum est de jure quo rex eos invitos alienare non potuit.   Item dato quod rex alienasset terram de Garviach cum tenentibus, tamen clerici sub nomine libere tenencium non essent comprehensi, per id quod legitur et notatur de privilegiis ex parte abbatisse juxta ver. clerum et populum, nam cum clerus et populus sint diverse professionis xij. q. 1. duo, xcvj. di. duo : xix. q. 1. due de ma. et obe. solite, in expressione unius alius non continetur facit c. si sentencia interdicti de sen. ex. li. vj° : et licet transtulisset clericos, monachi tamen non essent comprehensi, nam clerici et monachi sunt re et nomine diversi, ne cle. et mo. in R^{cis} xvi. q. 1. legi.   Item rex David suam donacionem interpretatus fuit et declaravit expresse quod illos religiosos vel terras eorum

soribus, manifestat predictos religiosos ad compariciones, sectas, vel fidelitatem sibi vel suis successoribus non teneri, que | manifestacio habet vim siue† quia facta fuit cum cause cognicione: nota doctorum in c. fi. de rescrip. li°. vj : et non solum declaravit, set in satisfactionem vexacionis et injurie eis illatarum annuam pensionem octo marcarum de terris de Flandir in liberam et perpetuam elemosinam eis constituit, et omnia ista morte defuncti confirmatur post quod tempus non penitet heres. C. fami. hercisde v. filius. Et si dubium esset, tam favore elemosine etc. tam favore devocionis grate quam favore religionis esset talis interpretacio facienda, quia in donacionibus ad elemosinam et pro remedio animarum plenissima est interpretacio facienda : nota Ho. c. dilecti de doncs. Item dominus comes de douglas intravit et peciit jure comitis marrie qui recognovit se nullum jus habere loquendo de terris istis et de oneribus debitis racione eorum, et iuri coherenti cause et rei renunciavit, ergo nomine suo vel petere possit in regis jure ; nemo plus juris etc. Item sicut approbat conquesicionem factam de terra de Garviach per comitem marrie, Ita recognicionem de istis non sibi debitis approbare debet, alias non debet consequi beneficium per ipsum cuius factum studet multipliciter inpugnare, c. cum olim de sensi [censi], cum ibi notatis per doctores. Quia quod aliquis approbat pro se tenetur recipere contra se : c. iiij. q. iij. § si quis testibus. Item non est patronus quia ius patronatus est potestas representandi instituendum ad beneficium simplex et vacans, set Ho. in summa § i, alio modo dicitur ius patronatus quod acquiritur ex manumissione proprii serui ff. de iure patronatus in l. i. secundum Hostien. neutro modorum istorum est ipse patronus ergo etc. Item est heres qui in vniuersum ius defuncti succedit et talis vocatur sucessor iuris, ff. de ħe insti. l. quociens § hered.; et excepcio que competebat contra defunctum competet contra talem successorem. ff. de contra. eꝑ.

[fo

Nota d Marcis Comes in satis tionem nobis c Flandr

loco heredum non habentur, quia heredes tenentur pro defuncti debitis respondere, ergo non respondent ut heredes qui heredes non sunt.   Cum igitur dominus Comes de Douglas quo ad comitem de Huntyngtoune sit donatarius et non successor in totum ius defuncti, sequitur clare quod non est heres, nec obsequia

|spiritualia sibi vt heredi sunt prestanda. Et cum sit successor vniuersalis comiti marrie qui informatus et cum cause cognicione ista declarauit ad se non pertinere, cuius morte ista confirmatur, sic quod non possit heres penitere, et dominus comes de Douglas habeat titulum lucratiuum et vtitur a successione re ex persona a[u]ctoris sicut ista excepcio repelleret comitem Marrie si viueret, Ita repellat dominum comitem de Douglas qui vtitur iure suo, et cuius factum non debet impugnare, ex quo magnum fructum consequitur ab eodem.

Item quia dominus rex Dauid declarauit expresse se istas vel alias eorum possessiones non transtulisse in comitem marrie et acciones personaliter alieui competentes eeiam re alienata, cuius nomine competunt apud eundem remanent; ·ff. de accio. et obli. v. quecunque, et ff. de furtis v. inter omnes.

Item in generali alienaccione vassalli non continentur inuitis vassallis, et maxime minori domino, sicut nec ius filiacionis inuito filio, et licet tenentes venissent clerici non venirent, et licet clerici non monachi.   Et cum vna carta et donacione vnica ipsi habeant istas possessiones et omnia alia loco vnius feudi, et pro vno feudo vassallus plures dominos non cogitur habere, et per cclx annos regi fidelitatem fecerint et nulli alii, et sic rex ipsos prescripserit, et hoc voluit rex Willelmus, sequitur quod ab inpeticione comitis sunt absoluendi.   Ista causa non solummodo pro libertate monasterii facit set exprimit ius regium, et corone regie iusticiam tuetur ne in regem monasterii lesio redundat, in c. cum olim. ij. § fi. de priuilegiis; spe. ti. ti. de. actore, versus, Item illustris pᵃ et in ti. de reo ṽs, Item consul etc. Item cum feudum inuenitur sine fidelitate, vt per pactum remissa, et liberum et immune, et hec concedantur in liberam etc. et sine omni seruicio et exaccione seculari non obstat si

scriptum speciale in terris istis set obsequium prestandi oraciones
que ad animarum salutem debetur heredi vniuersali, et est
scriptum in tota successione non in re singulari, nec obstat
quod dicitur abbas approbauit processum ibi processu trium
dierum stante vt valido, quia non approbauit processum set
ordinem procedendo non inpugnauit, et ibi ly vt non est
veritas expressum set propter similitudinem facti aliqua
numerantur inter ea de quorum numero non sunt; xxvij. q̃. i.
quotquot; notatur in c. nuper de biga.

(Abstract)

'DAVID, EARL of HUNTHYNGTON.'

[NOTE. The document here inscribed in the pages of the Chartulary, like that which follows it (CL.), differs wholly in character
from the general contents of the volume. It is simply the opinion
of a skilled ecclesiastical lawyer on a disputed point of law. Such
documents are not very common among the ecclesiastical remains of
Scotland in the mediæval period; and that which is now before the
reader is interesting, not only for the subject matter dealt with, but as
affording a very full specimen of the form and style in which such legal
opinions were drawn up. The opinion is manifestly the work of one
who was well versed in the civil as well as in the canon law, and who
was familiar with the writings of several of the most eminent of the
mediæval jurists.

The numerous references to the Pandects, the Codex of Justinian, the
Decretals of Gregory IX., and the great legal commentators, have been
mostly identified, and they will be found dealt with in the Notes and
Illustrations. In the following Abstract it has not been thought necessary to give these references, and the aim has been to exhibit the
argument, leaving the authorities cited to be examined by the curious.
That the reader may understand the situation it may be explained that
David II. had given (see CXLVII.) the lands of Garioch to his cousin,
Thomas, Earl of Mar. Mar had at first claimed from the abbot and
monks of Lindores, as from his other freeholders in Garioch, homage,
fealty, and compearance and suit at his courts (see CXLVIII.); but on
learning the facts of the case more fully, he formally acknowledged

recognise him as their 'patron.' This claim not being admitted, the earl took proceedings (*processum fecit*) against the abbot, the proceedings extending over three days. And while the action was still pending (*processu stante et valido*) the abbot 'promised that on the next day assigned by the earl as the fourth day of the action he would compear and do all that he was bound to do on the fourth day.' On the fourth day the abbot appeared, and immediately 'disclaimed the earl,' and appealed to the king (*dominum nostrum regem invocavit*), and thereupon departed from the earl's court. Afterwards the Earl of Douglas caused the lands held by the monks to be, in the language of feudal law, 'recognosced in his hand,' that is, forfeited by the monks and resumed into his possession as superior. Thereupon the abbot, within the legal limit of time, sought from the king to be restored in full to the lands. The king, responding to the claim of the abbot, ordered the lands to be restored, inasmuch as the founder of the abbey, Earl David, had given the lands and churches in Garioch to the monks 'in free, pure, and perpetual alms, and free from all service, custom, and temporal exaction,' and because King William had in express terms confirmed all their rights in these respects, and because the monks had done fealty to the king and to none other for thirty years and more. This narrative being premised, the reader will be in a better position to understand the arguments of the legal adviser of the monks in replying to the query put to him, 'Are the monks bound to do fealty to the Earl of Douglas?']

The opinion begins with a recitation at length of the pertinent parts of Earl David's Great Charter (II.), and of the confirmation of Earl David's grants by King William (CXXXVIII.), noticing in both that nothing was to be demanded from the monks but prayers for the weal of souls. Our lawyer also points attention to the fact that while in Earl David's charter it was said that 'none of my *successors*' should demand anything save prayers, King William in his confirmation says that 'none of the *heirs* of the said earl, my brother,' should demand anything save prayers. And the lawyer argues that we have in this change of phrase an interpretation of how the word 'successors' was to be understood.

It is next stated that after the donation of the lands of Garioch the monks held them in free regality (*in libera regalitate*), confirmed and privileged by the Apostolic See. And so they held them during the lifetime of Earl David, of his son, John of Scotland, and of his three sisters and their sons, to whom at length succeeded King David [II.] by right of blood and kindred. King David gave the land of Garioch to his cousin, Thomas, Earl of Mar, with its freeholders, villeinages (*bondagiis*), and services, as freely and fully in all things as David, Earl of Huntington, had and held it.

It is next related that the Earl of Mar claimed from the monks com-

burdens (*onera*) aforesaid, and publicly declared the same for himself, his heirs, and his successors, by 'his letters patent to all,' dated in the year 1359 (see CXLVIII.).

King David [II.], in the twenty-ninth year of his reign (1357), (see CXLVII.) had taken the monks, their monastery, and their possessions throughout Scotland, under his protection, patronage, right, and royal majesty, without any intermediary (*nullo medio*), declaring that the monks should recognise no claim of superiority in any one save himself. He further declared that although he had transferred his land of Garioch to his cousin, the Earl of Mar, he did not surrender (*ab eo abdicare*) the said monks, their lands, or rents. He further forbade the Earl of Mar and all others to disturb the monks by reason of any grant made, or to be made, by the king, hereafter, under pain of full forfeiture.

The Earl of Douglas succeeded to the Earl of Mar as lord of the land of Garioch; and his claims and his action towards the abbot and monks of Lundors is then recited (as related in the preliminary Note). The abbot's appeal to the king, and the king's restoration of the lands to the monks, are then recounted. After which follows the question, 'Are the monks bound to do fealty to the earl?'

The answer is, 'It seems that they are not bound.' And the reasons for this opinion are set forth at great length. (1) A vassal is not compelled to have more lords than one for one fee (*vassalus non cogitur pro uno feodo plures dominos habere*). Now the land which the monks held in Garioch was given to them in one charter, and so was to be regarded as one fee. And for thirty years and more (actually, as stated in a later part of the opinion, for no less than two hundred and sixty years) the monks had recognised no other feudal superior than the king, and to him only had done fealty; therefore they were not bound to do fealty to another. (2) But, again, it is laid down in the Feudal Law (*Consuetudines Feudorum*) that if any one holds anything in fee and renders due service to the superior, or lord of the fee, for thirty years, he was to be defended in his possession by prescription, even though he had never been invested. And King William seems to have recognised this kind of possession by the monks of their land of Garioch, for where Earl David had said that the monks were to hold the lands 'of him and his heirs,' the king in his confirmation of the grant omits these words, and declares that the monks were to hold the lands for their own use and maintenance. (3) Again, during the whole time while the lands of the monks in Garioch were 'outside the hands of the Kings of Scotland,' that is, after the lands had been transferred to the Earl of Mar, the monks had adhered to none but the king, and done fealty to him as immediate

immune), which gives rise to such a common expression as 'I hold this castle in free fee.' And in such cases the holder is not bound to any obligation save simple recognition, that is, acknowledgment of the superior. But this agreement seems indicated by Earl David and King William granting the lands in free alms, without any service and secular exaction. But fealty is a 'service,' and it seems to have been remitted by the clause which prescribed that none of the successors of the Earl David should presume to exact anything from the monks save only prayers for the weal of the soul. (5) Again, it is recognised in feudal law that a feudal lord cannot alienate a fee if the vassal who holds the fee is not a consenting party. Nor can vassals be held to concur in a general alienation, unless they concur expressly and by name. (6) Again, let it be assumed, for the sake of argument, that the king had alienated the land of Garioch 'with its tenants,' yet the word 'tenants' occurring in the charter must not be held to include the 'clergy.' This it is sought to establish by passages where the 'clergy' are distinguished from the 'people.' And even had the word 'clergy' occurred in the charter, it could not be inferred that 'monks' were included, for monks and clergy are distinct both in name and in fact. (7) Again, King David [II.], when transferring the lands to the Earl of Mar, interpreted his own gift by expressly declaring that he had not transferred the monks and their lands to the earl, and this is in accord with the maxim that 'from whence the law proceeds the interpretation of the law ought to proceed,' and again, 'Princes are wont to interpret princely benefactions.' (8) Again, the Earl of Mar himself, the donee (*dotarius*), acknowledged for himself, his heirs, and his successors, that the religious of Lundors were not bound to render compearance, suit, or fealty; and this was done after a full knowledge of the question in dispute. And not only did he make the declaration, but, as satisfaction for the vexation and injury caused the monks by his making the claim, he even agreed to pay to the monks an annual pension, in perpetual and free alms, of eight marks out of his land of Flandir. All this was confirmed by the death of the Earl of Mar, for after the death of him who bequeaths, according to the legal maxim, 'the heir cannot repent,' that is, the heir cannot alter the disposition of the property as he has received it. Even if there were doubts as to the contention of the 'opinion,' yet the favour shown to the grants of alms, the favour shown to devotion, and to the monastic life, indicate that such an interpretation ought to be made, for in the matter of gifts of alms, and for the relief (*remedio*) of souls, the most ample and favourable interpretation is to be allowed. (9) Again, the Earl of Douglas entered heir to the land of Garioch, and

rule of law, 'No man can transfer to another a larger right than he had himself.'[1]

(10) Again, as the Earl of Douglas assents to the acquisition of the land of Garioch made by the Earl of Mar, he ought to assent to the acknowledgment that these obligations were not due from the land. Otherwise he ought not to enjoy the benefit of the land, on the ground of the possession of which he seeks to make various attacks on the rights of the monks. 'Because what any one assents to when it is in his favour he is bound to receive when it makes against him.' (11) Again, the Earl of Douglas is not the patron of the monks of Lundors, as he claims, for the right of patronage is the power of presenting any one for institution to a simple benefice when vacant. In another sense of the words, 'right of patronage' is said to be acquired by the manumission of one's own slave (as in the *Pandects*). But in neither of these ways is the Earl of Douglas a patron, therefore his claim falls to the ground. (12) Again, an heir is one who succeeds to the whole right (*jus*) of one deceased, and as such is called successor of right (*saccessor juris*); and an exception which is competent against the deceased is competent against such a successor. But such an exception was objected to the deceased Earl of Mar, and the Earl of Douglas cannot make another exception in law because he has a 'lucrative title,' that is, a title by bequest, bringing a gain with it. And the principle is illustrated by the case of a purchaser using a purchase which the seller had obtained by fraud (as discussed in the *Pandects*), in which case the purchaser is liable to suffer loss. (13) Again, a donee and other legatees are not responsible to creditors in the matter of the property which has come to the successor in law. Therefore donees are not to be accounted as heirs, because heirs are bound to answer for the debts of the deceased. Those who are not heirs are not responsible as if they were heirs. Since therefore the Earl of Douglas is, as regards the Earl of Huntington, a donee and not a successor to his whole right (*successor in totum jus defuncti*), it follows clearly that he is not an heir, nor is there any obligation to render to him the spiritual observances (*obsequia spiritualia*) that were due to the heir. And since the Earl of Douglas was universal successor to the Earl of Mar, who on full information acknowledged that the services he had claimed were not due by the monks, it is plain that he, as his successor, cannot make this claim; nor ought he to impugn the Earl of Mar's action since he reaps great advantage from the succession.

The 'opinion' then sums up and repeats the arguments which had

---

[1] I have ventured on the supposition that the words '*nemo plus juris, etc.*,' indicate the passage from Ulpian, which will be found in the lib. l. tit. xvii.

been already set forth, and then adds that this view of the case not only makes for the liberty of the monastery, but expresses the royal rights, and defends the just claims of the crown, which would suffer injury by the harm which would be inflicted on the monastery in admitting the claim of the Earl of Douglas.

The Earl of Douglas cannot contend that he is entitled to raise the claim on the ground that a personal right conveyed by writ is transferred to a singular successor, inasmuch as in this case there is no special right conveyed by writ in respect to these lands, except the obligation on the part of the monks of offering prayers, which prayers are due to the universal heir (heir general); and in the written charters it is to the general succession, not to a succession of a part, that this obligation refers.

Nor can an objection be raised on the ground that the abbot acknowledged the validity of the Earl of Douglas's processes at law by appearing at the earl's court, because he in no way assented to the process at law, though he did not impugn the order of the proceedings.[1]

CL

25.]   Casus.

Monasterivm de Lundors, diocesis Sancti Andree, habens quasdam ecclesias parrochiales infra dioceses de A. de B. sibi vnitas, de quibus abbas et conuentus eiusdem recipiunt grossos fructus, videlicet decimas garbales ad utilitatem monasterii sui, que quidem ecclesie in se habent curatos per abbatem et conuentum etc Episcopo presentatos, et per ipsum receptos, et ad curam et administracionem earundem admissos, ut moris est in ceteris.

ro.   Hic queritur si abbas de Lundoris, Sancti Andree diocesis, ad Synodos episcoporum A. et B. venire teneatur racione ecclesiarum supradictarum, et eisdem episcopis obedienciam et alia facere que episcopo pertinent, Videtur quod sic : per c. conquerente de off. Ord et c. quod super hiis de ma. et ob. xviij q̃. ii. c.

---

[1] This abstract (omitting all the references to the *Corpus Juris Civilis*, the *Corpus Juris Canonici*, and the legal commentators, which will be found, so far

Abbates. Contrarium tamen verum esse videtur, per jura alle-
gata que intelliguntur de Episcopo in cujus diocesi situatum est
monasterium de L. et infra quam dictus Abbas populum habet
et administracionem, Et non sic in casu proposito, quia monasterium de L. infra diocesim Sancti Andree, nec ejusdem Abbas
infra diocesas A. et B., nec populum nec administracionem
habet unde teneri videtur etc. Item nec quisquam ad Synodum
alicujus episcopi venire tenetur nec eidem juramentum facere
nisi qui sub eodem curam animarum vel rerum ecclesiasticarum
administracionem habet : ut c. nullus, de jurejurando: xxiij. di.
c. quamquam, xxii. qu. ultima, §. ultimo. Et cum dictus
Abbas de L. infra dioceses A. et B. nec populum nec administracionem set nec ullam curam habere videtur unde ad hujusmodi non tenetur : ut xviij q. ultima § canonicam et
juribus allegatis. Item omnes religiosi in favorem religionis
videntur esse exempti, xviij. q. ultima. § canonicam allegat
xviij. di. c. Episcopus etc. ex ore sedentis, de privilegio in fi.
c. dilectus, de off. orđ. glo. ii. circa medium. Set racione
administracionis perpetue et populi quem habent abbates et
prelati alii religiosi, subsunt episcopo loci et ad hujusmodi
tenentur : ut c. quod super hiis de ma. et ob. xviij. q̃. ii.
Abbates et sic hujusmodi non habentes non tenentur : et cum
venire et alia hujusmodi facere sunt onerosa et odiosa restrin-
genda sunt, de illa regula juris li. vj. odia etc. Item, si dicatur
quod quamvis ecclesia cum clericis suis ita exempti sint quod
non veniant ad Synodum nec excommunicari vel interdici non
possunt, tamen si aliquis clericorum loci illius privilegiati
aliam ecclesiam parrochialem, curam et populum habentem,
obtineat, per hoc subest episcopo loci, et posset in eum suam
jurisdiccionem exercere non obstante privilegio suo, non obstat
hoc casui isti. Item, ad hoc quod quis ad Synodum venire
teneatur et episcopo alia incumbencia facere requiritur quod
eidem subsit aut lege diocesana aut lege jurisdiccionis in
quibus legibus totum jus et potestas et episcoporum consistit,

Andree, quod est manifeste verum, nec idem abbas eisdem episcopis subesse videtur lege jurisdiccionis quia nullam curam, nullam administracionem, locum, vel populum infra dioceses A. et B. habet dictus Abbas propter que eisdem episcopis subesse videtur, aut qua racione in persona sua jurisdiccionem habere possit quisque eorum.

Et hoc potissime cum ecclesie parrochiales infra dictas dioceses, monasterio de L. annexe, in se habent curatos qui subsunt episcopo loci qui ad modum patrie dicuntur vicarii, set pocius veri rectores sunt ; ut c. suscepti re. de preh. li. vj, qui ad Synodum veniunt, episcopo respondent, obediencias et alia incumbencia pro et de ipsis ecclesiis episcopo faciunt, in quibus si velit possit episcopus suam jurisdiccionem communem exercere, et per hos rectores episcopo per abbatem et conven-tum | presentatos, per ipsum ad earum curam receptos et admissos, exoneratur abbas de L. Et si non exoneratus esset sequeretur in quociens et daretur religiosi evagandi extra claustrum, materia quod contrarium est religioni et jure satis prohibitum. Non negatur tamen quin episcopus de istis ecclesiis possit ab abbate caritativum subsidium petere : secun-dum quod jure traditur c. conquerente, de off. ord., nisi privilegio fulciantur.

26.]

(*Abstract*)

NOTE.—This, like Charter CXLIX., is a legal opinion on a disputed question. The passages of the Canon Law referred to will be found in Notes and Illustrations. The letters C.J.C. = 'Corpus Juris Canonici,' have been inserted in square brackets to indicate where references to the Canon Law occur.

'A CASE.'

'THE monastery of Lundors, in the diocese of St. Andrews, has united to it certain parish churches within the dioceses of A[berdeen] and B[rechin], from which parishes the abbot and convent of the same receive the great fruits (*grossus fructus*), to wit, the garbal tithes, for the use of their monastery. The parish churches have in them curates [*i.e.* vicars perpetual with cure of souls], who have been presented to the bishop by the abbot and convent, and, having been received by him, have been admitted to the cure and administration of the same, as is the

Yet the contrary seems to be true. For the laws just alleged are to be understood of the bishop in whose diocese the monastery of L. is situated, and within which diocese the abbot has his people and administration. But it is not so in the case proposed. For the monastery of L. is within the diocese of St. Andrews, and the abbot of the same has neither his people nor administration within the dioceses of A. and B.

Again, no one is bound to attend the synod of any bishop or to take the oath [of canonical obedience] to him, unless he has, under that bishop, cure of souls, or the administration of things ecclesiastical [C.J.C.]. And since the said Abbot of L. has neither people, nor cure, nor administration, within the dioceses of A. and B. he is not bound.

Again, all religious seem to be exempt, by reason of the favour shown to religion [C.J.C.]. But by reason of a perpetual administration and of the people which they have, abbots and other monastic prelates are subject to the bishop of the place and are bound to the duties of the kind in question [C.J.C.], and abbots who have no such people or administrations are not bound.

And since to attend synods and perform the other things mentioned are ' odious and onerous,' they are to be restrained by the rule of law [C.J.C.].

Again, if it be said that, although the Church with its clerks are exempt, so that they need not come to the synod, nor are liable to be excommunicated or interdicted by the bishop, yet if any of the clerks of the privileged place should obtain another parish church which has people and the cure of souls, he on that account is subject to the bishop of the place, who is able to exercise his jurisdiction over him, notwithstanding his privilege, such a statement raises no obstacle in

(*curatos*), who are subject to the bishop of the place. These are called, after the manner of this country, 'vicars,' but more truly they are 'rectors,' [C.J.C.]; and these attend the synod, answer to the bishop, render obedience, and perform the other things incumbent, for and of the said churches. On these rectors the bishop, if he wishes, can exercise his common jurisdiction, and by reason of these rectors, received and admitted to their cure by the bishop, the Abbot of L. is exonerated from attendance, etc.

But if the abbot is not exonerated it follows that cause would be given for a religious wandering outside his cloister [in attending the synods], which is contrary to monastic rule (*quod contrarium est religioni*), and is sufficiently prohibited by law. Yet it is not denied that the bishop is entitled to claim, on account of these churches, a 'benevolence' (*caritativum subsidium*) from the abbot, according to the law [C.J.C.].

CLI

Carta terre seu tenementi quondam Magistri Thome Rossy jacentis in nouo burgo.

In dei nomine, Amen: per hoc presens publicum instrumentum cunctis pateat evidenter quod anno ab incarnacione ejusdem millesimo quadringentesimo septuagesimo octavo, die vero mensis Februarij septimo, indictione xij, pontificatus Sanctissimi in Christo patris et domini nostri, domini Sixti divina providencia pape quarti, anno octavo, In mei notarii publici et testium subscriptorum presencia personaliter constitutus discretus vir Magister Thomas Rossy, vicarius ecclesie parochialis de Inchestur, Sancti Andree diocesis, tanquam vir multum prudens, et anime sue ferventer cupiens et ardenter, ut apparuit, salubriter providere salutem, veraciter sperans et confidens quod per pias oraciones et missarum celebraciones peccata dimitti, purgatoriique penas molliri et ab eisdem defunctorum animas frequencius liberari et ad gaudia paradisi feliciter deduci: Hine est quod dictus Magister ipse Thomas, non vi [salutem], sponte voluit, dedit, concessit, nominavit, et a corde donavit, ac presentis instrumenti per tenorem vult, dat, concedit, nominat, et pro perpetuo irreuocabiliter donat venerabilibus et Religiosis viris, suppriori et conuentui dicti monasterij modernis, et eorum successoribus in parte augmentacionis suarum petanciarum, prius, vt Religiosus vir, frater Andrea Wynton, tunc temporis huius loci predicti su[p]prior, affirmauit, speciali licencia eorum magistri et abbatis ad hoc petita et obtenta, et integras terras suas cum quadam domo lapidea sumptibus et expensis ipsius magistri thome, vt asseruit, sieut stat constructa et erecta, cum earundem vniuersis pertinenciis infra nouum burgum ex parte boreali et ad finem orientalem eiusdem, inter terras Stephani caluart ad occidentem ab vna et terras arabiles dicti monasterij ad orientem partibus ab altera jacentes ; Que quidem terre cum pertinenciis prius erant pro dicto monasterio et sibi dicto magistro Thome, prout publice et palam ibidem fatebatur et cum effectu affirmabat, ad edificandum et construendum dictam domum, pro suo vsu, vtilitate, et quiete, durante tempore vite sue, ex speciali gracia et non alias concesse et donate extiterunt ; Tenendas et habendas totas dictas terras et domum cum pertinenciis suis suppriori et conuentui modernis et eorum successoribus in dicto monasterio nunc et futuris temporibus existentibus, in puram et perpetuam elimosinam, in omnibus commoditatibus, libertatibus, asiamentis, ac iustis suis pertinenciis qnibuscunque ad predictas terras et domum cum pertinenciis spectantibus seu iuste spectare valentibus quomodolibet in futurum, in feodo et hereditate inperpetuum, adeo libere, quiete, plenarie, integre, honorifice, bene et in pace sicut alique terre siue domus cum pertinenciis in regno scocie dantur aut conceduntur siue poterunt dari vel concedi in puram et perpetuam elimosinam liberius, quiecius, plenarius, et integrius, honorificencius, melius, seu pacificencius, sine quacunque contradiccione aut reuocacione aliquali ; Reseruato tamen sibi ipsi magistro Thome et saluo remanente pro toto tempore

Jacobi sui auunculi, vnam missam specialem de requiem solempniter cum nota, et uigilias mortuorum cum ix lectionibus in nocte precedente deuote, in ecclesia monasteriali apud magnum altare, pro anima ipsius dicti Thome, necnon anima dicti sui auunculi, et animabus omnium defunctorum celebrare et indesinenter perficere, et inperpetuum inuiolabiliter obseruare. Tuncque et incontinenter idem frater andrea, supprior predictus, ad omnia predicta perimplenda et deuote annuatim, vt premittitur, perficienda onus pro se et conuentu moderno, durante tempore suo, et pro eorum successoribus sponte in se assumpsit, ac fideliter et deuote ad perficienda absque fictione promisit. Super quibus omnibus et singulis dictus supprior nomine suo et conuentus predicti et dictus magister Thomas hinc inde a me notario publico sibi pecierunt publicum seu publica instrumentum seu instrumenta. Acta erant hec apud dictum burgum et infra predictam domum, hora quasi 3ᵃ post meridiem, anno, die, mense, indiccione, et pontificatu quibus supra. Presentibus ibidem Alexandro spens de Pettincreffe, domino Valtero Anderson, Jacobo Philp cum diuersis aliis, ad premissa vocatis specialiter et rogatis.

(Abstract)

'Charter of the Land, or Holding, of the late Master Thomas Rossy, which is situated in Newburgh.'

In the name of God. Amen. By this present public instrument let it be plainly known to all men that in the year from the Incarnation of the same mccccLxxviii.,[1] on the eighth day of the month of February, Indiction xii., in the eighth year of the pontificate of our most Holy Father and Lord in Christ, Lord Sixtus iv., by divine providence, Pope, in the presence of me, notary public, and of the witnesses underwritten, compeared in person, the discreet man, Master Thomas Rossy, vicar of the parish church of Inchestur, in the diocese of St. Andrews, as being a very prudent man, and earnestly and eagerly desirous, as appeared, to provide in wholesome wise for the weal of his soul, hoping in truth and trusting that by pious prayers and the celebration of Masses sins were remitted, the pains of purgatory mitigated (*molliri*), and that from the

circumvented by any, but of his own assured knowledge and spontaneous wish, moved by the impulse of pious devotion, to the praise and honour of Almighty God and of the glorious Virgin Mary, His Mother, and of all saints, and for the weal of his own soul, and of the soul of his dearest uncle, the late James de Rossy, of good memory, formerly Lord Abbot of Lundoris, and the souls of all the faithful departed, of his own accord willed, gave, granted, named, and gifted from his heart, and, by the tenor of this present instrument, wills, gives, grants, names, and for ever irrevocably gifts to the venerable religious, the present sub-prior and convent of the said monastery, and to their successors, to the end that their pittances might be increased, having first obtained the special leave of their master and abbot (as the religious, Brother Andrew Wynton, at that time sub-prior of the place aforesaid, affirmed), the whole of his lands, together with a house built and erected of stone at the cost and charges of the said Master Thomas, as he asserted, with all the pertinents of the same, within Newburgh at the northern part and at the western bound of the same, lying between the lands of Stephen Calvart on the one side to the west, and the arable lands of the said monastery to the east on the other side.

These lands with their pertinents had been formerly granted and given by special favour for the said monastery and for himself, the said Master Thomas, as he publicly and openly acknowledged and effectively affirmed, for the building and constructing of the said house, for his use, service, and convenience (*quiete*), during his life. They were now given to be had and held with their pertinents by the present sub-prior and convent, and by their successors, in pure and perpetual alms, with all their conveniences, liberties, easements, etc., in fee and heritage, as freely, quietly, fully, perfectly, honourably, well, and in peace, as any lands or houses in the kingdom of Scotland are given or granted, or could be given or granted, in pure and perpetual alms, most freely, fully, etc., without any gainsaying or revocation, yet reserving and saving to himself, the said Master Thomas, for his whole life, the freehold of the said lands and house with their pertinents. But on the condition that the said sub-prior and convent, and their successors, shall be strictly bound once every year in all future time, on the day of the anniversary of the late abbot, his uncle, to celebrate one special Mass of requiem, solemnly, with music (*cum nota*),[1] and, on the night preceding, the vigils of the dead with nine lessons, in the church of the monastery, at the great altar, for the soul of the said Thomas, the soul of his uncle, and the souls of all the faithful departed.

Whereupon, immediately the same Brother Andrew, the sub-prior

Thomas, each, severally, craved from me, notary public, a public instrument, or public instruments.

These things were done at the said burgh, and within the aforesaid house, at about the third hour after noon, the year, day, month, indiction, and pontificate, as above. Present—Alexander Spens of Pettincreffe, Sir (*domino*) Walter Anderson, James Philp, with divers others specially called and summoned for the purpose (*ad premissa*).

CLII

27.]

De Nouo Burgo.

VNIVERSIS sancte matris ecclesie filiis ad quorum noticias presentes litere peruenerint, Johannes permissione diuina abbas monasterii sancte Marie de Lundoris, ordinis beati benedicti, sancti Andree diocesis, et eiusdem loci conuentus, salutem in omnium saluatore. Et quia cartis et munimentis infeodacionis nostrorum burgensium noui burgi per guerras, ignem, vel alia mundi discrimina negligenter distructis et peremptis, Ideo continuis precibus et crebris instanciis, pro innovacione infeodacionis dicti burgi cartarumque suarum reformacione, predicti burgenses sepissime et indefesse per se ac per nonnullos alios probos ac circumspectos viros nobis, tanquam eorum dominis superioribus, humiliter institerunt et supplicarunt, Nos vero prefati abbas et conventus tandem attendentes et pie considerantes supplicaciones eorum continuas fore justas et racioni consonas, capitulari tractatu, consilioque maturo ac unanimi deliberacione prehabitis, necnon commodo et utilitate dicti nostri monasterii in omnibus prepensatis, dictis nostris burgensibus et suis heredibus innovacionem infeodacionis antedicte, unacum cartarum et munimentorum suorum reformacione meliori modo quo poterimus de novo duximus concedendam. Noverit igitur universitas vestra nos prefatos abbatem et conventum unanimi consensu et assensu dedisse, concessisse, et confirmasse, ac presentis nostre carte tenore dare, concedere, et confirmare dilectis et fidelibus nostris burgensibus, suis heredi-

tenementa, tam in fronte quam in cauda, cum omnibus justis suis pertinenciis, solitis et consuetis, pure et simpliciter in liberum burgum, et forum in eodem cum libera et plenaria facultate emendi et vendendi victualia, vinum, ceram, pannos lineos et laneos, lanam, carnes, pisces, pelles, coria, ac illas et illa fruniendi, piscandi, brasiandi; ballivos, serjandos, ac alios officiarios quoscunque creandi, eligendi, continuandi, deponendi, et in eorum locis alium vel alios singulis annis eligendi et statuendi, curias tenendi, leges burgales exercendi, statuta racionabilia condendi, transgressores debite puniendi, et si opus fuerit eosdem expellendi, amerciamenta levandi, mercimonia quecunque propinandi, liberandi, et mensurandi, ac omnia alia et singula, actus et officia, de jure et consuetudine dictum burgum concerñencia, faciendi et exercendi, nundinas infra dictum burgum die Sancte Katrine Virginis annuatim proclamandi et tenendi, eschaetas et amerciamenta exinde|levandi, exigendi,   [fo et recipiendi, et delinquentes in eisdem debite puniendi, cum omnibus aliis et singulis libertatibus, commoditatibus, et asyamentis prefato burgo de jure vel consuetudine pertinentibus, et quas nos possidemus et illis concedere valemus secundum formam et tenorem carte serenissimi principis quondam, bone memorie, regis Alexandri nobis et nostris successoribus super dicto burgo, caritatis intuitu, graciose concesse in nostrisque archivis conservate : Tenendum et habendum dictum nostrum novum burgum cum omnibus suis pertinenciis in liberum burgum, et forum in eodem, quolibet die martis singularum ebdomadarum cujuslibet anni, et inperpetuum nostris predictis burgensibus et suis heredibus ac successoribus de nobis et successoribus nostris in feodo et hereditate inperpetuum, Adeo libere, quiete, plenarie, honorifice, bene, et in pace sieut nos et predecessores nostri possedimus et habuimus, per omnes et singulas suas antiquas metas rectas et divisas, et aliis suis justis pertinenciis quibuscunque dicto novo burgo spectantibus, seu de jure spectare valentibus quomodolibet in futurum, Et tam

Necnon et prefati burgenses sui heredes et successores reddendo nobis et successoribus nostris annuatim firmas burgales, videlicet; vj. denarios monete currentis pro qualibet virgata seu perticata terre ad terminos solitos et consuetos : Reservando nobis et successoribus nostris omni anno itinera justiciarie et camerarie unacum custumis in dicto burgo contingentibus.   Item volumus quod nullus extraneus extra dictum burgum moram trahens exceptis heredibus legitimis in burgensem recipiatur seu admittatur nisi prius ad hoc noster consensus expresse requiratur et eciam optineatur.   In cujus rei testimonium sigillum commune capituli nostri apud dictum nostrum monasterium, hora capitulari, vicesimo quarto die mensis Maij, Anno domini M°. cccc°. quinquagesimo septimo, presentibus est appensum, etc., quod ff.   R. K.

(Abstract)

' OF NEWBURGH.'

To all the sons of Holy Mother Church to whose notice the present letters shall come, John, by divine permission abbot of the monastery of St. Mary of Lundoris, of the order of Blessed Benedict, in the diocese of St. Andrews, and the convent of the same place, greeting in the Saviour of all men.   Inasmuch as the charters and muniments of infeftment of our burgesses of Newburgh have through negligence perished, and been destroyed, by wars, fire, and other hazards of this life (<i>alia mundi discrimina</i>), and inasmuch as the burgesses aforesaid by continual prayers and frequent and urgent intreaties have by themselves, and by other good and circumspect men, with unwearied persistence humbly urged and supplicated us, as their lords superior, for a new infeftment of the said burgh, and the renewal (<i>reformatione</i>) of their charters, we the aforesaid abbot and convent at length giving ear to them, and considering that their continual supplications were just and agreeable to reason, after discussion in our chapter, and mature counsel, and unanimous deliberation, having carefully weighed what concerned the convenience and advantage of our monastery, have judged that a renewal of the infeftment aforesaid should be granted to our said burgesses and their heirs, together with the renewal (<i>reformatione</i>) of their charters and muniments, in the best way in our power.   Be it known therefore to all of you that we, the aforesaid abbot and convent, have by unanimous consent and assent, given, granted, and confirmed, and by the tenor of our present charter, give, grant, and confirm, to our beloved and faithful

and accustomed, purely and simply, as a free burgh, and a market in the same with free and full power of buying and selling victuals, wine, wax, linen and woollen cloth, wool, flesh, fish, skins, and hides, and of tanning the skins and hides, of fishing, and of brewing. They shall have also full and free power to make and elect bailiffs, sergeants, and other officers, to continue them, depose them, and in their places to elect and appoint one or more; to hold courts; to administer burgh laws; to enact reasonable statutes; to duly punish offenders, and, if need be, to expel the same; to levy fines; to expose for sale, weigh, and measure merchandise of all kinds, and to do and exercise all other and singular acts and offices which by law or custom affect the said burgh, to proclaim and hold every year, on the feast of St. Katherine the Virgin, [Nov. 25] a fair within the said burgh, to levy, exact, and receive escheats and fines therefrom, and to duly punish delinquents in the same, together with the other liberties, conveniences, and easements, all and singular, which by right or custom pertain to the aforesaid burgh, and which we possess and are capable of granting them, according to the form and tenor of the charter of the late most serene prince, of good memory, King Alexander, which, at the prompting of love, was graciously granted to us and our successors anent the said burgh, and which is preserved in our archives. Our said Newburgh to be held and had with all its pertinents as a free burgh, and the market in the same every Tuesday of each week throughout the year, and for ever, by our aforesaid burgesses and their heirs and successors, of us and our successors, in fee and heritage for ever, as freely, quietly, fully, honourably, well, and in peace, as we and our predecessors possessed and had it by all and singular its ancient right meiths and marches, and with its other just pertinents of every kind pertaining to the said New-burgh, or which can of right pertain to it in any way in future, and as freely and quietly as any like burgh within the realm of Scotland is given, granted, or possessed, the said burgesses, their heirs, and successors doing homage to us and our successors, and making three suits of court in the year at our three head-courts to be held within the said burgh, and also the said burgesses, their heirs, and successors, rendering to us and our successors yearly at the usual and customary terms the burgh rents, to wit, six pence of the current money for every rod or perch of land, reserving to us and our successors the justice and chamberlain ayres, together with the customs pertaining in the said burgh. Likewise we will that no stranger (*extraneus*) from outside the said burgh, tarrying there [?], should be received or admitted as a

CLIII

2.] Instrumentum Saysine terre quondam Magistri
Thome Rossy Jacentis in nouo burgo.

IN dei nomine, Amen. per hoc presens publicum instrumentum cunctis pateat evidenter quod anno ab incarnacione eadem millesimo quadringentesimo septuagesimo nono, die vero
mensis Martii vicesimo sexto, indictione duodecima, pontificatus Sanctissimi in Christo patris ac domini nostri, domini
sixti divina providencia pape quarti, anno octavo in plena
curia burgali novi burgi tenta apud ipsum burgum, infra capellam ejusdem, per probos viros, Michaelem de Inch et Ale-
xandrum Michelsen dicti burgi ballivos, comparuit discretus vir
Magister Thomas Rossy, vicarius ecclesie de Inchthur, Sancti
Andree diocesis, qui nec metu ductus nec coactus, nec in aliquo
errore, ut asseruit, lapsus, set ex sua certa scientia ac mera et
spontanea voluntate universas et singulas terras suas et domum
suam lapideam desuper constructam et erectam, cum earundem
pertinenciis vniuersis infra dictum burgum ex parte boreali
eiusdem, inter terras stephani caluart ad occidentem ab vna, et
terras arabiles dominorum abbatis et conuentus monasterii de
Lundoris ad orientem partibus ab altera Jacentes, in manibus
predictorum balliuorum per tradicionem cuiusdam parue
virgule sursum dedit, pureque et simpliciter resignauit ; saluo
tamen sibi dicto magistro thome dictarum terrarum et domus
cum pertinenciis pro toto tempore suo libero tenemento.
Quaquidem resignacione, sic, ut premittitur, facta et admissa,
prefati balliui, finita dicta curia, ad dictas terras et domum
cum pertinenciis, recto tramite, vnacum me notario publico et
testibus subscriptis, accesserunt, et ibidem Michael, balliuus predictus, de dictis terris et domo cum earundem pertinenciis statum
et saisinam hereditariam Religiosis viris fratribus Andree
Wyntoun, suppriori dicti monasterii, et Johanni Cambal,
monachis eiusdem loci professis, tanquam veris et legittimis

lapidis in eorum manibus donacionem, vt moris est in burgo, saluo iure cuiuslibet, tradidit et deliberauit, ac eosdem procuratores nomine et ex parte tocius dicti conuentus in realem actualem et corporalem possessionem traduxit, et realiter inuestiuit de eisdem: Super quibus omnibus et singulis prefatus supprior, nomine et ex parte tocius dicti conuentus, a me notario publico infrascripto sibi fieri peciit vnum seu plura publicum vel publica Instrumentum seu Instrumenta. Acta erant hec anno, mense, die, Indiccione, locis, et pontificatu quibus supra hora vndecima vel eocirca ante meridiem, presentibus ibidem dicto magistro thoma, Johanne Wrycht, Stephano crukschank, Patricio Coule, Jacobo Philip, Nicholao Grynlaw, Dauid arbroth, Alano arbroth, Thoma Wyntoun, Jacobo Kok, Johanne Wemis et Willelmo Zung, cum diuersis aliis testibus, ad premissa vocatis specialiter et rogatis.

(*Abstract*)

'INSTRUMENT of SASINE of the LAND of the late MASTER THOMAS ROSSY, lying in NEWBURGH.'

IN the name of God. Amen. By this present public instrument let it be clearly manifest to all that in the year of the same Incarnation [1] one thousand, four hundred, and seventy-nine, on the twenty-sixth day of the month of March, the twelfth indiction, the eighth year of the pontificate of our Most Holy Father and Lord in Christ, the Lord Sixtus IV. by Divine Providence, Pope, in the full burgh-court of Newburgh, held at the same burgh, within the chapel of the same, by the good men Michael of Inch and Alexander Michelson, bailiffs [2] of the said burgh, compeared the discreet man, Master Thomas Rossy, vicar of the church of Inchthur, in the diocese of St. Andrews, who not led nor forced by fear, nor, as he asserted, having fallen into any error, but of his certain knowledge and pure and spontaneous inclination, gave back into the hands of the aforesaid bailiffs by the delivery of a small twig, and purely and simply resigned, all and singular his lands and his house of stone erected and built thereon, with all pertinents of the same within the said burgh, at the northern part of the same, lying between

pertinents for the whole of his time. On the resignation being made and admitted, as stated above, the aforesaid bailiffs, on the said court having been finished, went by the straight road, together with me, notary public, and the witnesses underwritten, to the said lands and house with their pertinents, and there Michael, the bailiff aforesaid, gave and delivered, by the giving of earth and stone into their hands, as the custom is in the burgh, state and heritable sasine of the said lands and house with the pertinents of the same to the religious, Brothers Andrew Wyntoun, sub-prior of the said monastery, and John Cambal, being professed monks of the same place, as to true and lawful procurators for the whole convent of the same monastery, specially admitted by the said bailiffs in the aforesaid court, for this purpose, according to the form of the said resignation and the tenor of the charter executed thereanent by the said Master Thomas, and put the same procurators in the name and on the part of the whole said convent, into real, actual, and corporal possession, and gave them real investiture of the same. On which things, all and singular, the aforesaid sub-prior, in the name and on the part of the whole said convent, craved of me, the notary public underwritten, that a public instrument or public instruments should be made for them. These things were done in the year, month, day, indiction, places, and pontificate as declared above, at the eleventh hour, or thereabouts, before noon. There being present at the same place the said Master Thomas, John Wrycht, Stephen Crukschank, Patrick Coule, James Philip, Nicholas Grynlaw, David Arbroth, Alan Arbroth. Thomas Wyntoun, James Kok, John Wemis, and William Zung, with divers other witnesses specially called and summoned to the premises.

CLIV

1.] ## [Fragmentum Instrumenti Publici.[1]]

In Dei nomine amen; per hoc presens publicum instrumentum cunctis   secunda Indictione vij[a] pontificatus sanctissimi in christo patris ac domini nostri
et testium subscriptorum presencia personaliter. constitutus discretus uir du   singulos procuratores suos super consilii infrascripta potestate cum   predictam permittandi Reuocando et quos extunc Reuocantur de Butyll, archidiaconum candide case, sacri palacij.[2]

Carric Ricardum Cady et dominum Johannem de
auchynleke a   actores factores et negociorum suorum
gestores d.d. resigna   parochialem de Kynnetlys
predictam quam secundum fac
Roberto de Dryden, Rectore dicte ecclesie de mukart, in
            supradicti uel alterius cuiuscunque ab eodem
monasterio propria   ac in ipsius constitucionis
animam iurandum et juramentum
niaca prauitas uel illicita pactio   Et generaliter
            si particulariter interesset eciam si talis huc
que in iudicum . . . stipulanti tanquam persone publice
      et nomine omnium   a aliquis in premissis duxerit
faciendum sub ypotheca   singulis premissis
Idem dominus hugo a me notario publico
Sancti Andree sub anno die mense Indiccione et pontificatu
supradictis Glasguen. et Brechynen. canonico Johanne Scheues
. . . sancti andree diocesis ecclesiarum Rectoribus Johanne de
Cameron   vocatis et requisitis in
testimonium omnium et singulorum
[Signum Notarii,] Et ego Willelmus.

[FRAGMENT of a PUBLIC INSTRUMENT.

NOTE.—The sense of this fragment cannot be gathered, the document
having been cut lengthwise, so that the latter part of each line is wanting.
Indeed it seems highly probable from the discoloration of the parchment
that the leaf had been at one time pasted down on the oaken board
which formed the front cover of the little volume. The *verso* side is
blank. Some conjectures as to some of the persons named will be found
in the Notes and Illustrations. One of them was, almost certainly, at a
later date, Bishop of Galloway.]

NOTES AND ILLUSTRATIONS

The Notes with the initials [A.G.] added are from comments furnished by Mr. Alexander Gibb, F.S.A. Scot.

I

Date. This may be determined as between 1178 and 1182. Of the witnesses, Hugh was appointed Bishop of St. Andrews not earlier, at least, than 1178 (*Chron. de Mailr.* s.a.), while Earl Waldeve (Earl of Dunbar) died in 1182 (*Chron. de Mailr.* s.a.).

Page 1. *Probis hominibus.* The familiar phrase *probi homines* is perhaps to be understood as signifying 'the smaller tenants-in-chief.' See Rait's *Scottish Parliament*, p. 15.

Comitatum de Leuenaus. 'Alwyn, second Earl of Lennox, being very young, William I. gave the ward of the Earldom of Lennox to David, Earl of Huntingdon and Garioch' (Douglas, *Peerage*, ii. 81). In *Scotichronicon* (lib. ix. cap. 27) we do not find Lennox mentioned among the grants made by William to Earl David. It is there said that after returning from his captivity in England (1175) King William gave to his brother David the earldom of Huntingdon and the earldom of Garioch, with the lordship of Strathbolgi, the royal vill of Dundee, together with Inverbervie and the lands of Langforgrund, with other wide and spacious lands and possessions. On the other hand the same authority elsewhere (lib. ix. cap. 33) when recording Earl David's death describes him as 'Earl of Huntingdon, of Garioch, and of Lennox.' And the comparison of the two entries falls in with a late date (such as that of our charter) for the donation of Lennox. We learn (*Registr. Monast. Passelet*, pp. 166-168) that when Earl David held and possessed

to the treaty for the marriage of the Maid of Norway (Palgrave's *Documents* (Scotland), i. 32).

Dunde. This, so far as the editor is aware, is the earliest notice of Dundee in authentic history.

Forgrund. This is presumably the 'Langforgrund' in the account of the grants made by King William to Earl David as given in *Scotichron.* (lib. ix. cap. 27). If this identification is correct the Forgrund of this charter (which is in the Carse of Gowrie) is to be distinguished from the Forgrund (Forgandenny) near Exmagirdle, of No. LXVIII.

Petmothel. This name seems to have disappeared. 'Mothel' or 'Moethel' (the modern Muthill) is frequent in the Chartulary. On the prefix 'Pet' (= a portion of land), see Skene, *Four Ancient Books of Wales,* i. 157.

Neutyle. Earl David seems to have given land at Newtyle (in Forfarshire) to his (natural) daughter Ada, wife of Malise, son of Ferteth, Earl of Strathern, from which she made a grant of Balemagh. Compare p. 4 and p. 38.

Most of the Aberdeenshire place-names are obvious, as Fintreth (Fintray), Inuerurin (Inverury), Monkegyn (Monkeigie), Boverdyn (Bourty), Durnach (Durno),[1] Uuen (Oyne), Arduuen (Ardoyne). The editor hesitates to offer conjectures as to Rothiod. In the bulls of Celestine III. and Innocent III. (pp. 103, 109) we find that Inverurie and Monkegie were then chapels of the church of Rothket or Rothketh ; perhaps this is the same place as 'Rothiod.' In a charter of King William to Earl David, preserved in *Registrum Aberdonense* (i. 9) we have Rothkes mentioned together with Durnach, Monkegyn, Fyntrach, and Bourdyn. The name 'Rothket' as applied to a parish church seems to have disappeared at an early date. In No. II. 'Inverury' is the parish church and 'Monkegie' its chapel. Rothket does not appear in the old valuation (*Regist. Aberdon.* ii. 51-56), nor in Boiamund's roll (Theiner's *Monumenta,* 109-116).

Mertonam. 'Mertona' is to be identified with the lands which lie south and west of Liberton, near Edinburgh, and have retained a form of the name in the modern 'Mortonhall.' Dr. J. Maitland Thomson has been good enough to furnish the following references. In 1357-8 David II. grants to William Sinclair the lands of 'Mertona' and 'Merchamystona' (Merchiston), in the sheriffdom of Edinburgh, on the resignation of them by William Bisset (*Reg. de Neubotle,* Append. p. 295). The *Register of Neubotle* contains earlier notices of Merton in connection with the Bissets, but none reaching to the time of Earl David. In 1404 Robert III. grants to Henry Sinclair, Earl of Orkney,

also *Regist. Mag. Sigil.* (A.D 1306-1424), p. 23, No. 15; and the same, vol. ii. No. 1271.

Cum saccu et socca, cum tol et tem et infangenthefe, etc. Any discussion of the sense of these familiar, but really obscure, terms of feudal infeftment would be out of place here. Reference may be made, among the older feudalists, to Skene's *De verborum significatione,* and Craig's *Jus Feudale,* and among more recent writers to the *Glossarium* in Wilkins's edition of *Leges Anglo-Saxonicae,* Bishop Stubbs's Glossary to *Select Charters,* and Mr. Cosmo Innes's *Scotch Legal Antiquities* (pp. 55-58).

Testibus, etc. Hugh, *capellanus regis,* was intruded into the see of St. Andrews by King William (after the canonical election of John, the Scot), probably in 1178. Hugh died 4th Aug. 1188 (*Scotichron.* vi. 41 and viii. 44). Joceline, fourth abbot of Melrose, was elected to the see of Glasgow, 23rd May 1174, and died 17th March 1199 (*Chron. de Mailr.* s.a.). Matthew was consecrated Bishop of Aberdeen, 2nd April 1172 (*Chron. de Mailr.* s.a.), and died 20th August 1199 (*ibid.* s.a.). Simeon (or Simon) de Tonei, a monk of Melrose, abbot of the Cistercian monastery of Coggeshall (in Essex), who had returned to Melrose, was elected to Moray in 1171 (*Regist. Morav.* 359). He died 17th Sept. 1184 (*Chron. de Mailr.* s.a.). Andrew, Bishop of Caithness, witnessed a charter of David I. (†1153), see *Book of Deer,* p. 95. He died 29th Dec. 1184 (*Scotichron.* viii. 33), or 30th Dec. 1195 (*Chron. de Mailr.* s.a.).

Comite Dunecano: Duncan, sixth Earl of Fife; consented to Convention of King William with Henry II. at Falaise, 1174; founded nunnery of North Berwick; died in 1203. His son, Malcolm, also witnesses this charter. [A. G.]

Comite Gileberto: Gilbert, third Earl of Strathern; founded the abbey of Inchaffray, 1198; was alive in 1219; and appears to have died shortly after. [A. G.]

Comite Waldevo: Waldeve, fourth of his family called earl; and the first styled Earl of Dunbar. He was a hostage for King William, and died in 1182. His son, Patrick, is also a witness to this charter. [A. G.]

Malcolmo Comite Ethol: Malcolm, second Earl of Athole. Gave to the monks of Scone the church of Logen-Mahed; to the abbey of Dunfermelyn the tithes of the church of Moulin, for the weal of his own soul, the soul of his spouse, and the souls of the Kings of Scotland, his predecessors—he being a descendant of King Donald Bane.[1] To the priory of St. Andrews he gave the patronage of the church of Dull for the weal of the soul of Hextilda his spouse. [A. G.]

G. Comite de Anegus: Gillibrede, second Earl of Angus; is said to have died *circa* 1180. It is impossible to tell whether 'G' here be Gillibrede

Gartnait, his wedded wife (a ben phusta), he gives to Drostan, and Columcille and Peter the Apostle (that is to the Columban monastery of Deer) a four davachs' share of what would come on the chief monasteries of Alba (Scotland). The deed is witnessed by the gentry of Buchan at Eilan (Ellon), which long continued to be the seat of the courts of the Earldom of Buchan. Mr. Joseph Robertson judges the charter to have been granted about the year 1150.[1] The fortunate occurrence of his name in this charter gives an earlier earl than hitherto known, and extends the earldom back for fifty years; also furnishes an instance of the Scottish 'mormer' being changed to 'comes' or earl.

Earl Colban of Buchan appears to be the Earl Colbein who brought a considerable force to Caldenlé' [Caddon-Lea] to swell the host with which King William made his disastrous raid into Northumberland in 1173.

l. 472.   'De Ros e de Muraive unt grant ost banie.
          Certes, le Cunte Colbein ne s'e ublia mie.
          Seigneurs, le Cunte d'Anegus i vint od tel aie,
          Plus de treis mil Escoz aveit en sa baillie.'

          'From Ross and from Moray they have a great host gathered,
          Certainly Earl Colbein did not forget himself there.
          Lords, the Earl of Angus came there with such aid,
          More than three thousand Scots he had in his command.'[2] [A. G.]

Ricardo de Moreuille, Constabulario : Richard of Morville, Constable of Scotland. Richard de Morville was made Constable of Scotland by King Malcolm about 1163, and continued in that office till his death in 1189. The family had considerable possessions in Cumberland, about Burgh-upon-Sands, etc., and in Lauderdale in Scotland. He was much about court, and is a frequent witness to charters. [A. G.]

Roberto de Quincy: This is the first de Quincy that appears in record in Scotland. Dugdale says the family do not appear earlier than the reign of Henry II. in records in England (1154-1189). Robert de Quinci married Orabilis, daughter and heiress of Ness, the son of William, and got with her a large estate of Locres (Leuchars) and Lathrisk. A charter by Seyer de Quinci about Dauch Icthar Hathyn (modern form would be Auchter Eden) mentions that the lands were given to the priory of St. Andrews by his mother. Robert de Quinci, *patre meo*, and Stephan [de Quinci], parson of Locres, witness this charter; *ante* 1208 as Seier is not styled Earl of Winchester.[3] After her husband's death Orabilis married Duncan, the eighth Earl of Mar, and became Countess of Mar. Duncan died 1238. [A. G.]

Waltero Olifer : the third son of David Olifard, who was ancestor of the Lords Oliphant. See No. II. *infra.* [A. G.]

Alano, etc. : Alan, son of Walter the Steward ; Walter, Steward of Scotland, died 1177. Alan, his son, also Steward, died in 1204, and was buried at Paisley. [A. G.]

Willelmo de Haya : the first de Haya on record that possessed the lands of Herrol (Errol), in Gowrie, which he obtained by charter from King William. [A. G.]

Radolpho de Vere : Radulphus de Vere is witness to a confirmation by King William to the abbey of Cambuskenneth before 1214. He was ancestor of the Weirs of Blackwood. [A. G.]

Ricardo de Munfichet : this name has crumbled down to Mushet. John of Drummond, Lord of Concrag, is said to have got Stobball and other lands in Perth by marriage with a Munfichet heiress. A respectable family of Mushet possessed considerable estates in Menteith. [A. G.]

Willelmo de Lindesey : William de Lindesei. See No. II. p. 235.

Rand[olpho] de Solis: Members of the family of Solis, Soulis, Sules appear frequently in early Scottish charters. We find Randulph witnessing charters of Malcolm the Maiden (*Regist. Glasguen.* i. 15 ; *Regist. Priorat. S. Andree,* 198), and, still earlier, charters of David I. (*Regist. Priorat. S. Andree,* 182, 183, 189). William de Soulis was Justiciar of Lothian in 1284 (*Regist. Glasguen.* i. 196). See for more as to William de Soulis (*Scotichron.* x. 29).

II

Date. The date of this charter can be fixed with more exactness than many undated charters of the period. Roger, Bishop of St. Andrews, is a witness. He was not consecrated till the First Sunday in Lent, 1198 (*Chron. de Mailr.* s.a.). The First Sunday in Lent fell on 15th Feb. in that year. But again, Hugh, 'chancellor of the king,' is also a witness. He died on vi. Id. Julii (10th July) 1199 (*Chron. de Mailr.* s.a.). The charter accordingly belongs to some date between 15th Feb. 1198 and 10th July 1199. There must have been a charter of like tenor before 8th March 1194-5. See Celestine's *Confirmation* (No. XCIII.).

The charter from the Denmyln MSS. in the Advocates' Library (hitherto regarded as the foundation charter), which is printed by Turnbull in *Liber Sancte Marie de Lundoris* (pp. 37-8) is of a later date, which can be shown to be 1202 or 1203.

Magister Thomas. This was doubtless the priest of the parish of Lindores.

Rivuli descendentis de magno lacu. See Introduction, p. xxxix. note.

Redinche. See Introduction, p. xxxix.

Omnia que pertinent ad molendinum. See Introduction, p. lxxxix.

Iharam. A *yair* or *yare*, a stake-net. In Sir John Skene's old vernacular version of the statutes of Robert I. the word is used together with 'cruves.' See Introduction, p. xl.

Cum omni secta sua means all those tenants of lands astricted or thirled to that mill, who were known in Scotland as *suckeners.* *Sequela* is sometimes used as equivalent to *secta.* The multure was ordinarily paid in grain or in flour. Erskine (*Institutes*, Book II., tit. ix. 19), interprets, incorrectly, *sequelae* as the payments made to the servants of the mill over and above the multure paid to the lord. See Craig's *Jus Feudale* (lib. II. dieg. viii. 12), and Ducange (sub *Secta ad molendinum*).

Et multura. Multure dues. The payments due to the lord of the mill for the privilege of having corn ground there. See Introduction, p. lxxxv. ff.

Ultra muneth. 'The Mounth' is the name applied to the mountainous range running from the west with a northerly trend, and terminating in the north of Kincardineshire.

Lethgauel et malind. In the fifteenth century rental of the abbey (Laing's *Lindores Abbey*, p. 416) Mellensyde appears. It is the Malinsyd of the map (1654) of Gordon of Straloch. The identification of Lethgauel must be left to those better versed than the editor in the topography of the Garioch. Charter cxvii. (assuming Lethgauen to be a variant of the name) is a clue to its position.

Pramet. For this and the names of other churches in the Garioch, see Introduction, p. xli.

Page 4. *Mota canum.* The word *mota* still survives in the French terms *meute de chiens, chef de meute*, etc.

Curiam . . . et dignitatem pacis. 'Curia' is the abbot's court of secular jurisdiction; 'dignitas ¦pacis' is perhaps the privilege of asylum, the right of affording protection (for a time) to criminals craving the *pax ecclesiae.*

Vivariis. The *vivarium*, or fish-pond, where fish caught, if not immediately needed, were placed, was an usual adjunct of the religious houses. The word has been a fruitful source of mistakes, the second 'u' being often read as 'n.' Hence more 'vineyards' (*vinariae*) have been imagined to exist than facts justify. See Cosmo Innes's *Scotch Legal*

the king, William's mother Ada being sister to the earl. He was consecrated 15th Feb. 1189 (*Chron. de Mailr.* s.a.). He died 7th July 1202 (*Scotichron.* vi. 42). John, Bishop of Dunkeld, is 'John the Scot' who had been ousted from St. Andrews by King William. He was confirmed in Dunkeld by the Pope in 1183. He died in 1203 in the monastery of Newbottle, where he assumed the habit on his death-bed (*Scotichron.* vi. 41).

Hugone cancellario regis. Hugh of Roxburgh, afterwards elected to the bishopric of Glasgow after the death of Joceline (17th March 1199). He died, probably before consecration, 10th July 1199.

Comite Patricio. Patrick, fifth Earl of Dunbar, from 1182 (*Chron. de Mailr.*) till 1232 (*ibid.*) He founded a monastery of Red Friars at Dunbar in 1218. In 1184 he married Ada, a natural daughter of King William the Lion. [A. G.]

Roberto de Lundors. So the MS. reads. This is doubtless Robert of London, natural son of King William. In Celestine's bull (p. 104) he is 'Robertus de Lundres, filius prefati regis' (*sc.* Willelmi); he is 'Robertus de Lundoniis' in No. LXXXV. (p. 91).

Seier de Quinci: son of Robert de Quinci and Orabilis, daughter of Ness, son of William. Was made Earl of Winchester in 1208 (Dugdale). [A. G.]

Philippo de Valuniis. This family took their surname from Valones or Valoignis, in Costatyn, in Normandy. Peter de Valoniis was an eminent follower of William the Conqueror, and obtained many manors from him. His son, Roger de Valoniis, had six sons, of whom Philip de Valoniis came to Scotland about the end of the reign of King Malcolm IV. He was one of the hostages for the liberation of King William the Lion in 1174 ; in recompence the king gave him the manors of Panmure and Benvie in Forfarshire, and appointed him High Chamberlain about 1180. He died on the 5th of November 1215, and was interred in Melrose

Roberto Basset; also a frequent witness to Earl David's charters. Families of this name had great possessions in the Midland Counties of England, such as Drayton, etc. [A. G.]

Henrico filio comitis. He is either Henry of Striuelyn, or Henry of Brechin, both illegitimate sons of Earl David. For the last, see also No. LXI., *infra.* [A. G.]

III

Date. John, Bishop of Aberdeen, a witness, was consecrated certainly before 6th Dec. 1201, when he appeared as 'bishop of Aberdeen' at the council held by Cardinal John, of Salerno (*Regist. Glasguen.* i. 81). He died in 1207—Oct. 13. (Gawan's *Epistolare* in *Regist. Aberdon.* ii. 247). Radulph, Bishop of Brechin, another witness, was consecrated in 1202 (*Chron. de Mailr.* s. a.). As a third witness Osbert, abbot of Kelso, died in 1203, (*Chron. de Mailr.* s. a.). The charter must be dated as in 1202 or 1203.

The original of this charter is in the Denmyln collection, preserved in the Advocates' Library, and has been printed (not very accurately) by Turnbull in the Appendix to *Liber S. Marie de Lundoris,* pp. 37-38. The variations from our text are few and unimportant.

Page 8. *Osberto abbate Kelchoensi* : prior of Lesmahago ; succeeded to Kelso in 1180 ; died 1203.

Henrico abbate de Aberbrodoc. Henry was second abbot of Arbroath, and succeeded in 1179.

Simone archidiacono de Aberdoen, Roberto decano de Aberdoen. Both these ecclesiastics are witnesses to a charter of Bishop Matthew de Kyninmond (*Regist. Aberdon.* i. ii.). Robert, dean of Aberdeen, is a witness of No. v.

Normanno filio Malcolmi. Of the family afterwards known as that of Lescelin (Lesley). See Introduction, p. lvi.

IV

Date. There is nothing that enables us to fix the date of this charter of Earl David within very narrow limits. It was probable like others of the minor charters shortly after the date of the great charter (No. II.)

Page 9. *Cum eorum sequela.* See Introduction, p. lvii.

Page 10. *David de Lindeseie.* One of the ancestors of the family of the Earls of Crawfurd, acquired Crawfurd estates by marriage, and died 1230. [A.G.]

V

Date. Between about 1200 or 1201, and 1207, when John, Bishop of Aberdeen, died.

Salvo cano. The small tribute, custom, or cane, referred to as due to the Bishop of St. Andrews, had not been commuted or exchanged, as were certain tithes and customs due to the Bishop of Aberdeen out of Durno, Rothkes, Monkegie, Fintray, and Bourtie, which in the time of Bishop Matthew had been exchanged for two ploughgates of land in Kinethmond given to the bishop by Earl David (*Regist. Aberdon.* i. 9).

Page 11. *Malisio filio comitis Fertheth.* See Introduction, p. xxxiv.

Duobus Henricis filiis comitis. Henry of Stirling and Henry of Brechin. See Introduction, p. xxvi.

VI

Date. Before the death of Earl Duncan in 1204 (*Chron. de Mailr.* s.a.) and if 'A.' abbot of Dunfermline is Archibald (Erchinbald) before his death in 1198 (*ibid.* s.a.).

Mr. Turnbull printed this charter, from an inferior text, in *Liber S. Marie de Lundoris,* p. 8. 'Malisio comite Fertheth,' as printed by him is an obvious error. 'R. de Anas' should, as we learn from our Chartulary, be 'N. de Anas.' In No. VII. Nicholaus de Aness appears as a witness.

Page 11. *Ad colcrike.* The name Colcrick seems to have disappeared. Charter LXXVI. may help towards determining its locality.

VII

Date. Probably before the foundation charter, but there is nothing to determine the date within narrow limits.

This is printed in *Liber S. Marie de Lundoris* (p. 24) with a few trifling variants in the spelling of the names of witnesses.

In quarrario meo in hyrneside. Mr. Alex. Laing (*Lindores Abbey,* p. 53, note) writes : 'The quarry, which is now covered up, was of old red sandstone ;—it was about a mile east from the abbey, on the farm of Parkhill. The track of a small canal for conveying the stones to the abbey was said to be discernible in recent times.' On the etymology of

text. It is the Witstones of the fifteenth century rental (*Lindores Abbey*, p. 411). The lands all lie close together in the south of Kincardineshire on the sea-coast.

Eglesgirg, 'ecclesia Cyrici.' See Bishop Forbes's *Kalendar of Scottish Saints*, pp. 319-20. In modern times the name St. Cyrus has been given to the parish. For St. Cyriacus, see Smith and Wace, *Dict. of Christian Biography*, s.v. (3). This saint is commemorated in *Breviarium Aberdonense* together with St. Julitta (his mother) on 16th June. By an error the Kalendar of this Breviary reads 'Ceriaci et Julitti,' as if the name of the latter saint was Julittus. Ceres, in Fife, has been supposed to be derived from the name of this saint. In the forms Girrig, Gerrig, Gwrig, the name appears in some Welsh place-names, as in Llangwrig, or Llangirrig in Montgomeryshire. The more common form in Wales is Curig. See Forbes's *Kalendar of Scottish Saints*, pp. 319-20; Rees's *Welsh Saints*, pp. 82, 307.

Pethergus, Pethannot. These names have perished. The Kaim of Matheres is a crag overlooking the sea, with the ruins of a fortlet upon it. The burn of Matheres appears to be the burn east from the village, where the wild Falls of Den-Finella are seen. In the charter of erection of the lordship of Lindores, dated at the burgh of Perth, 31st March 1600, Wicheston appears as Wistoun; and among the lands we find Pittargus and Pittannous. [A. G.]

IX

Date. Perhaps before No. ii., in which the grant is confirmed with others.

Page 13. *Balemawe.* Mr. Laing writes : 'Balmaw in the parish of Newtyle' (*Lindores Abbey*, p. 460). This charter shows that Mr. Laing is in error as to the original grantor of Balmaw. In No. xxxvi., the grant of a ploughgate of land, 'cum corpore meo,' in the vill of Balemagh, is made by Ada, natural daughter of Earl David. In a rental, which Mr. David Laing assigned to about 1580, we find, 'Balmaw and Newtyld yeirlie sevintyne poundis viijs' (*Lindores Abbey*, p. 423).

Henrico abbate de Aberbrothoc. He appears in No. xi. as 'Abbot of St. Thomas,' that is, of Arbroath, dedicated to St. Thomas of Canterbury. His tenure of office was from 1179 till (certainly) 1202, and perhaps later.

X

Averia. 'Beasts of burden,' here distinguished from horses, though in other documents it includes cart-horses, and, in the later Scottish vernacular, an 'aver' was a 'cart-horse.'

XI

Date. Apparently between 8th March 1195 and 20th March 1198; for the grant of the church of Whissendene is not confirmed in the hull of Celestine III., but is confirmed in that of Innocent III.

Wissendene. See Introduction, p. 1.

[Mr. A. Laing (*Lindores Abbey*, p. 54, note) states that Mr. Scott, son of Sir Gilbert Scott, who had charge of the restoration of Whisendine church (1868), is of opinion that the north transept, which still stands, was built about A.D. 1220.—A. G.]

XII

Date. See No. XI.

The duplication of this charter, as also of that relating to Conington (No. XIV.), was perhaps for exhibition in England to the Bishop of Lincoln or his official. The witnesses differ slightly from those of No. XI.

See Introduction, p. 1.

XIII

Date. Before 1195; as the grant is confirmed in the bull of Celestine III. (No. XCIII.)

See Introduction, p. 1.

Page 16. Cunington, or Conington, lies in the north of the shire of Huntingdon, several miles south from Peterborough. Camden (1607) says Cunington was possessed by Waldeof, Earl of Huntingdon. By marriage with Isabel, daughter of David, Earl of Huntingdon, Cunington and other large estates fell to Robert Brus. From Brus's 'younger son, Bernard, who inherited Cunnington and Exton, Sir Robert Cotton, Knight, derives his [descent], a person who, besides other excellencies, is a great admirer and master of learning, and has here a collection of venerable antiquities from all parts.'—Gibson's *Camden* (1695), p. 423. [A. G.]

XV

Date. Between 1219, when John succeeded his father as Earl of Huntingdon, and 1232 when he succeeded to the earldom of Chester.

Page 19. *Roberto de Campaniis.* Dr. Maitland Thomson has informed the editor that 'the English printed records leave no doubt that *de Campania* is in the vernacular *de Champagne*, or *de Chaumpaigne* (there are numerous varieties of spelling).' This witness is probably the father of Robert de Campaniis, the grantor of No. cxiii., who appears to have succeeded his brother William de Campaniis, son of Robert, in the lands of Stokes in Leicestershire. See pp. 137-140.

Johanne de Brus. Robert de Brus (1215-1245) married Isabella, daughter of Earl David and sister of Earl John. This John may have been a son. There is a John de Brus, reputed ancestor of the Bruces of Clackmannan, and Earls of Elgin and Kincardine. See Wood's *Peerage,* i. 318. [A. G.]

Normanno constabulario. Norman, of the family afterwards known as Lescelyn (Leslie), was constable of Inverurie Castle. See p. lvi.

Henrico de Dundemor. Dundemore, near Lindores, now whittled down to Dunsmoor or even Dinmuir. Its original name, Dun-dhu-mor, appears to be derived from the ancient British fort on Norman's Law. The family of Dundemore kept possession for a lengthened period, and took the Scottish side in the Wars of Independence. [A. G.]

Thoma de Lindeseia. Nothing is known of this Lindsay. [A. G.]

Nicholao de Inuerpeffyn. He appears frequently as a witness. [A. G.]

XVI

Date. Between 1219 and 1232. See No. xv.

All the witnesses appear in No. xv.

XVII

Date. After 1232, when John, Earl of Huntingdon, succeeded to the earldom of Chester, and before 5th June 1237, when he died.

Page 21. *Pontem de Balhagerdyn.* This is an early notice of a bridge in Aberdeenshire. Balhaggardy is north of Inverurie, near the river Ury. [A. G.]

Ad pietanciam, etc. It was very common for the founders of an 'anniversary' or yearly commemoration of some one defunct, observed ordinarily in the church by a Mass for the soul of the departed with

not with *pietas,* but with *picta,* a small coin first struck by the earls of Poitiers (Pictavia). See Ducange, s.v. In the *Chartulary of Coldstream* (P. 24) we find Walter, the chaplain, granting a toft or croft to the nunnery 'ad unam petanciam faciendam dictis monialibus' on the morrow of St. Laurence, for the soul of his mother.

H. Phyton. He is 'Dominus Hugo Phyton' in No. xix.

Simone de Garentuly. He witnesses No. xviii., which see.

XVIII

Date. Between 1232 and 5th June 1237.

Page 21. *Toftum in villa de Inverbervyn.* Towards the close of the fifteenth century 'the annewellis of Bervay' brought viiij s. to the monastery (*Lindores Abbey,* p. 411), and the same sum appears in the rental of the lands of Lindores about one hundred years later (*ibid.* p. 424).

Utting Cachepol. The latter word perhaps points to office. We find one Huttyngus, who was 'marescallus' of Brice, Bishop of Moray, 1203-1222 (*Regist. Morav.* p. 61).

Page 22. *Simone de Garentuli.* We find 'Simon de Garentuly' witnessing a charter, relating to lands in the diocese of Moray, on 25th April 1229 (*Regist. Morav.,* p. 26). Garentuli seems to be Grantuly, or Garntuly, or Gartly, in Strathbolgie. See *Regist. Morav.,* pp. 365, 366, 407. The parish was in the diocese of Moray, and was mensal of the bishop. See Theiner's *Monumenta,* p. 69. Simon was 'ballivus' of John, Earl of Chester and Huntingdon before 1234. See No. xxi. He gave the lands of Ederlarg to the monastery (No. lvi.). In No. lvii. he describes himself as 'miles,' and gives lands in exchange for 'second tithes.' He obtained leave to have a private chapel at his seat at Cremond near Inverurie (No. lxiii.)

XIX

Date. Between 1232 and 5th June 1237.

Page 22. *Tofto Sancti Clementis.* The position of St. Clement's Church in Dundee is still indicated by St. Clement's Wynd.

Page 23. *Portencrag.* Portincraig is now on the shore of Fife, opposite Broughty, at the opening of the mouth of the Tay. [The editor of the Register of Arbroath points out that Portincrag at first lay to the north

XX

Date. Between 1232 and 5th June 1237, probably after Whitsunday 1234.

XXI

Date. See No. xx.

XXII

Date. 20th April 1236.

Page 25. *Dunmernoch .   in Strathtay.* [Drummernoch in Strathtay cannot be identified.—A. G.]

Fedal in theynagio de Ouchyrardour. These lands are obviously the Westere Fedal of No. xxiii., the marches of which were determined by a jury in 1246, the result being fortified by the seal of the Justiciar of Scotland, Alan Durward. Thanages were crown-lands ordinarily let out at fee-farm. [The name Fedal persists in Feddal House, Mid Feddal, and Feddal Hill, north of Braco.—A. G.] On the thanages in Scotland see W. F. Skene's full note in his edition of *Fordun* (ii. 414-419). In Skene's long list of thanages we do not find Auchterarder (supplied by this charter). But he mentions Forteviot not far off.

P. Comite de Dunbar. Patrick, sixth Earl of Dunbar, succeeded his father in 1232. He died at Damietta in Egypt in 1248, in the crusade under Louis ix. of France. [A. G.]

W. Comnyn, Comite de Menethet. Walter Comyn became Earl of Menteith by marriage with the Countess of Menteith, one of the daughters of Maurice, third earl. He was earl from 1231 to 1258. He was the only Comyn who was earl. [A. G.]

R. de Quency, constabulario Scocie. Roger de Quency, or Quincy, became Constable of Scotland, by his marriage with Helena, daughter of Alan, Lord of Galloway, on whose death, in 1233, De Quincy succeded to the office and dignity. [A. G.]

W. filio Alani, senescallo, Justiciario Scocie. Walter succeeded his father, Alan, High Steward and Justiciar of Scotland, in 1204; was made Justiciar of Scotland in 1230, died 1246. [A. G.]

XXIII

Date. 1246.

Page 26. *Aldendoneche,* etc. The editor must leave to those versed in the topography of the district of Auchterarder to trace or guess at these

We find John de Haya as 'vicecomes de Perth,' 31st March 1226 (*Regist. Morav.* p. 22).

Hominibus quamplurimis Domini Joachim. No doubt this is Sir Joachim of Kynbuk, recorded in Nos. xxviii., xxxv., cxii. Sir Joachim was the first of the family of Kinbuck of that ilk, who held the lands of Kinbuck for several generations. In 1458 Marjorie, daughter of Malcolm of Kinbuck (apparently the last of the family) married Alexander Bruce of Stenhouse. See Rev. John Anderson's *Laing Charters* No. 143. [A. G.]

Kinbuck is some two or three miles north of Dunblane, and not very far from Feddal.

Comitis de Strathern. This would appear to be Malise, fifth earl, who succeeded about 1244, and died in 1270. [A. G.]

A. Hostiarii. Alan, the Door-ward (*Ostiarius, Hostiarius*) was appointed Justiciar in 1244 (*Scotichron.* ix. 61). He was reputed the *flos militiæ* (*ibid.* x. 1). He was married to a natural daughter of Alexander ii. (*ibid.* x. 4). He was appointed at Roxburgh (20th Sept. 1255) one of the fifteen guardians during the minority of Alexander iii. (*Foedera,* i. 566). He died in 1275 (*Scotichron.* x. 35). Bower's eulogium on Durward will be found in the same place.

XXIV

Date. In the time of Robert, Earl of Strathern, who is said to have died before 1244. See the Genealogical Table, Introduction, p. xxxiv.

Page 27. This is a commutation of second tithes (tithes of cane and rent) due to Lindores (by the grant of Malise, husband of Ada, daughter of Earl David) from the lands in Strathern and Hure by means of an exchange of them for 'Fedal in Kathermothel,' which exchange was 'made by Sir Fergus, son of Earl Gilbert, and nephew of Malise. In addition to the land, permission to cut timber in his wood was granted by Sir Fergus. This land I take to be the 'Eister Feddellis' of the fifteenth century rental (*Lindores Abbey,* p. 412).

De exercitu, etc. See Introduction, p. lxxiii.

Kathermothel. Till a few years ago Muthill included, as a parish, the parts now separated into the parish of Ardoch. 'Cathair,' or, as here, Kather, is the Gaelic word for a 'fort'; and there can be no reasonable doubt that Kathermothel means that part of Muthill where the Roman camp forms such a conspicuous feature. Keirburn still perpetuates the

seventh Earl of Strathern, who succeeded in 1296, gives a donation of 8s. silver yearly from his territory *de Magna Hure*. In the semi-Saxon English of that time the word 'Micel' or 'Mucel,' great, was reputed fashionable, and Magna Hure became Micel-Hure, now Meiklour, in the nook betwixt Ilay and Tay. See also Nos. xxxiv. and xxxv. [A. G.]

> Page 28. *Waltero de Rotheuen.* See under No. xxvi.
> *Henrico de Aschirche.* Nothing known of him. [A. G.]
> *Rogero de Leuuethot.* See No. xxvi.

XXV

Date. Earl Robert, the grantor of this confirmation, is said to have died before 1244. And as Innocent, afterwards abbot of Inchaffray, was appointed prior in 1220 we can roughly approximate to the limits of the date.

Page. 29. *Innocencio abbate de insula missarum.* This is doubtless the canon of Scone who in 1220 was made prior of Inchaffray, 'amoto quodam Scotico propter insufficientiam' (*Scotichr.* ix. 36), and who was afterwards elevated to the rank of *abbot* of Inchaffray.

Gilberto archidiacono Dumblanensi. He appears again as a witness in No. xxvii., xxx., xxxi. (G. archidiacono de Strathern), and xxxii.

Gilescop de Cletheueys. Cletheueys (Clavage). [A. G.]

XXVI

Date. In the time of Earl Robert. See No. xxv. and before the end of 1234, about which time William became Earl of Mar. As Clement, Bishop of Dunblane, is a witness, the date is probably towards the end of 1233 or sometime in 1234.

Page 29. *Beny*: now Bennie. [On the east side of the Knaik above the village of Braco.—A. G.] Concrag (not named in the text of the charter) was probably what is described as the land 'pertaining to Beny,' near the land of Roger de Luvethot. 'Beney' brought a rent of x lb, xiijs. iiijd. at the close of the fiteenth century (*Lindores Abbey*, p. 412). [It can hardly be the Concraig on which Drummond Castle was afterwards built. The name has now perished.—A. G.]

Militis mei. See Introduction, pp. lxxiii-lxxvi.

Page 30. *Clemente Dunblanensi episopo.* Clement, a Dominican friar, was consecrated for Dunblane, 4th September 1233 (*Chron. de Mailr.* s.a.): he died in 1258 (*ibid.* s.a.), or, according to Bower (*Scotichr.* x. ii.) in

Willelmo filio Duncani Comitis de Mar. William succeeded his father about 1234, and died shortly after 1270. [A. G.]

Luuethot. The same name as Louthit. Has this name been filed down to Loutfut? [A. G.]

XXVII

Date. Time of Robert, Earl of Strathern, who died *circa* 1244, and after 1233, when Clement, Bishop of Dunblane, was consecrated.

XXVIII

Date. Time of Malise fifth Earl of Strathern, before 1258, when Clement, Bishop of Dunblane, died. The charter is between about 1244 and 1258.

Page 31. *Cotken.* This name appears in Great Seal Charters and Retours as Cathkin. It appears to have been the moor and low hill to the north or north-east of the Roman Station at Ardoch. Tacks of Benee (Beny) and Catkin or Caitkin made to Sir John Stirling of Keir in 1516 and 1532 will be found in *The Stirlings of Keir*, pp. 310, 346.

J. Abbot of Lindores. See Appendix, p. 303.

N. Is abbot of Inchaffray. This is an abbot not hitherto known. He must have immediately preceded Alan. See *Liber Insule Missarum*, p. xiv.

Domino W. de Rotheuen. Was alive in 1267 ; of the family of whom came the Earl of Gowrie. [A. G.]

G. filio suo. Sir William de Rotheuen had a son named Gilbert. [A. G.]

XXIX, XXX, XXXI, XXXII, XXXIII, XXXIV

This group of charters concern the lands of Rathengothen (Ratengothen, Rathargothen). The exact position of these lands is uncertain.

[Rathengothen appears to be now Redgorton in the shire of Perth, on the river Almond, some miles north from the city. Under the form Redgorton and other spellings it appears frequently in *Liber de Scon.* —A. G.]

Dates. The original grant (No. xxix) is made to the abbey by Malise, son-in-law of the founder, in the time of Gilbert, Earl of Strathern, and

be paid by the heirs of Malise, the original grantor, to the chapter of the cathedral in the time of Bishop H[ugh], that is, between 1214 and 1228, who confirmed the quitclaim of the chapter (No. xxxiv.).

Witnesses to No. xxix.

Page 32. *Waltero Olifard.* Sir Walter Olifard was Justiciar of Lothian. He married in 1200 Christian, daughter of the Earl of Strathern, and got with her the lands of Strageath. He died in 1242. [A. G.]

David de Lindeseia. He witnesses charters to Newbotle, etc, 1200-1227; married the heiress of Crawford, and with her acquired large estates in Lanarkshire; was knighted; died in 1230. [A. G.]

Walkelino filio Stephani. He appears to have belonged to Northampton. He is probably the 'Walkelino braciatori meo' ('my ale-brewer'), to whom King William gives a charter of Innerpefir (*Lib. S. Thome de Abirbrothic*). [A. G.]

Willelmo Wascelyn. A frequent witness. Probably a Huntingdon name. The modern form might be Wesley. [A. G.]

David Olifard. Probably the brother of Sir Walter. [A. G.]

XXX

Abraham (witness) was Bishop of Dunblane before 1217. See Theiner's *Monumenta*, No. vi. Between him and Osbert, who died in 1231, there was a Bishop Ralph.

XXXI

Abraham, Bishop of Dunblane, is a witness. See above.

XXXII

Abraham, Bishop of Dunblane, is a witness.

XXXIII

Before No. xxxiv., which see.

XXXIV

Date. Before 1229 and after 1214.

H. · · · episcopus Dunkeldensis. Hugh de Sigillo, known as 'pauperum episcopus' (*Scotichr.* ix. 47). He died in 1228 (*ibid.*)

Domino Gilberto de Glencarny. An agreement was made (12th Sept. 1232) between Andrew, Bishop of Moray, and Gilbert son of Gilbert, Earl of Strathern, respecting a half davoch of Kyncarny in feu-farm (*Regist. Morav.* 89). By gift of King William (*c.* 1180) Earl Gilbert got Kinnebethin (Kinveachie) in Strathspey, and conferred the lands on a younger son. The cadet family retained Glencairnie till 1391 when they exchanged it for Fochabers (*Grant Book,* vol. iii.) [A. G.]

Domino Joachim. No doubt Sir Joachim of Kinbuk. See No. xxiii.

Domino Nicholao Canonico de Incheaffray. Inchaffray was a house of Austin Canons.

XXXVI

Date. Ada's grant is confirmed in Earl David's foundation charter, but it does not appear in the hull of Pope Celestine iii., but one ploughgate of land in the vill of Newtyle is confirmed by Innocent iii. This charter is therefore to be dated between 8th March 1195 and 20th March 1199.

Page 38. *Balemagh.* We find Neutile in the foundation charter, p. 4, and Balmaw among the lands confirmed to Lindores by David ii., 1364 (*Reg. Mag. Sig.* (folio) p 36, No. 92). [The name of a place in or close to Neutile. Gaelic, *Baile,* a town, *Magh* a plain : here no doubt Strathmore.—A. G.]

Cum corpore meo. See Introduction, p. lxxxii.

Malcolmo filio Bertulfi. See No. lxxxiv.

XXXVII

Date. This, like No. xxxvi., is an early charter. Though the name of Mabel, wife of William, is not mentioned in No. x., it is plain that No. x. is a confirmation of the grant made in the present charter. See note on No. x.

Page 39. *David de Haya,* who succeeded William de Haya in Errol, *c.* 1200. For this name, and Thomas his brother, and Robert, parson of Errol, see notes on Nos. lxxvi.-lxxix.

David oiselario. 'Oiselarius' is a 'bird-catcher,' 'fowler'; Fr. *oiseleur.* It may be here an indication of occupation, or, possibly, already an equivalent of the family name, Fowler.

XXXIX

Date. This is a confirmation of William Wascelyn's oxgate in New-tyle. See No. xxxvii. Griffyn perhaps came into possession of Wascelyn's estate by marriage with his widow Mabel. Mr. A. Gibb in his notes offers the same conjecture. G[ilbert?] is abbot of Arbroath, so the charter must be dated before 1226.

XL

Date. Before 9th August 1248, when the grant was confirmed, No. xli., and after 1237, when John Earl of Chester and Huntingdon died, whose property was divided between his sisters.

Page 42. Isabella was the second daughter of Earl David, married to Robert de Brus, Lord of Annandale.

This charter is printed from an inferior text (and with errors of the editor added) in Turnbull's *Liber S. Marie de Lundoris*, p. 14.

The barony of Cragy is east of the town of Dundee.

Miltown of Cragy is well known.

The vill of Abraham has not been identified.

Willelmo de Brechyn, son of Henry of Brechin, Earl David's son. He died about 1284. [A. G.].

XLI

Date. This charter is dated at its close, 9th August 1248.

Robert de Brus, the grantor, was grandfather of King Robert. See Dunbar's *Scottish Kings*, p. 67.

Page 43. *Alexandro Cumyn, Comite de Buchan.* The second Cumyn, earl (1240-1289), Constable of Scotland.

Thoma de Lascelis. A knight.

The *Registrum Prioratus S. Andree* supplies many names of members of this family. Thomas is not among them.

The Bishops of St. Andrews and Dunkeld and the abbot of Dunfermline are commanded by the Pope (Innocent iv.), in 1250, to assign a suitable sum of money to Alan de Lasceles who is going, with Richard called Giffard, kinsman of the King of Scotland, to the Holy Land (Theiner's *Monumenta*, p. 52).

Gilberto de Haya. See notes on Nos. lxxvi.-lxxix.

XLII—LIII

This group of charters relates to Eglesmagril, in a later form Exmagirdle, in the parish of Dron, in the south-east of Perthshire. For a consideration of the question of the origin of the word and the saint whose name has been supposed to be indicated by 'magril,' the reader is referred to the discussion (not quite conclusive) by the late Dr. W. F. Skene in the *Proceedings of the Society of Scottish Antiquaries*, vol. iv. p. 318. There is a roofless church with a burying-ground, still occasionally used, close to the old mansion-house of Exmagirdle.

Some observations on the early Earls of Strathern will be found in the Introduction, p. xxxiv, ff.

Dates. The litigation between Guido, the first abbot, and Abraham, Bishop of Dunblane (No. XLII.), shows that the grants of land and of the church had been made at an early date. The dispute, which also involved questions as to the church of Muthill, was temporarily settled in the time of William Malvoisin, Bishop of St. Andrews (1202-1238), and in the time of Earl Gilbert (†c. 1223). See also what is said below on Simon, prior of St. Andrews, and of John, prior of May, which restricts the date to 1211-1214.

No. XLIII. is obviously of about the same time as No. XLII.

No. XLIV. is Earl Robert's confirmation of No. XLIII., and is after 1233 (4th Sept.), when Bishop Clement was consecrated, and before 1256, when he died. If Earl Robert died before 1244, the limits are further abridged.

No. XLV. is earlier than the preceding. It is a grant of Abraham, Bishop of Dunblane, and is mentioned in the hull of Innocent III., dated 23rd January 1215.

Nos. XLVI., XLVII., XLVIII., and XLIX. are also early, and in the lifetime of Bishop Abraham (1214-1223).

No. L. is dated 16th April 1235, and is an amendment of an error in the decree arbitral (No. XLII.) of more than ten years before.

No. LI. is dated 7th May 1235; and Nos. LII. and LIII. must be very soon after.

Page 43. *Cletheueis* (in No. XLIX. Clethues) seems to be now the lands of Clavage in the neighbouring parish of Dunning. [A. G.]

Elphini, prioris de Incheaffran. [Elphin or Elpin, prior of Inchaffray, has been hitherto unknown. He appears again in Nos. xlv. and xlix ——— A. G.]. He must come in between Malise and Innocent, who from prior was raised to the dignity of abbot by the Papal Legate (*Scotichron.* ix. 36).

Willelmi bone memorie. The phrase *bonae memoriae* is ordinarily used of deceased persons. We may conjecture that it was added by the scribe who engrossed the record.

XLIII

Page 47. *Bricio persona de Crefe et eius filio Malisio.* It must be remembered that Brice may not have been in Holy Orders. But even if he were, the mention of his son would not at this date have been regarded as unusual. The sons of priests are frequent in the records of the time ; and several Scottish bishops were such.

Rogero de Mortimero. This is, presumably, the Roger de Mortimer, sheriff of Perth, who in 1209 was sent with a brother of the Temple on an embassy to King John of England (*Scotichron.* viii. 70). He appears as a witness to charters of King William in the *Registrum Priorat. S. Andree,* and in *Liber de Melros,* vol. i.

XLIV

Page 48. *Domino C. episcopo nostro.* Clement, a Dominican friar, was consecrated for Dunblane, 4th September 1233 (*Chron. de Mailr.* s.a.). He died in 1256 (*Scotichron.* x. ii.) or 1258 (*Chron. de Mailr.* s.a.). 'Our bishop' is a peculiar phrase. It must be remembered that the Earls of Strathern were 'patrons' of Dunblane. See p. 57.

Malisio persona. Malise, brother of Earl Robert, was parson of Gask (No. liii).

Malisio filio meo. Afterwards fifth Earl of Strathern. See Introduction, p. xxxiv.

XLV

This charter is of Bishop Abraham (*c.* 1214–*c.* 1224).

XLVI

Page 49. *Macbeth, Rex scolarum.* We find the expression *Rex scolarum* in connection with Muthill in No. xlvii. The editor is not acquainted with any other examples of the use of this term. He has

English Dictionary says, 'Ancient Celtic Law : Ancient Irish, *Coinmeadh* in Tigernach, 1163, *Counmedh*, . . . billeting,' etc. O'Brien makes *Comhmheadh* equal to 'free quarters.' In modern Gaelic *Comaith* means messing together. Dr. Skene says *Conveth* came to signify a night's meal or refection, given by the occupiers of the land to their superiors when passing through their territories, and was due four times a year. It is interesting to find Conevet in operation in Perthshire. The Scologs and Clerici, on their way perhaps to Abernethy or St. Andrews, got a night's board and lodgings, or perhaps for a longer time. [A. G.]

The editor would only add to Mr. Gibb's note the suggestion that just as a *procuratio* in the ecclesiastical world meant originally an entertainment of bed and board given to the bishop or archdeacon on his visitation, and was soon commuted for an allowance in money, so perhaps in the cases referred to in these charters Conveth had been commuted into a charge on the lands.

Drumendufelis. Place unknown. [A. G.]

XLVIII

Page 50. *Clerici de Methfyn.* Perhaps students or scholars as in Nos. xlvi. and xlvii. See Introduction, p. liv.

L

Dated, 16th April 1235.

Page 52. *Willelmus   . episcopus . .   Glasguenses.* William de Bondington, Chancellor of the king in 1231 (*Scotichron.* ix. 48); elected to Glasgow, 1232 (*ibid*); consecrated at Glasgow, 11th September 1233 (*Chron. de Mailr.* s.a.) ; died 10th November 1258 (*ibid.* s.a.)

Gregorius : Gregory ix. This mandate does not appear in Mr. Bliss's *Calendar of Papal Registers.* But it may be mentioned as a confirmation of the genuineness of the document dated at Perugia, 3rd November 1234, that while the Papal writs of the earlier part of 1234 are dated from the Lateran, we find that towards the end of October the Pope had moved to Perugia, where he seems to have remained till at least the middle of July 1235. See *Calendar of Papal Registers,* vol. i. pp. 141-148.

Page 53. *Venerabili viro Episcopo Sancti Andree.* The Bishop of St. Andrews at this date was William Malvoisine, who died 9th July 1238.

Apud Lyston. Listun, or Liston, was a parish in the Deanery of Linlithgow (*Regist. Priorat. S. Andree,* p. 29).

Perhaps this is the place called at a later period Temple-Liston, now Kirkliston, in the shire of Linlithgow. [A. G.]

LI

Dated, 7th May 1235.

Page 55. *Clemens E ˙   us.* Bisho of Dunblane 4th Se tember 1233-

R. Abbas. This is the R[obert], abbot of Arbroath, in No. LII. Perhaps he was the same Robert who, in 1267, was expelled by the monks, and appealed to the Apostolic See (*Scotichr.* x. 21). There is a charter of Abbot Robert, dated 1261, in *Regist. Priorat. S. Andree,* p. 287. For the history of the succession of the abbots of Arbroath our charter is valuable.

J. Abbas. This is the J. [nnocent?], abbot of Inchaffray, of No. LII.

P. Abbas. The abbot of Cambuskenneth. See No. LII. There was a 'Peter,' abbot of Chambuskenel, in 1240 (*Regist. Priorat. S. Andree,* p. 162), probably the person who subscribed this charter.

Hugo, Abbas de Sancto Seruano. This is an abbot of St. Serf's, Culross. This entry will serve to correct a date in Walcott's *Ancient Church of Scotland,* p. 271. The religious house of St. Serf in Lochleven was only a priory.

Vicarius ecclesie de Methel. The parish was in the deanery of Fothri, and the name appears as Methkil in *Regist. Priorat. S. Andree,* p. 33, and in Theiner's *Monumenta,* p. 110.

LII

Date. Shortly after that of No. LI.

Page 57. *Patroni nostri.* See Introduction, p. xxxviii.

The confirmation by the whole clergy of the diocese as distinct from that of the chapter (No. LIII.) is interesting. The abbots of Arbroath, Culross, and Cambuskenneth appear perhaps as holding churches in the diocese or canonries in the cathedral.[1]

LIII

Probably soon after No. LI.

If *bone memorie* (p. 58) was not inserted afterwards, it must be dated after the death of William, Bishop of St. Andrews, 9th July 1238.

LIV

This charter is dated 7th April 1239.

For the place-names, see p. 244.

Page 59. *De novalibus suis et de nutrimentis animalium suorum.* See Introduction, p. xxxviii.

Ad mensam . . . Dumblanensis episcopi. The incomes of the bishops

went to the bishop. Such churches were called 'mensal.' In some dioceses such a disposal of parishes was extensive. Thus in Moray some eleven or twelve parishes were 'mensal' of the bishop.

Quocunque nomine censeantur. Ordinarily tithes were divided into 'great' and 'small,' the great tithes, or 'garbal tithes,' being the tithe of grain, and the small tithes the tithe of lambs and calves, milk, butter, cheese, eggs, etc. Very commonly the great tithes went to the rector or the corporate body (in the case of appropriate churches) representing the rector, while the small tithes went to the vicar. In the present case it was agreed that tithes of all kinds out of the lands of Fedal, Beny, and Concrag, in the parish of Muthill, should go to Lindores, and that Lindores was to pay to the parish churches six marks yearly.

H. abbate de insula missarum. This charter adds a name hitherto unknown to the abbots of Inchaffray. He comes in between Innocent and Alan.

Dompno W. Decano Dumblanensi . . . Dompno Adam priore de Abberbrodoc. The form 'Domnus' or 'Dompnus,' rather than 'Dominus,' was affected by some. For the reasons, see Ducange s.v. *Domnus.*

Andrea priore de Abernythyn. That is prior of the Keledei of Abernythyn. See the witnesses of No. LI.

Gask crist. Probably *Gask Christi,* presumably what is now Trinity Gask. It is not uncommon to find churches dedicated to the Trinity, commonly called Christ Church.

LV

Dated 30th August 1245.

The original is in the Denmyln Charters (29) in the Advocates' Library. From this the text was printed by Mr. Turnbull (*Lib. S. Marie,* etc., p. 42), with the extraordinary error in the date of 'tercentissimo.' The date in the original is written exactly as in our Chartulary.

This charter is helpful towards determining the position of Rathmuriel.

Page 61. William of Brechin, son of Henry of Brechin (Earl David's son). He was one of the fifteen regents and guardians during the minority of Alexander III., appointed at Roxburgh (1255).

Johanne de Haya. Probably Sir John de Haya of Ardnaughton, ancestor of the Hays of Naughton, in Fife, and son of William de Haya, first of Errol on record. [A. G.]

Gilberto de Haya. Probably third of Errol; witnesses a charter by Alexander III. to the Priory of St. Andrews, 1250-51. [A. G.]

Willelmo de Haya de Balcolmi. Unknown; perhaps son of the first

LVI

Date. Perhaps about the middle of the thirteenth century.

Among the witnesses is Norman, son of Norman (the constable). The following document relating to the grantor of the present charter is dated 1252.

Simon de Garentuly. See *ante*, p. 241.

Ederlarg. Edderlick lies in the parish of Premnay. In a charter of 1600 it is called Etherlik. [A. G.]

LVII

Dated 7th July 1250.

Page 62. *Creymund* (Cremond, LVIII.). Hill of Crimond, and Nether Crimond appear, in the ordnance map, in the parish of Keithhall and Kinkell. [A. G.]

Edengerroke. There is now an Edingarrach in the parish of Premnay; and this Edengerroke (though mentioned along with Creymond) is probably the same place. [A. G.]

Tolaukery (*Tholachkere*). Tillykerrie lies just across the march in the parish of Fintray. [A. G.]

Sir Simon of Garentuly, the grantor, witnesses a charter on 25th August 1243 (No. LXXXIII.).

LVIII

Date. In the time of Abbot John, that is 1218-*c.* 1244.

On private chapels, see Introduction, pp. lxviii-lxxiii.

LIX

Date. 'G.', Bishop of Aberdeen, one of the witnesses, must be Gilbert of Stirling, who was elected in 1228 or 1229, and died in 1238 or 1239.

Page 65. *Sancti Drostani de Inchemabani.* For St. Drostan, see Forbes's *Kalendar of Scottish Saints*, pp. 326-7.

Ravengille. The name has perished. [A. G.]

Gillandreston : now Glanderston in the parish of Kennethmont, near the march of Insch. [A. G.]

Weredors : now Wardhouse. The site of the castle is marked in the parish of Insch. [A. G.]

LX

Date. After 1218, when G[regory], Bishop of Brechin, was elect. The date of Gregory's death is unascertained. He was Bishop of Brechin till at least 1242.

The date of Henry of Brechin's death is uncertain.

Page 66. *Juliane sponse mee.* In 1204 King John was promised by Earl David 1000 marks for granting him the marriage of the great heiress Matilda de Cauz for his son Henry.[1] Mr. Bain assumes, perhaps rightly, that this Henry was Henry of Brechin. The marriage was not effected and John remitted the fine. In July of the following year King John commanded Reginald de Cornhill to give to Henry, son of Earl David, or his authorised messenger the daughter and heiress of Ralf de Cornhill whom he (the king) has given with the land pertaining to her to the said Henry.[2] This lady is presumably the 'Juliana' of our charter.

LXI

Date. The charter belongs to the time of David de Bernham, Bishop of St. Andrews.

Page 67. *Ad festum sancti martini in hyeme.* In this familiar formula designating Martinmas term the words *in hyeme* appear to distinguish this feast (Nov. 11) from the feast of St. Martin's translation (July 4). The latter is found as a feast of nine lections in the *Aberdeen Breviary.*

LXII

Date. Third Sunday in Lent (22nd March) 1248.

Page 68. *David dei gracia episcopi Sancti Andree.* David de Bernham, Bishop of St. Andrews; consecrated 22nd January 1239-40; died 26th April 1253 (*Fordun,* vi. 42).

Page 69. *Inchemurthach.* One of the manors or palaces of the Bishop of St. Andrews; now Inchmurdo, near Boarhills in Fife. Bishop William Malvoisine died at this house, as did also Bishop Gameline.

Dominica qua cantatur oculi mei. The Third Sunday in Lent was known as *oculi mei* (or simply as *oculi*) so called from the beginning of the 'office' (or introit) of the Mass on that day, which consisted of two verses from Psalm xxiv. (A.V. Psalm xxv. 15, 16). See *Missale de Arbuthnott,* p. 86.

The hull of Innocent III. among the pertinents of the church of Lindores mentions 'capellas de Dundemor' (P. 108).[1] See Introduction, p. lxx.

Dominum Henricum de Dundemor. Some notices of the Dundemores of Dundemore will be found in Laing's *Lindores Abbey*, pp. 85, 434, 435, 474, 475.

Page 70. *Officialis Sancti Andree.* The 'official' was the judge ordinary in the bishop's court.

LXIV

Date. 11th May 1253, nearly five years after the ordinance of the synod at Perth directing the monastery to find 'once' the required *ornamenta* of the chapel of Dundemor. It will be noted that in the interval Sir John has succeeded Sir Henry, an important date in the family history.

Page 71. *Missale.* On this book, remarkable in liturgical bibliography, see Introduction, p. lxx, note 5.

Page 72. *Vestimentum plenarium.* This expression is often employed to denote not only the chasuble of the celebrant and the stole, maniple, etc., but also the vestures of the deacon and subdeacon. But it is scarcely probable that at the chapel the celebrant was so assisted, at least on ordinary occasions.

LXV

Date. The chief clue is that Henry of Stirling, Earl David's son, is still alive.

Page 72. Monorgrund is a farm or farms called Monorgan, at Forgrund, now Langforgan, in the Carse of Gowrie. *Moine* [Fh]orgrund would mean the moss or marsh of Forgrund. [A. G.]

LXVI

Date. John de Haya is the grantor. Among the witnesses are David de Haya, and his brother, Robert de Haya, all doubtless of the family of the Hays of Errol. See above, p. 247. Nos. LXXVI.-LXXIX. give us three brothers, David, Robert, and Malcolm, with Gilbert, son of the first, and Nicholas, son of Gilbert, and Robert, a nephew of Gilbert, and apparently another David (No. LXXIX.). Earl Malise of Strathern is a contemporary of the first Gilbert (No. LXXVIII.). Thomas de Haya, brother of David, appears in No. XXXVII.

LXVII

editor suspects this may be a very early charter granted, perhaps, by one of the English followers or servants of Earl David. One Richard de Leicestria witnesses a charter of Roger de Beaumont while he was ' elect of St. Andrews,' that is, between 13th April 1189 (*Chron. de Mailr.* s.a.) and 15th February 1198 (*ibid.* s.a. ; Fordun, vi. 42). His name appears towards the end of a group of inferior witnesses, such as 'Hugo de pincerna,' 'Aldred pistor,' etc. (*Regist. Priorat. S. Andree*, p. 153). Our Richard de Leycestre may have been the same person. Among the witnesses is 'John de la Batayle.' Norman sobriquets survived indeed after the time of Earl David, but they were common at an early period.

Page 74. *Johanne filio Leue.* This person had a toft in Perth (No. lxxiv.). Perhaps a burgess.

LXVIII

Date. Sir Henry of Stirling, son of Earl David, is a witness.

Page 74. *Rogerus de Berkeley.* The name Berkeley (Berclay and many other spellings) is frequent in charters of the date of Malcolm, William the Lion, and Alexander ii. But the editor has not come across 'Roger.' Several members of the family of Berkeley figure in the later history of Scotland. See *Scotichronicon, Exchequer Rolls, Register of the Great Seal,* etc.

Forgrund (Forgrunt). From the text it appears that this land was near Exmagirdle. The name Forgan, a village in the parish of Forgandenny, is the modern form of the word. Mr. A. Gibb has independently come to the same conclusion.

Page 75. *Meo maro.* The *marus* was an officer who executed the summons of his lord's courts. See *Regiam Majestatem,* lib. i. cap. vi. § 7, and lib. iv. cap. viij. § 3 ; Skene's *De Verborum significatione,* s.v.

LXIX

Date. Roger de Berkeley. See No. lxviii.

Page 75. *De dimidia petra cere firmitatis.* The word (or words) of the rubric represented in the printed text by 'firmitatis' is blurred. A con-scribe may have erroneously written 'firmitatis' for 'firme terre.' But one would expect 'de firma terre.'

LXX

Date. In the time of William Malvoisine, Bishop of St. Andrews (1202-1238), which is narrowed by Abraham being Bishop of Dunblane (1216?-1224?).

Page 76. *Reginaldus de Warenna.* He has brothers, Adam and Roger, among the witnesses (Nos. LXX., LXXII.), and a nephew (or ? grandson, *nepotem*) Adam (No. LXXI.). This Adam has a brother David and a *nepos* called John. Reginald is styled 'Dominus' (No. LXVIII.).

Decano de Perth, that is 'dean of Christianity,' or rural dean.

LXXI

Date. Probably a little later than No. LXX.
On the family, Reginald de Warrenne, see notes on No. LXX.

LXXII

Date. Probably later than LXX.

Page 78. *Dunbernyn,* Dunbarny.
Petcathelin, Pitcaithly.
W. preposito nostro. There is no clue as to the place of which W. was provost. The word *nostro* suggests the conjecture that the deed was drawn by one of the monks of Lindores, and that W. was provost of Newburgh, elsewhere styled 'our burgh,' while the townsmen are called 'our burgesses of Newburgh' (No. CLII.).

LXXIII

Date. The materials do not enable us to be very precise. The charter was granted in the time of Abbot John (1219—after 1242). But Alan Durward first appears as Earl of Athol in a confirmation of a deed of gift to Arbroath, 12th October 1233. He succeeded to the earldom by right of his marriage with the eldest daughter of Earl Henry, who is 'quondam Comes de Athoyle' at the date of this charter. But Earl Henry may have died some time before 1233; and Conan's grant may have been some years after his death.

in a Retour (1672) of Robert Stewart of Tulloch, is said to be in the lordship of Cupar and earldom of Atholl. One of the Tullochs lies directly opposite Blair. [A. G.]. Conan's son Ewyn is a witness, and so is Hath, son of Gilbrid, his son-in-law.

It may be well to transcribe a summary of the charter referred to by Mr. Robertson, as cited above by Mr. Gibb. This summary is printed in Dr. Rogers's *Rental Book of the Cistercian Abbey of Cupar Angus* (i. 334), taken from the manuscript *Breviarium Antiqui Registri Monasterii de Cupro in Anegus* in the Advocates' Library :—'Carta donationis Cumingi, filii Henrici comitis Atholiae, Deo, Sanctæ Mariae, et monachis de Cupro, de asiamenta [? asiamentis] bosci mei de toto Glenherthy et de Tolikyne. Testibus Domino Roberto de Haya, Johanne Capellano eius, Magistri Johanne phisico, et Petro clerico eius.'

Ligna que dicuntur Wrawes de bule et de auhne. The difficulty of interpreting this perplexing passage was laid by the editor before Dr. T. G. Law, who speedily enlisted the services of quite a considerable body of charter-scholars. It must suffice here to note what seem to the editor the most probable of the conjectures offered. There was almost a complete *consensus* of opinion that 'auhne' is nothing else than the French *aune*, the alder. On 'bule' there is more variety of opinion; but there seems little doubt that, as suggested by Dr. J. Maitland Thomson and Rev. John Anderson, it is the birch-tree (*bouleau*: the form *boul* being given by Godefroy). The main difficulty lies in the word 'wrawes'; and though various conjectures, more or less attractive, have been offered, the editor prefers to leave the word for the investigation of others. The Rev. J. Wilson, vicar of Dalston, has been kind enough to furnish, as illustrative of *bule*, 'felics de bulo pro biga' : Finchale Accounts.

LXXIV

Date. Uncertain.

Page 80. *Malcolmus de Kinspinithin.* He had land in the town of St. Andrews (*Regist. Priorat. S. Andree*, p. 285).

Kinespinedyn and *Kinspinithin*: now Kilspindy. [A. G.]

LXXV

Date. Probably at the close of the twelfth or early in the thirteenth century. See below.

Page 81. *Willelmus de Munford.* We find a William de Munfort

present charter, we get some notion as to its date, which must have been early in the history of the abbey.

Munford seems to be a form of Montford (de Monteforti).

LXXVI

Date. Perhaps before 1215. See confirmation of Innocent III. (No. xcv.), where a fishery 'in Sabulo' is mentioned. Sir David de Haya, the second of Errol, succeeded his father William before 1199, and was alive in 1237. [A. G.]

This charter is printed from an inferior and imperfect text by Turnbull in *Liber S. Marie de Lundoris*, p. 9.

Page 81. *Glasbani* (*Glesbanyn, Glesbanin*). Clashbennie on the north bank of the Tay, nearly opposite Lindores.

Rugesablyn (*Rugesablun*). Not identified. The word suggests that it represents a Norman-French equivalent of Red-sands. [These red sands may have given its name to the Isle of Red Inch.—A. G.]

Page 82. *Colcric.* Not identified.

This and the three following charters give us three brothers, Sir David, Robert, and Malcolm de Haya (LXXVI., LXXVII.). David was twice married, first to Ethna, secondly to Eva (LXXVI.). [This charter enables the peerage books to be corrected, where his wife is called Helen.—A. G.] His son, who succeeds him, is Gilbert, whose wife is Edoyna (LXXVIII.). Robert and Malcolm are described as rectors of the church of Errol (LXXIX.). They are succeeded in the rectorial rights by (another) David, perhaps a brother of Gilbert (*ibid.*). Lastly, Gilbert styles Malise of Strathern 'consanguineus meus' (LXXVIII.). Gilbert, son of David, second of Errol, has a son Nicholas (No. LXXVIII.).

In the account of this family given by Douglas (*Peerage,* vol i. p. 544), we learn that the first known of the family was William de Haya, 'pincerna regis' in the time of Malcolm IV. To his eldest son, David, King William, the Lion, granted, between 1189 and 1199, the lands of Errol. This David is the first David of our charters. His mother was Helen, daughter of Gilbert, Earl of Strathern. It is presumably thus that Malise of Strathern, afterwards earl, was 'cousin' of Gilbert de Haya.

LXXVII

Date. About the same date as last. The witnesses are almost the

' for the future' (*de caetero*) there should not be more than one parson (*i.e.* rector) for each church (Wilkins, *Concilia*, i. 652). It is quite likely that neither Robert nor Malcolm was in Holy Orders, a case contemplated in express terms in the constitution referred to.

LXXVIII

Date. Probably on Gilbert de Haya succeeding his father, David, whose charter (No. LXXVI.) is here confirmed, together with the additional grant of the third part of the fishings of the draw-nets at Joymersandes (not identified).

Ricardo Cumyn filio Ricardi Cumyn. Two generations of Cumin. Probably there should be two Richards. [A. G.]

Nicholao filio meo. Nicholas succeeded his father in Errol. [A. G.]

Roberto de Haya nepote meo. The uncertainty attaching to 'nepos' makes it impossible to say what was the relation of this witness to Sir Gilbert.

The wife of Sir Gilbert is said to have been a daughter of William Cumin, Earl of Buchan. This charter gives her name, 'Edoyna.' [A. G.]

LXXIX

Date. Probably on David de Haya succeeding Robert and Malcolm in the rectory of Errol. This is a confirmation of No. LXVII., with the addition of the grant of the tithe of the monks' draw-nets at Joymersandes. This place has not been identified.

LXXX

Dated, 4th July 1251.

Page 85. *Alanus Ostiarius, Justiciarius Scocie.* Alan Durward was made Justiciar of Scotland in 1243 (*Scotichron.* lib. ix. cap. 61). It would seem that later in this year (1251), or early in 1252, Durward was deprived of his office of Justiciar; but he was restored in 1255.

Margerie. Durward's wife, Margery, was a natural daughter of

LXXXI

Date. In the time of John, Bishop of Aberdeen (1200-1207).

Page 88. *Normannus.* The Constable (No. xv.) of Inverury Castle. His son Norman is the grantor of No. lxxxiv.

A. uxoris mee. A ms. (1695), of doubtful value, on the Sirname of Lessley, from which Macfarlane makes extracts, describes this Norman's wife as a daughter of the Lord of Lorn (*Genealogical Collections,* Scottish History Society, vol. ii. p. 424).

Confining attention to our charters we find mention of four generations :—

(1) Bertolf, referred to as father of Malcolm (No. xiii.).

(2) Malcolm (No. xiii.) before 1195.[1]

(3) Norman, son of Malcolm, called the Constable (Nos. lxxxi., lxxxii.). He has a brother, Malcolm (No. lvi.).

(4) Norman, son of Norman, (Nos. lvi., lxxxiii., lxxxiv.).

LXXXII

Date. Soon after lxxxi., and before the death of John, Bishop of Aberdeen (1207).

LXXXIII

Dated, 25th August 1243,

Page 90. *Radulfo Aberdonensi episcopo.* Ralph de Lambley (1239-1247).

LXXXIV

Dated, 12th July 1253.

Normannus de Lescelin filius Normanni constabularii. This will correct Macfarlane (*Genealogical Collections,* ii. 455), who makes this Norman the son of Alfornus, who (according to Macfarlane) was successor of Norman, son of Malcolm, son of Bartholff. It is possible that Alfornus (as an elder brother) intervened between the two Normans. The charter, cited by Macfarlane, as of Alexander iii., must be a charter of Alexander ii. ; and its date must be 4th December 1247, the very first day of the thirty-fourth year of that monarch.

Of the second Norman, Macfarlane (*ibid.*) writes that it was ' he who, I

Page 91. *Omnem sequelam.* See Introduction, p. lvii.

Andrea de Lescelin. This is an early Sir Andrew of Leslie. Andrew was afterwards a frequent name among the Leslies.

Willelmo Theyno de Kintor. The property of Thainston exhibits a survival of the term thanage applied to the royal lands of Kintore.

LXXXV

Date. Before 8th March 1195, for the grant is recorded in Celestine's bull (P. 104).

Robertus de Lundoniis. See Notes on No. 11.

Inverkaithin. It is observable that Robert styles Inverkeithing 'my burgh.'

Page 92. *Comite Patricio.* Earl of Dunbar. The first named Patrick. He succeeded his father, Earl Waldeve, in 1182 (*Chron. de Mailr.* s.a.). He was married to Ada, illegitimate daughter of William, the Lion. He was a generous benefactor of the Church, and died, in the dress of a monk, in 1232 (*ibid.* s.a.)

Simone de Seyntliz. Simon (III.) de Senliz, Earl of Northampton, is said to have had a brother Simon (Nicolas's *Historic Peerage of England,* p. 415); perhaps our witness.

LXXXVI

Date. Time of Earl David, probably before 1215.

Willelmus de Camera. [Unknown : de Camera is the older form of the word Chalmers, later Chambers.—A. G.] He refers to Earl David as 'dominus meus,' and presumably held land of him. Hamildune is mentioned in the hull of Innocent III. of 23rd January 1215 as a possession of Lindores.

Hamildune. [Unknown.—A. G.] It is possible that this is an English Hamilton, Hambleden, or Hambleton. In Rutlandshire there is Hambleton, Middle Hambleton, and Nether Hambleton. One of the latter two is marked as 'Little Hambleton' in the map of Rutlandshire in Gibson's edition of Camden's *Britannia.* Little regard is had in the papal writs to the grouping of names, and the fact that the bull of Innocent III. places the possession in the order 'Ratengoden, Neutile, Hameldune, et Mernes' must not be considered as conclusive against the

LXXXVII

Date. Between 1232, when John succeeded to the earldom of Chester, and 5th June 1237, when he died.

Stokes. (Stoke, LXXXVIII.) lies south of Market-Bosworth in Leicestershire. [A. G.]

Willelmus de Campania. (Champneys, or Champaingne.)

Page 94. *Domino Anketyn.* Perhaps Sir Anketill de Foleville who appears as a witness (No. XC.).

LXXXVIII

Dated, 17th June 1248.

Turleston. There is a parish of Thurlaston in Leicestershire. It is spelt Thurleston in Morden's map in Camden's *Britannia.*

Quadraginta solidos argenti; the three marks of the preceding writ.

Domino Alano tunc celarario de Suleby. The abbey of Sulby, in Northamptonshire, was of Premonstratensian monks. The cellarer was a monastic officer of large power and influence, whose duties extended far beyond the cellar of the house. On account of the practical business habits acquired in office the cellarer was not infrequently elected to the post of abbot.

Henrico le frankeleyn de Norhamton. The English franklin held direct of the Crown. He was ordinarily of English (as distinguished from Norman) origin, and a man of good estate.

LXXXIX

Date. The time of Abbot Thomas, who died in 1273. The date of his appointment is unknown, but it was after 1244.

Page 95. *Laurencio de monte alto clerico.* We find 'Dominus Laurencius de Montealto' [Mowat.—A. G.] witnessing in 1267, or somewhat earlier, the foundation charter of the Messyndew (*Maison Dieu*) at Brechin, granted by William of Brechin (*Regist. Brechin,* p. 7). Dundee was in the diocese of Brechin.

On the places, see notes on No. XIX.

XC

This, with some unimportant variations in the spelling of proper names, is a repetition of No. XIX., which see.

Page 98. *Ade de Malcharwiston.* Adam witnesses charters in the time of David de Bernham and Gamelin, Bishops of St. Andrews (*Regist. Priorat. S. Andree*). See Notes on CXLI.

XCII

Dated, 24th June 1375.
On this charter, see Introduction, p. xlv.

XCIII

Dated, 8th March 1195.
See Introduction, p. lxxvi.

Page 105. *Duos bisancios.* In 1282 we find Pope Martin IV. sending Master Geoffrey de Veçano as nuncio to collect cess and other dues. St. Thomas's monastery at Arbroath has to pay 2 bezants; Lindores, 2 bezants; Kelso, 1 mark, etc. (*Calendar of Papal Registers : Letters,* i. 476).

XCIV

This bull was printed by Baluze in his *Papae Innocentii III. Opera* (Paris, 1682), i. 337, and from that source was reprinted by Turnbull in the appendix to his *Liber S. Marie de Lundoris* (p. 39). The variants in the text are mostly unimportant, the text of our Chartulary being obviously preferable. Thus 'Bundamer' appears for 'Dundemor'; 'Mineth' for 'Moneth' (the Mounth); 'Cuningrove' (which gave Mr. Alex. Laing much fruitless trouble in the endeavour to identify the place) for 'Cuningtone,' in the diocese of Lincoln; 'Ritcheth' for 'Rothket.' Baluze did not print the subscription of the cardinals. With the help of Chacon (Ciaconius) in his *Vitae et Res Gestae Pontificum Romanorum et S. R. E. Cardinalium,* with the notes Agostino Oldoini (*Romae,* 1677), every name has been identified; but it would be burdening these pages to notice the histories of these numerous cardinals. The reader, however, may be cautioned against identifying Pandulphus, cardinal-presbyter of the Basilica of the Twelve Apostles, with Pandulphus, the Papal Nuncio, to whom King John, of England, did homage in 1213. Matthew of Westminster and, long afterwards, Bishop Godwin

XCVI–XCVII

Of the dispute here referred to we have no other notice. Earl David's gift (No. v.) safeguarded the 'cane' of the Bishop of St. Andrews.

XCVIII

This bull is printed, from the copy in the Advocates' Library, by Mr. Turnbull, in *Liber S. Marie de Lundoris,* p. 18. No doubt the copy referred to is correct in giving 'filiis' after 'dilectis' in the first line of our bull (P. 116). On the other hand our text is more likely to be correct in reading (line 7) 'postulacionibus' for 'petitionibus,' and in reading (line 9) 'vacatis' for 'vacatur.' Turnbull's 'ad eam' should of course, be 'ad eum' as in our print.

Turnbull prints (P. 17) an instrument of Gregory, Bishop of Brechin, in which he states that with the assent of his whole chapter he puts the abbot and convent of Lindores into corporal possession of the church of Dundee, reserving for the vicar 10 lbs. sterling. The grant is obviously only a continuation of the grants of his predecessors Turpin, Ralph, and Hugh. Bishop Gregory's grant must be dated before 1226. In connection with No. xcix. it may be noted that Bishop Gregory's charter is witnessed by 'M. priore Keledeorum de Brechin.'

XCIX

Dated, 18th February 1250.

This bull marks the substitution of secular canons for Keledei as the chapter of Brechin. The older writs in the times of Bishops Turpin Ralph and Hugh had, presumably, mentioned that the concession of the Bishop of Brechin had been with the consent of the Keledei, and it is plain from the next bull (No. c.) that difficulties had been raised because the name of the members of the chapter was now no longer Keledei.

C

Dated, 20th April 1250. According to a common practice the Pope commissions certain ecclesiastics, presumably disinterested, to give effect to his ruling as expressed in No. xcix.

CI

This in order of time precedes Nos. xcix. and c. It is dated 4th

CIII

Dated, seven days later than No. c. The violence and lawlessness described is remarkable. More light on the particular occasions of these offences is lacking.

CIV

Dated as No. ciii. Commission is given to the same two ecclesiastics as in No. c. to give effect to the Pope's ruling in No. ciii.

CV

Dated as No. c.

CVI

Dated as No. c.

It will be noticed that all the above bulls of Innocent iv. are dated from Lyons. He had fled there in 1244 from the vengeance of the Emperor Frederick, and continued to reside mainly in that city till April 1251.

CVII

Date. Roger de Beaumont was consecrated 15th February 1198, and died 7th July 1202. There is uncertainty as to the date of the consecration of John, Bishop of Aberdeen, but it is probable that it was not till 1200 or 1201. Radulph, Bishop of Brechin, was not consecrated till 1202 (*Chron. de Mailros,* s.a.). Osbert, abbot of Kelso, died in 1203 (*Chron de Mailr.* s.a.). The charter must belong to the first half of the year 1202.

Page 129. *Personatum.* The rights of the *persona,* which term is applied to the rector, as distinguished from the vicar.

Conrediis. The word *conredium* (which appears also in the forms *conradium, corredum, corodium,* etc.) was an allowance of meat and drink, or its equivalent in money, made to persons not being members of the house. The word was also applied to grants demanded by the bishop ; and to special demands made in England by the king upon the religious houses of his realm. On these and other applications of the

Sinodalibus. See Introduction, p. lxi.

Can et conveth. See Introduction, p. liv.

A comite de Fyfe, M. filio eius. One can only conjecture that the scribe mistook 'D' for 'A.' Duncan, Earl of Fife, died in 1204 (*Chron. de Mailr.* s.a.), and was succeded by his son Malcolm.

CVIII

Date. William, Bishop of St. Andrews, is doubtless, William Malvoisine, the successsor of Roger, the grantor of No. cvii. He was postulated (from Glasgow) 20th September 1202, and died 9th July 1238. But the appearance of Thomas, prior of St. Andrews, restricts the date of the charter to before 1211.

CIX

Date. David de Bernham (1239-1253); probably early in his episcopate; but the absence of the testing clause makes it impossible to say more.

CX

Dated, the Saturday [20th Dec.] next before Christmas, 1259.

Page 132. 'G,' the prior of St. Andrews, was Gilbert, who died 1263.

Officiario nostro. 'Officiarius' occurs occasionally in mediæval writs in the sense of the more common word 'officialis.' The bishop's official heard causes and acted as judge in the bishop's ecclesiastical court. The archdeacon also had his official to whom authority was delegated in matters pertaining to the archdeacon's jurisdiction. The official of the archdeacon of St. Andrews is referred to in No. cxi. (p. 134).

CXI

Dated, 3rd February 1256.

Robert, called the brother of Steward of Strathern.

Perhaps 'senescallus' is here to be taken simply as the title of office. In No. xxiv. Fergusius is 'senescaldus meus' of Sir Fergus. In No. xxx. Malise is 'senescallus meus' of Earl Gilbert. From the Seneschals of Strathern the house of Tullibardine is descended (Cosmo Innes, *Early Scotch History*, p. 218).

In No. xxiv. we learn that Sir Fergus, son of Earl Gilbert, had granted leave for the taking of timber from his wood in Fedal in Kathermothel,

His place corresponded to that of the treasurer of a cathedral. He had custody of the gold and silver plate and jewels, the reliquaries, and the rich vestments. His duties at the Benedictine monastery of St. Augustine, at Canterbury, will be found very fully detailed in the *Customary of St. Augustine's*, edited (1902) by Sir E. M. Thompson for the Henry Bradshaw Society, i. 101-121.

Glenlitherne, or *Glenlicherne.* Glenlicherne is the glen running from Braco and Ardoch along the Knaik Water to the north-west towards Comrie. [A. G.].

CXII

Dated, January 23rd 1261.

Page 136. *Curelundyn.* This place must obviously be not far from the Fedals, it is described as 'in Stratherne'; but it is left to others to identify the spot. Kynbuc (Kinbuck), from which Sir Joachim took his name, is some three or four miles north of Dunblane on the Allan Water.

[Curelundyn is now unknown. It is said to be in Strathern, but that probably then included Strathallan, or part of it. *Lundyn* (Gaelic, *Lointean*) means marshes; and *cure* may be for *corrie*, a hollow. Curelundyn may have been somewhere in the hollow and marshy ground between Greenloaning and Blackford.—A. G.]

CXIII

Dated, 27th March 1260.

Page 137. *Noverit universitas vestra,* etc. See No. LXXXVII., of which this contains the exemplification.

Page 138. *Castleton de Borg in Galwythia.* Borg, now Borgue, some three miles south-west of Kirkcudbright.

CXIV

Dated, the Saturday next after the feast of St. Martin in winter 1261, which Saturday fell in that year on the 12th November.

Page 142. *Willelmum de Brechynch,* son of Henry of Brechin, and grandson of Earl David.

Bondington. This has not been identified.

Kyndeloich. Probably Kinloch, near Collessie.

hundred years later appears among 'the Maillis of the landis in the Mernis' as coming from Bervie (*ibid.* p. 424).

David de Cambrun. 'Cambrun' is a form of 'Cameron.' See *Regist. Priorat. S. Andree* (Index s. v.).

Lundynrothery. [Probably Linton-Roderick, now West Linton, in the shire of Peebles.—A. G.] Mr. Gibb's conjecture is doubtless correct. A reference to *Origines Parochiales,* i. 188, 516, 517, will show the name in the forms 'Lyntounrᴏthryk,' 'Lintonrothirrikis,' and, what is more pertinent, 'Linton Rotheri' (between 1243-1254) in *Lib. de Calchou,* p. 351.

CXVI

Date. Richard de Potton, or Pottock, was Bishop of Aberdeen between 1256 and 1270 (*Scotichr.* x. 28) or 1272 (Gawan's *Epistolare, Regist. Aberdon.* ii. 247). But from another source we can determine the date to be probably July 1261. In the *Charters of the Duchy of Lancaster* (Box A. No. 120) is the quitclaim of the second tithes in exchange for 'villa Willelmi' made to Sir Robert de Brus, Lord of Annandale, by Thomas, abbot of Lindores. This is given in abstract in Bain's *Calendar of Documents,* etc., vol. i. No. 2267. The deed was executed at Lindores on the Sunday after the feast of St. Peter *ad vincula* [1st Aug.] 1261. This Sunday in that year fell on 7th August. The quitclaim probably followed soon upon Bruce's charter. And the next charter (No. cxvii.) is the confirmation by the king on 29th August 1261.

The grantor was, as we learn from the charter itself, a grandson o Earl David. See Introduction, p. xxv. I take it that Bruce grants two lands (1) that of Williamstown (which grant united the monks' lands of Lethgaven and Wrangham), and (2) that of Bondes near Casky-ben. This settles the locality of Lethgaven.

Isabelle sponse nostre. Isabella, daughter of Gilbert de Clare, Earl of Gloucester (Dunbar's *Scottish Kings,* p. 67).

Page 146. *Villa Willelmi,* etc. Williamston and Wrangham are marked on the Ordnance Map (Sheet 86), a mile or two south and west of Kirkton of Culsalmond. Lethgaven must have been east of Williamston, near Mellenside. Bondes I take to be what is now called Boynds, a little more than a mile north of the ruins of the castle of Caskieben, both marked on the Ordnance Map (one inch to the mile), Sheet 76.

CXVII

Page 147. Dated, 29th August 1261.
See what is said above, No. cxvi.

Johanne de Dundemor.
Sir John was one of the regents during the minority of Alexander III.
Several notices of the family will be found in Laing's *Lindores Abbey*,
pp. 434, 435.

CXVIII

Page 148. *Date.* The absence of the testing clause is to be regretted.
The grantor was Henry de Hastinges, grandson of Earl David, and one
may conjecture that as this is, like No. cxvi., a commutation of second
tithes, it may be about the same date as that charter. It is confirmed
by Alexander III.

Flandris (*Flandres*) *in Garviach.* The name seems to be retained in
the form of Flinder, Little Flinder, New Flinder, Old Flinder, some
three or four miles west of Insch.

CXIX

Page 150. *Date.* The testing clause is absent. The grantor is
Alexander III. It may probably be of about the same time as No. cxvii.

CXX

Page 150. *Date.* No. cxxi. shows that this is a confirmation of
Alexander II. The testing clause and date are lacking, but may be
supplied from the *Great Seal Register* (p. 36, No. xcii.), where it appears
in an *inspeximus* and confirmation of David II. (granted at Dundee 20th
September 1361). After the word 'Testibus' the language of the *inspeximus* runs, 'Willelmo filio alani senescalli, Justiciario Scocie, Willelmo
Olifer, Justiciario Laodonie, bernardo fraser, Waltero byseth, iohanne
de Haya. Apud Castrum puellarum, xij° die nouembris. Anno Regni
domini Regis tercesimo tertio [*i.e.* 1247].'

We must not be led away here by the puzzle presented by '*William*
Olifer, Justiciar of Lothian.'

CXXI

Page 151. *Date.* We can only say that this is a charter of Alexander III.
(1249-1286). The testing clause is lacking.

Page 153. *In molendino suo de Inveralmeslei.* Now Inveramsay. The mill of Inveramsay is marked on the Ordnance Map (Sheet 76).

Balhagerdi. Balhaggerdy, a mile or so south-east of Inveramsay mill.

Inchemabani. Now Insch.

Donidor. The ruins of the ancient castle of Dunnideer are still visible, a little more than a mile west of Insch.

Unum par cirotecarum albarum. A pair of gloves was not an infrequent form among the curious *blench-duties* of feudal tenures. See Cosmo Innes, *Scotch Legal Antiquities*, pp. 64, 65.

Page 154. *In modum cirograffi.* The word *chirographum* is ordinarily used in writs of this period, in a restricted sense, for a deed twice written on the same parchment. A space was left between the two copies, on which space the word 'Chirographum,' or the letters of the Alphabet in large characters, or sometimes some ornamental devices were drawn with the pen. Through these letters or devices the parchment was cut, sometimes straight across, sometimes in zig-zags, and each party to the agreement received a part. The genuineness of either part could always be proved by bringing the parts together and seeing that the teeth of the indentures fitted into one another, or that the parts of the lettering or device fitted together. There were varieties in the way in which the parchment was cut. It was sometimes cut with a waving line, and hence the term *charta undulata*, but the teeth-like division was the favourite in England and Scotland. More particulars on this subject in A. Giry's *Manuel de Diplomatique*, pp. 510-513.

CXXIV

Page 155. *Date.* Andrew, abbot of Cupar, ruled from 1272 to 1296, when (17th December 1296) he was provided to the see of Caithness (Theiner's *Monumenta*, No. ccclix). The grantor, Alexander, Earl of Buchan, died in 1289.[1] William Wiseheart, Bishop of St. Andrews, was not consecrated till 15th October 1273. It may be doubted whether we can be more precise than in placing the charter between that date and 1289.

Alexander Cumyn, Comes de Buchan. This is the third Earl of Buchan; grandson of Fergus, whose only child, Margaret, or Margery, married William Cumyn, who became earl in right of his wife. Alexander succeeded his mother between 1236 and 1240. He was appointed Justiciar of Scotland in 1251; removed from that office, at the instigation of Henry III. of England, in 1255, but was re-appointed in 1257; and held the office till his death. He married Elizabeth, second daughter of Roger de Quincy, Earl of Winton. On the death of De Quincy in 1264,

possessions in Galloway and elsewhere. He was one of the six guardians on the death of Alexander III.[1]

Page 155. *Kelle (Kelly) in Buchan.* Kelly, in the parish of Methlick. In the possession of Alexander Cummin, Earl of Buchan, as early at least as 1261. In that year he founded an hospital in Newburgh in Buchan, the charter being dated 'apud Kelly in Buchan, die Veneris proxima post festum S. Matthaei, 1261.'[2] Another hospital (*domus elemosinaria*) founded by the earl was that of Turreth (Turref). The charter is dated 'apud Kelli,' 1273 (*Collections, Aberdeen and Banff,* p. 470). In 1287 he bound himself to pay to Arbroath half a mark for finding two tapers to be lighted before the altar of St. Mary in the monastery. This was in exchange for a 'particula terre inclusa infra parcum nostrum de Kelly' (*ibid.* pp. 322-23). The Gordon family appears to have come into possession of the lands of the Park of Kelly from David Annand of Ouchterellon in 1483 (*Historical Commission Report,* v. 608). See Dr. Temple's *The Thanage of Fermartyn,* pp. 2, 3.

Page 156. *Absque aliqua replegiacione.* The right of possessors of a private jurisdiction to reclaim, to be dealt with in their own courts, persons or goods, subject to their jurisdiction, was styled the right of 'replegiation.' It would seem that what the Earl of Buchan intended in this case was to renounce any right he might possess to reclaim cattle or goods taken by distraint from his lands of Kelly by the monks.

Privilegio crucesignatis vel crucesignandis indulto. Persons who took the cross, whose vow to go on crusade was often commuted, were taken under the protection of the Church (see *Statuta Ecclesie Scoticane,* ii. 20; *Regist. Aberdon.* ii. 15); and they were entitled to plead many of the exemptions of the clergy. Hence we occasionally meet in old charters a disclaimer of pleading such privileges, which imposed many difficulties in the event of a recourse to law.

Page 157. *W. episcopus Sancti Andree.* From what has been said above as to the uncertainty as to the date of this charter, we cannot say whether 'W' was William Wiseheart (15th October 1273-28th May 1279), or his successor, William Fraser (1279-20th August 1297).

Andrea Abbate de Cupro. See above, in discussion of the date of the charter.

Kyneth de Neuticbyr. The place-name may perhaps be that found in a list of homages in the *Ragman Roll,* where we find 'Richard de Neutebere' (Bain's *Calendar,* ii. p. 205).

CXXV

Dated, 25th January 1281.

Kynard (*Kynhard*), now Kinnaird, a property about two miles to the south-east of the abbey of Lindores. Mr. A. Laing (*Lindores Abbey,* p. 440) supplies an interesting note from the ms. of Sir James Balfour, Lyon King of Arms, who was owner of Kinnaird. 'These lands for merlie belonged to David, Earll of Huntindone, who dysponed the tyndis anno 9 regis Willelmi [*i.e.* 1174, a date which is certainly wrong], under the tenour, Omnes decimas ville nostre de Kynnaird Beate Marie et monochis de Londres in Sylvis, which he himself founded not a yeir befoir, and the lands within 3 yeiris following to Gilbert, Earll of Stratherne his cousigne, quhos son Madoc, Earl of Stratherne, with consent of his son Malise, dated [doted] the property of the said land to the Prioress and Holy Virgins of Elchok in the reign of Alexander II. A.D. 1214-1247.' To which more is added as to the later history of the successive owners. Sir James was specially interested in this property, and probably had special sources of information at his command; but there are some obvious errors in the above statement.

Page 159. *N. Abbate de Dunfermelyn.* The Register of Dunfermline does not supply an abbot with a name commencing with 'N' at this date. But there is nothing that contravenes the existence of an abbot named Nicholas in the scanty records of the abbey of that time.

On the subject-matter of the charter, see Introduction, p. lxxxvi.

CXXVI

Date. The reign of Robert I. (27th March 1306-7th June 1329). Perhaps before the death of Edward Brus (25th May 1315).

Page 163. *Kynmuk, Balbuthan, Hathirwych.* [These lands are all in the same neighbourhood, on the east of the Don, in the parish of Keithhall and Kinkell.—A. G.] The names now appear as Kinmuck, Balbithan, and Heatherwick.

Bernes in le Garviauch. [Mill of Barnes appears on the map near Kirkton of Premnay.—A. G.] 'Barnes (or Netherhall) lately possessed by Gordon of Barnes, but formerly by the Forbeses of Barnes; and

CXXVII

Date. This is an early charter granted by Malise, son of Earl Ferteth of Strathern, and son-in-law of Earl David. It was granted before 20th March 1198, as the church of Mothell is mentioned in the hull of Innocent III. of that date (p. 109). As Muthill is not mentioned among the churches of Lindores in the bull of Celestine III., dated 8th March 1195, this charter may probably be placed between the dates of the two bulls. Henry, abbot of Arbroath, one of the witnesses, fits in well with the proposed date.

CXXVIII

Dated, 1st March 1291, ' the Thursday next after the feast of St. Mathias the Apostle, 1290.' The feast of St. Mathias is 24th February ; so that the year intended is probably 1290-91. The Thursday referred to fell in that year on March 1st. The grant seems to be made with special reference to the weal of the soul of Alexander, Earl of Buchan, who had died shortly before (in 1289), and who is styled by the grantor ' dominus meus.'

Page 165. *Radulphus de Lascellis.* Here he is described as ' miles,' and as having been married ; so probably (though not necessarily) he is not to be identified with ' Radulphus Lasselis, clericus,' who witnesses a charter of Alexander Comyn, Earl of Buchan, in 1261 (*Regist. Aberdon.,* ii. 277). We find Sir Radulph de Lascellis witnessing a charter of Patrick, Earl of Dunbar, between 1273 and 1276 (*Regist. Prior. S. Andree,* p. 380).

The submission and fealty of ' Rauf de Lasceles, Chevalier' to Edward I. (1296), will be found in Sir Francis Palgrave's *Documents and Records* (Scotland), i. 161.

Huchannane Locherton. [Unknown.—A. G.] The land was held by Lascellis of the Earl of Buchan.

CXXIX

Page 166. *Date.* Time of King William. David de Lindesey is justiciar of the King.

Page 167. *Hugo Brito.* The exchange of Connington for lands in the Garioch points to Brito (or Britain) being one of the English vassals of

am now satisfied that 'propter' is right, signifying 'on account of,' *i.e.* in exchange for.

CXXX

Dated Thursday next after the feast of St. John before the Latin Gate, 1278, which Thursday in the above year fell on June 9.

Page 168. *Reginaldus de Chen pater,* more commonly known as Reginald *le* Chen (Cheyne, Chien, Chene). Both the father and Sir Reginald, his son, were figures of some importance in their day. In 1242 Reginald was sheriff of Kincardine. In 1267 he was appointed chamberlain (*camerarius*) of Scotland by King Alexander III. (*Scotichr.* x. 22), but he retired from the court in 1269 (*ibid.* x. 26).

Sir Reginald (the son?), in 1286, held the thanage of Fermartyn as 'firmarius,' the 'firma' or rent being 120 marks (Skene's *Celtic Scotland,* iii. 252). He submitted to Edward I. at Aberdeen, 17th July 1296. See the submission of 'Renaud le Chien, Chivaler,' in Palgrave's *Documents,* i. 175. But he is found among the signatories of the famous anti-English letter to the Pope drawn up in the Parliament at Arbroath on 6th April 1320.

Tholaukery, Cremund, Doesblare.

Cremund, now Crimond, lies in the parish of Keithall and Kinkel. Tholaukery, now Tillikerie, and Dis-blair in the neighbouring parish of Fintray. [A. G.]

CXXXI

Seher de Quence, earl of Winton, and Robert, his son, of forty shillings of annual rent from his land at Colesyn : witnesses, Sir Roger de Quence, Seher de St. Andrew, the donor's brother, etc. (2) Confirmation [1210-1218] of the preceding by Seher de St Andrew : witnesses, Sir Roger de Quence, Roger de St Andrew, etc.

Page 170. *Adam de Malcarreston* (Malcariuston, Malcarston, Malkarstoun). He was official of Gamelin, Bishop of St. Andrews, in 1259. We find him here as rector of Collessie, which he, provost of the church of St. Mary in the city of St. Andrews, resigns in June 1262 (No. cxlii.). He is found provost of the same church, 29th January 1266 (*Reg. Priorat. S. Andree*, p. 311); see also No. cxxxv. He had witnessed charters of Bishop David de Bernham in 1241 and 1246 (*ibid.* pp. 168, 169). He was evidently an ecclesiastic of some note, as in the year 1263 he, being then rector of Syreys (Ceres), in the diocese of St. Andrews, is appointed by Pope Urban iv. a papal chaplain (*Cal. Papal Registers*, i. 391).

CXXXII

Dated, 25th December 1263.

Page 171. Gamelin, Bishop of St. Andrews, postulated, not (strictly speaking) elected, on account of illegitimacy, 29th February 1254 ; confirmed by Pope Alexander iv., 1st July 1255 (Theiner's *Monumenta*, No. 176). He is still 'elect' 20th September 1255 (Bain's *Calendar*, i., No. 2013). He was consecrated 26th December 1255 (*Scotichr.* vi. 43). Died 29th April 1271 (*Scotichr.* vi. 43).

Richard, Bishop of Dunkeld. Richard of Inverkeithing (1250-1272).
Robert, Bishop of Dunblane. Robert de Prebenda (1259 ?-1284 ?).

CXXXIII

Dated, 22nd January 1300.

Page 172. *Johannes de Mubray, miles, dominus de Methfen.* Once an opponent but afterwards an adherent of Edward i. (?). See Tytler, *History of Scotland*, i. 100, 183-5, 232 ; *Scotichron.* xii. 13 ; Palgrave's *Documents and Records*, etc., vol. i., should also be consulted.

CXXXIV

Dated, 29th March 1342.

Page 173. *Thome de Carnoto.* Sir Thomas of Charteris (of Kinfauns), was Chancellor of Scotland in 1340. See *Exchequer Rolls*, i. 464, and

Bruce; was guardian of David II.; and died (as some suspect, of poison) at Musselburgh on 20th July 1332 (*Scotichron.* xiii. 22, and Fordun's *Annalia*, No. 146, Skene's edition). On 13th November 1329 Pope John XXII., in a letter addressed to Randolph, replies favourably to a petition of his that his heart might be extracted after his decease and buried in one place, and his body in another (Theiner's *Monumenta*, No. 489). One may conjecture that Bruce's bequeathing his heart to be buried at Jerusalem, 'apud sepulchrum Domini,' suggested the wish to Randolph. A discussion as to the cause of Randolph's death will be found in Dalrymple's *Annals*, iii. 52-54. 'Black Agnes,' wife of Patrick, ninth Earl of Dunbar, was his daughter.

Dilectum nepotem nostrum. This is an example of the loose way in which *nepos* was sometimes used. I have rendered the word by 'cousin' as in accordance with the facts. David elsewhere styles Randolph 'consanguineum nostrum' (*Reg. Morav.* pp. 157, 158).

Quondam Jacobi . . tunc Episcopi S. Andree. James Bene (Ben, Bane) was 'provided' to St. Andrews by the Pope, 1st August 1328 (Theiner's *Monumenta*, No. 472). He fled from Scotland shortly after the battle of Dupplin (12th August 1332), and died at Bruges in the following month (22nd September). As King Robert I. died 7th June 1329, we can within tolerably narrow limits fix the date of the Parliament referred to as held at Scone. A passage quite pertinent to the subject is to be found in the *Statuta Secunda Roberti Primi* (cap. i. § 4), which are undated. As printed by Skene in his addition to *Regiam Majestatem*, it runs thus : ' Et si Abbates, Priores, Custodes hospitalium, aliarum domorum fundatarum a Domino Rege, vel ejus antecessoribus, alienaverint tenementa domibus illis ab ipso, vel progenitoribus suis collata, tenementa illa in manibus Domini Regis capiantur, et ad voluntatem suam teneantur, et emptor amittat suum recuperare, tam de tenemento quam de pecunia quam pacavit.' See also the following sections. This is most probably the act referred to in our Chartulary. And the persons named show that the Parliament was held late in 1328, or early in 1329. Of this Parliament at Scone this charter seems to be our sole evidence, and thus adds an important fact to the history of Scotland. Hitherto the last Parliament of Robert I. has been supposed to be that of Cambuskenneth in 1326.

Apud monasterium de Kynlosse. David II., after seven years in France, had landed in Scotland, 2nd June 1341. We find him still at Kinlos six days later than the date of our charter, namely on 4th April 1342 (*Regist. Morav.* p. 127). This falls in well with the date of our charter.

CXXXV

Page 175. *Cheminagium* (chymnachium): from the old French *cheminage*, was commonly used for the payment or tolls demanded by the owners of forest for the passage of horses and wagons. 'Liberum cheminagium' is permission of passing without toll through the wood.

Page 176. *Magistro W. Wyscard, archidiacono Sancti Andree*, etc. He was elected to the see of Glasgow in 1270, and, while 'elect of Glasgow,' elected (2nd June 1271) to St. Andrews (*Chron. de Mailr.* s.a.).

CXXXVI

Dated, at Lindores, 24th August 1302.
Sir William of Brechin, son of Sir Henry (son of Earl David), married the fourth daughter of Alexander, Earl of Buchan. See No. cxxiv. (Douglas, *Peerage.*) From No. lxi. we learn that Sir William had lands at Lindores, and from No. lxii. that he had a castle there.

CXXXVII

Dated, at Dysart, 8th March 1247-8.
There is a confirmation of this grant by King Robert in the Haddington collection of charters (in the Advocates' Library). It has been printed by Mr. Turnbull (*Liber S. Marie de Lundoris*, p. 41). It is undated and the testing clause is lacking. Mr. Turnbull is in error in making Robert the *First* the confirmer ; but he had not material for correcting the rather natural conjecture.

CXXXIX

See No. xv., of which this is a later transcript, with omission of the names of the witnesses.

CXL

Date. The witnesses appear to belong to the time of William of Brechin. Here we have Hugo de Beaumys ('miles') and Robertus Mabilie. In William of Brechin's charter, No. lxi., we find 'Hugo de Beaumys' and 'Robertus filius Mabilie.'

Page 185. *In magnum lacum.* [The great loch is the loch of Rossie,

CXLII

Dated, Dervasyn (Dairsie), 5th June 1262.

Dairsie, a couple of miles east of Cupar in Fife, was one of the minor manors of the Bishop of St. Andrews. We find Gamelin dating a charter there in 1266-7 (*Regist. Priorat. S. Andree*, p. 311).

CXLIII

Dated, at Lindores on the Saturday next after the feast of St. Barnabas (11th June), that is on Saturday, 17th June 1262. This resignation into the hands of Thomas, abbot of Lindores, is dated six days after the confirmation by the chapter of St. Andrews (No. CXLIV.) and twelve days after the bishop's grant (No. CXLII.).

CXLIV

Dated, at St. Andrews, 11th June 1262.

Gilbertus *Prior cathedralis ecclesie.* Gilbert, formerly treasurer, became prior on 19th August 1258, and died 17th March 1263-4. He is described as 'vir religiosus, et gratiosus in temporalibus, licet non evidenter literatus' (*Scotichron.* vi. 51).

CXLV

Dated, at Monimel, Friday next after the Epiphany, that is Friday 7th January, 1277.

This is an *inspeximus* and confirmation. Possibly some defect was suspected in the formalities of the resignation that had been made: see the clause 'et supplemus defectum,' etc., and also No. CXLVI.

Willelmus. W. Wiseheart, postulated 2nd June 1271; but not consecrated till Sunday, 15th October 1273. He died 28th May 1279.

Monimel. Monimail, a few miles north-west of Cupar and not far from Lindores, was a lesser manor of the Bishop of St. Andrews.

CXLVI

There is nothing to determine the date. The charter is most probably by Wiseheart (15th October 1273-28th May 1279), who here confirms Gamelin's charter (No. CXLII.), as in No. CXLV. he confirmed No. CXLIII., and the date is probably the same as that of No. CXLV. A confirmation of Roger de Quincy's grant of Collessie by Pope Nicholas IV., 13th December 1288, is printed by Stevenson (*Documents*, etc., i. 68) and by Theiner (*Monumenta*, No. 308).

Page 197. *Thomam, Comitem de Marre.*   Thomas succeeded his father, Donald (the Regent who fell in the slaughter at Dupplin), in 1332.   He obtained the lordship of Garioch, in 1355, on the death of his grandmother, Christian Bruce, on whom it had been conferred by King Robert I. He died without issue in 1377.   His sister, Margaret, was married to William, first Earl of Douglas, who, in right of marriage, became Earl of Mar.

CXLVIII

Dated, at the castle of Kyldromy, 19th August 1359.

Page 199. *Thomas, Comes de Marre.*   See notes on No. CXLVII.

Apud castrum nostrum de Kyldromy.   For an account (about 1725) of the ruins of Kildrummy castle, see Macfarlane's *Geographical Collections* as cited in *Collections on the Shires of Aberdeen and Banff*, pp. 590-591. About two years after the granting of this charter David II., for some reasons not explained, besieged and took the castle and placed a garrison in it.   Mar obtained leave to quit the kingdom, but was soon received again into the royal favour.   See Dalrymple's *Annals*, ii. 302-3.

CXLIX

The date of this legal opinion is after the accession of William, Earl of Douglas, to the Earldom of Mar by marriage with Margaret, sister of Earl Thomas, *i.e.* after 1377.

For the references to the Civil and Canon Law and the commentators see Appendix V.

CL

The date of this legal opinion is uncertain.

A. and B. stand for Aberdeen and Brechin.

For the citations from the Canon Law, see Appendix V.

CLI

Dated, at Newburgh, 7th February 1478-9.   Sasine is given on 26th March.   See No. CLIII.

Page 216. *Vicarius ecclesie parochialis de Inchestur.*   Inchture in Gowrie.

unimportant: in line 9 'predicti' (burgenses) is read 'dicti'; in line 6 (P. 221) 'fruniendi' is misspelled 'frumiendi'; in line 9 from foot 'possedimus' is read 'possidemus'; 'nostras' in the last line (P. 221) is omitted. There is an exemplification of it in a charter of Abbot John, dated 13th July 1457, preserved in the charter-chest of Newburgh, of which Mr. Laing gives an English translation (*Lindores Abbey*, pp. 479-483).

Page 220. *Johannes . . abbas.* See Appendix IV. p. 310.

Page 221. *Secundum formam et tenorem carte . . . regis Alexandri.* King Alexander's charter is not found in our volume; but it was copied from the MS. transcript in the Advocates' Library and printed by Turnbull (p. 8). It grants to the abbot and convent and their successors that they should have for ever 'villam eorum que dicitur Novus burgus juxta monasterium de Lundoris in liberum burgum, et forum in eodem burgo quolibet die Martis cum libertatibus burgi et fori. Salvis in omnibus burgorum nostrorum libertatibus.' It is dated 'apud Strivelyn quarto die Marcii, anno regni nostri septimo decimo.' That the king was Alexander III. (not Alexander II.) we gather from the presence of 'William, Earl of Mar, chamberlain,' among the witnesses. The year, therefore, was 1266. Mr. Alexander Laing has made a curious slip in rendering 'quolibet die Martis' 'any day in March' (*Lindores Abbey*, p. 142). The concession is for a market on *Tuesdays* throughout the year. And so it is expressed in our charter. But the slip is corrected at p. 481.[1]

CLIII

Dated, Newburgh, 27th March 1479. See No. CLI.

Page 224. *Infra capellam ejusdem.* We find that in 1473 there was a chapel at Newburgh dedicated to St. Katherine (*Lindores Abbey*, p. 168). Compare No. CLII., where we find that the yearly fair was held on St. Katherine's day, 25th November. The bailies and council of the burgh seem to have commonly transacted burgh business in the chapel (*ibid.* pp. 175, 510). Mr. Alexander Laing has collected some curious information about this chapel and its chaplains in his volume *Lindores Abbey*.

CLIV

Fragment of a Public Instrument.

The year of this fragment is not given, yet we can infer it, with reasonable confidence, from the following data. An ecclesiastic, named De Butyll, appears as Archdeacon of Candida Casa. He also holds some office at the papal court (*sacri palacij . . .*). Now we find a certain

Thomas de Butyl (or Butill) in 1388 Provost of the Chapel of St. Mary, Maybole (*Calendar of Papal Registers: Petitions*, i. 570). In 1390 he is still holding the same office (*ibid.* p. 574), but we find him petitioning in that year for the archdeaconry of Whitherne (*ibid.* p. 575). In 1412 we find Thomas de Butyl, Doctor of Canon Law and Papal Auditor, archdeacon of Whiteherne and chaplain of St. Mary's, Maybole (*ibid.* p. 595). In 1413 he is described as archdeacon of Whiteherne and papal chaplain and auditor, and for him Benedict XIII. (Anti-Pope) reserves 'the church of Abernith' in the diocese of Dunkeld (*ibid.* p. 599). In 1415 Benedict XIII. provides him to the church of Kinkel (valued, with its chapels, at £100), in the diocese of Aberdeen, and also to the canonry and prebend of 'Inverkethny,' in Moray (*ibid.* p. 602). Later in the same year he is promoted to the see of Candida Casa. It would thus appear that this instrument should probably be dated some time between 1412 and 1415. But we find remaining in the MS. just enough of the date to establish that the Instrument was drawn up in the 'Seventh Indiction.' This practically fixes the year as 1414.[1]

Among the other names occurring in the fragment are Richard Cady, Robert de Dryden, and John Scheves. Ecclesiastics bearing these names are found among the many Scottish petitioners to the Pope about this time. John Scheves, of the Instrument (if we may venture to identify him with the petitioner), rector of the University of St. Andrews and official, petitioned Benedict XIII., in 1418, for the archdeaconry of Teviotdale, and his petition was granted (*Calendar of Papal Registers: Petitions*, i. 609). In 1394 there was one Robert de Dryden, a priest in the diocese of Glasgow (*ibid.* p. 617). Richard Cady, priest of the diocese of Dunkeld, was a petitioner in 1409 (*ibid.* p. 594); again in 1411 (p. 597); and again (now a Bachelor in Common Law) in 1417 (p. 606).

---

[1] The year 1399 was also the 'Seventh Indiction'; but Butyll does not appear as holding an office in the 'sacred palace' till 1412.

APPENDIX I

THE following charter, which in the opinion of the editor is the earliest known writ connected with Lindores, is among the Campbell Charters (xxx. 16) preserved in the British Museum. A fragment of the seal remains attached. The transcript was made by Dr. J. Maitland Thomson, Curator of the Historical Department in H.M. General Register House, Edinburgh, and supplied for this volume.

'Nouerint omnes presentes et futuri quod ego O. abbas et conuentus ecclesie Kelchoensis quietum clamauimus ab omnimoda subiectione et obedientia dompnum Guidonem electum in abbatem ecclesie Sancti Andree de Lundores · nec propter hoc quod monachos nostros illi ad edificandum locum illum accommodauimus aliquam potestatem aliquo tempore aliquis abbas de Kelchou habeat super domum vel super abbatem predicte ecclesie Sancti Andree de Lundores · nec abbas de Kelchou maiorem potestatem habeat in abbatem vel in predictam ecclesiam Sancti Andree de Lundores quam abbas Sancti Andree de Lundores in abbatem vel in ecclesiam de Kelchou · Igitur sola caritas familiaritas et orationes uigeant et ineternum permaneant inter predictas domos et earum personas nulla uero dominatio vel potestas · salvo ordine et habitu nostro.   Hiis testibus · Willelmo rege Scotie · comite Dauid fratre regis Scotie qui predictam ecclesiam fundauit · Rogero electo Sancti Andree · Jocelino episcopo Glasguensi · Matheo episcopo Aberdonensi · J. episcopo de Dunkeld' · Hugone archidiacono de Sancto Andrea et cancellario domini regis · Dunecano comite de Fife · comite Patricio · G. comite de Stradhern · Serlone de Quinti · Roberto de Lundres filio regis · Malcholmo filio comitis Dunekani · Alano dapifero · Willelmo de Lindesya · Waltero de Berchelay · Willelmo Cumino ·

(Abstract)

Let all present and to come know that I, O[sbert], abbot, and the convent of the church of Kelso have quitclaimed from subjection and obedience of every kind Sir Guido, elected to be abbot of the church of St. Andrews of Lindores. Nor shall any abbot of Kelso have at any time any power over the house or over the abbot of the aforesaid church of St. Andrew of Lindores by reason of our having lent our monks to him for the building of that place. Nor shall the abbot of Kelso have greater power over the abbot or over the aforesaid church of St. Andrew of Lindores than the abbot of St. Andrew of Lindores has over the abbot or over the church of Kelso. Therefore may love only, friendship, and prayers flourish and remain for ever between the aforesaid houses and those having authority in them [*earum personas*; but, possibly, *personae* is here used in a non-technical sense, meaning simply 'their members'] but no lordship or power, saving our order and habit. These being witnesses

The charter printed above is probably the earliest writ extant relating to the monastery of Lindores. It exempts from the jurisdiction of the abbot of Kelso Guido 'electum in abbatem ecclesie Sancti Andree de Lundores.' The form of expression suggests that it was written when Guido was only 'elect,' that is, when he had not yet received the benediction to his office.[1] This, as well as the general character of the contents, points to a date earlier than the first *dated* document, the bull of Celestine III., of 8th March 1195, which is addressed to the 'abbot and convent.' As is well known, Roger de Beaumont, one of the witnesses, was for many years 'elect of St. Andrews' before his consecration. He was elected 13th April 1189 (*Chron. de Mailr.* s.a.), and not consecrated till 15th February 1198 (*ibid.* s.a.). In the present charter he appears as 'elect of St. Andrews,' so that a pretty wide margin is allowed for the dating of the document; nor is it limited by the histories of the other witnesses.

But we find Guido as 'abbot' at least as early as 1194 (see Appendix IV.), so I would place this charter before that date, and perhaps it may be as early as 1191.

APPENDIX II

DESCRIPTION OF THE MS. BY J. MAITLAND THOMSON, LL.D., CURATOR OF THE HISTORICAL DEPARTMENT OF H.M. GENERAL REGISTER HOUSE.

The Register consists of (1) five gatherings containing respectively, 6, 3, 6, 8, and 3 leaves, in all 26 leaves; (2) five gatherings of 12 leaves each, in all 60 leaves. The whole is paged continuously according to its present arrangement, from fol. 3 to 87—one leaf between fols. 81 and 82 having been overlooked in paging.

The second of the two sections clearly ought to precede the other, and does so in the print. The greater part of it (fols. 29 to 74 *verso*, except 64 and part of 63 *verso*—comprising rather more than half of the whole Register) is in one handwriting, assigned by Dr. Dickson to about A.D. 1260. Each charter has an initial letter in red or blue, the illuminator having begun with making them red on one side of the leaf and blue on the other, and afterwards preferred to make them red and blue alternately: but neither rule is strictly adhered to, and several initials have not been filled in at all. There are contemporary rubrics to each charter up to fol. 58, and again fols. 65 to 73. Each page contains 25 lines.

Fol. 74 *verso*, and up to fol. 78, are written by a different scribe, contemporary with the first, or not much later. Here there are no coloured initials, and the titles are in black; but every important word has its initial touched with red. The usual number of lines to the page is 26.

The contents of fol. 63 *verso*, 64, 78 to the end, and 4 to 17 inclusive, seem all to have been engrossed in the first half of the fourteenth century; but there is a great variety of handwriting, and no uniformity of style. The number of lines to the page varies from 16 to over 40. Rubrics and coloured initials occur fols. 8 to 10 only. Five leaves have been cut away between fols. 8 and 9, but they probably did not form part of the Register—

87, and in some cases the handwriting may be identified—compare especially fol. 81 ff. with fol. 12 ff. The latest, but not the last engrossed, charter in this section belongs to the year 1342. On fol. 17 *verso* a charter ends abruptly, and something may have been lost.

The two gatherings which form fols. 18 to 28 are later. Fols. 18 to 24 are in an early fifteenth century hand; fols. 25 to 27 are in different hands of the end of the same century. Fol. 27 is written by the same scribe who supplied titles missed by the rubricator in the earlier portions of the Register, and added sundry notes. Three leaves are cut away between fols. 25 and 26, but there is no lacuna.

I think that what has been described is all that the Register contained when arranged, bound and paged as at present. It will be seen that the pagination begins with fol. 4—three blank leaves may have been left at the beginning for supplementary matter, one of which was filled up by a sixteenth century scribe with the instrument which, in the edition, concludes the Register. The other two may have been removed. There is a fly-leaf, cut out of an instrument not relating to Lindores which, from what remains of it, must belong to either 1399 or 1414; the proof being (1) that it is of the seventh indiction; (2) that Thomas de Butill is named as archdeacon of Galloway, a benefice to which he was provided in 1391, and which he held till 1415.

APPENDIX III

A CLUE-CATALOGUE OF SOME CHARTERS AND OTHER WRITS, RELATING TO LINDORES, NOT FOUND IN THE CHARTULARY.

The documents indicated below concern the abbey, its rights, privileges, and property, down to the time of the Reformation.

relating to the Abbey. The volume of the Abbotsford Club is indicated by *LL.* Theiner's *Vetera Monumenta* is indicated by *T.* ; *The Calendar of Papal Registers* by *C.P.R.* ; The *Registrum Magni Sigilli* by *R.M.S.* ; of the latter the writs up to A.D. 1424 are cited from the folio edition of 1814.

Of the documents printed by Mr. Turnbull, very full abstracts (in English) may be found in Mr. A. Laing's *Lindores Abbey,* pp. 467-483, in which volume also will be found abstracts of charters in the Charter-chest of Newburgh. The latter chiefly concern the burgh, but a few relate to the abbey or the abbots. The former are not noticed here : the latter are indicated here only in the briefest way ; and those who desire details are referred to Mr. Laing's volume.

(1.) *Before* 1194 (?).—Quitclaim of obedience and subjection of Guido, abbot-elect of the church of St. Andrew of Lindores, by O[sbert], abbot of Kelso.—British Museum, Campbell Charters, xxx. 16. See Appendix I.

(2.) *Before 8th March* 1195, *Selkirk.*—King William grants full tofts in his burghs of Berwick, Stirling, Crail, Perth, Forfar, Montrose, and Aberdeen ; to be held ' in liberam elemosinam.' [1]— *LL.,* p. 9.

(3.) *A few years (c.* 1202) *later than our No. II.*—The foundation charter given again with a few variants, and other witnesses.— Original in the Advocates' Library (29 Denmyln A. 3. 22): printed in *LL.,* pp. 37-38. See p. 233.

(4.) *Between 1st January* 1219 *and* 1225.—Gregory, Bishop of Brechin, confirms to Lindores the grant made by his predecessors of the church of Dundee with its chapels, lands, and pertinents, *ad proprios usus.* The vicar is to be presented by the monastery, and to receive ten pounds sterling *per an.,* out of which he is to pay the bishop's dues (*episcopalia*). The monastery is to have the right of appointing to the schools of Dundee.—*LL.,* p. 17.

(5.) 1248, *April* 20, *Lyons.*—Pope Innocent [IV.] states that a petition had been presented to him by the abbots of Kelso and Lindores and the prior of the cathedral church of St. Andrews, with respect to their churches in the diocese of Aberdeen ; and

from the vicars, and had taken lands and other possessions belonging to the vicarages for their own use. The Pope commits to the Chancellor of Moray, the Treasurer, and Master John de Everley, Canon of Dunkeld, to inquire into the revenues of the said churches, to assign fitting portions to the vicars, and to restrain any from molesting the said abbots and prior, after the judgment of the commissioners had been pronounced.—*Registr. Aberdon.*, i. 20-21. Compare No. xcii. in our Chartulary.

(6.) 1251, *May* 20, *Kinghorn.*—King Alexander [iii.¹] grants to the abbot and convent of Lindores their whole wood in the fee of Fintray to be held 'in liberam forestam.' No one to cut timber or hunt in said wood without the leave of the abbot and convent. —*LL.*, p. 10.

(7.) *Early* (?) *in* 1252.—Admission by Albin, Bishop of Brechin, of William Mydford to the vicarage of Dundee on the presentation of the abbot and convent of Lindores, under the reservation to the bishop of the 'taxatio' of the vicarage. Monday before Ash Wednesday, 1252, was assigned for the 'taxatio.' The parties appeared on the day appointed, and the bishop, after careful inquiry, on the advice of 'probi viri,' pronounced sentence that the vicar should receive the whole altarage, and pay at Easter every year ten marks sterling to the abbot and convent.—*L.L.*, p. 10.

(8.) 1256, *March* 18, *Lateran.*—Pope Alexander [iv.] to the abbot and convent of Lindores. He confirms the 'taxatio' of the Bishop of Brechin; for, although the vicar had appealed against it, he had failed to prosecute the appeal within the lawful time.—*L.L.*, p. 13.

admonished, was not careful to pay the ten marks. The monks of Lindores had obtained Apostolic Letters to the prior of May and the provost of St. Mary's church, St. Andrews ; and the vicar had obtained similar letters to the official of Aberdeen and his colleague. The vicar alleged that he had to pay so much to the abbot and convent that he could not be suitably maintained on the residue. While litigation was pending before the official and his colleague, Mydford the vicar retired from the suit. The prior and provost proceeded in the case before them, approved of the bishop's 'taxatio,' and gave definitive sentence to that effect. Mydford appealed from this sentence, and obtained Apostolic Letters to the abbot of Kynloss and his colleagues. But while the appeal was pending before these judges, Mydford appeared before the Bishops of Dunblane and Brechin and other prelates, in the church of the Friars Preachers, at Perth, on Saturday next after 14th Sep tember 1256 [*i.e.* on Sept. 16], agreed to the payment of the ten marks, and submitted himself to the judgment of the Bishops of Dunblane and Brechin as regards damages and costs. The bishops adjudged him to pay the arrears, and also fifty marks for damages and costs (although they really came to more), and remitted the vicar to the special grace of the abbot and convent. Sealed with the seals of the two bishops.—*LL.*, pp. 14-16.

(11.) 1257, *February* 10, *Lateran.*—Pope Alexander [iv.] to the abbot and convent. Prohibits the bishop or archdeacon of Brechin exacting anything from that portion of the revenues from the church of Dundee which belonged to the abbot and convent, or sequestrating the same. The vicar had been assigned a portion from which he was to bear the *episcopalia* and other burdens.— *LL.*, p. 16.

(12.) 1257, *September* 13, *Rome, St. Peter's.*—Pope Alexander [iv.] confirms the sentence of 'taxatio' of the parishes in the diocese of Aberdeen appropriated to Lindores, which sentence had been pronounced at Banquhory Terny on the Thursday next after the feast of St. Peter *ad vincula* [1 Aug.], 1250, by the commissioners appointed [see No. 5]. The 'taxatio' detailed in full.—*Reg. Aberdon.*, i. 23-26.

(14.) 1261, *August* 7.—Quitclaim by Thomas, abbot of Lindores, and the convent to Sir Robert de Brus, lord of Annandale, of the second tithes of the lands of the latter beyond the Mounth.—Record Office. See Bain's *Calendar*, ii. No. 2267.[1]

(15.) 1265, *March* 14, *Lindores.*—King Alexander [III.] grants that the whole wood of the monks, with the lands at Lindores, should be held ' in liberam forestam.' No one to cut or hunt in the said wood without the leave of the abbot and convent.—*LL.*, p. 11.

(16.) 1266, *March* 4, *Stirling.*—King Alexander [III.] grants and confirms to the abbot and convent that they should have their vill which is called New Burgh ' in liberum burgum,' with a market every Tuesday, and the liberties of burgh and market, ' saving the liberties of our burghs.'—*LL.*, p. 8.

(17.) 1282, *March* 15, *Orvieto.*—Pope Martin [IV.] notifies the amount of cess payable by certain monasteries in England and Scotland. The abbey of Lindores was to pay 2 bezants.—*C.P.R.*, i. 475-76.

(18.) 1288, *December* 13, *at St. Maria Maggiore.*—Nicholas [IV.] to the abbot and convent, confirms the grant of the church of Collessie made by Roger de Quency. [See Nos. CXLI.-CXLV.].—*T.*, p. 140.

(19.) 1289, *March* 15, *at St. Maria Maggiore.*—Nicholas [IV.] to the abbot and convent. In answer to a petition stating that Scotland is a cold region, and that some of the monks had suffered from being bare-headed when on certain solemn festivals they were vested in albs and silk copes, grants permission that they should use caps (*pileis*) on these festivals and in processions, provided that due reverence was done at the reading of the Gospel [in the Mass] and at the Elevation, and in all other things.[2]—*T.*, p. 141; *LL.*, pp. 24-25.

(20.) 1290, *September* 13, *Orvieto.*—Nicholas [IV.] to the abbot and

place-names], and declares that the present letter should have all the force of the original and might be exhibited in courts of law or elsewhere.—*T.*, p. 141.

(21.) 1309-10, *February* 19, 'the Thursday next before the feast of St. Peter's Chair' (Feb. 22), *Lindores.*—Memorandum of a controversy between the abbot and convent of the one part, and the men of the New Burgh of Lindores of the other part, as it was debated in the chapter-house before Sir Robert of Keith, Marshal of Scotland, and Justiciar from the water of Forth to the mountains of Scotland. Continued on the following day, Friday, in the presence of the Bishop of St. Andrews and others. The men of the burgh had withheld their fermes for five years. Decision in favour of the monastery.—*LL.*, pp. 11-13. [This writ is translated at length in *Lindores Abbey*, pp. 474-75, and presents an interesting illustration of the legal procedure of the time.]

(22.) 1306-1329.—An undated charter of King Robert (presumably Robert I.) confirming No. cxxxvii. of our Chartulary. The witnesses are not recorded. Printed by Turnbull (from a charter in Haddington's Collection in the Advocates' Library) in *LL.*, p. 41.

(23.) 1345, *June* 24, *Villeneuve, near Avignon.*—Pope Clement VI. grants to Simon Young (*Juvenis*) of the diocese of Aberdeen the reservation of a benefice, value twenty marks with cure of souls, or fifteen marks without cure, in the gift of the abbot and convent of Lindores.—*C.P.R.*, iii. 185 [compare *C.P.R.* ' Petitions,' i. 95].

(24.) 1345, *December* 7, *Avignon.*—Pope Clement VI. to the Abbot of Lindores and the Prior of Abernethy to make provision to Walter de Coventre, M.A., Licentiate of Civil Law, canon of Ross and Abernethy, of the archdeaconry of Dunblane.—*C.P.R.*, iii. 198.

(25.) 1350, *March* 17 [or March 16, in exemplification, No. 27], *Lindores.*—Duncan, Earl of Fife, grants *in proprios usus* to Lindores the parish church of Ochtirmokadi (Auchtermuchty), in fulfilment of a vow made when he was taken prisoner by the English at the battle of Durham [Neville's Cross, 17 Oct. 1346]. From the exemplification in a confirmation by King David.—*Haddington's*

(27.) 1354, *December* 3, *Avignon.*—Pope Innocent VI. confirms the grant of the parish church of Ochtirmokadi (Auchtermuchty) in the diocese of St. Andrews, by Duncan, Earl of Fife. This writ contains exemplifications of Nos. 25, 26.—*C.P.R.*, iii. 539-540.

(28.) 1355, *November* 19, *Lindores.*—Sir David de Lyndesay of Crauford grants to Lindores six stones of wax to be paid annually for finding a light to be burned daily in the choir of the abbey-church at the tomb of Lady Mary, his late wife, and of himself at certain services. For finding the wax he grants 2 marks out of his lands of Pitfour.—As exemplified in *R.M.S.*, p. 36, No. 94.

(29.) 1355-57.—Undated charter of Thomas, Earl of Mar, granting to Sir Robert de Erskyne, knight and his wife, Cristiana de Kethe, certain lands in Garioch, together with four marks annual rent due by the abbot and convent of Lindores out of the land of Flandres.—*Collections for History of Aberdeen and Banff*, p. 536.

(30.) 1358, *July* 31, *Dundee.*—King David II. confirms Earl Duncan's grant, No. 25.—From Haddington's Collection of Charters in Advocates' Library. Printed by Turnbull in *LL.*, p. 43.

(31.) 1364, *August* 3, *Lindores.*—King David II. confirms, with exemplification, Sir David de Lyndesay's grant of Nov. 19, 1355. —*R.M.S.*, p. 37, No. 94.

(32.) 1364, *August* 3, *Lindores.*—King David II. grants to Lindores half the land of Estir Cragy in the barony of Parnbogall (Barn-bougle), in the county of Edinburgh, which was resigned into his hands for the purpose by Bartholomew de Loone, knight, and Philippa, his spouse, daughter and heiress of Philip de Moubray, knight, on condition that a Mass should be said at the altar of St. Michael in the abbey-church for the souls of the donors, etc. —*R.M.S.*, p. 39, No. 101.

(33.) 1364, *September* 20, *Dundee.*—King David II. confirms the charter of King Alexander II. (exemplified with witnesses) which

marks annual rent paid by Lindores out of the land of Flandres.—
Collections, Aberdeen and Banff, 539.

(35.) 1380.—Petition to the Pope by William of Angus, abbot
of Lindores :—(1) For a faculty to hear confessions (because
mortality was rife in Scotland) of all persons, secular and regular,
lay and clerical, and to absolve them even in cases reserved to the
Apostolic See, and to enjoin suitable penance ; (2) On behalf of
Thomas de Kilconkar for a canonry in Moray, notwithstanding
that he has the church of Monymel ; (3) On behalf of Augustine
de Gogare, priest, for a benefice in the gift of Dunfermline, notwithstanding that he has the church of Gogare.—*C.P.R.,* Pet. i.
557.

(36.) 1382, *October* 1, *Chateauneuf, in the diocese of Avignon.*—
Clement VII. (Anti-Pope) to the Bishop of Brechin and the officials
of St. Andrews and Dunkeld, to summon those concerned in a
dispute between John Steil who had intruded himself into the
office of abbot and the abbot William. Further, to take order in
respect to Lindores (various details).—*C.P.R.,* iv. 248-49.

(37.) 1392, *March 23, Perth.*—King Robert III. confirms to David
of Abirkedor the security of certain rents in Dundee belonging
to the monastery for a loan of 7 marks made by the said David
to the monastery.—*R.M.S.,* p. 207, No. 35.

(38.) 1402, *November 8, Kyndromi (Kildrummy).*—Isabella de
Douglas, Lady of Mar and of Garioch in her widowhood, for the
weal of her soul, etc., grants to Lindores the patronage and
advowson of the church of Codilstane (Coldstone) in Mar ; and on
the death or resignation of Simon, then rector, they might
convert the church *in proprios usus,* if confirmation of the grant
could be obtained. Warrandice against all deadly.—*Denmyln
Charters* in Advocates' Library : printed by Turnbull in *LL.,*
p. 49.[1]

(39.) 1414, *March 26, Tortosa.*—Benedict XIII. (Anti-Pope) in
answer to a petition grants that, whereas the monastery of St
Mary, Lindores, has its buildings ruined and its rents diminished
by reason of the nearness of the wild (*silvestrium*) Scots, the church

12lb., should be appropriated to it. This to take effect on the death of the rector, Laurence of Lindores; a perpetual vicar, with fit stipend, being then appointed.—*C.P.R.*, Pet. i. 601.

(40.) 1451, *May* 10.—King James [II.] grants to the abbot and convent the lands of Perkhill with the office of keeper (*custodia*) of the royal wood of Irneside, with the emoluments (*proficuis*) pertaining to said ofhce,—to be held in frankalmoign. *Reddendo,* devout prayers.—*R.M.S.*, ii. No. 445.

(41.) 1451, *May* 21, *Edinburgh.*—King James II. to the sheriffs of Fife. Inasmuch as he had granted to the abbot and convent of Lindores his lands of Parkhill, in the county of Fife, and also the office of forester of his wood of Earnside [see No. 40] in the lands of Parkhill, he commands these, conjointly or severally, to give sasine of the lands and office of forester to the abbot and convent or to their attorney bearing these presents.—*LL.*, 18-19.

(42.) 1457, *July* 4, *Lindores.*—John, abbot, and the convent grant to their burgesses of Newburgh by this indenture the land called Wodrufe and the hill contiguous to the south part of Wodrufe [marches detailed]. *Faciendo,* homage and service used and wont; *reddendo,* forty bolls of barley annually at Easter. In default of payment the grantors reserve right to distrain; and, in the event of failure to pay the full rent for three successive terms to resume the lands into their own hands until the arrears with expenses have been fully paid. Other details and limitations of the grant. —*LL.*, pp. 5-7.

burgh, to be held in fee and heritage. *Reddendo*, 8 shillings for the reparation of the said chapel and the maintenance of a chaplain to celebrate divine service therein, and 12 pence Scots to the abbot and convent for burgh mail.—Translated from original in Newburgh Charter-chest by Mr. A. Laing, *Lindores Abbey*, p. 510.

(45.) 1471, *July* 6.—David Spalding, burgess of Dundee, grants to Lindores, for the weal of his soul and of the soul of Isabella, his wife, his land in Market Street, Dundee; also 30 shillings annual rent from the toft of the abbey between the vennel called *Spalding's Wynd* and the land of the late Thomas Leis. He reserves the freehold for the lives of himself and wife. *Reddendo*, 3lb. 6s. 8d., and 20s.; the twenty shillings to be paid to the altar of St. Margaret, behind the great altar of the church of St. Mary, Dundee, and 3lb. 6s. 8d. for the reparation of the choir of the said church.—*R.M.S.*, ii. No. 1279.

(46.) 1474, *May* 18, *Lindores.*—John, abbot of Lindores, increases from 2lb. to 4lb. per annum the allowance made to his monks in priest's orders for their habits and *ornatus*. To this the consent of the ordinary Patrick [Graham], Bishop of St. Andrews, had been given at the time of his visitation.—*LL.*, pp. 23-24.

(47.) 1476, *April* 8, *Lindores.*—Andrew [Cavers], abbot of Lindores, and the convent, with unanimous consent lease to George Muncrefe of Tybermolloke the lands of Exmagirdle in the earldom of Strathern and county of Perth, the mills and multures, with all the garbal tithes, altarages and small tithes of the parish church, for George's life-time. He is to have the right to sublet to his mother, younger brothers, labourers and farmers, 'being less in power than George himself,' but to none others. Rent, 40 marks usual money, payable at the two usual terms, with four dozen fat capons (otherwise 12d. for each capon) and accustomed services. Other conditions.—*LL.*, pp. 21-22.

(48.) 1476-77, *February* 22.—David Spalding's grant (No. 45) is confirmed under the Great Seal.—*R.M.S.*, ii. No. 1279.

(49.) 1478, *May* 20, *Lindores.*—Andrew, abbot, and the convent grant a rood of land in their burgh [situation defined] to David Hathintown their quarrier for faithful service in the past, and

(50.) 1479, *May* 18, *Lindores.*—Andrew [Cavers], abbot, with the unanimous consent of the chapter, lets to their 'special friends,' Dionysius Chalmers (Cameris) and his son William, to each an eighth part of the lands of Grange in the parish of Ebdy and county of Fife. Rental and various conditions stated.—*LL.*, pp. 19-21.

(51.) 1481, *May* 25.—Charter of John Wyntoun, priest of the diocese of St. Andrews and burgess of Newburgh, granting to his brother, Thomas Wyntoun, also a burgess of Newburgh, his land and tenement in the burgh, to be held of the abbot and convent of Lindores.—*Charter-chest of Newburgh,* translated in Laing's *Lindores Abbey,* pp. 510-511.

(52.) 1493, *July* 25.—John de Covintre of Mukdrum had been adjudged by the Lords of Council to pay one hundred and sixty marks to Andrew, abbot, and the convent of Lindores. Having no moveable goods that might be distrained, eight mark-lands of the lands of Mukdrum were assigned to the monastery. But George, Earl of Rothes, refused infeftment to the abbey. The king, James IV., confirms the arrangement; Covintre and his heirs to be allowed to resume the land if the debt and expenses are paid within seven years.—*R.M.S.*, ii. 2168.

(53.) 1500, *November* 9, *Perth.*—John Oliphant of Drone, and lord of Petcaithley, sold and alienated for a sum of money half the lands of Petcaithley, which he held of the king in feu-ferme, to the abbot Andrew and the convent. *Reddendo,* a penny *pro alba firma.* As exemplified in next.

(54.) 1500, *November* 6 (*sic*), *Edinburgh.*—[The dates of the charter and confirmation exhibit some error.] James IV. confirms No. 53.—*R.M.S.*, ii. 2553.

(55.) 1501, *November* 6.—Decreet arbitral by Patrick Wellis, Provost of Perth, and eight others, judges arbiters 'commonly chosen' between Andrew, abbot of Lindores, the convent and their successors, on the one part, and the bailies, council, and

burgesses of Aberdeen, 283lbs. 6s. 8d. (Scots) for the payment to their proctor, Stephen Orme, in Flanders or Zealand before 10th August of 100lbs. of Flemish ' grossi.' The payment to the Aberdeen burgesses was to be spread over some time. On the 18th August they were to receive from the monastery two hundred marks [133lbs. 6s. 8d.] Scots ; at Martinmas 'or thereby' 75lbs. Scots; and at Whitsunday 'or thereby' in 1503, another 75lbs. Scots. The bond was over the goods of the monastery, moveable and immoveable. Common seal of chapter.—*LL.*, 27, 28.

(57.) 1502, *October 7, Lindores.*—Obligation of the abbot and convent to Andrew Charters to the amount of 60lbs. ' usual money of the kingdom of Scotland' for the payment by Andrew or his factors to them or their proctors of 20lbs. of ' grossi,' to be paid in Flanders or Zealand within six days of the sight of the obligation, the 60lbs. Scots to be paid within forty days after the receipt of the acquittance of the monks' proctors for the 20lbs. of ' grossi.' A similar obligation is made to Alexander Tyri, burgess of Perth, to the amount of 30lbs. Scots for 10lbs. of ' grossi.' A similar obligation to Robert Clerk *alias* Vobster, burgess of Perth, to the amount of 30lbs. Scots for 10lbs. of ' grossi,' all to be paid to the proctors of the monks in Flanders or Zealand. The bonds were over all the goods, moveable and immoveable, of the monastery.—*LL.*, 25-26.

(58.) 1502-3, *March 20, Lindores.*—Bond given by the abbot (Henry Orme) and the convent to John Quhitsum, burgess of Perth, his heirs and assignees, for 105lbs. 10s. Scots, on account of his causing to be paid 30lbs. of ' grossi' 3s. and 4 ' grossi ' (Flemish) to their procurator, Master Hugh Mertini (? Martinson), rector of Weym, and on account of a debt, previously due to Quhitsum, of 10lbs. Scots. Payment was to be made to Quhitsum, after the monks had seen the receipt of their procurator, on the feast of St. Laurence (10 August) of the same year (1503).—*LL.*, 28-9.

(59.) 1503, *October 23.   Confirmed* 1503, *November* 21.—William Cavers is granted by the abbot, Henry, ' duplam sive binam partem' of the lands of Mukdrum for 160 marks. *Tenend.* ' a

the 'duplam sive binam partem' of Mukdrum for rents estimated at 8 marks and 14 pence annually.—*R.M.S.*, ii. No. 2985.

(61.) 1508, *April* 5.—Instrument of sasine. Andrew Cavers, 'pensionary of Lindores,'[1] resigns certain lands in the burgh of Newburgh, and John Malcumsone, as procurator of a chaplain who was to serve in the new kirk to be built in the burgh to the honour of SS. Duthac, Katherine, and Mary Magdalene, is given sasine of the same.—*Newburgh Charter-Chest* ; given in translation in *Lindores Abbey*, pp. 511-512.

(62.) 1510, *November* 7.—King James IV. erects the lands of Lindores into a Regality.—*R.M.S.*, iii. No. 12.

(63.) 1513, *July* 12.—Confirmation to Thomas Fodringham of the lands of Haltoun and Pethous de Inverarite, from which 5 marks were to be paid yearly to the abbot and convent of Lindores.— *R.M.S.*, iii. No. 3861.

(64.) 1514, *April* 5.—The erection of the Regality confirmed in Parliament.—*R.M.S.*, iii. No. 12.

(65.) 1515, *May* 28, *Edinburgh.*—Balthasar Stuerd (Stuerdus), protonotary of the Apostolic See, gives authority to Walter Lesle and Henry White, canons of Dunkeld, to induct Walter Marsar, presbyter of the diocese of St. Andrews, into the vicarage of Auchtermuchty, to which he had been presented by the favour of the abbot of Lindores.—*Laing Charters*, No. 308.

(66.) 1516, *June* 6, *Edinburgh.*—Confirmation to Sir John Lundin of Lundin of a charter concerning the patronage of the parish church of Largo, which patronage, under certain circumstances, was to fall to the abbot and convent of Lindores.—*R.M.S.*, iii. No. 78.

(67.) 1516, *September* 16, *Lindores.*—Henry, abbot, and the convent grant a tack to Sir John Stirling of Keir, knight, of their

(for him and his convent) 'anent the debatable lands betwix Rothmaiss and Tulymorgond and the peit moss callit off Malyngsyd and Bonytoune of Rayne.'—*Regist. Aberdon.*, i. 386.

(69.) 1532, *October 5, Lindores.*—John, abbot, and the convent grant a tack to Sir John Stirling of Keir, knight, of their lands of Beny and Caitkin, together with the teind-sheaves for twelve pounds usual money, with multure, hariage and carriage. They also appoint him their bailie for the lands of Feddallis (Estir and Westir) and Beny : for which office he was to pay two marks usual money.—*Stirlings of Keir*, pp. 346-9.

(70.) 1535, *October 9.*—Tack granted by John, the abbot, and the convent of Lindores to David Weddirburne, burgess of Dundee, and Elen Lausoun, his spouse, and the heirs male of David, of half the lands of Hiltoun of Cragy [near Dundee]. Confirmed under Great Seal, 10 Feb. 1538.—*R.M.S.*, iii. No. 1913.

(71.) 1537, *March 16, Lindores.*—Tack by the abbot and convent to James Wod of Inchebrek and Giles (Egidie) Straithauchin, his spouse, of the lands of Hall of Witstoun, Fischerhill, and Hillend in the Mernes. Confirmed under the Great Seal, 8 April 1542.—*R.M.S.*, iii. No. 2636.

(72.) 1541, *September 29, Perth.*—Grant by the King to Patrick Balfoure of Dene-mylne of the mill called the Denemylne and other properties, for rent, reserving to the abbot and convent of Lindores an annual payment of 53 shillings and 4 pence, and a duplicand on entrance of heirs, etc.—*R.M.S.*, iii. No. 2460.

(73.) 1544, *April 29, Lindores.*—John, abbot, and the convent to Master Dionisius Chalmer and John Calvy, bailies of their burgh of Newburgh. Precept of sasine of certain lands in the burgh [described] to Henry Philp. *Charter-chest of Newburgh* : full abstract in *Lindores Abbey*, p. 487.

(74.) 1545, *June 26, Lindores.*—Charter of feu-ferme by the abbot John and the convent to William Galloway, brother's son of Master Alexander Galloway, canon of Aberdeen, of the lands of Kyrktoun of Culsalmond. Precept of sasine the same day.—*Regist. Aberdon.*, i. 430.

(76.) 1559, *January* 12, *Lindores.*—Abbot John and the convent grant a tack of the mill under the rock, called Craigmylne to John Carmichael and Euphame Murray, his putative wife. *Confirmed,* 1566-67, Feb. 24.—*R.M.S.,* iv. No. 1771.

(77.) 1560, *September* 8, *Lindores.*—Abbot John and the convent grant a tack of land near Newburgh to John Calve and Katherine Dysart, his spouse. *Confirmed,* 1574, Nov. 12.—*R.M.S.,* iv. No. 2326.

(78.) 1562, *May* 6, *Lindores.*—Abbot John and the convent grant a tack of the lands of Eglismagirl to George Halyburtoun and Elizabeth Leirmonth. *Confirmed,* 1568, Sept. 22.—*R.M.S.,* iv. No. 1832.

(79.) 1563, *February* 20, *Lindores.*—Abbot John and the convent appoint David Barclay of Cullerny and his heirs male bailies of the abbey-lands. *Confirmed,* 1567, April 26.—*R.M.S.,* iv. No. 1787.

(80.) 1564, *February* 10, *Lindores.*—Abbot John and the convent grant tack of lands, near Lindores, to Henry Orme of Mugdrum. *Confirmed,* 1576-7, March 20.—*R.M.S.,* iv. No. 2666.

(81.) 1564, *March* 2, *Lindores.*—John [Philp], abbot, and the convent grant, for money paid, 'to our beloved cousin James Philp of Ormestoun and Margaret Forrett, his spouse, their heirs,' etc., at feu-ferme, the wood, two rabbit-warrens, and the Quhyte Park [particulars as to locality], in our barony and regality of Lindores, within the shire of Fife. Rent 10lbs., and three suits at the three head courts in the burgh of Newburgh, etc.

Given in full, from a certified copy which belonged to David Laing, in *Lindores Abbey,* p. 488. A few other writs are noticed in Appendix vii.

APPENDIX IV

AN ATTEMPT TO ASCERTAIN THE SUCCESSION OF

founded the monastery of Lindores' (*Scotichron.* viii. 25). None of the documents extant go to support so early a date for the foundation of the latter monastery. Nor is Bower's statement consistent with his own subsequent account of the length of time during which the first abbot occupied the headship of the house. He represents Guido as dying on the very day on which the founder died, that is, Monday, 17th June 1219, adding that he had ruled the monastery vigorously for twenty-eight years (*ibid.* ix. 27). This latter statement, if we accept it, would place the appointment of Guido in 1191, which falls in tolerably well with what the documentary evidence would lead us to believe possible.

We find 'Wydo' (a variant of 'Guido') witnessing a charter together with Adam, abbot of Cupar (*Regist. Vet. de Aberbrothoc,* p. 146). But we learn on the authority of the *Chronicle of Melrose* (s.a.) that Adam resigned the abbacy of Cupar in 1194.[1]

Guido had been a monk of Kelso; and the quitclaim of his obedience and subjection granted by O[sbert], abbot of Kelso, which will be found printed at p. 284, is in the opinion of the editor the earliest notice yet discovered of the monastery. Guido is still only elect; therefore we are probably not wrong in considering it prior to the testing clause in the charter which has been already referred to, where he appears as abbot.

From Osbert's quitclaim we also learn that monks had been lent from Kelso for the purpose of erecting the buildings at Lindores.

The first papal confirmation, the 'Great Charter' of Pope Celestine III., is dated 8th March 1195. Besides the grants of Earl David this bull confirms grants by King William, and by Robert of London, 'as in the charters of the donors is contained.' There seems, on the whole, to be no good reason for questioning that, in accordance with Bower's second statement, the monastery had its inception in 1191. It is not improbable that Charters IV., VI., VII., XIII. XIV., LXXXV., and possibly some others, may be earlier than Celestine's bull.

The monastery was built from its foundations, and most of the outbuildings (*officinae*) were completed before the death of abbot Guido (*Scotichron.* ix. 27). There were twenty-six monks in the

---

[1] I owe this early reference to Mr. R. Aitkin.

In the *Registrum Monasterii S. Marie de Cambuskenneth* there is a charter of the prior of St. Andrews (dated by the editor as '*c.* 1215') which is witnessed by 'Y. abbate de Lundores.' This must no doubt be for 'Ydo,' for Wydo

house at the time of Guido's death; and the number never seems to have surpassed this figure.

In the year immediately preceding the death of Guido the monastery was visited by the prior of Durham. He, in company with the archdeacon of the East Riding of York, had been going through Scotland, at the command of the Papal Legate, Gualo, to absolve the country from the interdict, which had been inflicted on the whole realm on account of the support given by King Alexander to Louis of France in his contest with John, King of England. During this visit the chamber in which the prior of Durham and his attendant monks were sleeping took fire. Nearly suffocated by the smoke, he escaped with difficulty. Though much exhausted, he succeeded in travelling on his homeward journey as far as the monastery of Coldingham, where he expired (*Chron. de Mailr.* s.a. 1218). The fire is said by the chronicler to have been caused ' per incuriam et prodigalitatem pincernarum.'

On 9th November in the seventeenth year of the Pope's pontificate (*i.e.* 9th Nov. 1214) G[uido], abbot of Lindores, was appointed a judge-delegate by Innocent III. (*Regist. de Cambuskenneth,* p. 149).

2. John (I.), a monk of the house, succeeded Gualo, probably in 1219 (*Scotichron.* ix. 27). The length of his tenure of office is unknown; but we find John, abbot of Lindores, witnessing a charter between 1232 and 1237, and others in 1240 and 1244 (*Regist. Priorat. S. Andree,* pp. 303-4 ; *Collections for a History of the Shires of Aberdeen and Banff,* pp. 548, 565). ' J., abbot of Lindores,' is a papal judge-delegate in 1242 (*Regist. Priorat. S. Andree,* p. 382). He appears as abbot in our Chartulary in Nos. XIX., XXVIII., LIV., LVIII., and LXXIII.[1]

3. The third abbot was Thomas (I.) who, according to Bower (and he is not lavish of eulogy), was *vir magnae sanctitatis.* The date of his succession is not recorded, but we find him appointed a judge-delegate by Pope Alexander IV. on 13th January 1257 (*Regist. Prior. S. Andree,* p. 391). He had a dispute with the Bishop of Aberdeen as to the boundaries of certain lands in Garioch, which

In the time of Abbot Thomas, Alexander III., accompanied by the Justiciar of Scotland, Alexander Cumyn, Earl of Buchan, and the Great Chamberlain, William, Earl of Mar, visited the abbey (14th March 1265). On this occasion the king made a grant of the woods and lands of Lindores (already belonging the monks) as 'in liberam forestam' (*Lib. S. Mar. de Lundoris*, p. 11). This was probably a little return for the hospitality of the abbey.

Thomas had served as one of the auditors of the Royal Exchequer in 1264 (*Exchequer Rolls*, i. 11). Thomas died in 1273 (*Scotichron.* x. 33).

4. The prior of the monastery, John (II.), succeeded. He died in the following year, and was buried at Kelso (? 1274) (*Scotichron.* x. 33, 34).

The next abbot was Nicholas the Cellarer. In the Benedictine monasteries the office of cellarer was one of dignity and great influence. To a large extent the management of the property of the house fell under his hands. There are many examples of those holding the office of cellarer being advanced to the office of abbot, of their own or of another house. It was so at Jedde-worth (Jedburgh) in 1174, at Melrose in 1214, and at Newbottle in the same year, and again at Melrose, as also at Balmerino, in 1236. Nicholas was abbot in 1281 (No. cxxv.). It was probably in his time that the heir-apparent of the Scottish throne, Alexander, elder and only surviving son of Alexander III., died at Lindores on 28th January 1284, in his twentieth year, to the grief and consternation of the whole kingdom. The body of the prince was removed from Lindores to Dunfermline for burial (*Scotichron.* x. 37).

5. We find a new abbot, John (III.), in 1289. He was then carrying on a law-suit with Devorgulla de Balliol concerning the patronage of the church of Whissendene. See Introduction, p. l. ; Bain's *Calendar*, ii. No. 379, and Stevenson's *Documents Illustrative of the History of Scotland*, i. 94-5.

On 23rd July 1291, Edward I. of England visited the abbey; and John, the abbot, with others, having touched the Host, and

king, Edward I., was at Scone on 8th August 1296, when he ordered the removal of the coronation-stone of the Scottish kings to Westminster. He arrived at Lindores on the following day, and remained till the 10th.

6. By this time it would appear there was a new abbot. At all events a few weeks later, on 28th August, we find the abbot of Lindores, by name Thomas (II.), together with most of the Scottish abbots, swearing fealty to Edward at Berwick-on-Tweed (Stevenson's *Documents, etc.*, ii. 68 ; *Ragman Rolls*, p. 116).

7. On 12th July 1298, William Wallace gained an important victory over the English troops under Aymer de Valence, Earl of Pembroke, in the neighbourhood of the abbey, and thither the weary Scots resorted after the battle for rest and refreshment. Ironside, the site of the battle (the exact spot is disputed), is the ' Hyrneside ' of our Chartulary. According to Blind Harry

'The Priour fled and durst na recknyng bide ;
He was befor apon the tother syde.'
(Book ix. lines 1123-24).

The Prince of Wales (afterwards Edward II.) spent from Tuesday, 7th April, to Thursday, 9th April 1304, at Lindores (Bain's *Calendar*, ii. No. 1516).

On 30th April 1305 Edward I. gave a protection to the abbot and convent for one year (*ibid.* No. 1717).

Under the year 1306, Sir James Balfour, who as Lord of Denmylne had not improbably special sources of information as to Lindores, recounts, ' This zeire ther was a mutuall endenture made betwix Sir Gilbert Hay of Erole, Sir Neill Campbell of Lochaw, and Sir Alexander Setton, knights, at the abbey of Londors, to defend King Robert and hes croune to the last of ther bloodes and fortunes ; wpone the sealling of the said indenture, they solemly toke the sacrament at St. Maries altar in the said abbey-churche.' (*Historical Works*, i. 89). Macfarlane has a notice of an indenture between Sir Gilbert Hay, Sir Neil Campbell, and Sir *Christopher* Seton, assigned to 1310, and

were Maurice of Inchaffray, William of Lindores, and Michael of Cambuskenneth, canons of Dunblane (Theiner, *Monumenta*, p. 178). Maurice, abbot of Inchaffray, is well known to history; but Michael of Cambuskenneth and William of Lindores have not hitherto appeared among the abbots of these houses. Nor is the editor aware of any other evidence in favour of these two persons being abbots. Still it is worth calling attention to the facts stated, and to the conjecture that here we have the names of abbots of their respective monasteries.

9. The abbot of Lindores (his name is not recorded) was present in the Parliament held by Robert I. at Cambuskenneth (6th Nov. 1314), some months after the Battle of Bannockburn.

10. The succession of abbots at this time is obscure. The next notice of an abbot of Lindores is that of Adam, who witnessed (30th June 1331) a grant of John de Dundemor to the neighbouring monastery of Balmerino (*Lib. S. Marie de Balmorinach,* p. 41). We find Adam still abbot in 1342, when he is said to have witnessed a charter of David II. (Father Hay's *Scotia Sacra,* referred to in Turnbull's Introduction to *Lib. de S. Marie de Balmorinach.*) During Adam's tenure of office, or not long after, Duncan, Earl of Fife, in the year 1350, granted to Lindores the neighbouring parish church of Uchtermukedy (Auchtermuchty) *in proprios usus.* This gift was in fulfilment of a vow made after his escape from death at the battle of Durham in 1346. The original deed of Earl Duncan is dated at Lindores 16th March 1350. It was confirmed by King David, 31st July of the same year. So far, as regards the temporal conveyance of the church; but more was necessary, and William (Landels), Bishop of St. Andrews, with the consent of his chapter, confirmed the grant, 12th April 1352, while the ratification of the appropriation was not given till 4th December 1354 by Innocent VI. The various steps in the process of transfer may be traced from the writ of David's confirmation, printed from the original in *Lib. S. Marie de Lundoris,* p. 43, and the *Calendar of Papal Registers,* iii. 539, 540.

stones of wax for a light to be burned daily 'in quadam pelve' at 'our tomb,' that is of Lady Mary, his late wife, and of himself, in the choir of the abbey-church of Lindores, at the Mass, mattins, and vespers of our Lady, and all solemnities when copes were worn. This deed was executed at Lindores on 19th November 1355 (*Reg. Mag. Sig.* i. 36, No. 94). The editor has been unable to find the evidence for the statement of Mr. Alexander Laing (*Lindores Abbey*, p. 94), that Sir David de Lindsay 'retired to Lindores, and spent the last of his days in the quiet of its retirement.' It is to be hoped that the evidence is of a more satisfactory kind than what is alleged by Lord Lindsay in his *Lives of the Lindsays* (i. 50). After relating the mortification of the wax, Lord Lindsay adds ' he had probably retired thither (to Lindores) to die, as his name nowhere occurs subsequently to that period.' There may be evidence unknown to the editor for Mr. Laing's positive statement, but till it is produced one cannot but suspect that conjecture of Lord Lindsay, for which he certainly adduces nothing that deserves the name of evidence, has, by a process not unknown to the students of the methods by which history is created, become solidified into fact. The story is not unnaturally accepted in Mr. A. H. Rea's pleasing and popularly written *Lindores Abbey and its Historical Associations* (1902), where the account runs that Sir David, 'after a long active public career, retired to the seclusion of the monastery to pass the remainder of his days in peaceful meditation.' It is a pleasing and attractive picture, but one cannot but ask, ' Is it true ?'

It would seem that the instrument of Sir David de Lindsay was kept at Lindores awaiting a favourable opportunity for obtaining the royal confirmation. However this may be, King David II., who must have been visiting Lindores, gave his confirmation under the Great Seal on 3rd August 1364. On the same day, and at the same place (Lindores), the king similarly confirmed a grant to the monastery of the lands of Cragy, in the barony of Parnbogall (now Barnbougle), in the sheriffdom of Edinburgh, made by Sir Bartholomew de Loone and Philippa de Moubray, his wife, in return for which the monks were bound to say Mass for the souls of the

allowed for the expenses of the late king, when he kept Christmas at Lindores.

12. The succession of the abbots after Adam is not clearly ascertained. Mr. A. Laing (*Lindores Abbey*, p. 97) refers to a charter in the charter-chest of Pittodrie, printed in the *Collections for the Shires of Aberdeen and Banff*, pp. 537-8), as a proof that William was abbot of Lindores at some time between 1355 and 1357. But a reference to the text shows that the crucial words ' de Lundoris' have been supplied by the editor. There was an abbot of Lindores in Parliament at Scone on 7th September 1367; but unfortunately he is not named. There is an abbot named Roger, who is spoken of in the time when Stele held possession as 'the late abbot Roger' (*Cal. Pap. Regist.* iv. 249), and who witnessed an undated charter, which has been assigned to some time between 1373 and 1381 (*Historical Records of the Family of Lindsay*, i. 25).

13. John Stele (or Steil), formerly prior of Coldingham (*Scotichron.* xi. 24; he is described in the letter of Clement vii. (Anti-Pope) as a monk of Lindores), was appointed abbot about 1380, apparently in defiance of a provision obtained from Clement vii. (Anti-Pope) on behalf of one William. This William, who is styled 'William de Angus,' as abbot of Lindores petitioned Clement vii. sometime in 1380 for a faculty to hear the confessions of all persons, regular and secular, clerical and lay, and to absolve them, even in cases reserved to the Apostolic See, and to enjoin salutary penance. This he prayed for because mortality was rife in Scotland (*Cal. Pap. Reg.* (Petit.) i. 557). If we may venture on conjecture, Stele had been elected by the monks *more canonico*; and it is certain that William failed to obtain possession. It is plain that the majority of the monks were on the side of Stele, for from a letter of Clement vii. we learn that William himself, with three

Among other charges made against Stele to Clement VII. was that he had taken from one of the monks who adhered to William, his rival, besides books, vestments, and copes, a topaz valued at 20lb., which had been committed to the said monk's custody by Roger, the late abbot. But this charge can be easily set aside if Stele held that he was Roger's legitimate successor (Letter of 2nd March 1383, *Cal. Pap. Regist.* iv. pp. 246-249). William and his three followers were compelled to beg their bread for the space of two years; and for his immediate relief Clement assigned to William a pension of 20 pounds from the abbatial *mensa* of Dunfermline (*ibid.*). Considering the all but universal adherence of Scotland to the Anti-Popes, this is a very curious episode, as to which one cannot but wish for more information.

Whether this William is the 'William of Angus, abbot of Lindores,' who appears in a confirmation by King Robert III. (23rd March 1392) is uncertain. The confirmation unfortunately does not throw light on the date of the deed confirmed to which William was a party (*Reg. Mag. Sig.* i. 207, No. 35).

14. The unfortunate Duke of Rothesay came to his untimely and mysterious end at the neighbouring castle of Falkland on 26th (or early in the morning of 27th) March 1401. His body was removed to Lindores, and buried with little ceremony (*Scotichron.* xv. 12; *Wyntoun*, iii. 82).

15. The succession of the abbots still remains in much obscurity. But a glimpse is afforded of the distressed condition of the monastery in the early part of the fifteenth century by a notice of a petition addressed to Benedict XIII. (Anti-Pope). It was represented that the buildings were ruined and the revenues diminished by reason of the nearness of the wild (*silvestrium*) Scots; and a request was made that the parish church of Criech in Fife, not far from the abbey, should be appropriated to it. This petition was granted by Benedict in 1413, the appropriation to take effect on the death of the rector, Laurence of Lindores (*Cal. Pap. Reg.*

Dundee with regard to the repair of the choir of the parish church (*Regist. Brechin.* pp. 90-95). He appears again on 28th June 1445 (*ibid.* p. 103). This is the abbot for whose soul his nephew, Thomas Rossy, founded an anniversary in the abbey (No. cli.). His seal is reproduced and described by Mr. Macdonald, Appendix vii.

16. John (iv.) was the next abbot. If we count Stele, this John must be numbered John (v.). On 24th May 1457 he granted new charters to the burgesses of Newburgh (No. clii.). Other charters of his, of the same year, will be found in *Lib. S. Marie de Lundoris*, pp. 1-8, 23. He is a witness in 1466 (*Regist. Brechin.* i. 193). On May 24th, 1474, John increases the allowance to monks of the abbey being in priest's orders, for their habits and ornatus, from 2lbs. to 4lbs. per annum (*Lib. S. Marie de Lundoris*, pp. 23-4).

17. Andrew Cavers succeeded in 1475. On 26th June in that year he paid to the officials of the Roman Curia 187 gold florins and 25 shillings (Brady, *Episcopal Succession*, i. 197). Charters of abbot Andrew in 1476 and 1479 will be found in the *Liber S. Marie de Lundoris* (pp. 19-22). In 1485 we find Andrew witnessing the marriage-contract of William, Earl of Erroll, and Elizabeth Leslie, daughter of the Earl of Rothes (*Antiquities of Aberdeen and Banff*, iii. 138). He resigned before 12th June 1502 (see below), and after 27th March (*Regist. Mag. Sig.* ii. 559). He had been one of the monks of Lindores (*Ib.* ii. 257).

18. About 1484 James, ninth Earl of Douglas, and sixth Duke of Turenne, was compulsorily secluded in the abbey of Lindores, where he spent the remainder of his days, and died 15th April 1488. With him terminated the earlier branch of the noble house of Douglas.

19. Henry Orme was provided to the abbacy by the Pope on 12th June 1502, the vacancy being caused by the resignation of Andrew Cavers (Brady, *Episcopal Succession*, i. 197). We find Cavers alive, and styled 'Pensionary of Lindores,' at least as late as 1508.

During the incumbency of Orme all the possessions of the abbey in Scotland were erected by James iv. into a Regality (7th Nov. 1510). And this grant was confirmed by James v. in Parliament, 5th April 1514 (*Regist. Mag. Sig.* iii. No. 12).

The tenure of Orme's office extended to 1523. In the previous

Scotland, wrote to Pope Adrian vi., stating that Henry, abbot of Lindores, who had much enlarged the buildings of the abbey, was now oppressed by the infirmities of old age, and felt himself unable to cope with the greed of courtiers,[1] and so had chosen John Philp, a professed monk of the house, being in priest's orders, to whom he desired to resign the abbacy. The petition of Orme, supported by the entreaties of the duke, was that the Pope would accept Orme's resignation and appoint Philp, reserving to the former the revenues for his life, together with the right of *regressus*, that is, of resuming the abbacy in the event of Philp dying or resigning. The duke urges this course, as it had been the practice of abbots of Lindores to resign in their old age, and so the monastery had not suffered from incapable rulers (*Epist. Regist. Scot.* i. 330-332).

A favourable return is made to the request on 24th July 1523. The revenues and *regressus*, together with the presentation to benefices, are reserved to Henry during his life. The revenues are recorded as 1000 florins; and the 'taxa' is 333 florins (Brady, *Episcopal Succession*, i. 197).

20. On 6th June 1516, it was passed under the Great Seal that a lapse of patronage to a chaplainry at the altar of SS. John the Baptist and John the Evangelist in the new aisle of Largo Church should go first to the provost and two great canons of St. Salvator's College, whom failing to the abbot and convent of Lindores (*Reg. Mag. Sig.* iii. 78). And in the same year Henry, the abbot, and the convent granted a tack of the lands of 'Benee and Catkin' for nineteen years to Sir John Stirling of Keir (15th Sept. 1516) for 'twolfe pundis wsuale monee of Scotland' *per an.* (*Stirlings of Keir*, p. 309). In 1521 (23rd May) an agreement was made between abbot Henry and Gavin Dunbar, Bishop of Aberdeen, and subscribed by both parties at Aberdeen 'anent the debatable lands betwix Rothmais and Tulymorgond and the peit moss callit off Malyngsyd and Bonytoune of Rayne' (*Regist. Aberdon.* i. 386). Compare 'Malind' in Earl David's Great Charter, p. 3.

Orme survived the appointment of his co-adjutor for more than

1527-8. John Philp, or Philips (he appears as 'Joannes Philippi,' in the papal deed of provision), is found granting to Sir John Stirling of Keir a renewal of the tack of the lands of ' Beny and Caitkin,' with the teind-sheaves of the same, and appointing him the bailie of the abbey for the lands of Estir and Wester Feddallis, on 5th October 1532 (*The Stirlings of Keir*, pp. 346-349), and making a grant to another of the fee-ferme of abbey lands in Mernes, on 16th March 1537 (see the confirmation in *Reg. Mag. Sig.* iii. 2636). Certain lands, multures, etc., in the neighbourhood of the abbey were confirmed to Patrick Balfour, heir of John Balfour, of Dene-myle, in 1541 (29th Sept., *ibid.* 2460). While a little earlier we have the confirmation of the lease of lands in the neighbourhood of Dundee to David Wedderburne, burgess of that town (*ibid.* 1913 ; confirmation, 10th Feb. 1538). John (v.) Philp, abbot of Lindores, was one of the large assemblage of ecclesiastics at St. Andrews, who on 28th May 1540, condemned Sir John Borthwick for heresy. He appears frequently in Parliament, and was one of the Lords of the Articles in 1544.

The tack of lands granted to Sir J. Stirling (referred to above) is subscribed by the whole chapter of the monastery ; and from it we learn that the monks numbered at this time twenty-five beside the abbot.

During the tenure of office by Philp, the wave of popular feeling hostile to the Church was rising and gaining volume. It is remarkable that Lindores was the first of the ancient abbeys of Scotland to suffer from the violence of the mob. In the autumn of 1543 the populace of Dundee rose, and, after destroying the houses of the Black and Grey Friars in that town, made their way to Lindores, sacked the monastery, and turned out the monks. The immediate cause of this outburst is very obscure ; but the selection of Lindores rather than the somewhat nearer monastery of Balmerino for the display of the popular animosity, may perhaps be accounted for by differences between the abbey and the burgesses with respect to their parish church of St. Mary.

21. The monks probably soon resumed life in their old home.

preaching at St. Andrews, marched upon Lindores. Knox, writing a few days later than the scene he describes, says, ' The abbey of Lindores, a place distant from St. Andrews twelve myles, we reformed; their altars overthrew we; their idols, vestments of idolatrie, and mass-books we burnt in their presence, and commanded them to cast away their monkish habits.'

On 24th February 1566, Pope Pius v. granted the petition of John, abbot of the monastery of Lindores,' resigning in favour of ' John Leslie, clerk of the diocese of Moray, a Doctor of both Laws, one of the Council in Scotland.' This was the well-known John Leslie, afterwards (22nd April 1575) provided to the see of Ross, with a dispensation *super defectu natalium* (Brady, *Episcopal Succession*, i. 147).

The documents from the charter-chests of Leslie of Balquhain, communicated to Bishop Keith by the antiquary Macfarlane, and printed by the bishop in his *Catalogue* (pp. 198-200, Russel's edition), sufficiently explain the need of the dispensation referred to, and show that Knox, if he was coarse and offensive in his language, was not incorrect in styling Leslie 'preastis gett' (*Works*, i. 236).

22. We know little of Leslie's administration of the abbey. Mr. David Laing shows that in June 1557 he obtained a royal man date, and took an active part in regard to the confirmation of various feu-farms of lands pertaining to the abbey of Lindores (*Works of John Knox*, ii. 601). Mr. Alexander Laing adds that John Leslie of New Leslie, son of Andrew Leslie and Janet Leslie (natural) daughter of the bishop, was served heir to his father in certain lands in Aberdeenshire which formerly were the property of the abbey of Lindores (*Abbey of Lindores*, p. 129).

According to Macfarlane (*Genealogical Collections*, ii. 4), John Leslie left three daughters, whose marriages he records.

Leslie was the last ecclesiastic of the old faith who held the dignity of abbot of Lindores, and with him this sketch appropriately closes.

APPENDIX V

THE LEGAL AUTHORITIES CITED IN THE 'OPINIONS,'
CXLIX., CL.

1.

P. 203, l. 5. 'nota Hostien. in summa, de feu. c° ultimo v. set numquid tenebitur.'

The reference is to the *Summa Aurea* of Henry de Bartholomæis, or (from his birthplace) de Suze (Henricus de Segusio), Cardinal (1261 or 1262) of Ostia (Hostiensis). He died at Lyons, 6th November 1271.

The passage referred to above is in liber iii. of the *Summa*, rubric *De Feudis*, the last chapter, the verse beginning, 'sed nunquid tenebitur' (edit. Lugduni, 1548, folio 155, *verso*).

P. 203, l. 14. 'nam in li. feu^{orum} ti. si de feu. defunct.† fuerit c. si quis coll. x. dicitur si quis,' etc.

Through an error in transcription the words 'militis contentio' (which appear in a contracted form in the Lindores MS.) have been omitted from the Latin text, the discovery being made too late to allow of doing more than inserting a dagger†, which it is hoped will call attention to this correction. The reference is to *Consuetudines Feudorum*, lib. ii. tit. xxvj. § 4, where we find (almost *verbatim*) the words of the MS.

P. 203, l. 18. 'Si enim prescriptus †'

The text here has been read with difficulty, and there is much doubt whether it is rightly represented in the print. At any rate it is obviously corrupt.

P. 203, l. 19. 'C. de episcopis et cleris li. 1.'

I have not identified this reference. Perhaps it is to the Codex of Justinian, lib. i. tit. iii., 'De episcopis et clericis,' etc. The passage of this title that seems most clearly to illustrate the text is the last section of cap. 38, taken from the *Novels* (Collat. ix.

obligaverat' ('obligavit,' Lindores MS.) according to the arrangement of modern printed books appears under tit. xxviij.   As
quoted here it seems to have been a chapter of tit. xxvij.

P. 203, l. 23. 'de privilegiis c. cum olim, § per.'

This is Decretals, lib. v. tit. xxxiij. (*De Privilegiis et excessibus*)
c. 14 (*cum olim*).   The section designated by 'per' is that which
begins in the best printed editions with 'super hoc autem,' but
which, as noted by Pithæus, was read in some texts 'per hoc autem.'

P. 203, l. 23. 'C. ex ore § fi.' is c. 17 (*Ex ore sedentis*).

Of the same book and title at the end.

The argument proceeds that there is nothing to the contrary
to be derived from—

'C. de prescrip.' Decretals, lib. ii. tit. xxvi. (*De praescriptionibus*),
or Codex, lib. vii. tit. xxxiij. (*De praescriptione*, etc.).   I must
leave to others to trace 'contra libertatem,' etc.

P. 203, l. 25. 'ff. de alienacione, iu[dic]ii, m[utan]di, c[aus]a,
    facta, l. iij. § 1.'

Pandects, lib. iv. tit. vij. c. 3 § 1.   Here occur the words 'quia
Praetores faveant libertatibus.'   The Lindores MS. suggests a
variant, 'fovent.'

P. 204, l. 1. 'in libro feu. quantum fiat investitura, c. nulla.'

This is *Consuetudines Feudorum*, lib. ii. tit. iij. of which the
rubric in the printed texts is 'Perquos fiat investitura,' etc.   At
its close we have the exactly pertinent passage 'Nulla autem
investitura debet ei fieri, qui fidelitatem facere recusat, cum a
fidelitate feudum dicitur vel a fide : *nisi eo pacto acquisitum sit
ei feudum, ut sine juramento fidelitatis habeatur.*'

P. 204, l. 5. 'Hostien.'

The passage is to a large extent illegible.

P. 204, l. 12. 'Azo.'   Portius Azo (or Azzolinus) died 1200.

He taught law at Bologna, where the school of law could not

prohibita feudi alienatione per Fridericum), which begins with the words, ' Imperialem decet solertiam.'

The section referred to begins, ' Praeterea ducatus, marchia, comitatus,' etc.

P. 204, l. 16. ' t3 pe. de bel. per.'

I offer as a conjectural expansion of the above ' tenet Petrus de Bella Pertica.' Pierre de Belle-Perche was a distinguished teacher of civil law at Orleans, and was afterwards Bishop of Auxerre and Chancellor of France. He died in 1307. A treatise of his (*De Feudis*) is printed in the great collection of Zilletus (x. ii. 2). A pertinent passage will be found under tit. viii. 27, 28.

Line 17. ' ff. de adop. l. ij.'

That is *Pandects*, lib. i. tit. vij. (*De adoptionibus*); ' l. ij ' seems to correspond to the second section of the printed editions, where the law is laid down that he who is about to be adopted must give his consent.

P. 204, l. 17. ' Hostiensis de ma. et obe. dilecti.'

That is, the comment of Hostiensis on Decretals, lib. i. tit. xxxjv. (*De majoritate et obedientia*), c. 13 (*Dilecti filii*). Though in *Summa Aurea* he has a chapter *De majoritate et obedientia* (fol. 57, edit. Lugduni, 1548), the reference seems to be to his *Expositio in Sex Libros Decretalium*, a work much esteemed, of which editions in print are said to have appeared in Rome in 1470 and 1473, in folio, and at Venice, 1478, in folio; but the editor has not had an opportunity of seeing this book.

P. 204, line 18. ' et in summa de feu. ult. vers. set nequit.'

This reference is to the *Summa Aurea* of Hostiensis, the last chapter of *De Feudis*. The verse ' sed nunquid ' seems to be intended ; ' nunquid ' having been here misread by the scribe for ' nequit.' There is no verse in this chapter beginning ' sed nequit.'

P. 204, l. 19. ' et spe. ti. de feu., § 1. vers. xxix.'

' Spe. ' is a recognised abbreviation in mediæval law books for ' speculum,' ' speculator.' [1]

of great repute among the mediæval jurists. In the inventory of the Glasgow Cathedral library, made in 1432, it is noted that Master Alexander Lawedre had been lent a *Speculum Judiciale*, having deposited as a pledge a copy of the *Decretum* ; the book was to be returned at the will of the chapter of the cathedral (*Regist. Glasguen.* ii. 336).[1] There was another copy of the *Speculum Judiciale* (in pulchro volumine) in the Glasgow Library (*ibid.* p. 338). In the inventory (1436) of the Library of Aberdeen Cathedral (which was much richer in books on canon and civil law than Glasgow), we find three copies of the *Speculum Judiciale* (*Regist. Aberdon.* ii. 129, 130).

P. 204, l. 23. 'de privilegiis ex parte abbatisse juxta ver. clerum et populum.'

Decretals, lib. v. tit. xxxiij. (*De Privilegiis*) c. 13. (*Ex parte Abbatissae*) near the words 'clerum et populum.'

P. 204, l. 25. 'xij. q. 1 duo.'

Decretum, pars. ii., causa xii., quaestio i. cap. 7 (*Duo sunt genera Christianorum*). The two kind of Christians are the clergy and the laity (or *populus*).

P. 204, l. 25. 'xcvj. di. duo.'

Decretum, pars. i., distinctio xcvj. c. 7 (*Duo sunt quippe Imperator Auguste*, etc.).

P. 204, l. 25. 'xix. q. 1. duo.'

Decretum, pars ii., causa xjx., quaestio i. [this should be ii.] cap. 2 (*Duae sunt leges*). Under *quaestio* i. there is no chapter beginning with *due*; but a glance at the page will show how easily the eye might have run on to the next *quaestio*.

P. 204, l. 25. 'de ma. et obe. solite.'

Decretals, lib. i. tit. xxxiij. (*De Majoritate et Obedientia*) cap. 6 (*Solitae benignitates affectu*). The drift of the four preceding references is to show the distinction between laity and clergy ; this reference goes further and contends that the *Imperium* is not superior to the *Sacerdotium*, but is subject to it, and is bound to

P. 204, l. 27. 'c. si sentencia interdicti de sen. ex li. vj°.'

Liber Sextus Decretalium, lib. v. tit. xi. cap. 16 (*Si sententia inter-dicti*). It is here laid down that if a sentence of interdict is pronounced against the clergy, it is not to be understood (unless otherwise expressed) that the sentence applies to the people. Having established to his own satisfaction that the clergy and people are different, the jurist proceeds to show that clergy and monks are different.

P. 204, l. 29. 'ne cle. et mo. in R^{cis} xvj. q. 1 legi.'

There are here two places referred to. But, owing to the un-certainty as to whether ' in R^{cis} ' (= *in Rubricis*) refers to the first or the second, they are here exhibited as they stand in the text. 'ne cle. et mo.' is Decretals, lib. iii. tit. 1, of which the rubric is ' Ne clerici vel Monachi secularibus negotiis se immis-ceant,' and almost certainly it is this rubric that is referred to. It proves the point which our jurist is labouring to establish, that clergy and monks are distinct.

P. 204, l. 29. ' xvj. q. 1. legi.'

Decretum, pars ii., causa xvj., quaestio 1., c. 36 (*Legi epistolam*). The rubric of this is also pertinent : ' Ad clericatûs militiam non eligantur desertores Monasteriorum.' The text of the chapter is also pertinent.

P. 204, l. 33. 'de sen. ex. inter alia.'

Decretals, lib. v. tit. xxxjx. (*De sententia excommunicationis* (cap. 31 (*inter alia*). In this chapter we find the words 'unde jus prodiit, interpretatio quoque procedat.'

P. 204, l. 34. 'de judi. cum venissent.'

Decretals, lib. ii. tit. i. (*De Judiciis*), cap. 12 (*Cum venissent*). The pertinent words are ' Cum super privilegiis Sedis Apostolicae causa vertatur, noluimus de ipsis per alios judicari.'

P. 204, l. 35. 'per ƀ et alios suggestum de Dec.'

The letter printed 'ƀ' is by no means distinct in the MS. It may perhaps be read ' V ' (with a mark of contraction). What commentator on the Canon Law is referred to must be left to conjecture.

' Suggestum de Dec.' is Decretals, lib. iii. tit. xxx. (*De decimis,*

P. 205, l. 3. 'Habet vim siue † quia facta,' etc.

It has been suggested that the word read here as 'siue' should be read 'snie' (=sentencie), but the testimony of the script does not appear to yield this reading.

P. 205, l. 4. 'c. fi. de rescrip. li⁰. vj⁰'

Liber Sextus Decretalium, lib. i. tit. iii. (*De Rescriptis*) last chapter.

P. 205, l. 9. 'c. fami. hercisde v. filius.'

Codex Justin., lib. iii. tit. xxxvj. (*Familiae [h]erciscundae*). There is no chapter in the printed text of the Codex beginning with 'filius'; but 'c. 16 Filii' is doubtless the passage referred to. It runs 'Filii patris testamentum rescindendi, si hoc inofficiosum probare non possunt, nullam habent facultatem.'

P. 205, l. 13. 'nota Ho. c. dilecti de doncs.'

This reference I take to be Hostiensis on Decretals, lib. iii. tit. xxiv. (De donationibus). There is no chapter beginning with the word 'dilecti' in the printed texts; but cap. 6 (*Cum dilecti*) is perhaps intended.

P. 205, l. 22. 'C. cum olim de sensi.'

Decretals, lib. iii. tit. xxxix. (*De censibus*), cap. 19 (*Cum olim*).

P. 205, l. 24. 'C. iiij. q. iij. § si quis testibus.'

Decretum, pars ii. causa iv. quaestio iii. § 42 (*si quis testibus usus fuerit*). The point is that if any one makes use of witnesses, and these witnesses are produced against him in another suit, it will not be lawful for him to take exception to them, unless he can prove that they had become hostile to him since he employed them as witnesses on his behalf. This is quite in accord with the preceding sentence in our Chartulary : 'Quia quod aliquis approbat pro se tenetur recipere contra se.'

P. 205, l. 26. 'Ho. in summa § i., alio modo,' etc.

Hostiensis, *Summa Aurea,* lib. iii. cap. *De jure patronatus,* § 1., where we read (under the heading *Quid sit ius patronatus*) 'Dicitur

P. 205, 1. 32. ' ff. de contra. ep̄. l. dolia, § fi.'

Pandects, lib. xviii. tit. i. (*De contrahenda emptione*), cap. 76 (*Dolia in horreis defossa*) the last section. The point is the support given by prescription of long possession in a legal defence.

P. 205, 1. 32. ' Nota et Dynus in rᵃ juris si quis in jus succedit et ibi notatis.'

Dinus (or Dynus) de Rossonibus, surnamed Mugellanus, from his birthplace, Mugello, near Florence, taught law at Bologna, and acquired a great reputation. He died in 1303. Among his writings (the titles of which may be found in Cave's *Scriptorum ecclesiasticorum Historia Literaria*, tom. ii. ; Wharton's Appendix, p. 8, *edit.* Basileae, 1744-5)[1] is *Commentarius in Regulas Juris Pontificii* ; and it is presumably to this work (despite the fact that the contraction 'rᵃ' must be extended as 'regula') that the reference is made. In the inventory of the library of the Cathedral of Aberdeen (1436) among the books on canon law we find what appears in the Spalding Club edition of the *Registrum Aberdonense* (ii. 129), 'Dignus de regulis iuris.' One cannot but suspect that 'Dignus' here is an error of transcription for 'Dynus.'

P. 205, 1. 37. 'ff. de do. ma. et metus excep. l. apud celsum, § de a[u]ctoris.'

Pandects, lib. xliv. tit. iv. (*De doli mali, et metus exceptione*), cap. 4 (*Apud Celsum*), § 27 (*De auctoris dolo exceptio emptori non objicitur*). 'Auctor,' in the language of the jurists, was the 'seller' or 'vender.'

P. 205, 1. 39. 'In l. quociens, C. de hered. insti.'

Codex Justin., lib. vi. tit. xxjv. (*De heredibus instituendis*), cap. 13. (*Quoties*).

P. 206, 1. 18. ' ff. de accio. et obli. v. quecunque.'

Pandects, lib. xliv. tit. vij. (*De obligationibus et actionibus*) cap. 11 (*Quaecunque gerimus*).

P. 206, 1. 19. 'ff. de furtis v. inter omnes.'

Pandects, lib. xlvii. tit. ii. (*De furtis*), cap. 46 (*Inter omnes constat*).

P. 206, 1. 31. ' in c. cum olim. ij., § fi. de priuilegiis.

' cum olim ' means (as I understand it) the second of the two chapters of this title which begins with *cum olim* (for cap. xij. begins with ' cum olim essemus ').

P. 206, l. 31. ' Spe. ti. ti. de actore, versus Item illustris pa. et in ti. de reo v̄s. Item consul,' etc.

The reference is presumably to the *Speculum* of Durandus, which the editor has not had an opportunity of consulting.

P. 206, l. 37. ' ff. de aqua plu. ar. l. si tertius, § si quis prius.'

Pandects, lib. xxxix. tit iij. (*De aqua, et aquae pluviae arcendae*) cap. 6 (*si tertius*), § 4 (*si quis, prius quam*).

P. 206, l. 38. ' in c. ex literis de pig.'

Decretals, lib. iii. tit. xxj. (*De pignoribus et aliis cautionibus*), cap. 5 (*ex literis*). The pertinent passage seems to be ' bona   cum suo onere transierint ad quemlibet possidentem.'

P. 206, l. 39. ' et de decs. cum non sit.'

Decretals, lib. iii. tit. xxx. (*De decimis*), cap. 33 (*cum non sit in homine*). The pertinent words seem to be ' quoniam res cum onere suo transit.'

P. 207, l. 6. ' ly vt.'

Dr. Maitland Thomson has pointed out to me that this passage is a discussion of the sense in which the word ' ut' is to be understood in the preceding phrase, ' processu trium dierum stante *ut* valido.' The word 'ly,' ' lie,' ' le,' is familiar in mediæval Latin before vernacular words introduced into the text, as in modern English we might use inverted commas or italics when using a foreign word. It is the old French definite article with a somewhat more demonstrative sense than now attaches to ' le.' The inquiry is into the meaning of the *ut*, that is, the word ' ut,' in the phrase cited above, and counsel's opinion labours to show that the expression must not be assumed to imply that the proceedings taken

III. in the text is discussing the case of one who on his wife's death is advanced to holy orders, and then marries again, or (to be more accurate), 'cum secunda de facto contraxit et cognovit.' His answer is that clerks, who, so far as in them lay, joined themselves in matrimony with second wives, were not to be dispensed 'tanquam cum Bigamis' . . . 'licet in veritate Bigami non existant.' To the word 'tanquam' the note is added, ' Hoc *tanquam* non est expressivum veritatis, sed similitudinarium, juxta illud : *existis tamquam ad latronem,*' etc. For readers who are not familiar with the Vulgate, I may add that the last four words are from St. Matthew, xxvi. 55, and form a good illustration of this use of *tamquam.*

The Lindores MS. undoubtedly reads 'veritas expressivum,' but ' veritas' must be a slip of the pen for 'veritatis,' as in the note to the passage in the Decretals.

II.

NOTES ON THE LEGAL AUTHORITIES IN ' CASUS' (NO. CL.)

P. 212, l. 19 and elsewhere. ' de A. de B.'

In the diocese of Aberdeen were the parishes of the Garioch ; and in the diocese of Brechin, St. Mary's, Dundee.

P. 212, l. 2 from foot. ' Videtur quod sic.'

It was a common manner of treating questions, theological as well as legal, to first exhibit at length the various arguments in favour of the view which the writer finally rejects. This system of treatment prevails throughout the *Summa Theologica* of Thomas Aquinas ; and instances could be cited of careless and unwary writers alleging the arguments, afterwards replied to, as those of the author.

P. 212, l. 2 from foot. ' C. conquerente de off. Ord.'

Decretals, lib. i. tit. xxxj (*De officio Judicis Ordinarii*), cap. 16 (*Conquerente oeconomo monasterii*). By the rescript which is embodied in this chapter Honorius III. confirms to the bishop of a diocese in which a monastery is situated his rights to obedience, subjection, reverence, ' institution and destitution,' correction and reforma-

is subsequently answered very easily by showing that it had reference only to churches and chapels within the diocese in which the
monastery was situated.

P. 212, l. 2 from foot. ‘ C. quod super hiis, de ma. et ob.’

Decretals, lib. i. tit. xxxiij (*De majoritate et obedientia*), cap 9.
(*Quod super his*).

Here it is enjoined that abbots and priests subject to a bishop
by diocesan law, who refuse to come to his synod, should be compelled by ecclesiastical censure to attend the synod and render
due obedience. This, again, does not touch the case, for it refers
only to abbots and priests who were subject to the bishop ‘ diocesana lege,’ that is, who were subject to him as within his
diocese.

L. 212, last line. ‘ xviij. q̄. ii. c. Abbates.’

Decretum, pars ii. causa xviii.; questio ii. c. 16 (*Abbates pro
humilitate*). In this it is enjoined that abbots should once a year
assemble at the place which the bishop might choose. This canon
is no more pertinent than the two preceding passages from the
canon law.

P. 213, l. 10. ‘ c. nullus, de jurejurando.’

Decretals, lib. ii. tit. xxjv (*De jurejurando*), cap. 5 (*Nullus*).
This declares that no bishop can compel clerks to swear to him
except those to whom some administration of things ecclesiastical
has been committed.

P. 213, l. 10. ‘ xxiij. di. c. quamquam.’

Decretum, pars i. distinctio xxiij. c. 6 (*Quamquam omnes*).

P. 213, l. 11. ‘ xxii. qu. ultima, § ultimo.’

Decretum, pars ii. causa xxii. questio v. (the last *Quaestio* of
this *Causa*), § 23 (the last section of the last *Quaestio*). It runs, in
almost precisely the language which was repeated by Gregory ix.
in the Decretals, lib. ii. tit. xxjv. cap. 5, already referred to, as

P. 213, l. 17. 'xviij di. c. Episcopus,' etc.

Decretum, pars i. distinctio xviij. c. ii. (*Episcopus*). This is a *Palea* (or addition to the original compilation of Gratian). It runs, ' Episcopus non debet abbatem cogere ad synodum ire, nisi aliqua rationabilis causa existat.'

P. 213, l. 17, ' ex ore sedentis de privilegio in fi.'

Decretals, lib. v. tit. xxxiij (*De privilegiis*), cap. 17 (*ex ore sedentis*), at the end of the chapter. This is from a letter of Innocent III. (written about 1213) to the abbot and monks of Evesham as to a dispute between them and the Bishop of Worcester. The abbot desired to establish that he was exempt from attendance at the bishop's synod, and for this purpose had shown that he was entitled to have the first place after the Bishop of Worcester. The Pope argues that the abbot on his own showing was bound to attend the episcopal (*i.e.* diocesan) synod, because it would be absurd that he should rank next the Bishop of Worcester at general or provincial synods. But though the abbot and monastery was exempt from episcopal jurisdiction, the abbot was bound to show 'reverentiam et obsequium' to the bishop for the ' members' not exempt, by which was meant probably those who had cure of souls in parish churches belonging to the monastery.

P. 213, l. 18. ' c. dilectus de off. ord. glo. ii. circa medium.'

Decretals, lib. i. tit. xxxj. (*De officio Judicis Ordinarii*), cap. 18. (*Dilectus*), glos. ii.

P. 213, l. 21. ' c. quod super hiis de ma. et ob.'

Decretals, lib. i. tit. xxxiij. (*De majoritate et obedientia*), c. 9 (*Quod super his*).

P. 213, l. 21. ' xviij. q̄. ii. Abbates.'

Decretum, pars ii. causa xvii. quæstio ii. c. 16 (Abbates).

P. 213, l 24. ' de illa regula juris li. vj. odia, etc.'

Sext: lib. v. Appended at the end of the book will be found ' *De Regulis Juris.*' Of these *Regula* xv. runs thus :—' Odia restringi et favores convenit ampliari.'

P. 213. l. 35. ' c. dilectus, de off. ord. cum suis notatis.'

Decretals, lib. i. tit. xxxj. (*De officio Judicis Ordinarii*), cap. 18 (*Dilectus*). The summary of this chapter as given in the *Corpus Juris Canonici*, as edited by J. and F. Pithou (Pithœus), Parisiis,

P. 214, l. 10. ' c. suscepti re. de preb. li. vj.'

Sext: lib. iii. tit. iii. (*De præbendis et dignitatibus*), cap. i. (*Suscepti regiminis*).

The point of this reference is to establish that there is good authority for regarding the clergy presented by the monastery to benefices as rectors and not as vicars. The pertinent passage runs as follows :—' Verum (sicut nobis querela multorum frequens insinuat) Religiosi exempti de proventibus Parœcialium Ecclesiarum, in quibus jus obtinent patronatus, seu Rectorum presentatio pertinet ad eosdem, tantum percipiunt annuatim quod Rectores Ecclesiarum ipsarum non possunt de residuo commode sustentare, et Episcopalia jura persolvere, ac alia incumbentia eis onera supportare,' etc.

P. 214, l. 21. 'c. conquerente de off. ord.'

Decretals, lib. i. tit. xxxj. (*De officio Judicis Ordinarii*), c. 16 (*conquerente Œconomo*). The pertinent part is ' Tu autem his juribus in præfatis Ecclesiis contentus existens, non amplius ab eis exigas præter moderatum auxilium, quod juxta formam Lateran. Concilii, si manifesta et rationabilis causa extiterit, cum charitate postulandum, sicut ab aliis Ecclesiis ejusdem diœcesis, pro necessitate temporis, sustinemus.'

APPENDIX VI

Le Liure des trois filz de Roys, etc.

Mr. Archibald Constable, in the notes to his translation of John Major's *Historia Majoris Britanniæ* (Scottish History Society, vol. x. p. 165), .writes, 'Brunet (ed. 1862, vol. iii. col. 1126, s.a. *Livre*) quotes five editions of this work in French, of which the first four were printed at Lyons—in 1501, 1503, 1504, 1508—and the fifth

by merely transcribing the full title (as given by Brunet) of the Lyons edition, printed by Claude Nourry in 1503. It runs ·
‘ Le liure de trois filz de roys : cest assavoir De france, dāgleterre et descosse, lesq̄lz en leur ieunesse pour la foy crestienne soustenir au seruice du Roy de secille eurent de glorieuses victoires contre les turz, lequel roy de secille apres pour ses victoires et vaillances fut des electeurs de lempire esleu empereur, et espousa le filz du roy de france alors roy la belle Yolente fille de lempereur par quoy succeda au royaulme de Secille et en jouyst paisiblement, et le filz du roy dāgleterre espousa la fille du turc apres quelle fut crestienne, et le filz du roy descosse alors roy print a femme la seur du dict roy dāgleterre, et le filz du turc alors turc lautre seur, seur du roy dāgleterre.’

Mr. A. Francis Steuart has been so good as to supply the editor with notes on the contents of the book. From these it is evident that there are some points of resemblance between the romance and the story as told by Boece. The name of the Scottish hero is David ; he suffers shipwreck ; he is taken captive by the Turks. But, on the whole, the differences are so numer ous, that it is certain that either Boece had some other source for his story, or else that he indulged largely in the faculty for inven tion, with which he is, only too justly, credited.

No English translation is known to exist in print. But in the British Museum (*MSS. Harley*, 326) there is a MS. on vellum, assigned to about A.D. 1500, containing an English translation. The contents will be found described in Mr. H. L. D. Ward’s *Catalogue of Romances in the department of Manuscripts in the British Museum* (vol. i. pp. 782, 783). ‘ The three princes are Philip of France, Humphrey of England, and David of Scotland. Philip leaves his father [King Charles] secretly and serves against the Grand Turk under Ferant, the seneschal of the King of Sicily. Philip calls himself “ Le Despureu,” but the Princess Iolante of Sicily gives him the title of “ Le Surnome.” The King of Sicily appeals for help, and French, English, and Scotch companies are sent to him under David of Scotland. David is shipwrecked and cap- tured by the Turks ; but he escapes and serves under Ferant, calling himself “Athis.” Humphrey also joins the same service,

turned Christian, and married a sister of Humphrey, King of England; but that after his death his people abjured the faith, and that he left no children by the English princess.'

A French MS. of this romance was transcribed in 1463, by David Aubert, librarian of Philip the Good, Duke of Burgundy; and indeed the authorship of the work has been by some assigned to him. See Mr. Ward's *Catalogue* as cited above. In addition to the early printed editions noticed by Brunet may be mentioned an issue in quarto from the press of ' Michel le Noir,' Paris, 1504, and another from the press of ' La Veufe feu Jehan Trepparel,' Paris, which the British Museum *Catalogue of Printed Books* marks [' 1520 '?]. Perhaps the latter may be the same as that assigned by Brunet to 'about 1530.'

APPENDIX VII

NOTES ON SEALS CONNECTED WITH LINDORES ABBEY.

By WILLIAM RAE MACDONALD, F.S.A. Scot., Carrick Pursuivant.

1. Seal of David, Earl of Huntingdon, younger brother of Malcolm IV. and William the Lion, who founded the Abbey of Lindores, *circa* A.D. 1191, and died 17th June 1219.

The earl in armour on horseback to sinister with sword in his right hand, and shield on left arm charged with :—Three piles (for Huntingdon).

Legend : (Goth. caps.), SIGILL' DAVID COMITIS FRATRIS REGIS SCOCIE. Diameter, $2\frac{9}{16}$ inches.

Appended to Grant of a rent charge of 2s. 6d. to the Church of the Holy Trinity of London and Canons thereof, no date, but *c.* A.D. 1206-14. In Record Office. See Bain's *Calendar of Documents,* vol. i. No. 603; Laing's *Seals,* vol. i. No. 443 ; Birch's

holding in her right hand a lily, branch, or sceptre, and in her left the model of a church, while in her lap is seated the Child, front face with cruciform nimbus, His right hand raised in benediction, and His left holding an orb.

Legend: (Goth. caps.), SIGILLVM SANTE MARIE ET SCI ANDREE DE LVNDORS. Pointed oval, $2\frac{11}{16} \times 1\frac{14}{16}$ inches.

Appended to Release by Thomas (who died 1273) abbot of Lindores and the convent to Sir Robert de Brus, Lord of Annandale, of all the second tithes of his land beyond Moneth, dated at Lundores, 7th August 1261. In Record Office, see Bain's *Calendar of Documents*, vol. i. No. 2267 ; Laing's *Seals*, vol. i. No. 1073 ; Birch's *British Museum Seals*, vol. iv. No. 15374 ; Raine's *North Durham*, Appendix, p. 88 ; Dugdale's *Monasticon Anglicanum* (1846 edition), vol. vi. part ii. p. 1150. Engraved, incorrectly, on the title-page of *Liber Sancte Marie de Lundoris*, being the second part of *The Chartularies of Balmerino and Lindores*. Abbotsford Club, Edinburgh, 1841.

An interesting description, with engraving, of a bone matrix of this seal is given by the Rev. John Brand, Secretary to the Society of Antiquaries of London, in a letter dated 10th May 1797, printed in *Archæologia*, vol. xiii. p. 196, where he says, ' This matrix represents the *Virgin Mary* seated with our Saviour in her lap holding a branch in her right hand, and the abbey of Lundores in her left, pl. xiii., fig. 4. The inscription runs thus : *" Sigillum Sancte Marie et Sci Andree de Lundo * * *"* here a piece has been broken off; part of the *R* is however still visible, and there is no doubt but that the letters *e* and *s* followed it.'

3. and **4.** Seal of the Chapter of the Abbey.

Obverse.—Under a canopy of three gables is a figure of the Virgin crowned and seated on a bench holding on her left knee the Child with nimbus. On the dexter side is an abbot in profile in the act of kneeling holding in front of him his crosier, while issuing from his mouth is a scroll inscribed with the words, ' AVE MARIA.' On the sinister side is a group of four monks chanting with a scroll in front of them inscribed with the commencement of the hymn, 'SALVE. SCA. PARENS.' *Legend*

to his teaching, while on the sinister side a man on a ladder is binding the arm of the Saint to the cross. Above his head is a trefoiled arch with six stars and a crescent enclosing a star, and beneath him is the half-length figure of a man in profile to sinister with his hands raised in adoration between a star and a crescent. *Legend* (Goth. caps.), BIDVO PENDENS IN CRVCE BEATVS ANDREAS DOCEBAT POPVLVM. Diameter $2\frac{14}{16}$ inches.

Appended to a charter by John [Philp] abbot of Lindores and the convent of the same to Patrick Leslie, son of Alexander Leslie of Wardes, of the lands of Flanders. Dated 20th March 1554/5. Hutton's *Sigilla*, p. 82 ; Laing's *Seals*, vol. ii., Nos. 1160 and 1159, pl. XIII., figs. 5 and 4 ; Birch's *British Museum Seals*, vol. iv., No. 15,375, pl. VIII., fig. 6, *reverse only*.

Also to Charter by the abbot and monks of Lindores in favour of David Hathinton, their old quarrier, of a rood of land, dated 20th August 1478. See Alexander Laing's *Lindores Abbey*, p. 185, where a woodcut of the *obverse* is given.

Also to letters by John [Philp], abbot of the monastery of Lundoris and the convent of the same, met in chapter, to Master John Major, Professor of Sacred Letters, and Provost of the Collegiate Church of St. Salvator of St. Andrews, dated 15th August 1547. In General Register House, Edinburgh.

Also to Tack by John [Philp], abbot of Lundoris, and the convent of the same in favour of their servitor John Chalmer, son of the late John Chalmer, liferenter of Balbuthenne, dated 31st May 1549. In General Register House, Edinburgh.

5. Seal of Thomas, abbot of Lindores, appointed 1291-1294, died c. 1306.

The seal is divided into three parts. In the upper portion is represented a Gothic porch of three niches. In the centre niche is a figure of the Virgin crowned and seated, holding on her left arm the Child. In the niche on either side is an angel adoring.

dated 28th August 1296, see Bain's *Calendar of Documents,*
vol ii. p. 196, and Appendix iii., seal No. 138.   Described
in Laing's *Seals,* vol. i. No. 1074, where date given (*c.* A.D.
1270) is certainly erroneous; also in Birch's *British Museum
Seals,* vol. iv., No. 15,377.   A fairly accurate engraving of the
seal is given in *Liber Sancti Marie de Lundoris.*   Abbotsford Club,
Edinburgh, 1841.

6. Seal of James de Rossie, Abbot of Lindores, who was abbot
   from, at least, 1426 to, at least, 1445.

Under a Gothic canopy of three arches is a full-length figure
of the Virgin without nimbus or crown, holding the Child on her
left arm, and in the niches on each side of her a lily or other
flowering plant.   Beneath in a round arched niche is the figure
of a monk kneeling to dexter and looking up.   On the sinister side
of this niche is a shield bearing arms :—A chevron between two
escallops in chief and a trefoil slipped in base.   *Legend* (Goth. l.c.),
$\mathfrak{S}$ iacobi · de · rosgii · abbatis · de · lundoris.   Pointed oval $2\frac{7}{16} \times 1\frac{8}{16}$
inches.

Appended to charter by William of Cuninghame, vicar of Dun-
donald, granting lands to the parish church of Irvine, dated at
the monastery of Lundoris, 26th July 1426.   See *Muniments of
the Royal Burgh of Irvine,* printed for the Ayrshire and Galloway
Archæological Association, Edinburgh, 1890, vol. i. pp. 129-131,
where a woodcut of the seal is given.

7. Seal of John Leslie, Bishop of Ross, and Commendator of
   Lindores Abbey, appointed by the Pope, 24th February 1565/6.

An ornamental shield bearing arms :—On a bend three buckles,
with initials I.L. at sides of the shield, and E.R. at top.
Motto, on an escroll beneath shield, 'MEMENTO.'   *Legend* (caps.),
S · IOANNIS · E · ROSSEV · AC · COMMENDTARII · DE ·
LN.   Diameter $1\frac{7}{16}$ inches.

'Mackenzie Charters A.D. 1567.'   See Laing's *Seals,* vol. i.

8. A later seal of the same.

An ornamental shield bearing arms :—On a bend three buckles, with initials I.L. at sides of the shield, and at top E.R. with a buckle between them. *Motto,* on an escroll beneath shield, ' MEMENTO.' *Legend* (caps), S' IOHANNIS · E · ROSSEN · AC COMENDATARII · LVNDORS. Diameter $1\frac{13}{16}$ inches.

Appended to Charter by John [Leslie], Bishop of Ross, to Robert Leslie and Janet Elphinstone his spouse, of the lands of Ardersier, etc., in Nairn and Inverness, dated 9th June 1573. Cawdor Charters. See Laing's *Seals,* vol. ii. No. 1070 ; Birch's *British Museum Seals,* No. 15,097.

9. Seal of Patrick, second son of Andrew, fourth Earl of Rothes, who was created Lord Lindores by Charter in 1600, and by Parliament in 1606. This seal is added though belonging to a time subsequent to the dissolution of the Abbey.

A shield bearing arms:—Quarterly. 1st and 4th. On a bend three buckles (Leslie). 2nd and 3rd. A lion rampant (intended for Abernethy). In chief over the first and second quarters a label of two points. *Surtout,* a tower embattled (for the title of Lindores). *Crest,* on a helmet with mantling and wreath, an angel head with wings expanded. *Motto,* beneath shield, ' STAT PROMISSA FIDES.' *Supporters,* two griffins segreant. *Legend* (caps.), S' PATRICII DOMINI DE LVNDORIS. Diameter $2\frac{1}{16}$ inches.

Appended to Precept of Clare Constat in favour of Alexander Irvine of Drum, dated 8th July 1615. Communicated by Lord Lindsay. See Laing's *Seals,* vol. ii. No. 621 ; Birch's *British Museum Seals,* vol. iv. No. 16,481.

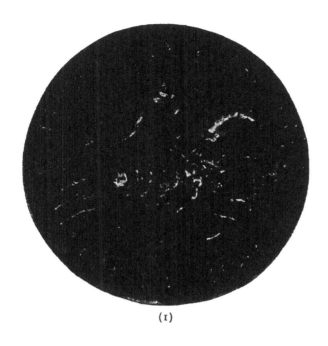

(1)

(2)

(1) SEAL OF DAVID, EARL OF HUNTINGDON.

(3)

(4)

(5)

(6)

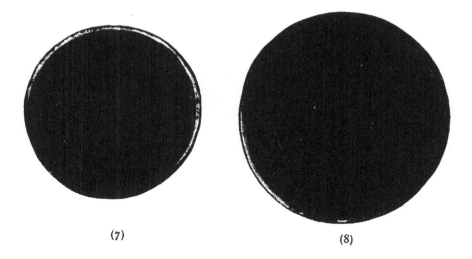

(7)   (8)

(9)

(7) SEAL OF JOHN LESLIE, BISHOP OF ROSS AND COMMENDATOR
  OF LINDORES ABBEY.
(8) A LATER SEAL OF BISHOP LESLIE.
(9) SEAL OF PATRICK LESLIE, LORD LINDORES.

INDEX

Camera, William de, 92, 93, 263.
Cameron, John de, 227.
Cameys or Cames, Radulf de, 12, 15-17.
—— Stephen de, xxix *n.*
Campania, Ralph de, 94, 138.
—— Robert de, lxiii, 19, 20, 23, 93, 97, 137-139, 240.
—— William de, lxiii, 93, 94, 137, 140, 240, 264.
Campbell charters, xvi and *n*, 284.
—— sir Neill, of Lochaw, 305.
Campsie, church of, 229 *n.*
Candida Casa or Whithorn, xv. 282.
Cane and conveth, xxxiv, liv, 129, 131, 132. *See also* Conveth.
Canterbury, xv, lxxiv, lxxxi *n*, lxxxiv.
Cantilupe, bishop of Hereford, lxxxiii. *n.*
Caps, privilege of wearing, by monks, lxxxiv, 291.
Cardynside, 184.
Carel, William, dean of, 131.
Carlingford, li.
Carmichael, John, 301.
Carnoto (Charteris), Thomas de, chancellor of Scotland, 132, 173, 277.
Carny, 306.
Carrick, lxvi.
Cartres, Adam de, 146.
Caskyben, 146, 147, 270.
Castello, Norman de, 42.
Castleton de Borg, 138.
Cathedrals, erection of, xiii.
Cather Mothyl. *See* Kathermothel.
Cathkin. *See* Cotken.
Cauz, Matilda de, 255.
Cavers, Andrew, abbot of Lindores, 296, 297, 299 and *n*, 310.
—— Dionisius, 298.
—— William, 298.
Cecilia, daughter of Gilbert, earl of Strathern, xxxiv *n.*
Celestine iii., pope, xl, xli *n*, xlii, lxxv, lxxvii, lxxxi *n*, 102, 288 *n*, 302.
Cellarer, the office of, 304.
Celtic church, decay of, xiii, xiv.
Ceres (Syreys), lix, 238.
Chalmer, Dionisius, bailie of Newburgh, 297, 300.
—— John, 329.
—— William, 297.
Charteris, sir Thomas of. *See* Carnoto.
Charters, Andrew, 298.
Cheeses, grant of, 113.
Chen, Reginald de, chamberlain of Scotland, 168, 276.

Chester, Hugh, earl of, xxi.
—— John, earl of. *See* Huntingdon.
—— Ranulph, earl of, xxi.
Chetewind, Philip de, 180.
Chirographum, 154, 272.
Christian, magister, 29, 48, 59.
—— daughter of Ferteth, earl of Strathern, xxxiv *n*, 246.
Cistercian nunnery at Elcho, lxxxvi, lxxxviii.
Clashbennie. *See* Glasbanin.
Claypottys, Dundee, 293.
Clement v., pope, 305.
Clement vi., pope, lxxvii, 292.
Clement vii., pope, 294, 308.
Clerk *alias* Vobster, Robert, burgess of Perth, 298.
Cletheueis (Clavage), 43, 44, 113, 249.
Cletheueys, Gilescop de, 29, 244.
Clinton, William de, earl of Huntingdon, lxxii *n.*
Clonyn, Madith of, 79.
Cockburn (Kokbrun), John de, 184.
Codilstane (Coldstone), 294 and *n.*
—— Simon, rector of, 294.
Coggeshall, monastery of, 231.
Cokyn, John, 74.
Colban, earl. *See* Buchan, earl of.
Colbrandspade, lxvi.
Colcrike (Colcric), 11, 82, 83, 85, 237, 260.
Coldingham monastery, 303.
Coldstream, xv.
Collessie (Cullessy), lviii-lx, 98, 169, 171, 184, 187, 189-194, 291.
—— John, chaplain of, 72.
Comyn, Walter. *See* Menteith, earl of.
Conan, son of Henry, earl of Atholl. *See* Glenorchy.
Concrag, lxxxii, 29, 30, 58, 59, 244, 253.
Conington or Cunington, l and *n*, 16, 103, 109, 167, 239, 275.
Conredium, 129, 267.
Consuetudines Feudorum, 315.
Conveth, 49, 50, 250. *See also* Cane and Conveth.
Cornhill, Juliana de, spouse of Henry of Brechin, lxxxii, 66, 67, 255.
—— Reginald de, 255.
Cotken or Cathkin, 31, 245, 299, 300, 311, 312.
Cotton, sir Robert, 239.
Coule, Patrick, 225.
Coventry, lxxiv.
—— John de, of Mukdrum, 297.

Crafford, Roger de, 180.
Cragmill, lxxxviii and *n*, 295, 301.
Cragy, in Barnbougle, 307.
—— Eister, in Barnbougle, 293.
—— or Cragyn (near Dundee), lands of, xxv, 41, 42.
—— Milltown of, 42, 248, 293.
Crail, 288.
Crailing, 235.
Crawfurd lands, 236, 246.
Crefe, Brice, parson of, 33, 34, 47, 49, 51, 250.
—— Malise, parson of, 31.
Cremond (Creymond), lxviii, lxix, 62, 64, 168, 241, 254, 276.
Criech, Fife, 294. 309.
Cristin, clerk to Robert, earl of Strathern, 31.
Crukschank, Stephen, 225.
Crusaders, privileges of, 156, 273.
Culross, 252.
Culsalmond (Culsamuel), xli, xlii, xlv, xlvii, xlix, lxi, 3, 8, 10, 18, 103, 109, 182, 184, 300.
Cumyn, Alexander. *See* Buchan, earl of.
—— Elena, spouse of William of Brechin, 176, 279.
—— Fergus, 157, 186.
—— John, 171.
—— Richard, 84, 261.
—— Robert, 177.
—— William. *See* Buchan, earl of.
—— —— 157, 284.
Cungertune, Walter de, 40.
Cunigburch, Thomas de, 86.
Cunigtone. *See* Conington.
Cunningham, lxvi.

Deer, monastery of, lxxviii, 232.
Den-Finella, falls of, 238.
Denmylne, lxxxvi, lxxxviii, 300.
Derech, Simon, 26.
Deruasyn. *See* Dairsie.
Dettauerley, Hugh de, 92.
Devorgulla, spouse of John Balliol, xxv, xxvi, lii *n*.
Doesblare (Dis-blair), 169, 276.
Dolepain or Holepen, Gilbert, 10, 15-17, 236.
—— William, 236.
Donidor (Dunnideer), 153, 272.
Donyn (Dunyn), Brice de, 29, 31.
Dornoch, lxxxii.
Douenald, brother of Kineth, 32.
Douglas, earl of, 202, 205, 206.
—— Isabella de, lady of Mar, 294.
—— James, 9th earl of, 310.
—— William, earl of, 281.
Drayton, 236.
Drem chapel, lxxiii.
Drostan, St., 65, 254.
Drumendufelis, 49, 251.
Drumgreve, Robert de, 186.
Drummond, John of, 233.
Dryburgh, xv.
Dryden, Robert de, 227, 283.
Dull, lxxxii, 231.
Dunbar, monastery, 235.
—— Gavin, bishop of Aberdeen, 311.
—— Patrick, 5th earl of, 5, 92, 235, 263.
—— —— 6th earl of, 25, 242.
—— —— 7th earl of, 275.
—— —— 9th earl of, 278.
—— Waldeve, earl of, 1, 229, 231,

Herring, grant of, 81.
Herrol. *See* Errol.
Hetun, John de, 35, 36.
Hextilda, spouse of Malcolm, earl of Athole, 231.
Heyham, Thomas de, 94.
Hillend in the Mernes, 300.
Hiltoun of Cragy, near Dundee, 300.
Holepen, Gilbert de. *See* Dolepain.
Holmcultram, xvi.
Holy, William de, 176.
Holyrood, xv, lxvi, lxxviii.
Honorius III., pope, lxxvi, 114, 115 and *n*, 322.
Hospitium, 129, 267.
Hostiensis, his *Summa Aurea*, 316, 319.
Huchannane Locherton, 166, 275.
Hugh, clerk, 94, 138.
—— 'pincerna,' 257.
—— notary public, 227.
Hugo, cardinal priest of St. Martin, 111.
Huntingdon, David, earl of, founder of Lindores, lvii, lxxxix, 7, 9-16, 39, 88, 89, 92, 117, 118, 128, 129, 131, 132, 146, 148, 168, 181, 197, 200, 206, 274, 284; notice of, xvii; the story of his alleged expedition to Palestine, xxx-xxxiv; his original endowment of Lindores, xxxviii, 2, 301; earl of Lennox, xxviii, 1, 229; his grants to Lindores, xxxviii-xlii, l, lxvii, *passim*; death of, xxiii; his seal, 327.
—— Henry, earl of. *See* Henry, son of David I.
—— John 'the Scot,' earl of, xxii, xxiv, xxvi, xxviii, lxiii *n*, lxvii, 18, 20-22, 24, 93, 94, 97, 138, 183, 201, 231, 240, 241, 248, 262 *n*, 264.
—— Simon de St. Liz, earl of, xxiv.
—— —— xxviii.
—— Waltheof, earl of, xxvii, 239.
—— William de Clinton, earl of, lxxii *n*.
—— castle, xix.
—— earldom of. xxvii.

Inchaffray, Elphin, prior of, 43, 48, 51, 250.
—— H., abbot of, 59, 253.
—— Innocent, abbot of, 29, 244.
—— J., abbot of, 55, 56, 252.
—— John, prior of, 33, 34.
—— Maurice, abbot of, 306.
—— N., abbot of, 31, 245.
—— Nicholas, canon of, 37, 247.
Inchcolm, xv, lxxviii.
—— Bower, abbot of, xxiv.
Inchemurthach (Inchmurdo), 69, 255.
Inchestur (Inchture), 216, 224, 281.
—— Michael de, 40, 224.
Inchmabanin (Insch), xli, xlvii, xlix, lxi, lxix and *n*, lxxxviii, 3, 8, 18, 65, 103, 109, 153, 182, 184, 274.
Innerleithen, lxxxii.
Innerpeffyr, Nicholas de, 19, 20, 22, 94, 138, 240.
Innocent III., pope, liii, lvi, lxxvi, lxxx *n*, 43, 107, 112, 247, 275, 303, 321-322, 324.
Innocent IV., pope, lxxvi, xcv, 117-126, 248, 267, 288, 293, 306.
Inveralmeslei (Inveramsay), 153, 272.
Inverbervyn (Bervie), 21, 145, 229, 241, 269.
Inverkaithin (Inverkeithing), 91, 92, 104, 263.
Inverkileder, Robert of, 13.
Inverurey, John, chaplain of, 88.
Inverury (Inverhuri), xli and *n*, xlvii-lix, lxi, 1, 3, 4, 8, 18, 20, 21, 64, 103, 109, 181, 182, 184, 230.
Iona, lxxviii.
Irish churches gifted to St. Andrews priory, li.
Irnsyde. *See* Hyrneside.
Irvine parish church, 330.
—— Alexander, of Drum, 331.
Isabella, daughter of Gilbert, earl of Gloucester, and spouse of Robert de Brus, 145, 270.
—— daughter of David, earl of Huntingdon, and spouse of Robert Bruce, lord of Annandale, xxv, lxiii, 41,

ERRATUM

Page 303, line 21, *for* Gualo *read* Guido.

REPORT OF THE SIXTEENTH ANNUAL MEETING OF THE SCOTTISH HISTORY SOCIETY

———•———

THE SIXTEENTH ANNUAL MEETING OF THE SOCIETY was held on Tuesday, October 28, 1902, in Dowell's Rooms, George Street Edinburgh,—The Right Rev. BISHOP DOWDEN in the Chair.

The HON. SECRETARY read the Report of the Council, as follows :—

The Council announce with regret that since the last General Meeting the Society has lost by death nine members, among whom should be particularly mentioned the eminent historian, Dr. S. R. Gardiner, who, as a corresponding member of our Council from the beginning, gave us his valuable support and advice, and moreover contributed an important volume to our series of publications; also Mr. Alexander Reid, of Auchterarder, who died shortly after the issue of his book, the *Diary of Andrew Hay.*

to these, *Inedited Narratives*, relating to Mary Queen of Scots, to be edited by Mr. John Scott, has been unavoidably delayed. One of the pieces intended for this volume was the facsimile of a long and interesting letter by Queen Mary to her uncle the Duke of Guise in 1562, the text of which was printed by Father Pollen in his *Papal Negotiations*. The letter contains some curious characteristics of the Queen's style of writing and spelling, and is thought to throw light on some of her disputed compositions. On account of the interest attached to the original document, Mr. Scott, in whose possession it is, now generously intends to issue the facsimile, with notes by Father Pollen and himself, as a separate volume, and to present it to members of the Society as a gift.

The publications in preparation for next year, 1902-1903, are :

1. *The Register of the Abbey of Lindores*, under the editorship of Bishop Dowden, the text of which is already in type ; and

2. A volume of Miscellanies.

This Miscellany will contain, in addition to the pieces mentioned in the Council's report of last year, the Statutes of the Scottish Nation at the University of Orleans in the fourteenth century, from a manuscript in the Vatican Library. Orleans was at that time a famous centre for the study of jurisprudence, and was much frequented by law students from Germany, Flanders, and Scotland. The statutes in question make mention of many Scottish names. Professor Kirkpatrick kindly offers to edit the document, with a translation.

Another paper to be included in the Miscellany will be ' *Ane Apologie for William Maitland of Lidington* against the lies and calumnies of Jhone Leslie, Bishop of Ross, George Buchanan, and William Camden—written by his onlie son,

coming volume of his *History of Scotland.* The Miscellany will also place in a more generally accessible form an interesting document in old French, descriptive of the Scottish king's household and the duties of the several officers of state in 1305, which was printed, from a manuscript in Corpus Christi College, Cambridge, with a translation and notes, by Miss Mary Bateson, in the *Juridical Review* of December last. As Miss Bateson remarks, 'It throws a welcome light on some of the obscurest places in Scottish history.'

Among the new materials offered to the Society for publication may be mentioned:

1. '*The Records of the Proceedings of the Justiciary Court* from 29th January 1661 to the end of 1678.' There are two manuscripts of this valuable collection known to exist. One formerly in possession of Thomas Maitland, Lord Dundrennan, and now the property of Mr. John Weston, has been kindly placed by him at the disposal of the Society. Another, in two volumes, covering the same ground, but with some slight variations, is in the Advocates' Library. By permission of the Faculty of Advocates, Mr. Weston's copy will be collated with and com pleted by the collection in their possession, and the work will be edited by Sheriff Scott Moncrieff. It will serve as a supplement to Pitcairn's well-known *Criminal Trials,* which came to an end with the year 1624.

2. *The Household Book of Cardinal Beaton.* This important ms. is also in the possession of the Faculty of Advocates, and is thus described in the manuscript catalogue of the

4

Professor Hume Brown, Dr. Hay Fleming, and Bishop Dowden retire by rule from the Council. It is proposed that Bishop Dowden and Professor Hume Brown be re-elected, and the Rev. Professor Flint, D.D., appointed in the place of Dr. Hay Fleming.

The Accounts of the Hon. Treasurer show that there was a balance at 31st October 1901 of £291, 8s. 11d., and that the income for the year 1901-1902 was £517, 10s. 7d. The expenditure for the same year was £422, 6s. 4d., leaving a balance in favour of the Society, as at 28th October 1902, of £386, 13s. 2d.

On the motion of the CHAIRMAN, seconded by Mr. W. K. DICKSON, Advocate, the Report was adopted; and on the motion of Mr. TRAQUAIR DICKSON, W.S., a vote of thanks was given to the Chairman and the Council.

5

ABSTRACT OF THE HON. TREASURER'S ACCOUNTS.

For Year to 28th October 1902.

I. CHARGE.

I. Balance in Bank from previous year—
   (1.) On Deposit Receipt, .   £250 0 0
   (2.) On Current Account,   .   41 8 11
                            £291 8 11

II. Subscriptions, viz.—
   (1.) 400 Subscriptions for
      1901-1902, . . .£420 0 0
      1 in arrear for 1900-01, and
      1 in advance for 1902-
      1903, ... 2 2 0

                   £422 2 0
      Less 6 in arrear and 10 in
      advance for 1901-1902, 16 16 0
                       405 6 0
   (2.) 75 Libraries, . . .£78 15 0
      3 in advance for 1902-1903, 3 3 0
                     81 18 0
   (3.) Copies of previous issues sold to New
      Members, ... 19 19 0

Brought forward,	£17	14	0			
(2) Stationery, Receipt, and Cheque Book, . . .	1	17	0			
(3) Making-up and delivering Publications, . . .	41	18	3			
(4) Postages of Secretary and Treasurer, ...	2	13	3			
(5) Clerical Work and Charges on Cheques, ...	4	4	9			
(6) Hire of room for Annual Meeting, ...	2	2	0			
				£70	9	3

II. *Papal Negotiations*—

Composition, Printing, and Paper,	£155	4	3
Proofs and Corrections, . .	52	17	0
Binding and Back-lettering 525 Copies, ...	18	5	0
Illustrations, ...	1	8	0
40 Copies of Introduction for Editor, ...	2	0	0
	£229	14	3

Less paid Oct. 27, 1900, £59 19 0						
„ „ 22, 1901, 142 3 6			202	2	6	
				27	11	9

III. *Diary of Andrew Hay*—

Composition, Printing, and Paper,	£62	10	0
Proofs and Corrections, . .	12	18	0
Binding and Back-lettering 520 copies, ...	18	1	8
	£93	9	8
Less paid, 22nd October 1901,	74	4	0

19	5	8

	£	s	d	£	s	d
Brought forward,	£102	4	6	£117	6	8
Transcripts,	2	2	0			
Indexing, .	3	0	0			
Binding and Back-lettering 520 copies,	17	18	2			
	£125	4	8			
Less paid, 22nd October 1901,	40	1	0			
				85	3	8

V. *The Remembrance—(Supplement to Vol. II. Scots Brigade)*—

	£	s	d	£	s	d
Composition, Printing, and Binding 60 Special Copies for Editor and Owner of MS.,	£8	19	0			
Less paid, 22nd October 1901,	4	13	6			
				4	5	6

VI. *The Loyall Dissuasive*—

	£	s	d	£	s	d
Composition, Printing, and Paper,	£76	0	6			
Proofs and Corrections,	25	14	6			
Facsimiles,	5	0	0			
Transcripts,	10	0	0			
Indexing,	3	5	0			
Binding and Back-lettering 540 copies,	18	11	6			
				138	11	6

VII. *Lindores Register*—

	£	s	d
Composition, etc., to date,	£37	1	0
Proofs and Corrections,	19	16	0

Brought forward,   £422   6   4

X. *Balance to next account—*

Sum due by Bank of Scotland on 28th October
1902—

 (1.) On Deposit Receipt,   £350   0   0
 (2.) On Current Account,   36 13   2
             386 13   2

        Sum of Discharge,   £808 19   6

EDINBURGH, 17*th December* 1902.—Having examined the Accounts of the Honorary Treasurer of the Scottish History Society for the year to 28th October 1902, of which the foregoing is an Abstract, we beg to report that we have found the same correct and properly vouched, closing with a balance of £386, 13s. 2d. in Bank, of which £350 is on Deposit-Receipt and £36, 13s. 2d. on Current Account.   RALPH RICHARDSON, *Auditor.*
WM. TRAQUAIR DICKSON, *Auditor.*

𝔖𝔠𝔬𝔱𝔱𝔦𝔰𝔥 𝔥𝔦𝔰𝔱𝔬𝔯𝔶 𝔖𝔬𝔠𝔦𝔢𝔱𝔶.

RULES

1. THE object of the Society is the discovery and printing, under selected editorship, of unpublished documents illustrative of the civil, religious, and social history of Scotland. The Society will also undertake, in exceptional cases, to issue translations of printed works of a similar nature, which have not hitherto been accessible in English.

2. The number of Members of the Society shall be limited to 400.

3. The affairs of the Society shall be managed by a Council, consisting of a Chairman, Treasurer, Secretary, and twelve elected Members, five to make a quorum. Three of the twelve elected Members shall retire annually by ballot, but they shall be eligible for re-election.

4. The Annual Subscription to the Society shall be One Guinea. The publications of the Society shall not be delivered to any Member whose Subscription is in arrear, and no Member shall be permitted to receive more than one copy of the Society's publications.

5. The Society will undertake the issue of its own publications, *i.e.* without the intervention of a publisher or any other paid agent.

6. The Society will issue yearly two octavo volumes of about 320 pages each.

7. An Annual General Meeting of the Society shall be held at the end of October, or at an approximate date to be determined by the Council.

8. Two stated Meetings of the Council shall be held each year, one on the last Tuesday of May, the other on the Tuesday preceding the day upon which the Annual General Meeting shall be held. The Secretary, on the request of three Members of the Council, shall call a special meeting of the Council.

9. Editors shall receive 20 copies of each volume they edit for the Society.

10. The owners of Manuscripts published by the Society will also be presented with a certain number of copies.

11. The Annual Balance-Sheet, Rules, and List of Members shall be printed.

PUBLICATIONS

OF THE

SCOTTISH HISTORY SOCIETY

For the year 1886-1887.

1. BISHOP POCOCKE's TOURS IN SCOTLAND, 1747-1760. Edited by D. W. KEMP.

2. DIARY AND ACCOUNT BOOK OF WILLIAM CUNNINGHAM OF CRAIG-ENDS, 1673-1680. Edited by the Rev. JAMES DODDS, D.D.

For the year 1887-1888.

3. GRAMEIDOS LIBRI SEX: an heroic poem on the Campaign of 1689, by JAMES PHILIP of Almerieclose. Translated and Edited by the Rev. A. D. MURDOCH.

4. THE REGISTER OF THE KIRK-SESSION OF ST. ANDREWS. Part I. 1559-1582. Edited by D. HAY FLEMING.

For the year 1889-1890.

8. A LIST OF PERSONS CONCERNED IN THE REBELLION (1745). With a Preface by the EARL OF ROSEBERY.

Presented to the Society by the Earl of Rosebery.

9. GLAMIS PAPERS: The 'BOOK OF RECORD,' a Diary written by PATRICK, FIRST EARL OF STRATHMORE, and other documents (1684-89). Edited by A. H. MILLAR.

10. JOHN MAJOR'S HISTORY OF GREATER BRITAIN (1521). Translated and edited by ARCHIBALD CONSTABLE.

For the year 1890-1891.

11. THE RECORDS OF THE COMMISSIONS OF THE GENERAL ASSEMBLIES, 1646-47. Edited by the Rev. Professor MITCHELL, D.D., and the Rev. JAMES CHRISTIE, D.D.

12. COURT-BOOK OF THE BARONY OF URIE, 1604-1747. Edited by the Rev. D. G. BARRON.

For the year 1891-1892.

13. MEMOIRS OF SIR JOHN CLERK OF PENICUIK, Baronet. Extracted by himself from his own Journals, 1676-1755. Edited by JOHN M. GRAY.

14. DIARY OF COL. THE HON. JOHN ERSKINE OF CARNOCK, 1683-1687. Edited by the Rev. WALTER MACLEOD.

For the year 1892-1893.

15. MISCELLANY OF THE SCOTTISH HISTORY SOCIETY, First Volume—

THE LIBRARY OF JAMES VI., 1573-83. Edited by G. F. Warner.—DOCUMENTS ILLUSTRATING CATHOLIC POLICY, 1596-98. T. G. Law.—LETTERS OF SIR THOMAS HOPE, 1627-46. Rev. R. Paul.—CIVIL WAR PAPERS, 1643-50. H. F. Morland Simpson.—LAUDERDALE CORRESPONDENCE, 1660-77. Right Rev. John Dowden, D.D.—TURNBULL'S DIARY, 1657-1704. Rev. R. Paul.—MASTERTON

For the year 1893-1894.

17. LETTERS AND PAPERS ILLUSTRATING THE RELATIONS BETWEEN CHARLES II. AND SCOTLAND IN 1650. Edited by SAMUEL RAWSON GARDINER, D.C.L., etc.

18. SCOTLAND AND THE COMMONWEALTH. LETTERS AND PAPERS RELATING TO THE MILITARY GOVERNMENT OF SCOTLAND, Aug. 1651—Dec. 1653. Edited by C. H. FIRTH, M.A.

For the year 1894-1895.

19. THE JACOBITE ATTEMPT OF 1719. LETTERS OF JAMES, SECOND DUKE OF ORMONDE. Edited by W. K. DICKSON.

20, 21. THE LYON IN MOURNING, OR A COLLECTION OF SPEECHES, LETTERS, JOURNALS, ETC., RELATIVE TO THE AFFAIRS OF PRINCE CHARLES EDWARD STUART, by BISHOP FORBES. 1746-1775. Edited by HENRY PATON. Vols. I. and II.

For the year 1895-1896.

22. THE LYON IN MOURNING. Vol. III.

23. SUPPLEMENT TO THE LYON IN MOURNING.—ITINERARY OF PRINCE CHARLES EDWARD. Compiled by W. B. BLAIKIE.

24. EXTRACTS FROM THE PRESBYTERY RECORDS OF INVERNESS AND DINGWALL FROM 1638 TO 1688. Edited by WILLIAM MACKAY.

25. RECORDS OF THE COMMISSIONS OF THE GENERAL ASSEMBLIES (*continued*) for the years 1648 and 1649. Edited by the Rev. Professor MITCHELL, D.D., and Rev. JAMES CHRISTIE, D.D.

For the year 1896-1897.

26. WARISTON'S DIARY AND OTHER PAPERS—

6   PUBLICATIONS

For the year 1897-1898.

29, 30. THE CORRESPONDENCE OF DE MONTEREUL AND THE BROTHERS DE BELLIÈVRE, FRENCH AMBASSADORS IN ENGLAND AND SCOTLAND, 1645-1648. Edited, with Translation, by J. G. FOTHERINGHAM. 2 vols.

For the year 1898-1899.

31. SCOTLAND AND THE PROTECTORATE. LETTERS AND PAPERS RELATING TO THE MILITARY GOVERNMENT OF SCOTLAND, FROM JANUARY 1654 TO JUNE 1659. Edited by C. H. FIRTH, M.A.

32. PAPERS ILLUSTRATING THE HISTORY OF THE SCOTS BRIGADE IN THE SERVICE OF THE UNITED NETHERLANDS, 1572-1782. Edited by JAMES FERGUSON. Vol. I. 1572-1697.

33, 34. MACFARLANE'S GENEALOGICAL COLLECTIONS CONCERNING FAMILIES IN SCOTLAND; MSS. in the Advocates' Library. 2 vols. Edited by J. T. CLARK, Keeper of the Library.

Presented to the Society by the Trustees of the late Sir William Fraser, K.C.B.

For the year 1899-1900.

35. PAPERS ON THE SCOTS BRIGADE IN HOLLAND, 1572-1782. Edited by JAMES FERGUSON. Vol. II. 1698-1782. (Nov. 1899.)

36. JOURNAL OF A FOREIGN TOUR IN 1665 AND 1666, AND PORTIONS OF OTHER JOURNALS, BY SIR JOHN LAUDER, LORD FOUNTAINHALL. Edited by DONALD CRAWFORD. (May 1900.)

37. PAPAL NEGOTIATIONS WITH MARY QUEEN OF SCOTS DURING HER REIGN IN SCOTLAND. Chiefly from the Vatican Archives. Edited by the Rev. J. HUNGERFORD POLLEN, S.J. (Nov. 1901.)

For the year 1900-1901.

38. PAPERS ON THE SCOTS BRIGADE IN HOLLAND, 1572-1782. Edited by JAMES FERGUSON. Vol. III. 1. Rotterdam Papers: 2. The Remembrance, a Metrical Account of the War in

For the year 1901-1902.

40. NEGOTIATIONS FOR THE UNION OF ENGLAND AND SCOTLAND IN 1651-53. Edited by C. SANFORD TERRY, Lecturer on History in the University of Aberdeen.   (March 1902.)

41. THE LOYALL DISSUASIVE. Memorial to the Laird of Cluny in Badenoch. Written in 1703, by Sir ÆNEAS MACPHERSON. Edited by the Rev. A. D. MURDOCH.   (July 1902.)

For the year 1902-1903.

42. THE CHARTULARY OF LINDORES, 1195-1479. Edited from the original MS. at Caprington Castle, Kilmarnock, by the Right Rev. JOHN DOWDEN, D.D., Bishop of Edinburgh. (July 1903.)

43. FACSIMILE OF QUEEN MARY'S LETTER TO THE DUKE OF GUISE [5TH JAN. 1562], with Notes by the Rev. J. H. POLLEN, S.J. *Presented to the Society by the late John Scott, C.B.*

44. MISCELLANY OF THE SCOTTISH HISTORY SOCIETY, Second Volume.

In preparation.

THE RECORDS OF THE PROCEEDINGS OF THE JUSTICIARY COURT FROM 29TH JAN. 1661 TO THE END OF 1678. Edited, from the MS. in possession of Mr. John Weston, by Sheriff SCOTT MONCRIEFF.

' MACFARLANE'S TOPOGRAPHICAL COLLECTIONS. Edited by Sir ARTHUR MITCHELL, K.C.B.

A TRANSLATION OF THE STATUTA ECCLESIÆ SCOTICANÆ, 1225-1556, by DAVID PATRICK, LL.D.

SIR THOMAS CRAIG'S DE UNIONE REGNORUM BRITANNIÆ. Edited,

REGISTER OF THE CONSULTATIONS OF THE MINISTERS OF EDINBURGH, AND SOME OTHER BRETHREN OF THE MINISTRY SINCE THE INTERRUPTION OF THE ASSEMBLY 1653, WITH OTHER PAPERS OF PUBLIC CONCERNMENT, 1653-1660.

PAPERS RELATING TO THE REBELLIONS OF 1715 AND 1745, with other documents from the Municipal Archives of the City of Perth.

A SELECTION OF THE FORFEITED ESTATES PAPERS PRESERVED IN H.M. GENERAL REGISTER HOUSE AND ELSEWHERE. Edited by A. H. MILLAR.

A TRANSLATION OF THE HISTORIA ABBATUM DE KYNLOS OF FERRERIUS, together with some inedited Letters of the Author. By ARCHIBALD CONSTABLE, LL.D.

RENTALE SANCTI ANDREÆ. The Household Book of Cardinal Beaton, 1539-1545. Edited, from the MS. in the Advocates' Library, by D. HAY FLEMING, LL.D.

POLICHRONICON SEU POLICRATIA TEMPORUM, or, the true Genealogy of the Frasers. By Master JAMES FRASER. Edited, from the original MS. known as THE WARDLAW MANUSCRIPT, in possession of the trustees of the late Sir Wm. Augustus Fraser, Bart., by WILLIAM MACKAY, Inverness.

MINUTE BOOK OF THE MANAGERS OF THE NEW MILLS CLOTH MANU-FACTORY, 1684-1690. Edited by W. R. SCOTT, Lecturer on Political Economy at the University of St. Andrews.